forkner SHORTHAND

SECOND EDITION

HAMDEN L. FORKNER, JR., ED.D.

FRANCES A. BROWN, M.A.

BARBARA JOHNSON, M.S.Ed.

MURRAY CUNNINGHAM, B.A.

Shorthand Outlines for Part B by Mary S. Lore

Nelson Canada

1120 Birchmount Road
Scarborough, Ontario
M1K 5G4

Originally published by Gage Educational Publishing Company. A Division of Canada Publishing Corporation

Canadian Cataloguing in Publication Data
Main entry under title:
Forkner shorthand

2nd ed.
ISBN 0-17-603630-X

1. Shorthand—Forkner. I. Forkner, Hamden L. (Hamden Landon), 1918 - .

Z56.2.F67F6 1990 653'.2 C90-095628-3

ISBN 0-17-603630-X

2 3 4 5 6 7 BP 6 5 4 3

Printed and Bound in Canada

TO THE TEACHER

Forkner Shorthand was introduced in 1952 after ten years of research. Today, it is taught in thousands of high school and college classrooms throughout the world.

Forkner Shorthand students succeed in business because they can write at high speeds and transcribe accurately. They consistently win awards for writing speeds and transcription accuracy in contests sponsored by national organizations.

Forkner programs succeed in secondary schools and colleges because the system is easy to learn to write. It combines 19 letters of the alphabet with a few symbols. Because Forkner Shorthand is based on what students already know—how to read and write longhand—they need not learn a whole new language to become competent in shorthand. Consequently, many high school students acquire a marketable shorthand skill in one year.

Motivation is high in Forkner programs because shorthand writing begins the first class period. Students make speedy progress toward their goals. Shorthand enrolments go up. These new materials are designed to equip the student to meet the current challenge of entry-level jobs in business and government.

This New Edition

Those who have taught Forkner Shorthand over the years will feel at home with this new generation of Forkner materials. We have retained the "rule discovery" approach in which students figure out the writing rules themselves. All materials are self-keyed, providing immediate reinforcement to the learner. Every fourth chapter provides a review and applies previously-learned theory through the medium of business letters. The *Study Guide* includes a self-test on each new writing principle and on transcription skills, so that both student and instructor can monitor progress.

New Features of the Second Edition

The textbook. This new two-semester text features the following improvements over earlier editions:

1. A new sequence of theory presentation gives students a more gradual introduction to shorthand theory.

2. The number of theory principles has been reduced. This reduction cuts even further the time required to learn Forkner theory. More class time is available for building speed and for teaching essential transcription skills.

3. For Semester One this new text presents the theory in 32 rather than in 37 chapters. Part A presents the theory along with correlated dictation material in every fourth chapter. Appendix A — Supplemental Letters for Dictation—provides 34 additional pieces of dictation, correlated chapter-by-chapter with Chapter 6 through 32. This Part provides over 20 per cent more dictation material than the previous edition. Semester Two, Part B, consisting of 16 chapters, provides a thorough review of the theory as well as English and transcription skills in Chapters 33 through 43. A review sentence, which incorporates all of the theory principles for the section reviewed, appears at the beginning of each review chapter; review charts appear in the consolidation chapters. The latter are Chapters 36, 40, 43, and 44. All chapters in Part B contain dictation material ranging from 300 to 500 words, providing over 80 per cent additional dictation material in Part B. Appendix B—Supplementary Correspondence for Dictation—provides, yet again, over 40 per cent more dictation material which may be used as sight dictation.

4. The number of abbreviated words has been reduced by some 40 per cent, thus lessening the memory burden.

5. Heavy emphasis is placed on transcription and on English skills. Most chapters provide a special section headed "Building Transcription Skills."

6. The *Study Guide* exercises are perforated so that out-of-class work may be checked periodically.

The Study Guide.

- Part A consists of self-tests which provide expanded drill and vocabulary while applying the principles learned in Chapters 1 through 32.

- Part B consists of various games which add variety and interest to developing shorthand skills and applying the principles learned.
  Both Parts provide a number of self-tests in English and transcription skills. Correlated chapter-by-chapter with the textbook, all 48 Units are completely self-keyed. Designed for out-of-class work, each unit requires approximately 30 minutes to complete.

- An exciting feature of this edition is that the *Study Guide* contains a set of examinations, all completely self-keyed. Following each four chapters, an examination is provided for the preceding section so that the student may self-test the learning that has taken place to that point in the course. A key to each examination appears at the back of the *Study Guide* , so that the student self-administers and self-corrects the level of performance before taking the teacher-administered examination provided in the *Teacher's Manual*.

The Examinations.

- Part A, set one, follows every fourth Unit within the *Study Guide*, as already explained, and is completely self-keyed. The second set is provided in the *Teacher's Manual*. There are eight examinations and one final theory examination in each set. The final examination tests the theory from Chapters 1 through 32. The format for each set is identical, but the content is, of course, different.

- Part B. Testing for this Part will consist of dictation for transcription which may be taken from the dictation material provided in Appendix B, the *Teacher's Manual*, and/or other programs in Forkner Shorthand which are compatible with this Second Edition.

Dictation Tapes.

Theory and Speed-Building Tapes in Forkner Shorthand are correlated with the text and *Study Guide*. For Part A, sixteen cassettes give students skill-building practice on all material presented in the 32 text chapters and correlated *Study Guide* units. A variety of speed-forcing dictation plans is used. Two additional cassettes for Part A provide compact reviews for use following Chapters 8, 16, 24, and 32. For Part B, all of the connected matter is dictated at various speeds for a duration of at least three minutes in length in a range gradually increasing by 10 words a minute from 80 through 120 words a minute. For Parts A and B there are more than 25 hours of dictation material, providing skill-building and dictation practice in shorthand either for in-class or out-of-class practice.

Other teaching aids for beginning classes. A complete range of materials is available for teaching beginning shorthand. These include the following: *Forkner Shorthand Dictionary for Beginners*—a dictionary that includes outlines for all words appearing in the first-year Forkner texts and workbooks, as well as additional words that appear in business correspondence.

ACKNOWLEDGMENTS

The authors and publisher of this edition of Forkner Shorthand are indebted to the late Dr. Hamden L. Forkner, Sr., who invented the system and who was an author of previous editions.

We are grateful to schools, colleges, universities, and educators everywhere who have used the four previous editions of Forkner Shorthand and who continue to hold workshops and conferences to acquaint teachers with the benefits of the Forkner Shorthand system.

H. L. F., Jr.
F. A. B.
B. J.
M. C.

CONTENTS

TO THE STUDENT

As you begin your study of Forkner Shorthand, you join thousands of other students throughout the world who are learning either the English- or French-language version of this scientific shorthand system. As you probably know, there is a strong demand for shorthand writers today, and employment experts say there will be a greater demand for people with shorthand skills in the future.

Recent studies show that *there will be a greater need for secretaries in the next 10 years than for any other occupational skill.*

Why study shorthand? Because a shorthand skill will *help you to*:

- *Land the job you want.* With a shorthand skill, beginning office workers can often select a stimulating job rather than settle for routine tasks.
- *Increase the size of your pay cheque.* Beginning and advanced-level office workers who are good at shorthand get better pay than those who do not have that skill.
- *Increase your chances for promotions and raises.* If you have good shorthand skills and show a willingness to work, you will probably find yourself at the top of the list for promotions and raises.

Developing writing speed

In order to write shorthand rapidly, you must be able to move your hand quickly. How fast can you write longhand?

To find out, write the following speed sentence in longhand as many times as you can in ten seconds (one-sixth of a minute). Your instructor will time you. Then multiply the total number of words you write by 6 to get your longhand writing rate. Try writing this sentence a number of times to see whether you can double your longhand writing rate.

Speed sentence: **They will make sure each page will look very good.**

Forkner Shorthand is easy to learn because it blends letters of the alphabet with a few symbols. If you follow your instructor's directions, you will soon have a skill that will give you an excellent start in your business career.

WRITING IN YOUR SHORTHAND NOTEBOOK

As a student of Forkner Shorthand, you will need a shorthand notebook in which to practice and to take shorthand dictation for transcription. Note that each page in your shorthand notebook has a line down the centre. When writing shorthand, begin at the top left edge of the page and write to the centre line. When you have completed the left column, begin at the top of the right column and write until all lines are filled. (See illustration below).

As you complete the right column, use your left hand to flip the left corner, ready to turn quickly to the next sheet. Turn the page and write *on the next sheet* (not on the back of the page just completed). Thus, you will write through an entire notebook in one direction and then turn the notebook over and write in the other direction. Write the current date at the bottom of each notebook page.

For efficiency, attach an elastic band to the cover of your notebook so that as shorthand is transcribed, pages are slipped under the band.

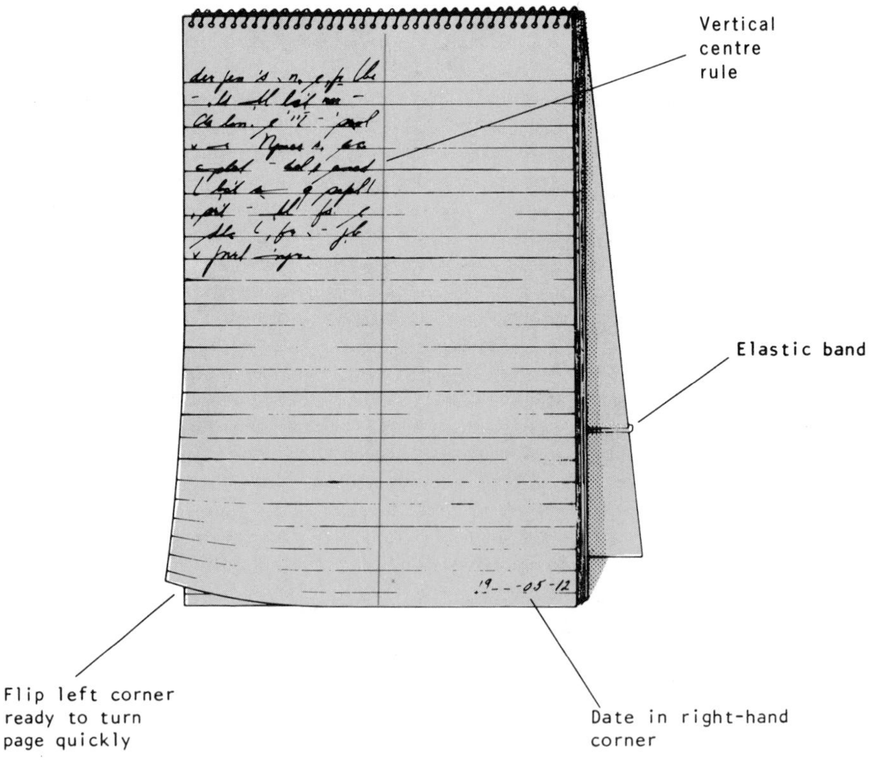
Vertical centre rule
Elastic band
19- -05-12
Flip left corner ready to turn page quickly
Date in right-hand corner

PART A

CHAPTER 1

WRITING SOUNDS OF LONG AND SHORT E AND LONG I

Assignment 1 — **Saving writing strokes**. Write the letters as they are written below until you can write them quickly and without hesitation. The samples below show how to eliminate unneeded strokes when letters are written *at the beginning of a word*.

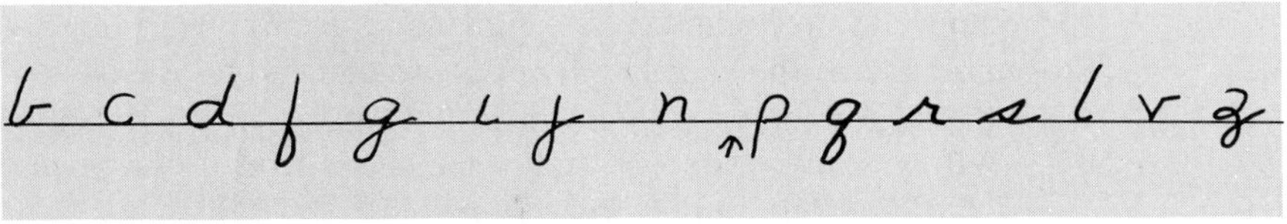

Learning tips:

1. Note that the usual beginning stroke is omitted from letters that begin a word or that stand alone.
2. When the letter *b* or *f* begins a word or stands alone, start at the top of the letter.
3. When *p* begins a word or stands alone, start below the line and make an upward stroke with the loop on the line.

The samples below show how to omit unneeded strokes in *letters that end a word*. Write each letter several times, remembering to omit the ending loop or stroke.

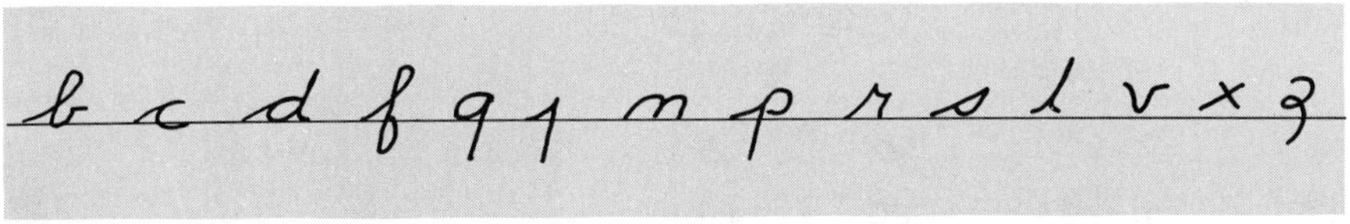

Assignment 2 — **Writing by sound**. When writing shorthand, you write only the sounds you hear. For example, in the word *leave*, you hear only three sounds, *l*, *e*, and *v*. Those are the sounds you would write in shorthand. In the word *light*, you do not hear the *g* or *h*; therefore, you write *l-i-t* in shorthand.

The silent letters in the words below have been crossed out. Study these examples and remember to write only what you hear when you write shorthand.

leave	day	goal	know
might	free	pay	scene
slow	own	sign	bright

Assignment 3 — **Rule discovery**. Follow the steps below to learn each writing principle.

Step 1. Examine both the shorthand and the print of the first group of words under the heading, Sounds of Long and Short E. Try to discover the rule for writing that group of words. When you think you have discovered the rule, check the writing principles that follow to see if you have made the correct discovery.

Step 2. Cover the print of each line of shorthand words and read the shorthand until you can read each line as rapidly as you can read the print. Use an index card as a shield.

Step 3. Cover the shorthand of each line of words and write each word in shorthand until you can do so rapidly and accurately. You will progress faster if the shorthand words are dictated to you as you write them. You may have the words dictated by your instructor, by a fellow student, or you may take them from *Theory and Speed-Building Tapes in Forkner Shorthand*.

SOUNDS OF LONG AND SHORT **E**

fe	del	feld	evn	se	ledr	pepl
fee	deal	field	even	see-sea	leader	people
ner	nvr	brd	srv	sd	sl	fl
near	never	bread	serve	said	sell	fell
ls	dd	eg	ern	rde	vre	ned
less	dead	egg	earn	ready	very	need
ded	les	sel	fel			
deed	lease	seal	feel			

Learning tips:

1. When you hear the *name* of the letter *e* in a word, you have a long *e* sound. For example, you hear the name of the letter *e* in *fee*; therefore, *fee* has a long *e*.

2. The final *y* in many words has a long *e* sound. See the words *very* and *ready* above.

3. Note that both *long* and *short* sounds of *e* are written at the beginning of a word. See *even*, *earn*, and *egg* above. You need the beginning sounds of all words in order to read them accurately.

4. When an outline stands for more than one word, as in *see-sea*, the meaning of the sentence tells you the correct word. When reading a shorthand outline, you should say all words which are represented by that outline.

SOUND OF LONG I

lif	lin	driv	sin	fin	rid	bi	i
life	line	drive	sign	fine	ride	buy	I-eye

idl	fil	fibr	finr	piplin	sirn
idle	file	fiber	finer	pipeline	siren

Learning tips:

1. Note that *i* is written with a short downward stroke when beginning a word or when it stands alone as in *idle* and *I*.
2. The final *y* in words such as *buy*, *fly*, and *cry* has a long *i* sound.

WRITING PRINCIPLES

LONG AND SHORT E — Write *e* for long *e* sounds. Omit *e* when the short sound of *e* occurs in the *body* of a word.

The letter *e* has two basic sounds: a long sound, as in *fee* and *deal*, and a short sound, as in *never* and *bread*. Note that the *e* is written when the short sound of *e* begins a word. See *earn* and *egg* on page 2.

LONG I — Write an undotted *i* for all long sounds of *i*.

The letter *i* has two basic sounds: a long sound, as in *sign* and *life*, and a short sound, as in *big* and *bill*. The short sound of *i* is presented in the next chapter.

Assignment 4 — **New vocabulary**. Some words that occur often are abbreviated in shorthand. These words are called *abbreviated words*. You must memorize abbreviated words so that you can read and write each one quickly and easily. The abbreviated words come first in each "New Vocabulary" section. They are also shown in italics and underlined with a solid line in color so you will know which words must be memorized.

Follow these steps to learn abbreviated words:

Step 1. Memorize the shorthand abbreviation for each word.

Step 2. Cover the print of each line of abbreviated words and read the outlines until you can read them as rapidly as you can read the print.

Step 3. Cover the shorthand of each line of words and write the outlines for each abbreviated word several times, saying the word to yourself each time you write it.

c	f	g	e	s	-
can	for	go-good	he	is-his-us	the

Learning tip: The outline for *the* is the cross of the letter *t* and is written above the line when it stands alone.

Assignment 5 — **Speed-building reading and writing**. Follow the steps below:

Step 1. Read each sentence from the shorthand until you can read it as rapidly as you can read from print. (These sentences are printed at the end of this chapter).
Write each sentence in shorthand until you can write each one rapidly and accurately.

1. - brd s vre g.
2. i c bi - brd f - ledr.
3. i c ern ern - vre g fe f - del.
4. e c nvr sl - feld.
5. s les f - fun feld s rde.
6. - ledr c sin - vre g les f s.
7. - pepl c se - ned f - fe.
8. i sd i nvr g ner - se.
9. e sd e s rde f - red.

Learning tips:

1. You do not begin a sentence with a capital letter when writing shorthand. Of course, you will capitalize the first word of a sentence when you transcribe.

2. To build your writing speed, place a sheet of notebook paper directly under the shorthand sentence you wish to practice. Then dictate the sentence to yourself as you write the shorthand, making your outlines like those in the book. When you can write the sentence rapidly and without hesitation, move on to the next sentence.

3. Note that sentences ending in a period are punctuated with a period in shorthand.

STUDY GUIDE ASSIGNMENT

Turn to Unit 1 of the *Study Guide* and complete the self-tests before you proceed with the rest of this chapter.

TAKING TAPE DICTATION

To write from dictation the words and sentences in this chapter, use Cassette 1 Side A of the *Theory and Speed-Building Tapes*. Your instructor will show you how to use the playback equipment.

IN-CLASS DICTATION AND TRANSCRIPTION

Assignment 6 — **Transcription**. Transcribe the shorthand sentences in Assignment 5 at your best typing or longhand writing rate. Do not number the sentences.

Assignment 7 — **Dictation**. Write from dictation the sentences in Assignment 5. Your instructor will dictate each group of 20 words to you at various speeds. In order to build speed, your instructor will often dictate at a rate faster than you can write comfortably. Taking dictation at speeds that "force" you to write faster is the best way to build your writing speed.

Note that the printed sentences at the end of this chapter include numbers in parentheses after certain sentences. These numbers indicate the number of standard words in the sentences up to that point. The numbers make it possible to dictate the sentences at a desired speed.

The table on page 6 gives a cumulative count of seconds for dictating 20-word groups at various speeds. For example, to dictate a passage at 70 words a minute the dictator should finish reading the first 20-word group in 17 seconds; the second 20-word group in 34 seconds; and the third 20-word group in 51 seconds. The fourth group should be completed when the stop watch reaches 1 minute and 8 seconds, and so on.

Speed of Dictation	50	60	70	80	90	100	110	120	130	140
Seconds Elapsed										
First	24	20	17	15	13	12	11	10	09	08
Minute	48	40	34	30	26	24	22	20	18	17
Second	12	60	51	45	40	36	33	30	27	25
Minute	36	20	08	60	53	48	44	40	37	34
	60	40	25	15	06	60	55	50	46	42
		60	42	30	20	12	06	60	55	51
			60	45	33	24	17	10	04	60
				60	47	36	28	20	14	08
					60	47	39	30	23	17
						60	50	40	32	25
							60	50	41	34
								60	51	42
									60	51
										60

To dictate for more than two minutes, simply repeat the cycle.

50 wpm--20 words every 24 seconds	100 wpm--20 words every 12 seconds
60 wpm--20 words every 20 seconds	110 wpm--20 words every 11 seconds
70 wpm--20 words every 17 seconds	120 wpm--20 words every 10 seconds
80 wpm--20 words every 15 seconds	130 wpm--20 words every 9 seconds
90 wpm--20 words every 13 seconds	140 wpm--20 words every 8 seconds

Assignment 8 — **Own-note transcription**. After you have taken the sentences in shorthand, select your best set of notes and transcribe them at your best typing or longhand writing rate. Do not number the sentences.

TRANSCRIPT OF SHORTHAND SENTENCES

1. The bread is very good.
2. I can buy the bread for the leader.
3. I can even earn the very good fee for the deal. (20)
4. He can never sell the field.
5. His lease for the fine field is ready.
6. The leader can sign the very good lease for us. (40)
7. The people can see the need for the fee.
8. I said I never go near the sea.
9. He said he is ready for the ride. (60)

CHAPTER 2

WRITING SOUNDS OF **A**, **T**, AND SHORT **I**

Assignment 1 — **Rule discovery.** Follow the steps below to learn each writing principle.

Step 1. Examine the shorthand and the print of the first group of words. Try to discover the rule for writing that group of words. When you think you have discovered the rule, check the appropriate writing principle in your text to see if you have made the correct discovery.

Step 2. Cover the print of each line of shorthand words and read the shorthand until you can read each line as rapidly as you can read the print. Remember to say all the words each shorthand outline stands for.

Step 3. Cover the shorthand of each line of words and write each word in shorthand until you can do so rapidly and accurately. You will progress faster if the shorthand words are dictated to you as you write them.

SOUNDS OF **A**

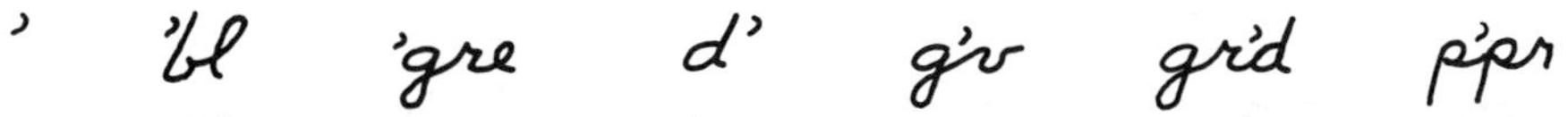

a able agree day gave grade paper

fall-fail pay sale-sail plan-plain-plane fair-fare-far

Learning tips:

1. In shorthand, a symbol is sometimes used to increase writing speed.
2. Write the *a* symbol first when it comes first in a word. Write it last at all other times.

SOUND OF **T**

date light rate-rat settle try type get eat

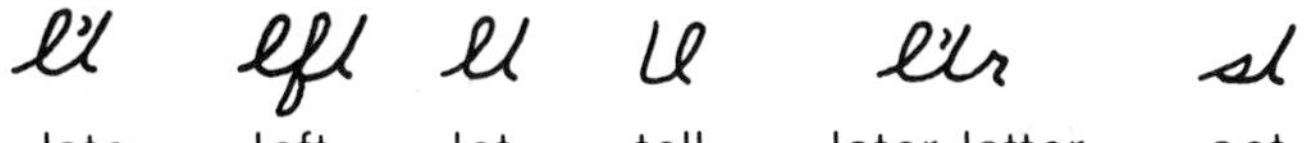

late left let tell later-latter set

Learning tip: Note that *t* is written with a downward stroke when it stands alone or when it begins a word, as in *try* and *type* on page 7.

SOUND OF SHORT I

big bill did give if trip little fill

WRITING PRINCIPLES

A Write an apostrophe for all sounds of *a*.

Write the *a* first when an *a* sound comes first in a word; write the *a* last at all other times.

The *a* is written like an apostrophe because it can be written much more quickly than the longhand letter *a*.

T Write the *t* without a cross.

SHORT I Where the sound of short *i* occurs, write a dot above the line.

Assignment 2 — **New vocabulary**. Follow these steps in learning new vocabulary words: (1) Study the print and the shorthand until you know the shorthand outline for each word. (2) Cover the print of each line of words and read the outlines until you can read them without hesitation. (3) Cover the shorthand of each line of words and write the outline for each word several times, saying the word to yourself each time you write it.

Remember, the abbreviated words that must be memorized are shown in italics and underlined in color.

all *be-but-by-bye* *it-at-to* *of* *your* today idea

final Ray Sally

Learning tips:

1. Note that the word *today* is made up of two words—the abbreviated word *to* and the word *day*. Words that are made up of an abbreviated word and another word or syllable are called *derivatives*. Derivatives are underlined with a dotted black line.

2. When writing shorthand, do not begin proper nouns with capital letters. Put a small check mark under the shorthand outline to show that it is to be capitalized when you transcribe the shorthand outline. It is not necessary to put a check mark

under the first word in the sentence because you know that word must be capitalized.

3. The *a* in *final* does not have an *a* sound. It has an indistinct neutral sound. Several longhand letters sometimes express this same indistinct sound. For example, the *i* in *possible*, the *o* in *method*, and the *u* in *butter* all have the same indistinct sound. To save writing time, we do not use a symbol or letter to express the neutral sounds in the body of a word. However, neutral vowel sounds must be expressed at the beginning and ending of a word.

Examples: above ; data 

Assignment 3 — **Phrases**. Joining two or more words when writing shorthand is called *phrasing*. Phrasing saves writing time. Cover the print of the following phrases and read them until you can do so rapidly. Then cover the shorthand and write the phrases from print, saying the phrase to yourself as you write it.

I can | of the | to go | to settle | he said | for the

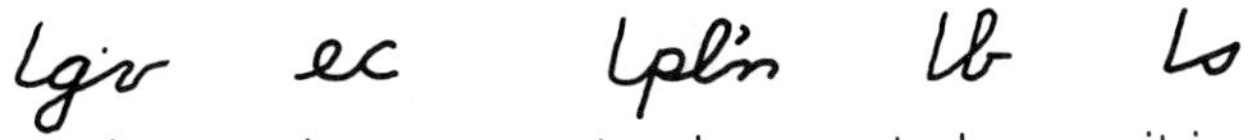

to give | he can | to plan | to be | it is

Learning tip: The outline for the phrase *it is* can also stand for *to us*, *to his*, *at his*, and *at us*. The meaning of the sentence will tell you the correct phrase.

Assignment 4 — **Reading and writing shorthand**. Read each sentence from shorthand until you can read it as rapidly as you can read from print. Write each sentence in shorthand until you can write each one rapidly and accurately.

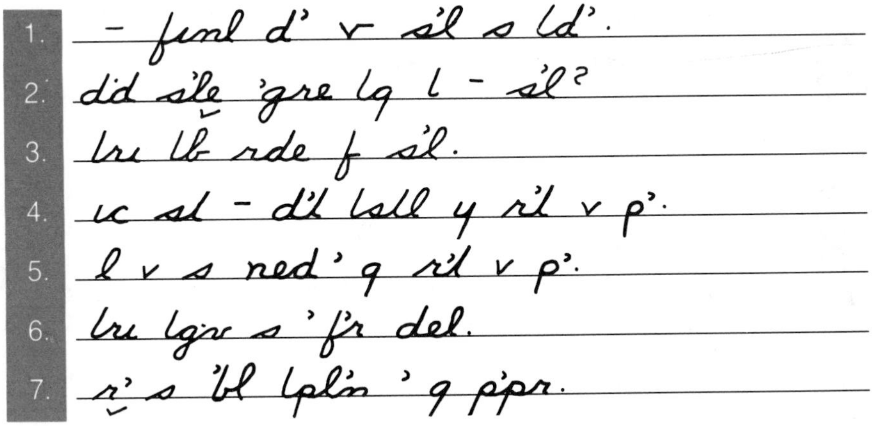

8. esd lg b se.
9. r' c gt ' g fnl grd f p'pr.
10. - ledr gv s ' g ide'.
11. ec p' f trip l'tr td'.
12. gv s - bl if ts rde.

BUILDING SHORTHAND SPEED AND TRANSCRIPTION ACCURACY

Assignment 5 — **Self-testing**. Complete Unit 2 in your *Study Guide* before you proceed with the rest of this chapter.

Assignment 6 — **Taking tape dictation**. To write from dictation the new words and sentences in this chapter, use Cassette 2 Side A from *Theory and Speed-Building Tapes*.

Assignment 7 — **Taking live dictation**. Write from dictation the sentences which are printed at the end of this chapter. Your instructor will dictate each group of 20 words to you at various speeds.

Assignment 8 — **Own-note transcription**. After you have taken the sentences in shorthand, select your best set of notes and transcribe them at your best typing rate. Do not number the sentences.

TRANSCRIPT OF SHORTHAND SENTENCES

1. The final day of the sale is today.
2. Did Sally agree to go to the sale?
3. Try to be ready for the sale. (20)
4. I can set the date to settle your rate of pay.
5. All of us need a good rate of pay.
6. Try to give us a fair deal. (40)
7. Ray is able to plan a good paper.
8. He said to go by sea.
9. Ray can get a good final grade for the paper. (60)
10. The leader gave us a good idea.
11. He can pay for the trip later today.
12. Give us the bill if it is ready. (80)

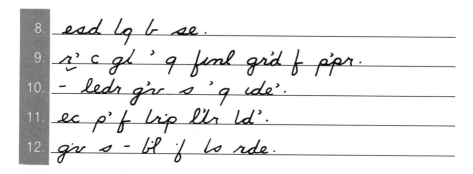

CHAPTER 3

WRITING SOUNDS OF HARD **C** AND **K**, **O**, AND SOFT **C**

Assignment 1 — **Rule discovery**. Follow the steps below to learn each writing principle.

Step 1. Examine the shorthand and the print of the first group of words. Try to discover the rule for writing that group of words. When you think you have discovered the rule, check the appropriate writing principle in your text to see if you have made the correct discovery.

Step 2. Cover the print of each line of shorthand words and read the shorthand until you can read each line as rapidly as you can read the print.

Step 3. Cover the shorthand of each line of words and write each word in shorthand until you can do so rapidly and accurately. You will progress faster if the shorthand words are dictated to you as you write them.

SOUND OF HARD **C** AND **K**

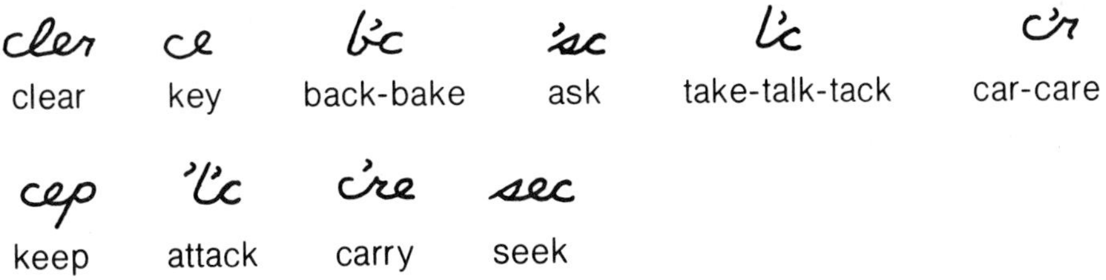

clear
key
back-bake
ask
take-talk-tack
car-care
keep
attack
carry
seek

SOUNDS OF **O**

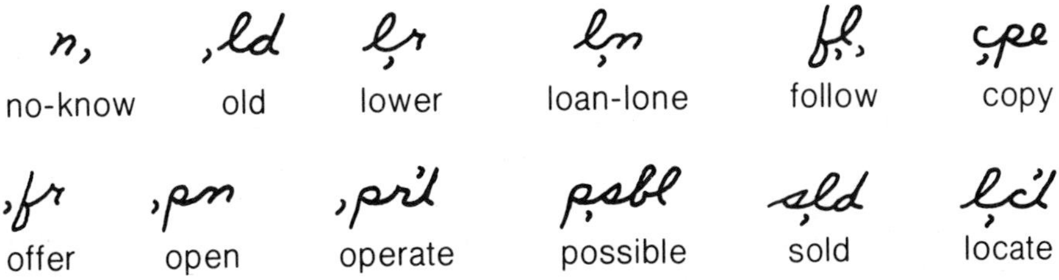

no-know
old
lower
loan-lone
follow
copy
offer
open
operate
possible
sold
locate

on-own lock bought-boat catalogue lot

factory course-coarse got sorry

SOUND OF SOFT C

face nice price office service notice policy

WRITING PRINCIPLES

HARD C AND K Write the longhand *c* to express the sound of hard *c* and *k*. The longhand *c* is used because it is much easier to write than *k*.

O Write a small curved stroke like a comma on or below the line of writing for all sounds of *o*.

SOFT C Write a longhand *s* when *c* has an *s* sound. When you write shorthand, you write what you hear.

Assignment 2 — **New vocabulary**. Follow these steps in learning new vocabulary words: (1) Study the print and the shorthand until you know the shorthand outline for each word. (2) Cover the print of each line of words and read the outlines until you can read them without hesitation. (3) Cover the shorthand of each line of words and write the outline for each word several times, saying the word to yourself each time you write it.

Remember, the abbreviated words that must be memorized are shown in italics and underlined in color.

n	nx	⌐	d	cn	den	nṭ
not	next	and	do	cannot	dean	note

icn	idid	in,	tp'	tsin	,n
I cannot	I did	I know	to pay	to sign	on the

Learning tip: Note how the *x* is written in *next* to save strokes. Simply add a tail to the *n* and cross the tail to form the *x*.

Assignment 3 — **Reading and writing shorthand**. Read each sentence from shorthand until you can read it as rapidly as you can read from print. Write each sentence in shorthand until you can write each one rapidly and accurately.

1. icn lcl y cpe v ,ld plse.
2. i d 'gre tp' - cllq pris f cr.
3. r' c ,pnl - ce ⌐ ,pn - ,ld lc.
4. in, ec gl vre q srvs l - fclre.
5. ls psbl l ,fr - crs l y ,fs.
6. - den sd - cllq c giv nts v crs.
7. - fclre srvs pln s ,pn l l pepl.
8. ic 'sc - fclre l ,fr ' lr pris.
9. sle sn rde l sin ' nt f ' ln l - ,fs.
10. - rl ,n nx nt s lr td'.

Learning tip: Some writers find they can omit many vowel symbols in words that *appear in a sentence* and still transcribe their notes accurately. Others find that they must insert most vowels. In the shorthand passages in this and later chapters, some vowel symbols have been omitted because the writer felt the passage could be accurately transcribed without them. In some cases, the writer has inserted a vowel in a word and later in the passage may have omitted the vowel in that same word. This was done because the writer felt the need for the vowel in some sentences and not in others.

The flexibility in the use of vowel symbols is an important feature of *Forkner Shorthand*. The more vowel symbols you can omit and still read your writing, the faster you will be able to take dictation.

All vowel symbols should be inserted when writing isolated words.

BUILDING SHORTHAND SPEED AND TRANSCRIPTION ACCURACY

Assignment 4 — **Self-testing**. Complete Unit 3 in your *Study Guide* before you proceed with the rest of this chapter.

Assignment 5 — **Taking tape dictation**. To write from dictation the new words and sentences in this chapter, use Cassette 3 Side A from *Theory and Speed-Building Tapes*.

Assignment 6 — **Taking live dictation**. Write from dictation the sentences which are printed at the end of this chapter. Your instructor will dictate each group of 20 words to you at various speeds.

Assignment 7 — **Own-note transcription**. After you have taken the sentences in shorthand, select your best set of notes and transcribe them at your best typing rate. Do not number the sentences.

TRANSCRIPT OF SHORTHAND SENTENCES

1. I cannot locate your copy of the old policy.
2. I do agree to pay the catalogue price for the car. (20)
3. Ray can operate the key and open the old lock.
4. I know he can get very good service at the factory. (40)
5. It is possible to offer the course at your office.
6. The dean said the catalogue can give notice of the course. (60)
7. The factory service plan is open to all people.
8. I can ask the factory to offer a lower price. (80)
9. Sally is not ready to sign a note for a loan at the office.
10. The rate on the next note is lower today. (100).

CHAPTER 4

BUSINESS LETTER DICTATION AND TRANSCRIPTION

No new writing principles are presented in this chapter. Instead, you will be taking business letters in shorthand and transcribing them. Because these letters *review* the writing principles you have already learned, you should concentrate on building your writing speed and transcription skills.

TRANSCRIBING BUSINESS LETTERS

Business letters are set up and typed according to certain guidelines. These guidelines will not be presented now because you should concentrate at this time on building speed in taking dictation and in transcribing your notes accurately. Therefore, do not type the letters in regular letter form until you are instructed to do so.

When you are ready to transcribe from the shorthand letters in the book or from your own notes, simply set your typewriter margins as directed and type the letters in the form shown under the heading, "Transcripts of Letters 1 and 2."

BUILDING TRANSCRIPTION SKILLS

Assignment 1 — **Correspondence Forms**. The *salutation* in a letter is the greeting that comes before the body of a letter. Some salutations are given below. Note that the salutation begins with a capital letter, usually includes the person's title (Mr., Mrs., Ms., Miss, Dr., etc.), and usually ends with a colon.

Dear Mrs. Jones:	Dear Miss Conti:	Ladies:
Dear Mr. Smith:	Dear Madam:	Ladies and Gentlemen:
Dear Ms. Taylor:	Gentlemen:	Mesdames:

The *complimentary close* comes after the body of a letter. Common complimentary closes include:

Yours truly,	Sincerely yours,	Yours sincerely,
Yours very truly,	Cordially yours,	

The first word in a complimentary close begins with a capital. A comma comes after the complimentary close if a colon is used after the salutation.

Assignment 2 — **Capitalization preview**. When transcribing, always capitalize days of the week, months, and names of holidays. Do not abbreviate days of the week or months when transcribing.

1. She will visit us the last Friday in August.
2. I believe that New Year's Day is on Sunday this year.
3. I will report for work on Monday.

Assignment 3 — **Using standard abbreviations**. Words that are commonly abbreviated in longhand are called *standard abbreviations*. To increase your writing speed, you should use these abbreviations. As you can see from the examples that follow, you apply the shorthand writing principles in writing standard abbreviations. Note that standard abbreviations are underlined with a dotted line in color.

Read and write the following standard abbreviations until you can do so rapidly and accurately.

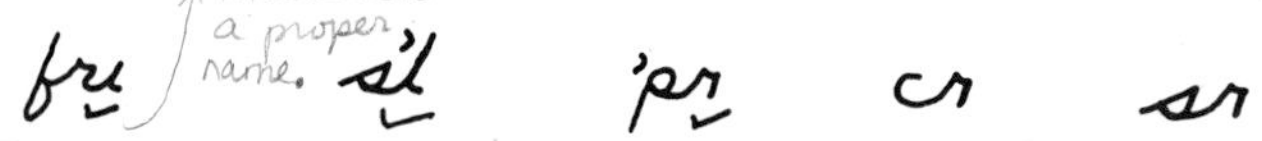

Friday Saturday April credit senior

BUSINESS LETTERS

Assignment 4 — **Letter 1**. Read and write each of the new words and phrases for Letter 1 until you can read and write each one rapidly and accurately. Then read and write the shorthand for Letter 1 until you can read and write it rapidly and accurately.

practice leave ticket given night say-saw

dear Debby play also class or-oar-ore

Yours truly paid-pad

Learning tip: *Yours truly* is an example of a *correspondence form*. Abbreviations for other complimentary closes and salutations will be introduced as they are used in the business letters. A list of correspondence forms is on page 15.

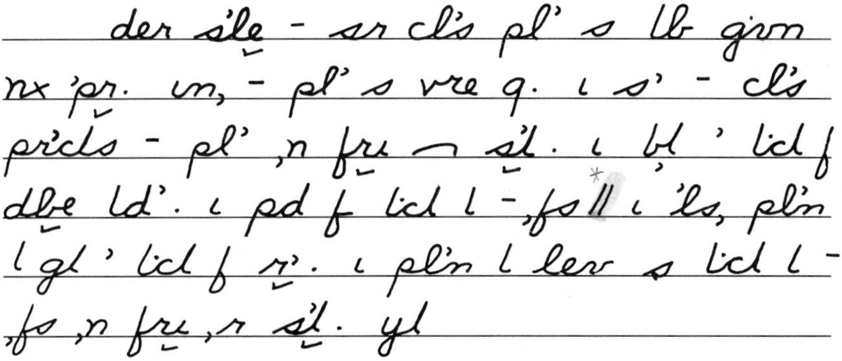

* **Learning tip**: When taking dictation, indicate a paragraph in your notes with two parallel diagonal lines as shown in the letter above.

Assignment 5 — **Letter 2**. Read and write each new word and phrase for Letter 2 until you can read and write each one rapidly and accurately. Then read and write the shorthand for Letter 2 until you can read and write it rapidly and accurately.

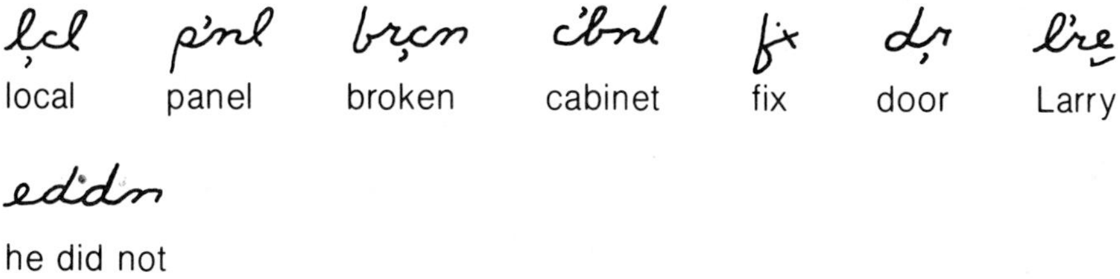
local
panel
broken
cabinet
fix
door
Larry
he did not

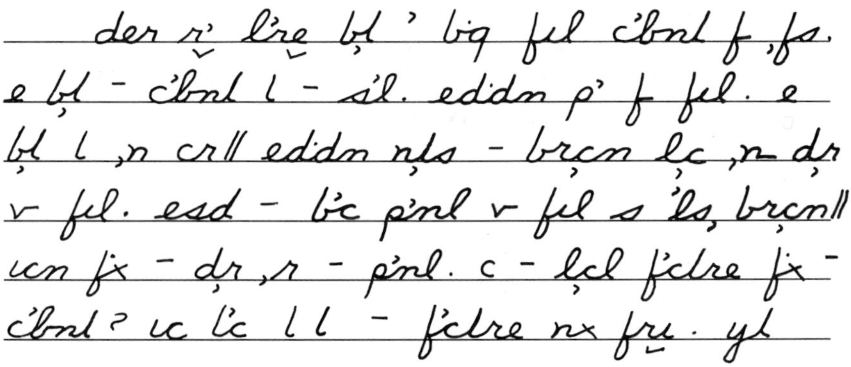

BUILDING SHORTHAND SPEED AND TRANSCRIPTION ACCURACY

Assignment 6 — **Self-testing**. Complete Unit 4 in your *Study Guide* before you proceed with the rest of this chapter.

Assignment 7 — **Taking tape dictation**. To write from dictation the new words and sentences in this chapter, use Cassette 4 Side A from *Theory and Speed-Building Tapes*.

Assignment 8 — **Taking live dictation**. Write from dictation the letters which are printed at the end of this chapter. Your instructor will dictate to you from these transcripts at various speeds.

Assignment 9 — **Own-note transcription**. Transcribe at your best typing rate an accurate copy of at least one of the letters you took in shorthand in Assignment 8. Type the letter in the form requested by your instructor. (See the model letter on page 154).

TRANSCRIPTS OF LETTERS 1 AND 2

Letter 1 Dear Sally: The senior class play is to be given next April. I know the play is very good. I saw the class (20) practice the play on Friday and Saturday. I bought a ticket for Debby today. I paid for the ticket at (40) the office.

I also plan to get a ticket for Ray. I plan to leave his ticket at the office on Friday (60) or Saturday. Yours truly, (65)

Letter 2 Dear Ray: Larry bought a big file cabinet for the office. He bought the cabinet at the sale. He did not pay (20) for the file. He bought it on credit.

He did not notice the broken lock on the door of the file. He said the back (40) panel of the file is also broken.

I cannot fix the door or the panel. Can the local factory fix (60) the cabinet? I can take it to the factory next Friday. Yours truly, (73)

EXAMINATION I

- Remove and complete Examination 1 which follows Unit 4 in your *Study Guide*, before proceeding to Chapter 5 of your textbook.

- Self-check with the Key to Examination 1 which appears at the back of the *Study Guide*.

CHAPTER 5

WRITING SOUNDS OF **U-OO**, **M**, AND **MENT**

Assignment 1 — **Rule discovery**. Follow the three-step plan to learn the new writing principles: (1) Discover the rule for each group of words. (2) Read the shorthand outlines until you can read them rapidly. (3) Cover the shorthand and write each word until you can do so rapidly and accurately.

SOUNDS OF **U-OO**

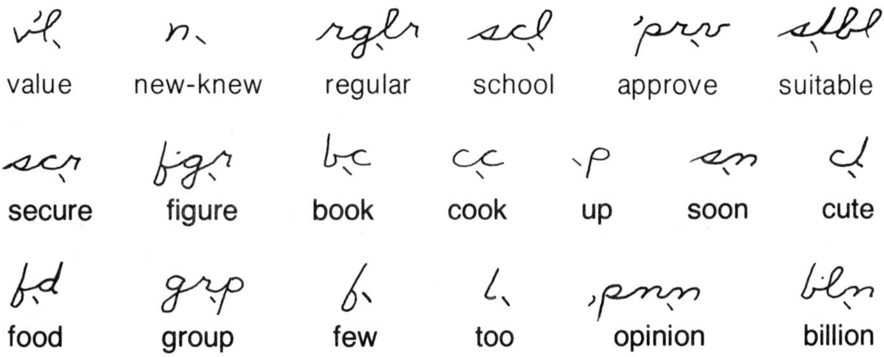
value
new-knew
regular
school
approve
suitable
secure
figure
book
cook
up
soon
cute
food
group
few
too
opinion
billion

SOUND OF **M**

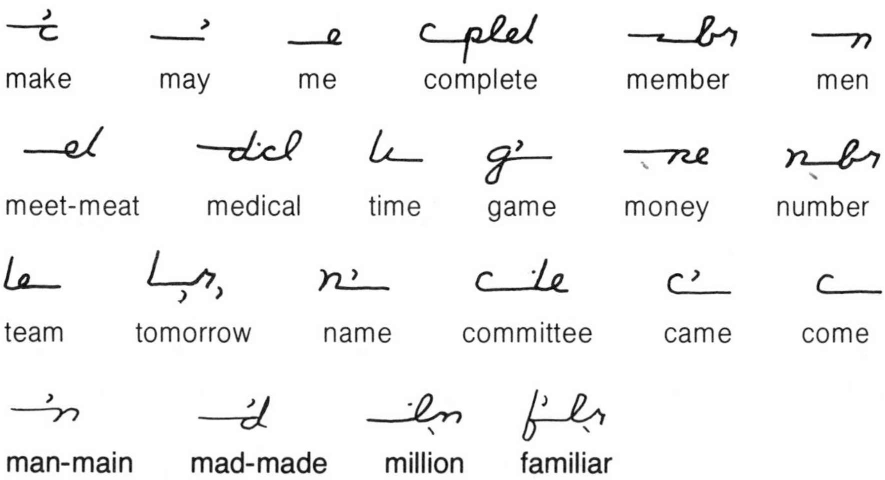
make
may
me
complete
member
men
meet-meat
medical
time
game
money
number
team
tomorrow
name
committee
came
come
man-main
mad-made
million
familiar

Learning tip: Note that the *m*'s in *member* are joined with a slight jog so that the two *m*'s can be easily recognized. Make the jog very small so it will not be mistaken for an *i*.

SYLLABLE **MENT**

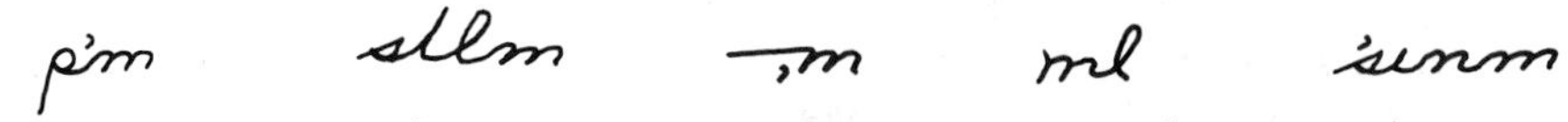

payment settlement moment mental assignment

agreement improvement movement commitment

WRITING PRINCIPLES

U-OO Write a short, slanted, downward stroke on or below the line of writing thus ` to express sounds of *u* and *oo*.

The following sounds illustrate various words in which the *u* stroke is written: *value, up, full, few.* The *u* stroke is also used for all *oo* sounds. Examples include sch*oo*l, b*oo*k, and st*oo*d. In some words a lightly sounded *y* comes before a *u* or other vowel sound. Examples include: *value, secure, familiar*, and *ammonia*. In such words, omit the lightly sounded *y* and write the *u* stroke.

M Write a long, straight line to express *m*. The long, straight line is used for *m* because longhand *m* takes too many strokes to write.

MENT Write a longhand *m* for the syllable *ment*.

Assignment 2 — **New vocabulary.** Read and write the following words and phrases until you can read and write them rapidly and accurately. Memorize the abbreviated words.

as right-write you like Mr. Mrs. company

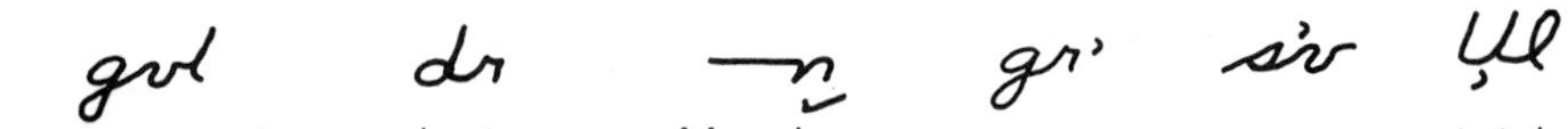

government doctor Monday gray save total

sun-son cut supply place low it is not

may be able as soon as to meet if you

Learning tip: Note that the *w* in *write* is silent. The *w* is silent in many other words. Examples include: *grow*, *sew*, *wrong*, and *wreck*.

Assignment 3 — **Reading and writing shorthand**. Read each sentence from shorthand until you can read it as rapidly as you can read from print. Write each sentence in shorthand until you can write each one rapidly and accurately.

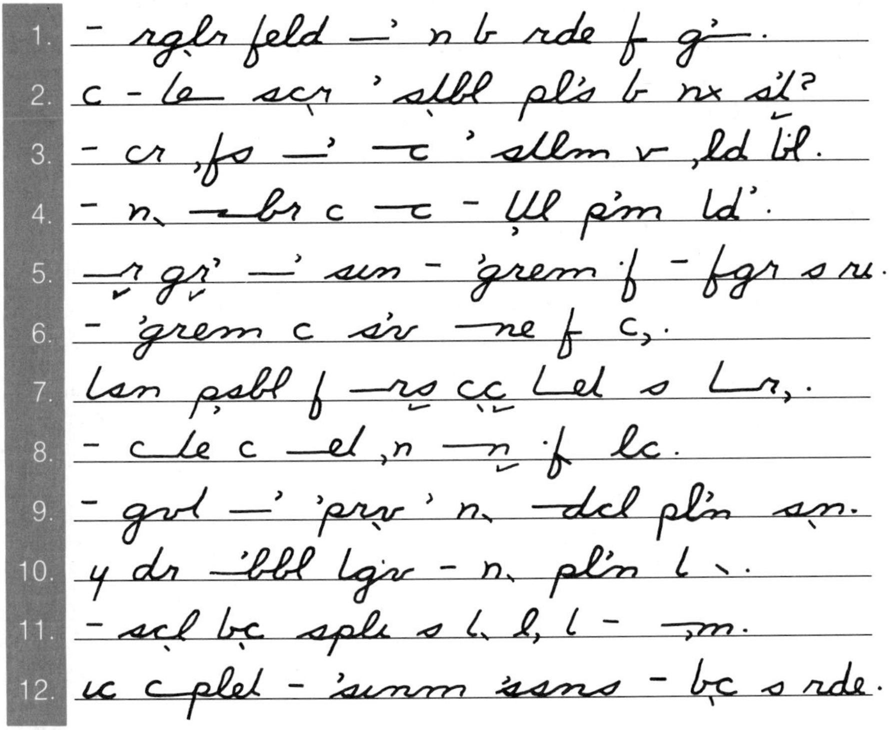

BUILDING SHORTHAND SPEED AND TRANSCRIPTION ACCURACY

Assignment 4 — **Self-testing.** Complete Unit 5 in your *Study Guide* before you proceed with the rest of this chapter.

Assignment 5 — **Taking tape dictation.** To write from dictation the new words and sentences in this chapter, use Cassette 5 Side A from *Theory and Speed-Building Tapes*.

Assignment 6 — **Taking live dictation.** Write from dictation the sentences which are printed at the end of this chapter. Your instructor will dictate each group of 20 words to you at various speeds.

Assignment 7 — **Own-note transcription.** After you have taken the sentences in shorthand, select your best set of notes and transcribe them at your best typing rate. Do not number the sentences.

TRANSCRIPT OF SHORTHAND SENTENCES

1. The regular field may not be ready for the game.
2. Can the team secure a suitable place by next Saturday? (20)
3. The credit office may make a settlement of the old bill.
4. The new member can make the total payment today. (40)
5. Mr. Gray may sign the agreement if the figure is right.
6. The agreement can save money for the company. (60)
7. It is not possible for Mrs. Cook to meet us tomorrow.
8. The committee can meet on Monday if you like. (80)
9. The government may approve a new medical plan soon.
10. Your doctor may be able to give the new plan to you. (100)
11. The school book supply is too low at the moment.
12. I can complete the assignment as soon as the book is ready. (120)

CHAPTER 6

WRITING SOUNDS OF SOFT **G** AND **J**, **IN-EN-UN**, AND **D** OR **ED** ADDED TO A ROOT WORD

Assignment 1 — **Rule discovery**. Follow the three-step plan to learn the new writing principles: (1) Discover the rule for each group of words. (2) Read the shorthand outlines until you can read them rapidly. (3) Cover the shorthand and write each word until you can do so rapidly and accurately.

SOUND OF SOFT **G** AND **J**

job college budget garage manager

management large page knowledge age general

June judge judgment

Learning tip: Remember to save time by omitting the final upward stroke in words ending in *j* or *g* (see *college* and *garage* above).

PREFIXES **IN-EN-UN**

increase indeed engine engineer unable-enable

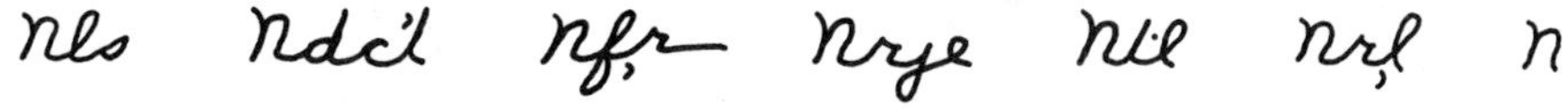

unless indicate inform energy until enrol in

income engage

D OR ED ADDED TO A ROOT WORD

pln	sbt	cnsl	dj	cplet
planned	submitted	cancelled	damaged	completed

sc	cl	Nvt	lcl	Nfr	pl
asked	called	invited	located	informed	played

Learning tip: Note that the short dash is written directly under the *a* in *played*.

WRITING PRINCIPLES

IN-EN-UN Write a longhand capital *N* thus N to express the prefixes *in-en-un*.

SOFT G AND J Write an undotted *j* for all soft sounds of *g* and *j*. You write what you hear in shorthand. The soft *g* in words like *edge* sounds like *j*.

PAST TENSE Make a short dash under the last letter or symbol in a word to show that *d* or *ed* is added to a root word to form the past tense.

This method of indicating past tense will help you transcribe accurately words that sound alike. An example: build bld billed bl

Assignment 2 — **New vocabulary**. Read and write the following words and phrases until you can read and write them rapidly. Memorize the abbreviated words.

csp	—	gr	pr
accept	am-more	great	opportunity

sls	gl	lc	Nsls	Nl
satisfy-satisfactory	glad	liked	unsatisfactory	into

Npd	gre	prv	prc	slre	dj
unpaid	agreed	improve	park	salary	damage

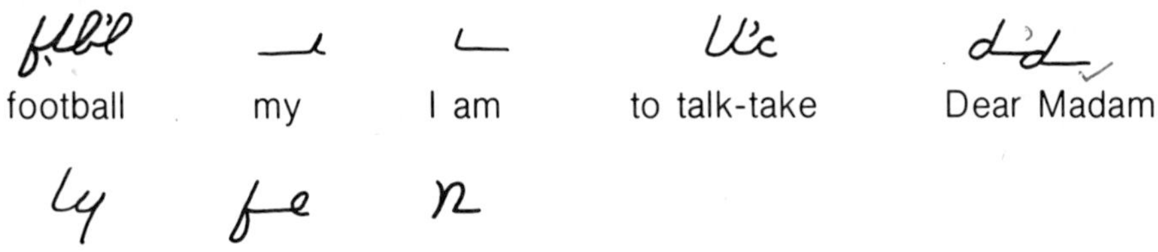

football | my | I am | to talk-take | Dear Madam

to your | for me | in the

Assignment 3 — **Reading and writing shorthand**. Read each sentence from shorthand until you can read it as rapidly as you can read from print. Write each sentence in shorthand until you can write each one rapidly and accurately.

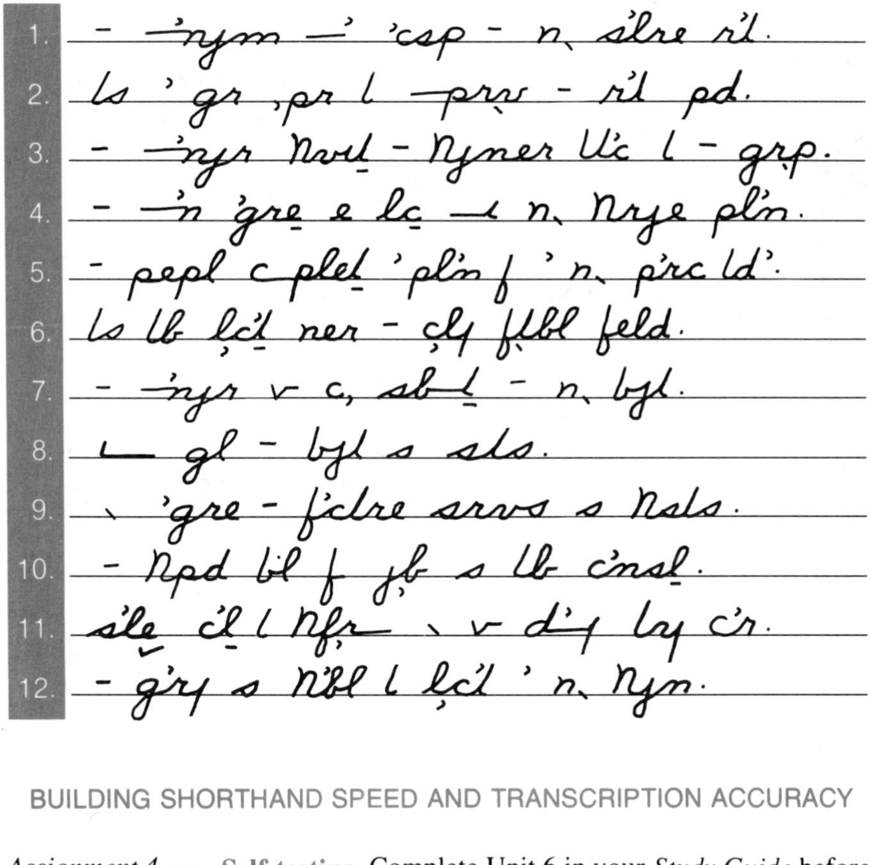

BUILDING SHORTHAND SPEED AND TRANSCRIPTION ACCURACY

Assignment 4 — **Self-testing**. Complete Unit 6 in your *Study Guide* before you proceed with the rest of this chapter.

Assignment 5 — **Taking tape dictation.** To write from dictation the new words and sentences in this chapter, use Cassette 6 Side A from *Theory and Speed-Building Tapes*.

Assignment 6 — **Taking live dictation.** Write from dictation the sentences which are printed at the end of this chapter. Your instructor will dictate each group of 20 words to you at various speeds.

Assignment 7 — **Own-note transcription.** After you have taken the sentences in shorthand, select your best set of notes and transcribe them at your best typing rate. Do not number the sentences.

Assignment 8 — **Supplemental business letters.** If instructed to do so, read and write the additional business letter for this chapter found in "Supplemental Letters for Dictation" in Appendix A.

TRANSCRIPT OF SHORTHAND SENTENCES

1. The management may accept the new salary rate.
2. It is a great opportunity to improve the rate paid. (20)
3. The manager invited the engineer to talk to the group.
4. The man agreed he liked my new energy plan. (40)
5. The people completed a plan for a new park today.
6. It is to be located near the college football field. (60)
7. The manager of the company submitted the new budget.
8. I am glad the budget is satisfactory. (80)
9. You agree the factory service is unsatisfactory.
10. The unpaid bill for the job is to be cancelled. (100)
11. Sally called to inform you of the damage to your car.
12. The garage is unable to locate a new engine. (120)

CHAPTER 7

WRITING SOUNDS OF **W-WH**, **AWA-AWAY**, AND **CON-COUN-COUNT**

Assignment 1 — **Rule discovery**. Follow the three-step plan to learn the new writing principles: (1) Discover the rule for each group of words. (2) Read the shorthand outlines until you can read them rapidly. (3) Cover the shorthand and write each word until you can do so rapidly and accurately.

SOUNDS OF **W-WH**

we week-weak warm warmer water-waiter when

way-weigh where-were why woman women wide

one-won white win work what-wait-weight

would-wood while wheel wire twice somewhere

Learning tip: When the *w-wh* stroke comes first in a word, begin the stroke below the line so the next letter rests on the line.

AWA-AWAY

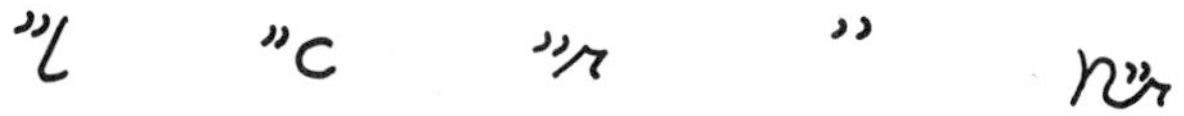

await awake aware away unaware

PREFIXES **CON-COUN-COUNT**

concern · concerned · consider · contain · consulted

council-counsel · county · considered · continue · country

WRITING PRINCIPLES

W-WH Write a long, upward, slanted line thus / for the sounds of *w* and *wh*.

AWA Write two *a* symbols thus ” for the combination *awa* and *away*.

CON-COUN-COUNT Write a capital C to express the prefixes *con*, *coun*, and *count*.

Assignment 2 — **New vocabulary**. Read and write the following words and phrases until you can read and write them rapidly. Memorize the abbreviated words.

after · any · are · will-well · arm · club · could

enough · noon · notify · package · invite · injured

yellow · matter · top · league · followed · some-sum

free · none · could not · I do not · we are · did not

we can · would be · Dear Sir

Assignment 3 — **Reading and writing shorthand**. Read each sentence from shorthand until you can read it as rapidly as you can read from print. Write each sentence in shorthand until you can write each one rapidly and accurately.

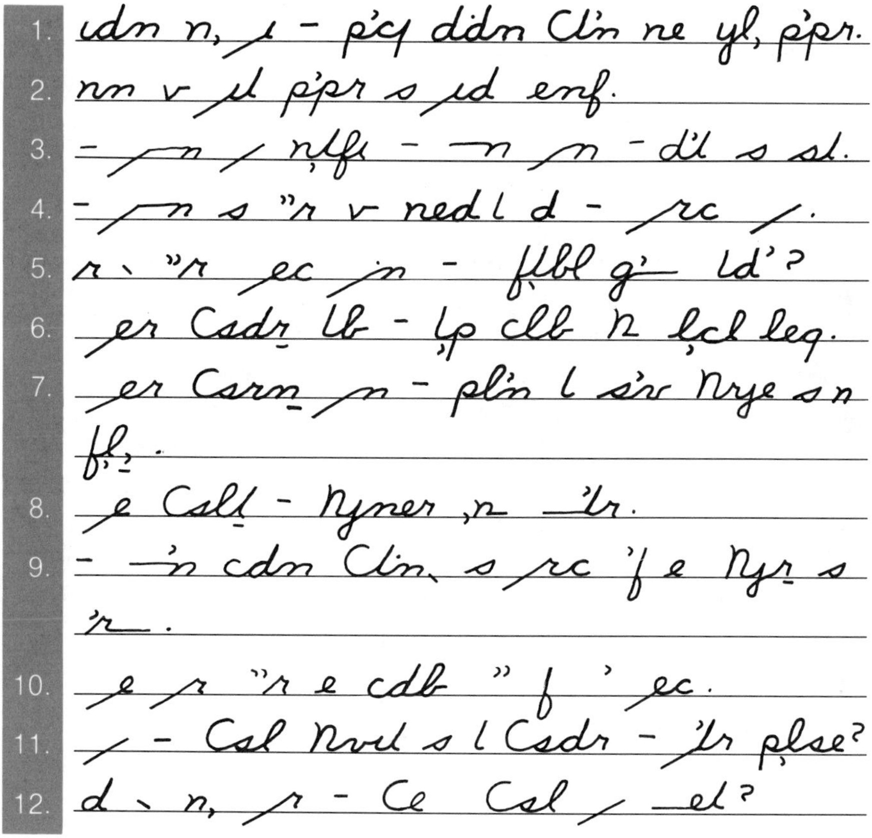

BUILDING SHORTHAND SPEED AND TRANSCRIPTION ACCURACY

Assignment 4 — **Self-testing**. Complete Unit 7 in your *Study Guide* before you proceed with the rest of this chapter.

Assignment 5 — **Taking tape dictation**. To write from dictation the new words and sentences in this chapter, use Cassette 7 Side A from *Theory and Speed-Building Tapes*.

Assignment 6 — **Taking live dictation**. Write from dictation the sentences which are printed at the end of this chapter. Your instructor will dictate each group of 20 words to you at various speeds.

Assignment 7 — **Own-note transcription**. After you have taken the sentences in shorthand, select your best set of notes and transcribe them at your best typing rate. Do not number the sentences.

Assignment 8 — **Supplemental business letters**. If instructed to do so, read and write the additional business letter for this chapter found in "Supplemental Letters for Dictation" in Appendix A.

TRANSCRIPT OF SHORTHAND SENTENCES

1. I do not know why the package did not contain any yellow paper.
2. None of the white paper is wide enough. (20)
3. The women will notify the men when the date is set.
4. The woman is aware of the need to do the work well. (40)
5. Are you aware we can win the football game today?
6. We are considered to be the top club in the local league. (60)
7. We are concerned when the plan to save energy is not followed.
8. We consulted the engineer on the matter. (80)
9. The man could not continue his work after he injured his arm.
10. We were aware he could be away for a week. (100)
11. Will the council invite us to consider the water policy?
12. Do you know where the county council will meet? (120)

CHAPTER 8

BUSINESS LETTER DICTATION AND TRANSCRIPTION

BUILDING TRANSCRIPTION SKILLS

Assignment 1 — **Punctuating introductory words, phrases, and clauses.** An introductory word or expression introduces the reader to the rest of the sentence. Place a comma after an introductory word, phrase, or clause.

The most common introductory words and expressions include: *therefore, however, nevertheless, even so, furthermore,* and *for example*. Introductory phrases and clauses usually begin with one of the following words: *if, since, when, after, although, as, because, in, unless, upon, whenever,* and *while*.

The letters in this chapter include introductory expressions that are set off by commas. Note how the punctuation rule for introductory expressions is applied in the following examples. Apply the rule when transcribing the letters.

1. If you accept the offer, we will make you a partner.
2. When you visit me in August, we can go to the lake.
3. While I was on vacation, my new car arrived.
4. Unless your paper is completed in time, you will get an incomplete.
5. However, exceptions will be made in case of illness.
6. Therefore, make every effort to get your paper in on time.
7. Furthermore, the term paper should be typed.
8. As you know, my car ran out of gas last night.

Assignment 2 — **Punctuating shorthand notes.** If time permits, you may insert commas and other punctuation during dictation. Circle the punctuation marks within a sentence so you can distinguish them easily when transcribing. Because periods and question marks do not come within a sentence, they need not be circled. Note how the commas are circled in Letters 1 and 2.

Assignment 3 — **Spelling review.** To transcribe accurately, a secretary must be able to spell correctly. When in doubt about the spelling of a word when transcribing, always look up the word in a dictionary.

This and later spelling reviews cover common words that are often misspelled when transcribing. Use the following steps to check your ability to spell these words correctly:

Step 1. Pronounce each word slowly, one syllable at a time, as you note how each word is spelled.

Step 2. Then write the shorthand outline for each spelling word in a column on the left side of your shorthand notebook. The outlines for all the words have been presented in previous chapters in your textbook.

Step 3. Close your textbook and write the transcript of each outline you have written in your notebook.

Step 4. Check your spelling of each word with the spelling in your textbook. Study any words you may have misspelled.

1. accept
2. budget
3. catalogue
4. committee
5. complete
6. damage
7. energy
8. engineer
9. follow
10. general
11. government
12. increase
13. knowledge
14. management
15. office
16. operate
17. people
18. policy
19. possible
20. ready
21. service
22. until

BUSINESS LETTERS

Assignment 4 — **Letter 1**. Read and write each new word and phrase for Letter 1 until you can read and write each one rapidly and accurately. Then read and write the shorthand for Letter 1 to build your writing speed.

engage capable motel approval offered so-sew

Jean we feel would like you are let me know

for us for his to buy you will be able

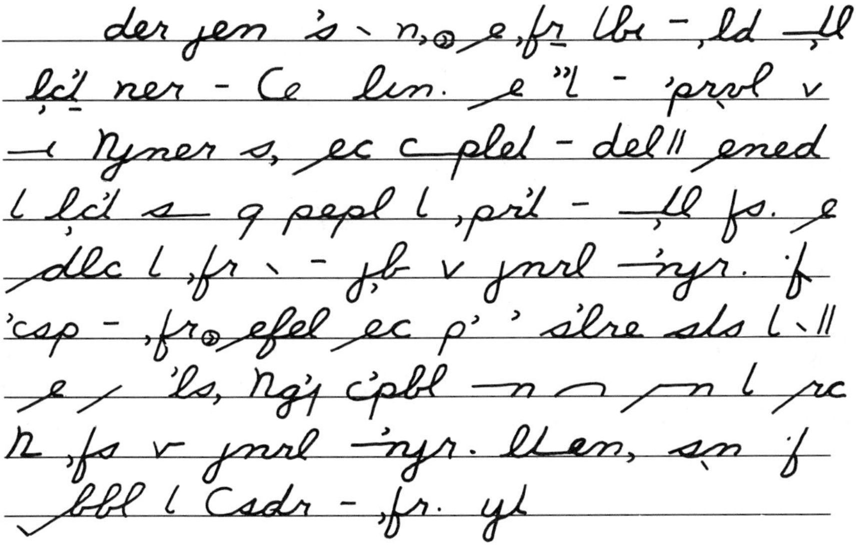

Assignment 5 — **Letter 2**. Read and write each new word and phrase for Letter 2 until you can read and write each one rapidly and accurately. Then read and write the shorthand for Letter 2 to build your writing speed.

mail-male made-maid worked desk clerk

summer tried call learned to know Dear Mrs.

to tell for you

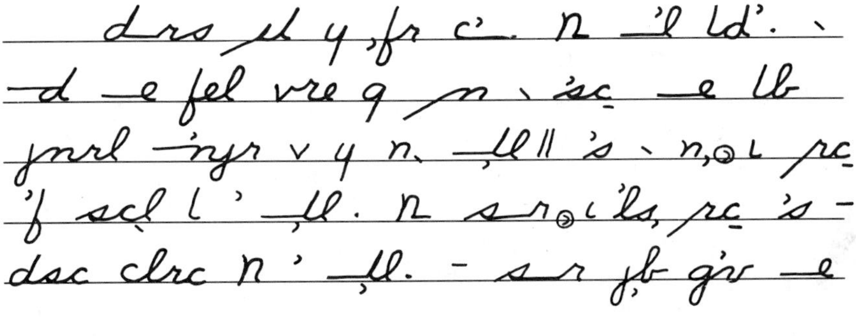

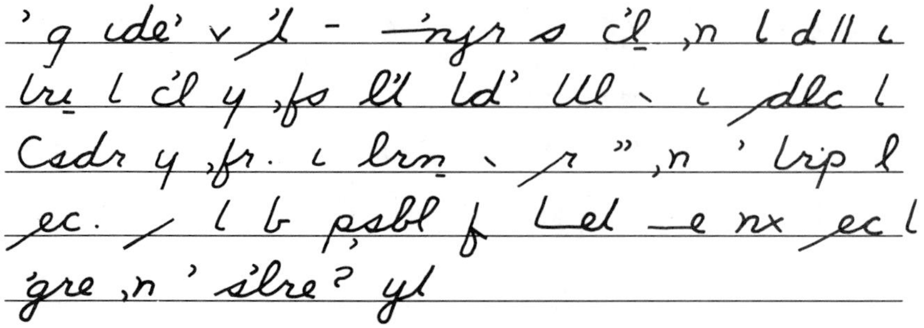

Assignment 6 — **Supplemental business letters**. If instructed to do so, read and write the additional business letters for this chapter found in "Supplemental Letters for Dictation" in Appendix A.

BUILDING SHORTHAND AND TRANSCRIPTION ACCURACY

Assignment 7 — **Self-testing**. Complete Unit 8 in your *Study Guide* before you proceed with the rest of this chapter.

Assignment 8 — **Taking tape dictation**. To write from dictation the new words and letters in this chapter, use Cassette 8 Side A from *Theory and Speed-Building Tapes*.

Assignment 9 — **Taking live dictation**. Write from dictation the letters which are printed at the end of this chapter. Your instructor will dictate to you from these transcripts at various speeds.

Assignment 10 — **Own-note transcription**. Transcribe at your best typing rate an accurate copy of at least one of the letters you took in shorthand in Assignment 9. Type the letter in the form requested by your instructor.

TRANSCRIPTS OF LETTERS 1 AND 2

Letter 1 Dear Jean: As you know, we offered to buy the old motel located near the county line. We await the approval (20) of my engineer so we can complete the deal.

We need to locate some good people to operate the motel (40) for us. We would like to offer you the job of general manager. If you accept the offer, we feel (60) we can pay a salary satisfactory to you.

We will also engage capable men and women to (80) work in the office of the general manager. Let me know soon if you will be able to consider the (100) offer. Yours truly, (104)

Letter 2 Dear Mrs. White: Your offer came in the mail today. You made me feel very good when you asked me to be general (20) manager of your new motel.

As you know, I worked after school at a motel. In the summer, I also (40) worked as the desk clerk in a motel. The summer job gave me a good idea of what the manager is called (60) on to do.

I tried to call your office late today to tell you I would like to consider your offer. I learned (80) you were away on a trip all week. Will it be possible for you to meet me next week to agree on a (100) salary? Yours truly, (103)

REVIEWING THE WRITING PRINCIPLES

All the writing principles, abbreviated words, and standard abbreviations you have learned in Chapters 1 through 8 are reviewed on Tape 17 Side A of the *Theory and Speed-Building Tapes*. Take dictation from this tape before completing Examination 2.

EXAMINATION 2

- Remove and complete Examination 2, which follows Unit 8 in your *Study Guide*, before proceeding to Chapter 9 of your textbook.
- Self-check with the Key to Examination 2 which appears at the back of the *Study Guide*.

CHAPTER 9

WRITING SOUNDS OF **H**, **SH**, AND **BE-DE-RE**

Assignment 1 – **Rule discovery**. Follow the three-step plan to learn the new writing principles: (1) Discover the rule for each group of words. (2) Read the shorthand outlines until you can read them rapidly. (3) Cover the shorthand and write each word until you can do so rapidly and accurately.

SOUND OF **H**

her help had hold high him home hot

hope hotel who head hire-higher hear-here

Learning tips:

1. Make the *h* dash short so you will not confuse it with the long line for *m*.
2. Note that *h* is joined to *m* in *him* and *home* with a very slight jog.
3. The *h* dash may be written on the line, as in *her*, or above the line, as in *hot*.

SOUND OF **SH**

she shall cash publish finish machine wish

shop official pleasure should show unusual

PREFIXES **BE-DE-RE**

believe delay deliver development receipt repair

return release become begin

WRITING PRINCIPLES

H	Write a short dash thus — to express the sound of *h*.
SH	Write an *h* dash through the *s* to express *sh*.
BE-DE-RE	Omit the *e* in the prefixes *be*, *de*, and *re*.

Assignment 2 — **New vocabulary**. Read and write the following words and phrases until you can read and write them rapidly. Memorize the abbreviated words.

appreciate
have
put-please
receive
ship-short
side
Wednesday
decide
before
decided
received
shipment
from
firm
bulletin
signed
cover
below-blow
should not
should be
we should
we shall
we believe
to see
to receive
I hope
we received

Assignment 3 — **Reading and writing shorthand**. Read each sentence from shorthand until you can read it as rapidly as you can read from print. Write each sentence in shorthand until you can write each one rapidly and accurately.

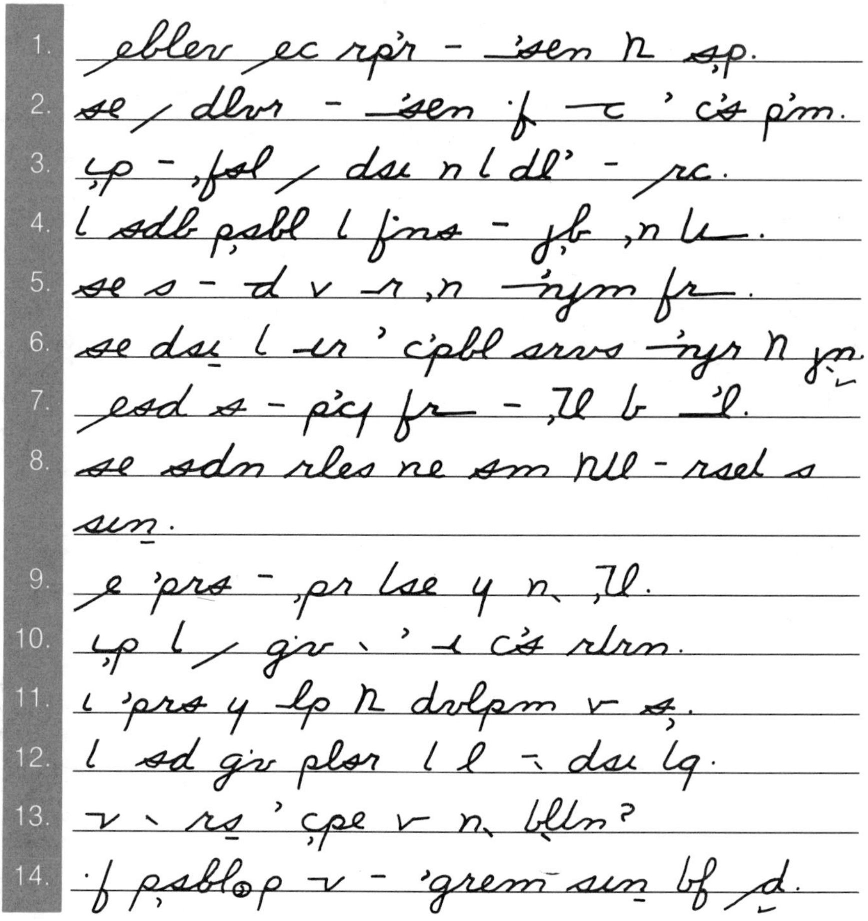

BUILDING SHORTHAND SPEED AND TRANSCRIPTION ACCURACY

Assignment 4 — **Self-testing**. Complete Unit 9 in your *Study Guide* before you proceed with the rest of this chapter.

Assignment 5 — **Taking tape dictation**. To write from dictation the new words and sentences in this chapter, use Cassette 9 Side A from *Theory and Speed-Building Tapes*.

Assignment 6 — **Taking live dictation**. Write from dictation the sentences which are printed at the end of this chapter. Your instructor will dictate each group of 20 words to you at various speeds.

Assignment 7 — **Own-note transcription**. After you have taken the sentences in shorthand, select your best set of notes and transcribe them at your best typing rate. Do not number the sentences.

Assignment 8 — **Supplemental business letters**. If instructed to do so, read and write the additional business letter for this chapter found in "Supplemental Letters for Dictation" in Appendix A.

TRANSCRIPT OF SHORTHAND SENTENCES

1. We believe we can repair the machine in the shop.
2. She will deliver the machine if you make a cash payment. (20)
3. I hope the official will decide not to delay the work.
4. It should be possible to finish the job on time. (40)
5. She is the head of her own management firm.
6. She decided to hire a capable service manager in June. (60)
7. We should ship the package from the hotel by mail.
8. She should not release any shipment until the receipt is signed. (80)
9. We appreciate the opportunity to see your new hotel.
10. I hope it will give you a high cash return. (100)
11. I appreciate your help in the development of the show.
12. It should give pleasure to all who decide to go. (120)
13. Have you received a copy of the new bulletin?
14. If possible, please have the agreement signed before Wednesday. (140)

CHAPTER 10

WRITING SOUNDS OF **CH**, **TH**, AND HARD **S** AND **Z**

Assignment 1 — **Rule discovery**. Follow the three-step plan to learn the new writing principles: (1) Discover the rule for each group of words. (2) Read the shorthand outlines until you can read them rapidly. (3) Cover the shorthand and write each word until you can do so rapidly and accurately.

SOUND OF **CH**

chair   charge   check-cheque   chapter   child   children

teach   much   which   such   attach   reach   church

teacher   picture   feature   future   fixture

Learning tips:

1. Be sure to write the *ch* sound as shown above. The word *church* illustrates the two ways that the *ch* sound is written.
2. Note that some words have a *ch* sound but do not have the letters *ch* in them. Examples: *feature*, *future*, *picture*. Remember to write what you hear.

SOUND OF **TH**

than   then   them   their-there   either   rather

leather   method   month   they   this   weather-whether

SOUND OF HARD S AND Z

busy | choose | close (v) | deposit | desire | visit

visited | does | season | use (v) | result | zoo | size

was | reason | these | those | cause

Learning tip: The *(v)* after *close* and *use* indicates that these are verb forms of the words.

WRITING PRINCIPLES

CH — Write an *h* dash through the *c* to express *ch*.

When writing *ch* at the beginning of a word, write the *c* first. Then write the dash through the *c*, joining the *h* dash to the next letter, as in the words *chair* and *charge*. When *ch* occurs in the body or at the end of a word, make the *h* dash *an extension* of the preceding letter. Then write the *c* through the *h* dash, as in the word *feature*.

TH — Join an *h* dash to the *t* to express *th*.

Most writers find it is easier to join the *h* to *t* by retracing the *t* part way up and then writing the *h* dash. Some writers prefer to write *th* thus . Either way is correct.

HARD S AND Z — Write a small longhand *z* to express the hard sound of *s*. This rule follows the principle of writing the sound you *hear* when you write shorthand.

Assignment 2 — **New vocabulary**. Read and write the following words and phrases until you can read and write them rapidly. Memorize the abbreviated words.

each | *merchandise* | *that-thank* | manufacture | remain

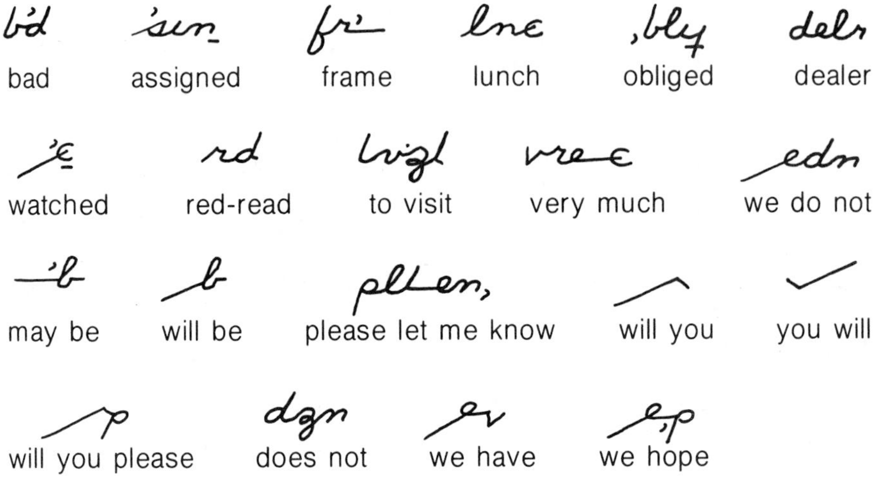
bad
assigned
frame
lunch
obliged
dealer
watched
red-read
to visit
very much
we do not
may be
will be
please let me know
will you
you will
will you please
does not
we have
we hope

Assignment 3 — **Reading and writing shorthand**. Read each sentence from shorthand until you can read it as rapidly as you can read from print. Write each sentence in shorthand until you can write each one rapidly and accurately.

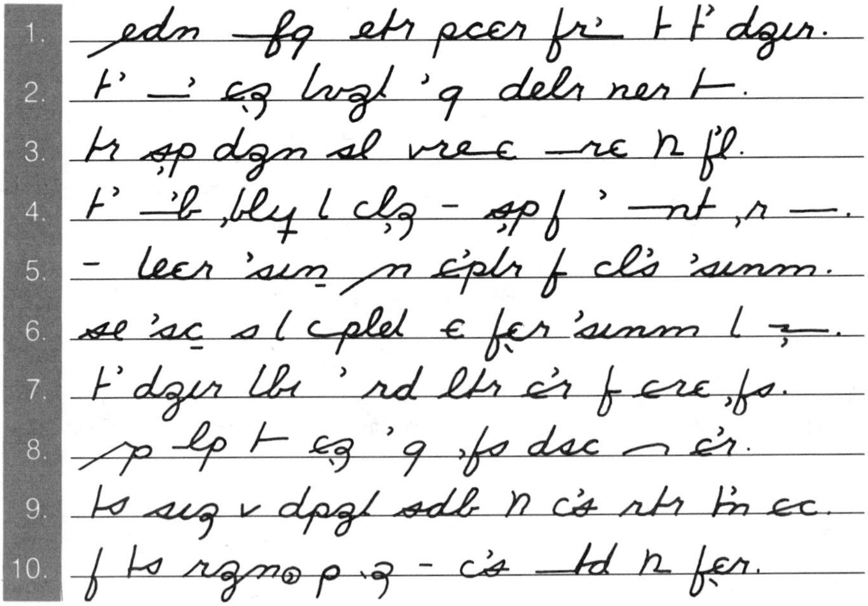
1.
2.
3.
4.
5.
6.
7.
8.
9.
10.

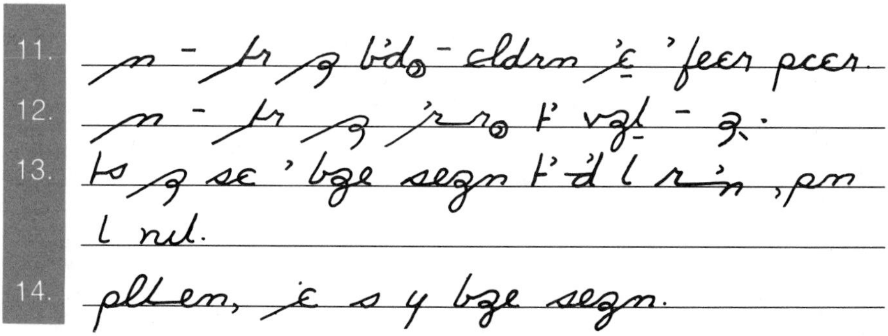

BUILDING SHORTHAND SPEED AND TRANSCRIPTION ACCURACY

Assignment 4 — **Self-testing**. Complete Unit 10 in your *Study Guide* before you proceed with the rest of this chapter.

Assignment 5 — **Taking tape dictation**. To write from dictation the new words and sentences in this chapter, use Cassette 10 Side A from *Theory and Speed-Building Tapes*.

Assignment 6 — **Taking live dictation**. Write from dictation the sentences which are printed at the end of this chapter. Your instructor will dictate each group of 20 words to you at various speeds.

Assignment 7 — **Own-note transcription**. After you have taken the sentences in shorthand, select your best set of notes and transcribe them at your best typing rate. Do not number the sentences.

Assignment 8 — **Supplemental business letters**. If instructed to do so, read and write the additional business letter for this chapter found in "Supplemental Letters for Dictation" in Appendix A.

TRANSCRIPT OF SHORTHAND SENTENCES

1. We do not manufacture either picture frame that they desire.
2. They may choose to visit a good dealer near them. (20)
3. Their shop does not sell very much merchandise in the fall.
4. They may be obliged to close the shop for a month or more. (40)
5. The teacher assigned one chapter for the class assignment.
6. She asked us to complete each future assignment at home. (60)
7. They desire to buy a red leather chair for the church office.

→ within.

8. Will you please help them choose a good office desk and chair. (80)
9. This size of deposit should be in cash rather than cheque.
10. For this reason, please use the cash method in the future. (100)
11. When the weather was bad, the children watched a feature picture.
12. When the weather was warmer, they visited the zoo. (120)
13. This was such a busy season they had to remain open at night.
14. Please let me know which is your busy season. (140)

CHAPTER 11

WRITING SOUNDS OF **NG-ING-THING**, **AD-ADD**, AND **TRANS**

Assignment 1 – **Rule discovery**. Follow the three-step plan to learn the new writing principles: (1) Discover the rule for each group of words. (2) Read the shorthand outlines until you can read them rapidly. (3) Cover the shorthand and write each word until you can do so rapidly and accurately.

SOUNDS OF **NG-ING-THING**

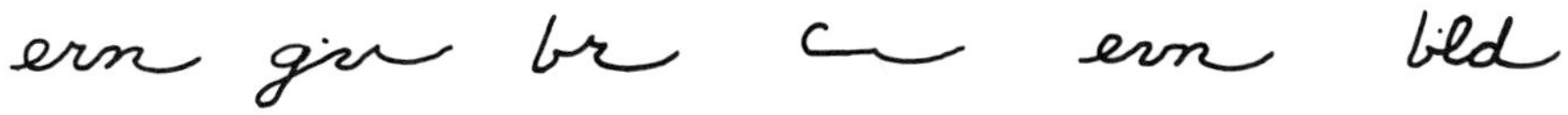

earning giving bring coming evening building

getting meeting among along selling reviewing

thing planning bank blank think long nothing

bringing something asking considering increasing

frank beginning morning opening looking

following young language English publishing

Learning tip: Some words ending in *nk* also have an *ng* sound before the hard *c*. See *bank*, *blank*, and *think* above.

PREFIX **AD-ADD**

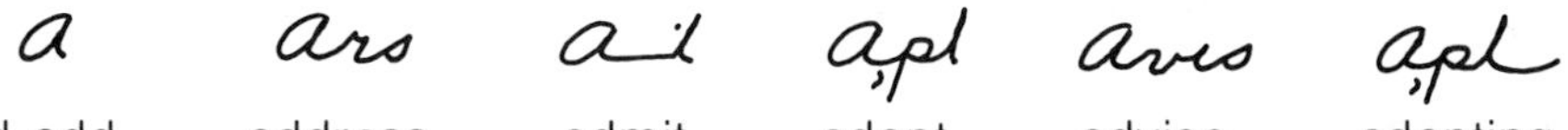

ad-add address admit adopt advice adopting

advise added advised adding

PREFIX **TRANS**

transfer transferred transferring transform transmit

transmitted transmitting translate

WRITING PRINCIPLES

NG-ING-THING Write a long, curved stroke thus to express the combinations *ng-ing-thing*.

AD-ADD Write a capital to express the prefix *ad-add*. Use this longhand form of *a* because it can be written quickly and joined easily to other letters.

TRANS Write a capital to express the prefix *trans*. Any form of capital *T* may be used. The *T* may be joined or disjoined. Example: *transfer*: or .

Assignment 2 — **New vocabulary**. Read and write the following words and phrases until you can read and write them rapidly. Memorize the abbreviated words.

advertise *has* *business* secretary being

advertising writing anything shipping writer

count
conserve
magazine
message
done
issue
review
he is
we think
to do
to bring
thank you
we shall be glad

Assignment 3 — **Reading and writing shorthand**. Read each sentence from shorthand until you can read it as rapidly as you can read from print. Write each sentence in shorthand until you can write each one rapidly and accurately.

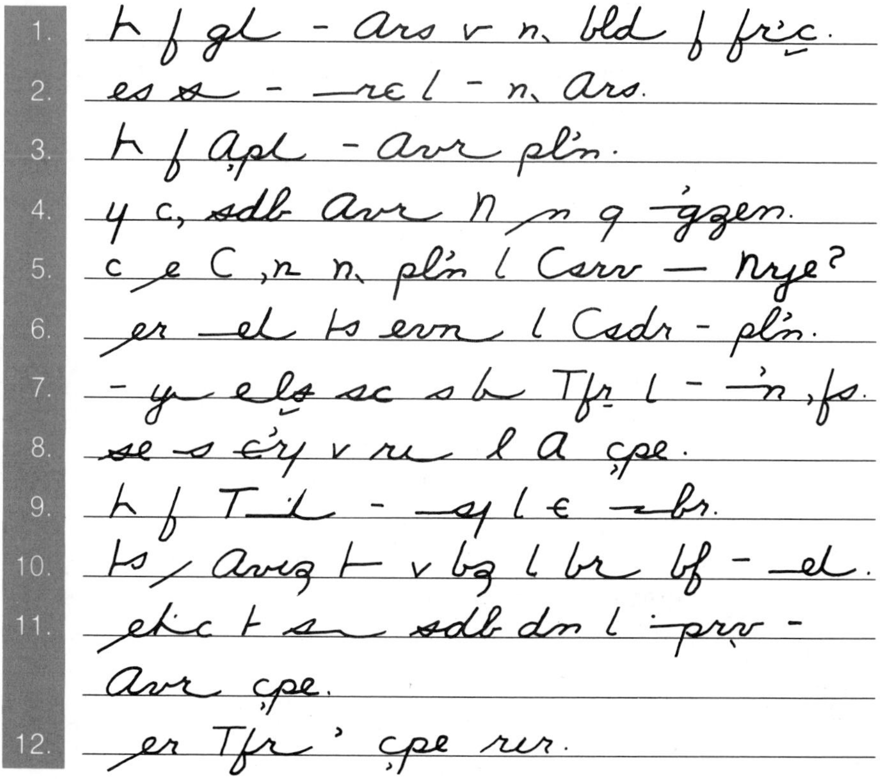
1.
2.
3.
4.
5.
6.
7.
8.
9.
10.
11.
12.

13.
14.

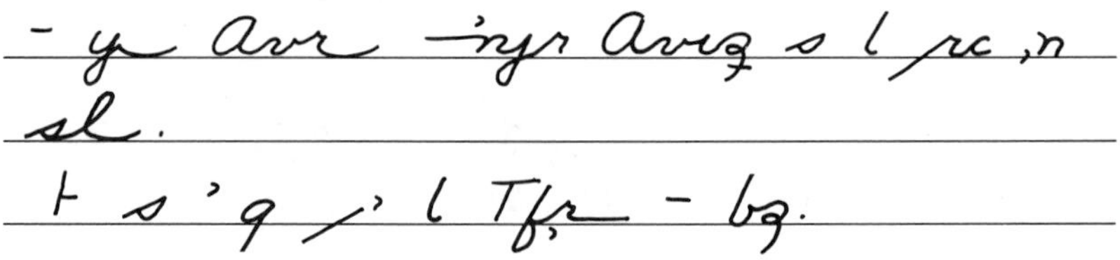

BUILDING SHORTHAND SPEED AND TRANSCRIPTION ACCURACY

Assignment 4 — **Self-testing**. Complete Unit 11 in your *Study Guide* before you proceed with the rest of this chapter.

Assignment 5 — **Taking tape dictation**. To write from dictation the new words and sentences in this chapter, use Cassette 11 Side A from *Theory and Speed-Building Tapes*.

Assignment 6 — **Taking live dictation**. Write from dictation the sentences which are printed at the end of this chapter. Your instructor will dictate each group of 20 words to you at various speeds.

Assignment 7 — **Own-note transcription**. After you have taken the sentences in shorthand, select your best set of notes and transcribe them at your best typing rate. Do not number the sentences.

Assignment 8 — **Supplemental business letters**. If instructed to do so, read and write the additional business letter for this chapter found in "Supplemental Letters for Dictation" in Appendix A.

TRANSCRIPT OF SHORTHAND SENTENCES

1. Thank you for getting the address of the new building for Frank.
2. He is shipping the merchandise to the new address. (20)
3. Thank you for adopting the advertising plan.
4. Your company should be advertising in one good magazine. (40)
5. Can we count on the new plan to conserve more energy?
6. We are meeting this evening to consider the plan. (60)
7. The young English secretary is being transferred to the main office.
8. She has charge of writing all ad copy. (80)
9. Thank you for transmitting the message to each member.

10. This will advise them of business to bring before the meeting. (100)
11. We think that something should be done to improve the advertising copy.
12. We are transferring a copy writer. (120)
13. The young advertising manager advised us to work on selling.
14. That is a good way to transform the business. (140)

CHAPTER 12

BUSINESS LETTER DICTATION AND TRANSCRIPTION

BUILDING TRANSCRIPTION SKILLS

Assignment 1 — **Punctuating parenthetical words and expressions**. Parenthetical words or expressions are those that can be omitted without changing the meaning of the sentence. Place a comma before and after parenthetical words or expressions. Common parenthetical words and expressions include: *indeed*, *also*, *however*, *therefore*, *perhaps*, *as you know*, *at any rate*, *I believe*, *I think*, *no doubt*, *of course*.

Study the examples below and apply the rule for punctuating parenthetical words and expressions in the letters that follow.

1. My car is, as you know, a terrible gas guzzler.
2. I can reduce my gas consumption, they tell me, if I replace my air filter.
3. I can't do that, I regret to say, because I have a slight financial problem.
4. I am, therefore, forced to wait until pay day.

Assignment 2 — **Punctuating a polite request**. A polite request asks for action rather than an answer. Use a period after a polite request, as in the examples that follow.

1. If you cannot come, will you please telephone me.
2. May I have your new address.
3. Will you please send the books by mail.

Assignment 3 — **Spelling review**. Follow these steps to check your ability to spell correctly the words on page 51.

Step 1. Pronounce each word slowly as you note how each word is spelled.

Step 2. Write the shorthand outline for each word in a column on the left side of your shorthand notebook.

Step 3. Close your textbook and write the transcript of each outline you have written in your notebook.

Step 4. Check your transcript of each word with the spelling in your textbook. Study any words you may have misspelled.

1. approval
2. attach
3. appreciate
4. beginning
5. believe
6. business
7. future
8. machine
9. manufacture
10. merchandise
11. owner
12. planning
13. pleasure
14. receipt
15. receive
16. secretary
17. something
18. summer
19. transfer
20. transferred
21. transferring
22. Wednesday
23. write
24. writing

BUSINESS LETTERS

Assignment 4 — **Letter 1**. Read and write each of the new words and phrases for Letter 1 until you can read and write each one rapidly and accurately. Then read and write the shorthand for Letter 1 to build your writing speed.

Tuesday
afternoon
satisfied
therefore
during
measured
recall
room
urge
hoping
telephone
bell
with
adopted
area
else
available
helpful
increased
determine
happy
informing
Ms.
can be
we should like
could be
to come
to be able
Dear Ms.
Very truly yours

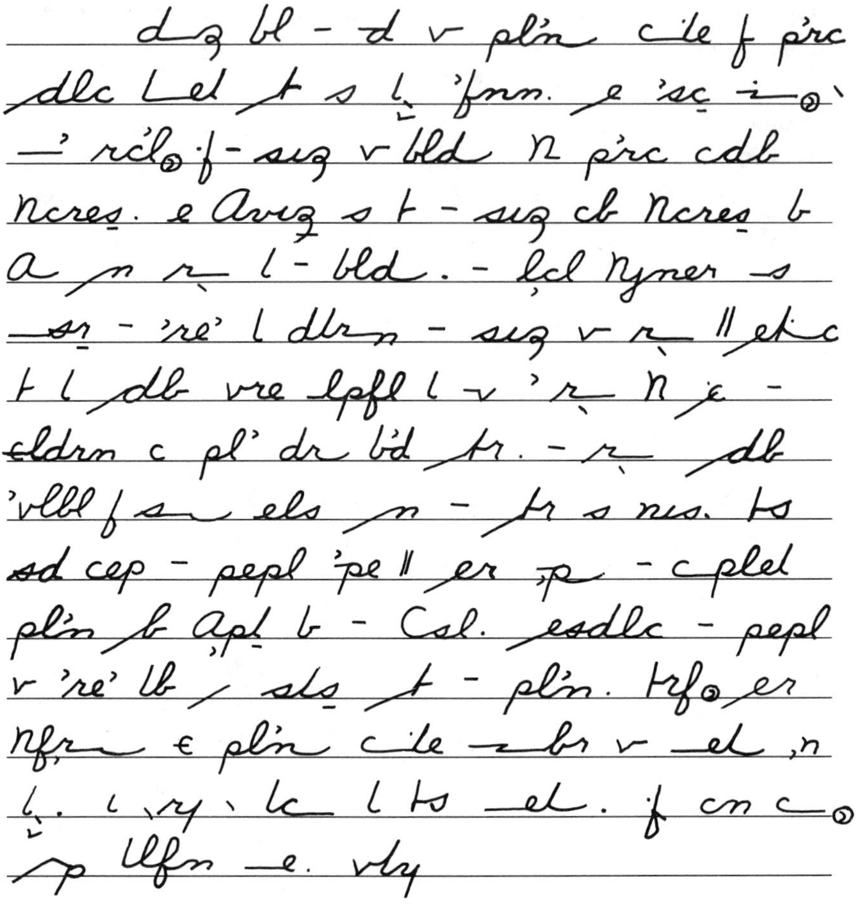

Assignment 5 — **Letter 2**. Read and write each of the new words and phrases for Letter 2 until you can read and write each one rapidly and accurately. Then read and write the shorthand for Letter 2 to build your writing speed.

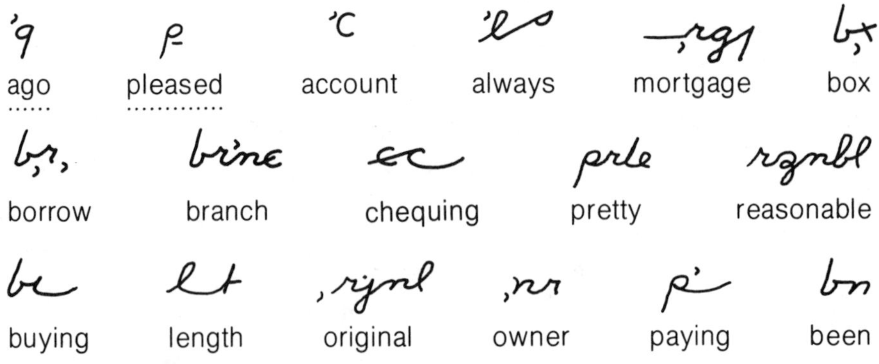
ago
pleased
account
always
mortgage
box
borrow
branch
chequing
pretty
reasonable
buying
length
original
owner
paying
been

thought safe banking same told we have been

Dear Mr. would have I shall some time at your

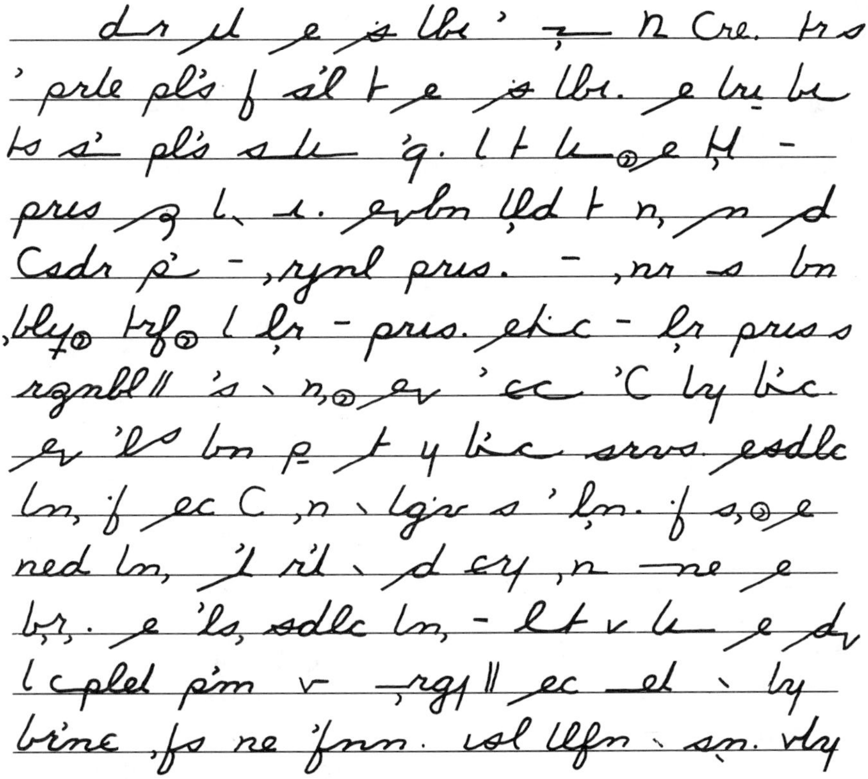

Assignment 6 — **Supplemental business letters.** If instructed to do so, read and write the additional business letters for this chapter found in "Supplemental Letters for Dictation" in Appendix A.

BUILDING SHORTHAND SPEED AND TRANSCRIPTION ACCURACY

Assignment 7 — **Self-testing.** Complete Unit 12 in your *Study Guide* before you proceed with the rest of this chapter.

Assignment 8 — **Taking tape dictation.** To write from dictation the new words and letters in this chapter, use Cassette 12 Side A from *Theory and Speed-Building Tapes*.

Assignment 9 — **Taking live dictation.** Write from dictation the letters which are printed at the end of this chapter. Your instructor will dictate to you from these transcripts at various speeds.

Assignment 10 — **Own-note transcription.** Transcribe at your best typing rate an accurate copy of at least one of the letters you took in shorthand in Assignment 9. Type the letter in the form requested by your instructor.

TRANSCRIPTS OF LETTERS 1 AND 2

Letter 1 Dear Ms. Bell: The head of the planning committee for the park would like to meet with us Tuesday afternoon. We asked (20) him, you may recall, if the size of the building in the park could be increased. He advised us that the size can be (40) increased by adding one room to the building. The local engineer has measured the area to determine (60) the size of the room.

We think that it would be very helpful to have a room in which the children can play during (80) bad weather. The room would be available for something else when the weather is nice. This should keep the people (100) happy.

We are hoping the complete plan will be adopted by the council. We should like the people of the area to (120) be well satisfied with the plan. Therefore, we are informing each planning committee member of the meeting on (140) Tuesday. I urge you to come to this meeting. If you cannot come, will you please telephone me. Very truly yours, (160)

Letter 2 Dear Mr. White: We wish to buy a home in the country. There is a pretty place for sale that we wish to buy. We (20) tried buying this same place some time ago. At that time, we thought the price was too high. We have been told that no one would (40) consider paying the original price. The owner has been obliged, therefore, to lower the price. We think the (60) lower price is reasonable.

As you know, we have a chequing account at your bank. We have always been pleased with (80) your banking service. We should like to know if we can count on you to give us a loan. If so, we need to know what (100) rate you would charge on the money we borrow. We also should like to know the length of time we would have to complete (120) payment of the mortgage.

We can meet you at your branch office any afternoon. I shall telephone you soon. Very (140) truly yours, (143)

EXAMINATION 3

- Remove and complete Examination 3, which follows Unit 12 in your *Study Guide*, before proceeding to Chapter 13 of your textbook.
- Self-check with the Key to Examination 3 which appears at the back of the *Study Guide*.

CHAPTER 13

WRITING **NT-ND**, **AN**, AND **DIS-DES**

Assignment 1 — **Rule discovery**. Follow the three-step plan to learn the new writing principles: (1) Discover the rule for each group of words. (2) Read the shorthand outlines until you can read them rapidly. (3) Cover the shorthand and write each word until you can do so rapidly and accurately.

NT-ND

end event find inventory attend want agent

confident demand recommend interview kind

handle different efficient guarantee depend paint

print send-sent printing dependable convenient

Learning tip: The word *interview* is written with the *nt* combination rather than the *in* prefix because the word is pronounced int-er-view.

PREFIX **AN**

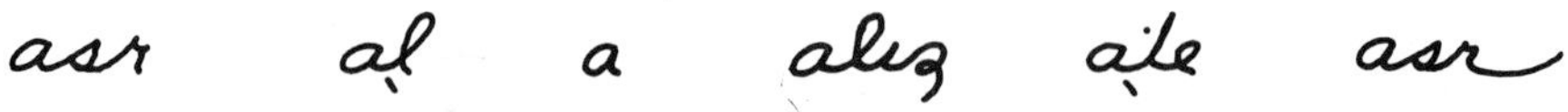

answer annual an analyze annuity answering

PREFIXES **DIS-DES**

discover discuss display discontinue discovered

desperate desolate

WRITING PRINCIPLES

NT-ND Write a curved stroke thus to express the combinations *nt* or *nd*. Note that this stroke is used for both *nt* as in *event* and for *nd* as in *end*.

AN Write a small longhand *a* to express the prefix *an*.

DIS-DES Write a Capital D thus to express the prefixes *dis* and *des*. Some writers prefer to write the capital D thus D. Either is correct.

Assignment 2 — **New vocabulary**. Read and write the following words and phrases until you can read and write them rapidly. Memorize the abbreviated words.

difficult-difficulty year represent-representative

gentlemen September Thursday memorandum

memo accountant discount sometime somebody

several Miss case sure mailed worker

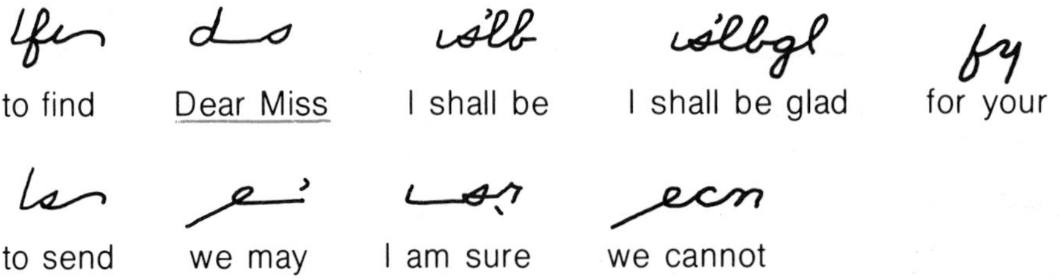
to find
Dear Miss
I shall be
I shall be glad
for your
to send
we may
I am sure
we cannot

Assignment 3 — **Reading and writing shorthand**. Read each sentence from shorthand until you can read it as rapidly as you can read from print. Write each sentence in shorthand until you can write each one rapidly and accurately.

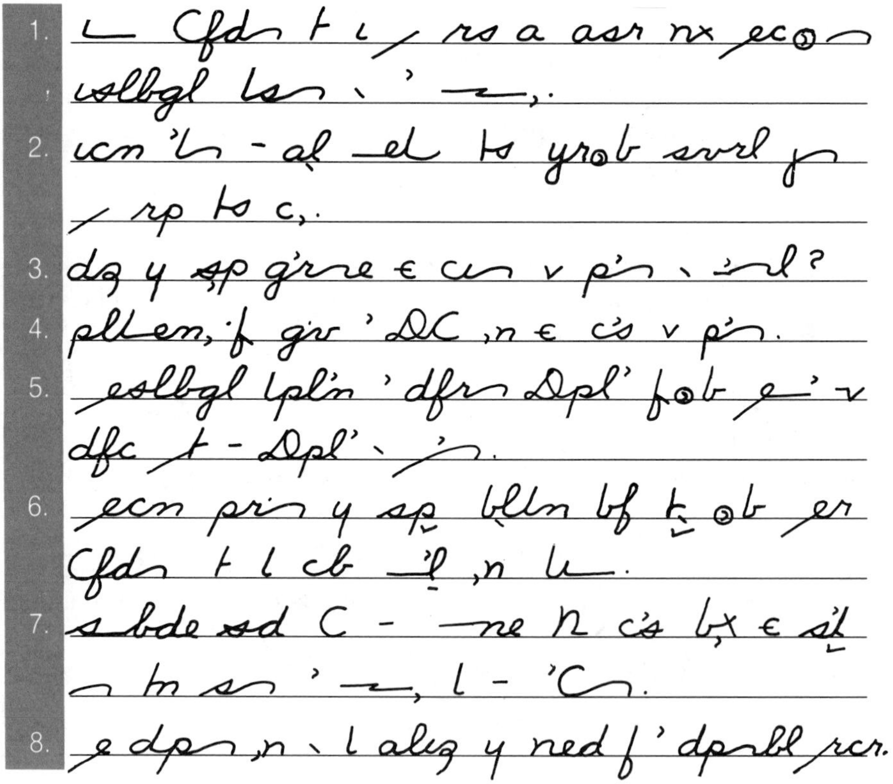
1.
2.
3.
4.
5.
6.
7.
8.

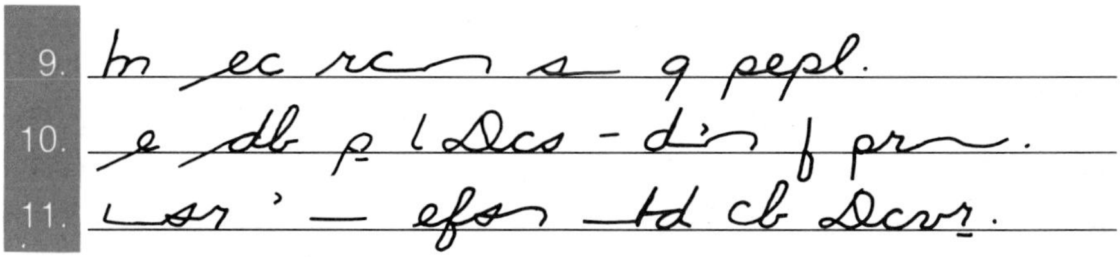

BUILDING TRANSCRIPTION SKILLS

Assignment 4 — **Punctuating compound sentences.** The shorthand sentences in Assignment 3 include *compound sentences*. Study the punctuation rule and examples that follow, and apply the rule when transcribing the sentences.

A compound sentence is two sentences joined together. The two sentences are usually joined by a connecting word (conjunction). Common connecting words are: *and*, *but*, *for*, *either*, *or*, *nor*, and *neither*. Place a comma before the connecting word in a compound sentence.

1. John overestimated his gas mileage, and he ran out of gas.
2. He will come to the meeting, but he may arrive late.
3. I will mail you a ticket to the game, or you may pick up your ticket at the box office.

BUILDING SHORTHAND SPEED AND TRANSCRIPTION ACCURACY

Assignment 5 — **Self-testing.** Complete Unit 13 in your *Study Guide* before you proceed with the rest of this chapter.

Assignment 6 — **Taking tape dictation.** To write from dictation the new words and sentences in this chapter, use Cassette 13 Side A from *Theory and Speed-Building Tapes*.

Assignment 7 — **Taking live dictation.** Write from dictation the sentences which are printed at the end of this chapter. Your instructor will dictate each group of 20 words to you at various speeds.

Assignment 8 — **Own-note transcription.** After you have taken the sentences in shorthand, select your best set of notes and transcribe them at your best typing rate. Do not number the sentences.

Assignment 9 — **Supplemental business letters.** If instructed to do so, read and write the additional business letter for this chapter found in "Supplemental Letters for Dictation" in Appendix A.

TRANSCRIPT OF SHORTHAND SENTENCES

1. I am confident that I will receive an answer next week, and I shall be glad to send you a memorandum. (20)
2. I cannot attend the annual meeting this year, but several gentlemen will represent this company. (40)
3. Does your shop guarantee each kind of paint you handle?
4. Please let me know if you give a discount on each case of paint. (60)
5. We shall be glad to plan a different display for you, but we may have difficulty with the display you want. (80)
6. We cannot print your September bulletin before Thursday, but we are confident that it can be mailed on time. (100)
7. Somebody should count the money in the cash box each Saturday and then send a memo to the accountant. (120)
8. We depend on you to analyze your need for a dependable worker.
9. Then we can recommend some good people. (140)
10. We would be pleased to discuss the demand for printing.
11. I am sure a more efficient method can be discovered. (160)

CHAPTER 14

WRITING **QU**, **INCL-ENCLOSE**, AND **LY**

Assignment 1 – **Rule discovery.** Follow the three-step plan to learn the new writing principles: (1) Discover the rule for each group of words. (2) Read the shorthand outlines until you can read them rapidly. (3) Cover the shorthand and write each word until you can do so rapidly and accurately.

QU

quote quality quite quoted acquainted equip

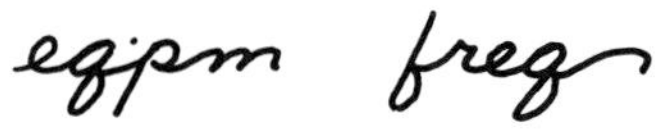

equipment frequent

INCL-ENCLOSE

include included including incline inclined

inclusive enclose enclosure enclosing enclosed

LY

easily quickly clearly daily surely monthly

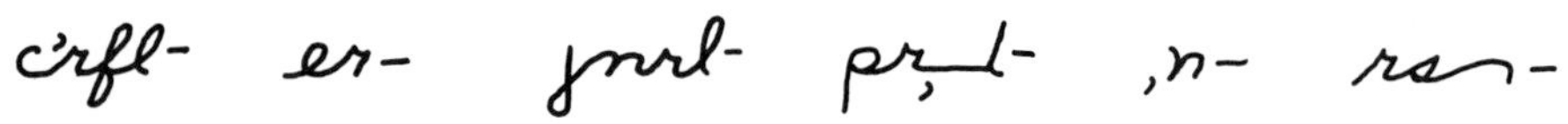

carefully early generally promptly only recently

weekly usually entirely kindly finally

WRITING PRINCIPLES

QU Write only *q* for the combination *qu*.

INCL ENCLOSE Write a capital longhand *I* thus *I* to express the combination *incl* and the following vowel and the word *enclose*. The capital *I* must be written so it cannot be confused with the longhand *l*. The form shown above is recommended.

LY Write a short, disjoined dash close to the word to which it belongs to express the ending *ly*. Write words in full that end in *l* and then add the *ly* dash, as in *carefully* c'rfl- and *fully* fl-.

Assignment 2 — **New vocabulary**. Read and write the following words and phrases until you can read and write them rapidly. Memorize the abbreviated words.

q'n	q	rq	dpl	g—	
quantity	question	require	department	going	
gr-	yr-	rq	rqm	gl-	f,r—
greatly	yearly	required	requirement	gladly	form
nr,lm	-prv	tx	lsn	rsn	f,r=
enrolment	improved	tax	lesson	recent	formed
nele		lasn	-erfr	ny	
any time - anytime		to answer	hear from	in your	
plle					
please let me					

Assignment 3 — **Reading and writing shorthand**. Read each sentence from shorthand until you can read it as rapidly as you can read from print. Write each sentence in shorthand until you can write each one rapidly and accurately.

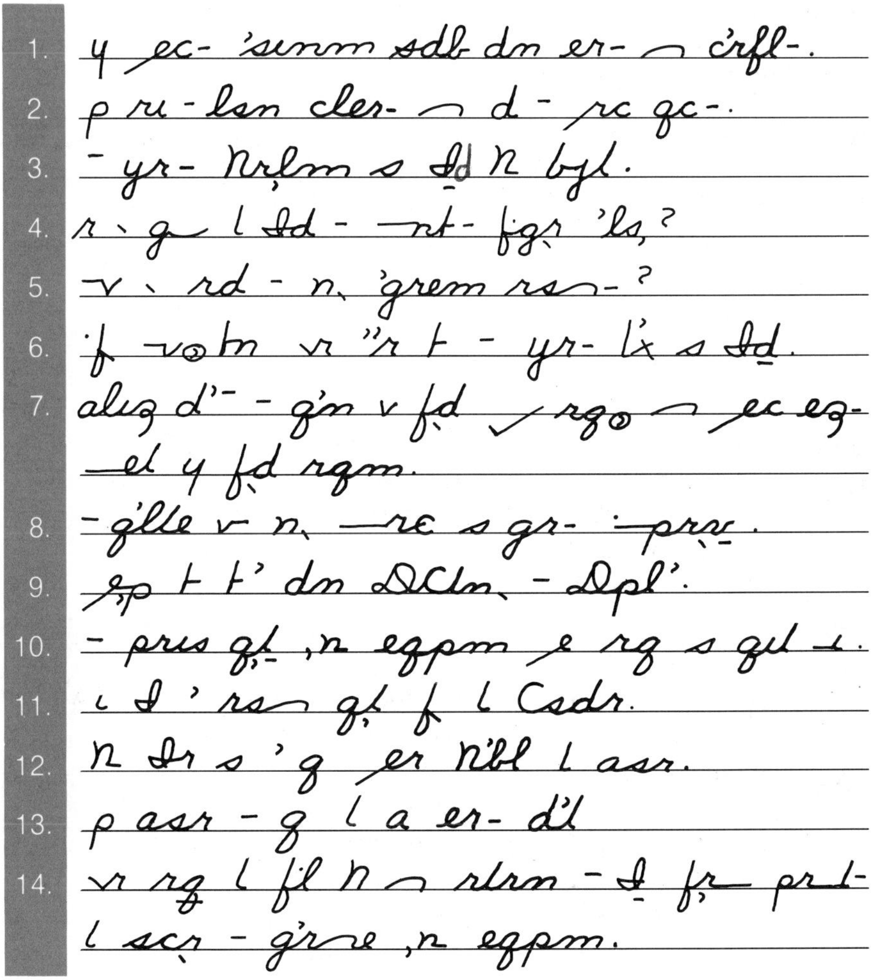

BUILDING SHORTHAND SPEED AND TRANSCRIPTION ACCURACY

Assignment 4 — **Self-testing.** Complete Unit 14 in your *Study Guide* before you proceed with the rest of this chapter.

Assignment 5 — **Taking tape dictation.** To write from dictation the new words and sentences in this chapter, use Cassette 14 Side A from *Theory and Speed-Building Tapes*.

Assignment 6 — **Taking live dictation.** Write from dictation the sentences which are printed at the end of this chapter. Your instructor will dictate each group of 20 words to you at various speeds.

Assignment 7 — **Own-note transcription.** After you have taken the sentences in shorthand, select your best set of notes and transcribe them at your best typing rate. Do not number the sentences.

Assignment 8 — **Supplemental business letters.** If instructed to do so, read and write the additional business letter for this chapter found in "Supplemental Letters for Dictation" in Appendix A.

TRANSCRIPT OF SHORTHAND SENTENCES

1. Your weekly assignment should be done early and carefully.
2. Please write the lesson clearly and do the work quickly. (20)
3. The yearly enrolment is included in the budget.
4. Are you going to include the monthly figure also? (40)
5. Have you read the new agreement recently?
6. If you have, then you are aware that the yearly tax is included. (60)
7. Analyze daily the quantity of food you will require, and we can easily meet your food requirement. (80)
8. The quality of the new merchandise is greatly improved.
9. We hope that they do not discontinue the display. (100)
10. The price quoted on the equipment we require is quite high.
11. I enclose a recent quote for you to consider. (120)
12. In the enclosure is a question we are unable to answer.
13. Please answer the question at an early date. (140)
14. You are required to fill in and return the enclosed form promptly to secure the guarantee on the equipment. (160)

CHAPTER 15

ADDING S TO ROOT WORDS AND WRITING EVER-EVERY

Assignment 1 — **Rule discovery**. Follow the three-step plan to learn the new writing principles: (1) Discover the rule for each group of words. (2) Read the shorthand outlines until you can read them rapidly. (3) Cover the shorthand and write each word until you can do so rapidly and accurately.

ADDING S TO ROOT WORDS

advises answers banks bills checks-cheques

thinks copies damages figures days says

ideas payments machines makes sales terms

transfers files funds gives forms taxes shows

assures

PREFIX OR SUFFIX EVER-EVERY

everybody everyone ever-every whenever everything

WRITING PRINCIPLES

ADDING S Write an upward, slanted, straight stroke joined to the last letter or symbol of a word to add *s* to a root word. This same stroke is used to add *s* to a word to form the possessive. (See punctuation of possessives in Chapter 16.) Note how the *s* symbol is joined to words that end in a vowel symbol. Some writers prefer to *double* the symbol to indicate *s* with such words. Examples: *days* d/ or d" ; *shows* s/ or s" .

EVER-EVERY Write a disjoined capital *V* thus V for the words *ever* and *every* and the prefixes and suffixes *ever-every.* Make the first stroke of the *V* with a straight slanted line so it will not look like a *t*.

Assignment 2 — **New vocabulary.** Read and write the following words and phrases until you can read and write them rapidly. Memorize the abbreviated words.

-p	-ed	prin
important-importance	*immediate*	*principal-principle*

-ed-	yr/	q/	bz/	c/
immediately	years	questions	businesses	companies
rqm/	y/	g/	rs/	s̲
requirements	yours	goes-goods	receives	shipped
t/	'c/	dsc/	d,	cpe
thanks	accounts	discounts	due	copying

Csidrbl	trd	-ne	cl'	lrjr	-
considerable	trade	many	claim	larger	and the
lt					
to make					

Assignment 3 — **Reading and writing shorthand.** Read each sentence from shorthand until you can read it as rapidly as you can read from print. Write each sentence in shorthand until you can write each one rapidly and accurately.

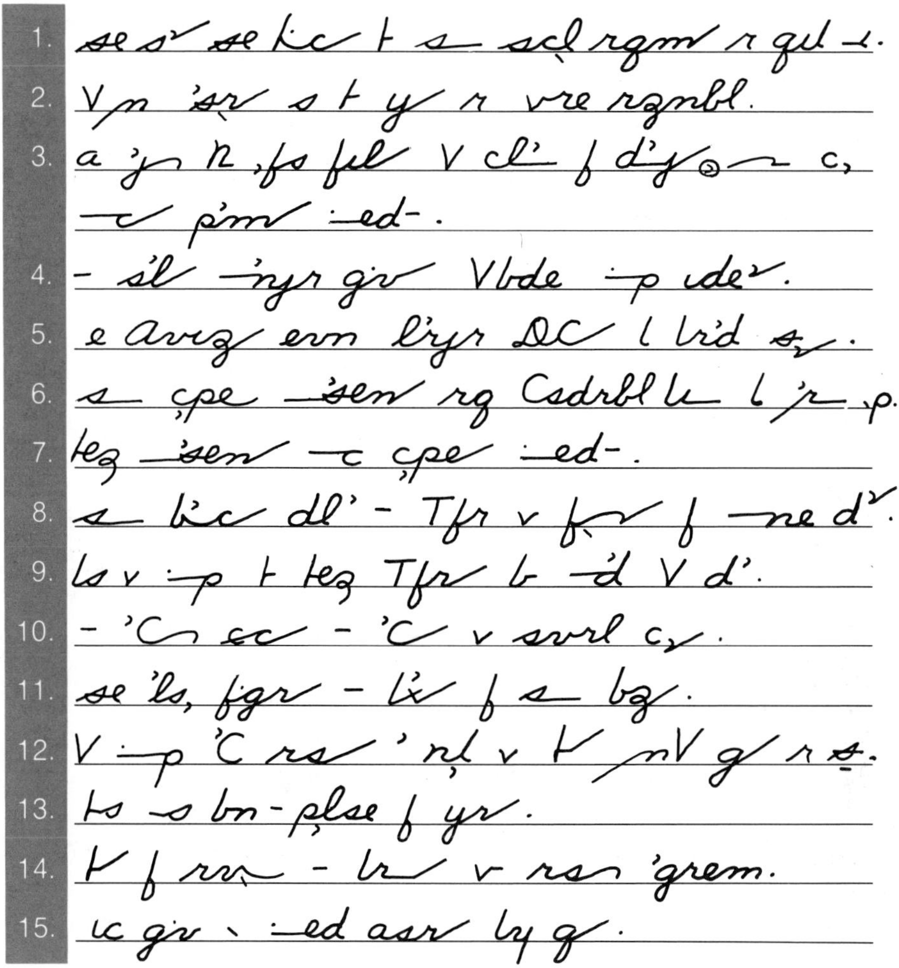

BUILDING SHORTHAND SPEED AND TRANSCRIPTION ACCURACY

Assignment 4 — **Self-testing.** Complete Unit 15 in your *Study Guide* before you proceed with the rest of this chapter.

Assignment 5 — **Taking tape dictation.** To write from dictation the new words and sentences in this chapter, use Cassette 15 Side A from *Theory and Speed-Building Tapes*.

Assignment 6 — **Taking live dictation.** Write from dictation the sentences which are printed at the end of this chapter. Your instructor will dictate each group of 20 words to you at various speeds.

Assignment 7 — **Own-note transcription**. After you have taken the sentences in shorthand, select your best set of notes and transcribe them at your best typing rate. Do not number the sentences.

Assignment 8 — **Supplemental business letters**. If instructed to do so, read and write the additional business letter for this chapter found in "Supplemental Letters for Dictation" in Appendix A.

TRANSCRIPT OF SHORTHAND SENTENCES

1. She says she thinks that some school requirements are quite high.
2. Everyone assures us that yours are very reasonable. (20)
3. An agent in the office files every claim for damages, and the company makes payments immediately. (40)
4. The sales manager gives everybody important ideas.
5. He advises even larger discounts at trade shows. (60)
6. Some copying machines require considerable time to warm up.
7. These machines make copies immediately. (80)
8. Some banks delay the transfer of funds for many days.
9. It is of importance that these transfers be made every day. (100)
10. The accountant checks the accounts of several companies.
11. She also figures the taxes for some businesses. (120)
12. Every important account receives a note of thanks whenever goods are shipped.
13. This has been the policy for years. (140)
14. Thanks for reviewing the terms of the recent agreement.
15. I can give you immediate answers to your questions. (160)

CHAPTER 16

BUSINESS LETTER DICTATION AND TRANSCRIPTION

BUILDING TRANSCRIPTION SKILLS

Assignment 1 — **Forming the singular possessive**. In the letters that follow are some words that require the possessive form. Study the rule and the examples and apply the rule when you transcribe.

To form the possessive of a singular word, add an *apostrophe* and an *s* to the word. In the examples, note that each possessive indicates "belonging to" or "of."

1. The boy's coat was torn. (coat belonging to the boy)
2. The company's balance sheet is printed. (the balance sheet belonging to the company)
3. The society is planning next year's meeting. (meeting of next year)
4. The manager's representative will meet you. (representative of the manager)
5. The customer's request came to the department head. (request of the customer).

Assignment 2 — **Spelling review**. Follow the steps outlined in Chapter 12 to check your ability to spell the following words correctly:

1. account
2. available
3. always
4. annual
5. answer
6. carefully
7. convenient
8. copies
9. different
10. difficulty
11. final
12. finally
13. generally
14. guarantee
15. immediately
16. mortgage
17. original
18. receiving
19. recommend
20. several
21. Tuesday
22. usually

BUSINESS LETTERS

Assignment 3 — **Letter 1**. Read and write each of the new words and phrases for Letter 1 until you can read and write each one rapidly and accurately. Then read and write the shorthand for Letter 1 to build your writing speed.

dissatisfied inside doing advertisements receiving

adequate shopping charges lighting reaching

areas growing appear pictures desirable rapidly

serves renting centre discussed buildings

services shown friend indicated modern design

talked retail appears rates touch kinds rent

Yours very truly

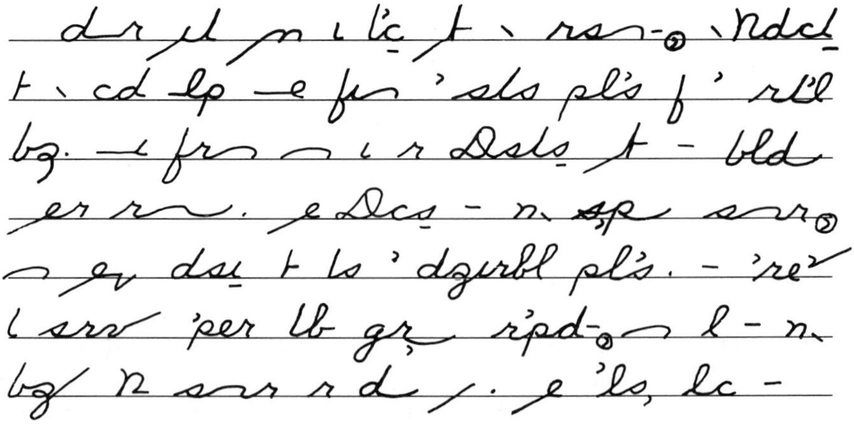

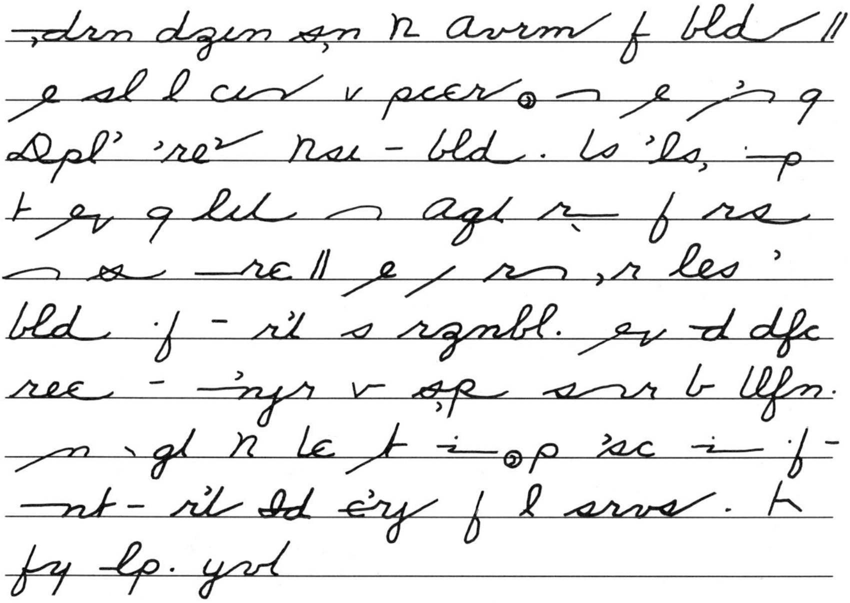

Assignment 4 — **Letter 2**. Read and write each of the new words and phrases for Letter 2 until you can read and write each one rapidly and accurately. Then read and write the shorthand for Letter 2 to build your writing speed.

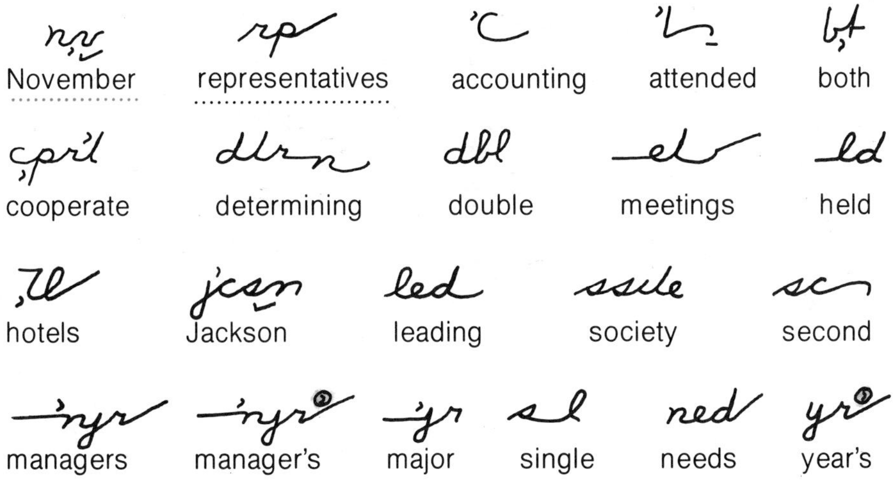
November
representatives
accounting
attended
both
cooperate
determining
double
meetings
held
hotels
Jackson
leading
society
second
managers
manager's
major
single
needs
year's

rooms | prices | please let us know | will be glad | have not

very much

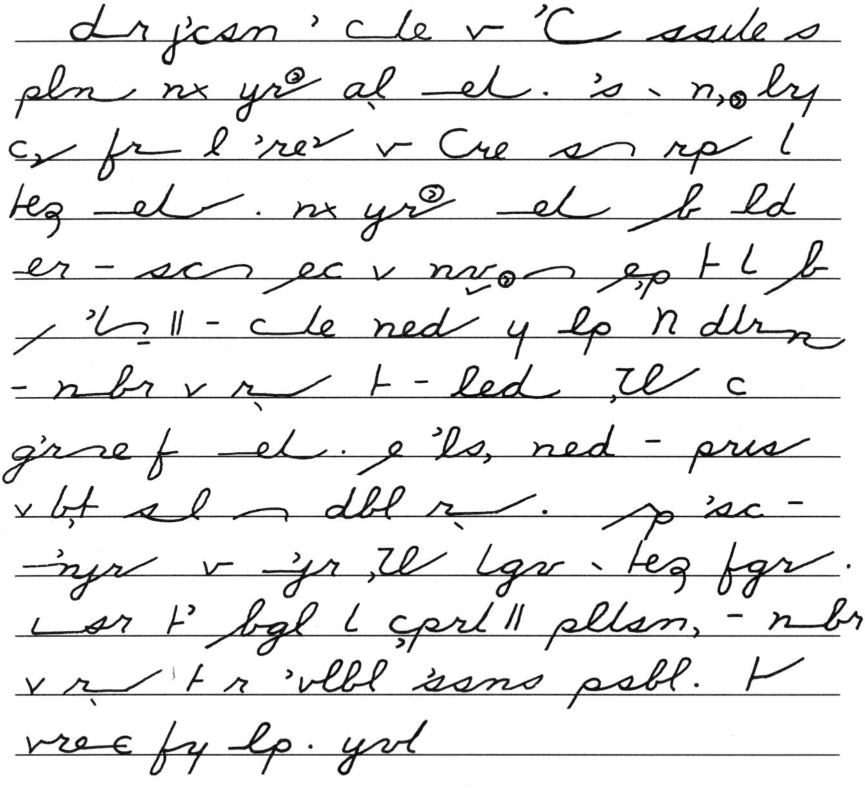

Assignment 5 — **Supplemental business letters**. If instructed to do so, read and write the additional business letters for this chapter found in "Supplemental Letters for Dictation" in Appendix A.

BUILDING SHORTHAND SPEED AND TRANSCRIPTION ACCURACY

Assignment 6 — **Self-testing**. Complete Unit 16 in your *Study Guide* before you proceed with the rest of this chapter.

Assignment 7 — **Taking tape dictation**. To write from dictation the new words and letters in this chapter, use Cassette 16 Side A from *Theory and Speed-Building Tapes*.

Assignment 8 — **Taking live dictation**. Write from dictation the letters which are printed at the end of this chapter. Your instructor will dictate to you from these transcripts at various speeds.

Assignment 9 — **Own-note transcription**. Transcribe at your best typing rate an accurate copy of at least one of the letters you took in shorthand in Assignment 8. Type the letter in the form requested by your instructor.

TRANSCRIPTS OF LETTERS 1 AND 2

Letter 1 Dear Mr. White: When I talked with you recently, you indicated that you could help me find a satisfactory (20) place for a retail business. My friend and I are dissatisfied with the building we are renting. We discussed (40) the new shopping centre, and we have decided that it is a desirable place. The areas it serves appear (60) to be growing rapidly, and all the new businesses in the centre are doing well. We also like the (80) modern design shown in the advertisements for the buildings.

We sell all kinds of pictures, and we want good display (100) areas inside the building. It is also important that we have good lighting and adequate room for (120) receiving and shipping merchandise.

We will rent or lease a building if the rate is reasonable. We have had (140) difficulty reaching the manager of the shopping centre by telephone. When you get in touch with him, please ask (160) him if the monthly rates include charges for all services. Thank you for your help. Yours very truly, (178)

Letter 2 Dear Mr. Jackson: A committee of the accounting society is planning next year's annual meeting. As (20) you know, large companies from all areas of the country send representatives to these meetings. Next year's meeting (40) will be held here the second week of November, and we hope that it will be well attended.

The committee (60) needs your help in determining the number of rooms that the leading hotels can guarantee for the meeting. We (80) also need the prices of both single and double rooms. Will you please ask the managers of the major hotels (100) to give you these figures. I am sure they will be glad to cooperate.

Please let us know the number of rooms that (120) are available as soon as possible. Thanks very much for your help. Yours very truly, (136)

REVIEWING THE WRITING PRINCIPLES

All the writing principles, abbreviated words, and standard abbreviations you have learned in Chapters 9 through 16 are reviewed on Tape 18 Side A of the *Theory and Speed-Building Tapes*. Take dictation from this tape before completing Examination 4.

EXAMINATION 4

- Remove and complete Examination 4, which follows Unit 16 in your *Study Guide*, before proceeding to Chapter 17 of your textbook.
- Self-check with the Key to Examination 4 which appears at the back of the *Study Guide*.

CHAPTER 17

WRITING **ST** AND **SITY-CITY**

Assignment 1 — **Rule discovery**. Follow the three-step plan to learn the new writing principles: (1) Discover the rule for each group of words. (2) Read the shorthand outlines until you can read them rapidly. (3) Cover the shorthand and write each word until you can do so rapidly and accurately.

ST

request
adjustment
cost
customer
customers
customer's
east
investigate
must
history
installing
largest
register
statement
stated
storage
staff
industry
steel
still
stock
store
strong
instant
list
registered
yesterday
stocks
west
install
costly
best
requests
most
past
just
last
demonstrate

SITY-CITY

capacity publicity university city simplicity

WRITING PRINCIPLES

ST Write a capital *S* thus to express the *st* combination. The use of the capital *S* for the combination *st* helps when reading shorthand notes because one knows immediately that there is no vowel between the *s* and the *t*. When one sees , a vowel must come between the *s* and the *t*.

SITY CITY Write a disjoined capital *S* thus to express the combinations *sity-city* and the preceding vowel. Write the disjoined capital *S* close to the word to which it belongs.

Assignment 2 — **New vocabulary**. Read and write the following words and phrases until you can read and write them rapidly. Memorize the abbreviated words.

administer because suggest acknowledge estimate

its it's estimated suggests greatest

manufacturing computer computing market limited

airline travel attends data apply small benefit

easy showed computers we must as well as

at this time

Learning tip: The outline for the contraction *it's* (meaning *it is*) should be written with an apostrophe inserted as shown on page 76. The apostrophe is a reminder to insert the apostrophe when transcribing. See Chapter 31 for more help with contractions.

Assignment 3 — **Reading and writing shorthand**. Read each sentence from shorthand until you can read it as rapidly as you can read from print. Write each sentence in shorthand until you can write each one rapidly and accurately.

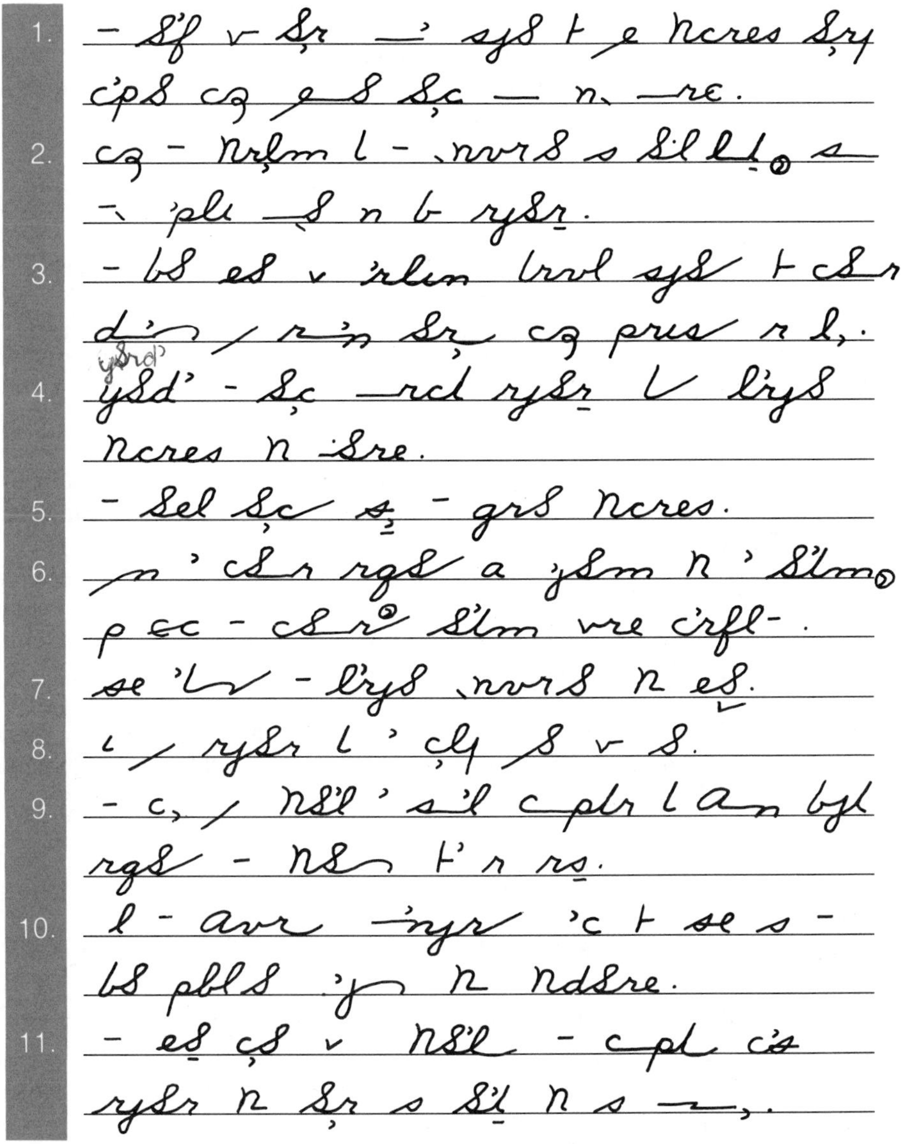
1.
2.
3.
4.
5.
6.
7.
8.
9.
10.
11.

BUILDING TRANSCRIPTION SKILLS

Assignment 4 — **Capitalizing geographical sections of a country.** Capitalize compass points when they name specific geographic regions. Apply the rule when transcribing.

1. She lives in the East.
2. Our geology class will visit the desert in the Southwest.
3. The Rocky Mountains are in the West.

Do not capitalize compass points when they indicate direction.

1. You drive west from Calgary to reach the Rocky Mountains.
2. To reach the restaurant, go north at the traffic light.
3. We live northwest of the college campus.

BUILDING SHORTHAND SPEED AND TRANSCRIPTION ACCURACY

Assignment 5 — **Self-testing.** Complete Unit 17 in your *Study Guide* before you proceed with the rest of this chapter.

Assignment 6 — **Taking tape dictation.** To write from dictation the new words and sentences in this chapter, use Cassette 1 Side B from *Theory and Speed-Building Tapes*.

Assignment 7 — **Taking live dictation.** Write from dictation the sentences which are printed at the end of this chapter. Your instructor will dictate each group of 20 words to you at various speeds.

Assignment 8 — **Own-note transcription.** After you have taken the sentences in shorthand, select your best set of notes and transcribe them at your best typing rate. Do not number the sentences.

Assignment 9 — **Supplemental business letters.** If instructed to do so, read and write the additional business letter for this chapter found in "Supplemental Letters for Dictation" in Appendix A.

TRANSCRIPT OF SHORTHAND SENTENCES

1. The staff of the store may suggest that we increase storage capacity because we must stock more new merchandise. (20)
2. Because the enrolment at the university is still limited, some who apply must not be registered. (40)
3. The best estimate of airline travel suggests that customer demand will remain strong because prices are low. (60)

4. Yesterday the stock market registered its largest increase in history.
5. The steel stocks showed the greatest increase. (80)
6. When a customer requests an adjustment in a statement, please check the customer's statement very carefully. (100)
7. She attends the largest university in the East.
8. I will register at a college west of the city. (120)
9. The company will install a small computer to administer budget requests the instant they are received. (140)
10. All the advertising managers acknowledge that she is the best publicity agent in the industry. (160)
11. The estimated cost of installing the computing cash register in the store is stated in his memo. (180)

CHAPTER 18

WRITING SOUNDS OF **OU-OW**, **OUT**, AND **SELF**

Assignment 1 — **Rule discovery**. Follow the three-step plan to learn the new writing principles: (1) Discover the rule for each group of words. (2) Read the shorthand outlines until you can read them rapidly. (3) Cover the shorthand and write each word until you can do so rapidly and accurately.

SOUND OF **OU-OW**

brown doubt allowed aloud amount found

house south ground now power how down

town voucher

PREFIX OR SUFFIX **OUT**

outlines outfit outlet outlined outstanding without

outlook outline outcome

PREFIX OR SUFFIX **SELF**

self-service himself myself themselves herself

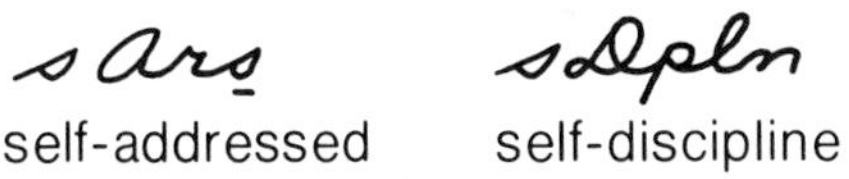
self-addressed
self-discipline

WRITING PRINCIPLES

OU-OW Write a small longhand *o* to express *ou-ow*. Write the longhand *o* in a clockwise direction thus [shorthand] so that you can form the *o* quickly.

OUT Write a small longhand *o* to express the prefix or suffix *out*.

SELF Write a small disjoined longhand *s* thus [shorthand] to express the prefix or suffix *self*. The suffix *selves* is expressed by adding the *s*-added stroke to the suffix *self*, as shown in the word *themselves*.

Assignment 2 — **New vocabulary**. Read and write the following words and phrases until you can read and write them rapidly. Memorize the abbreviated words.

about
first
our-out-hour
street
August
Sunday
outside
yourself
suggested
sending
catalogues
again
campus
returned
materials
rating
test
family
research
revised
teachers
wrong
live
study
schedule
consult
revise
generous

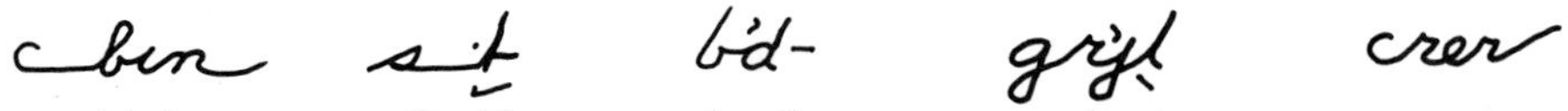

combining Smith badly graduate careers

counselor thinking had been

Assignment 3 — **Reading and writing shorthand**. Read each sentence from shorthand until you can read it as rapidly as you can read from print. Write each sentence in shorthand until you can write each one rapidly and accurately.

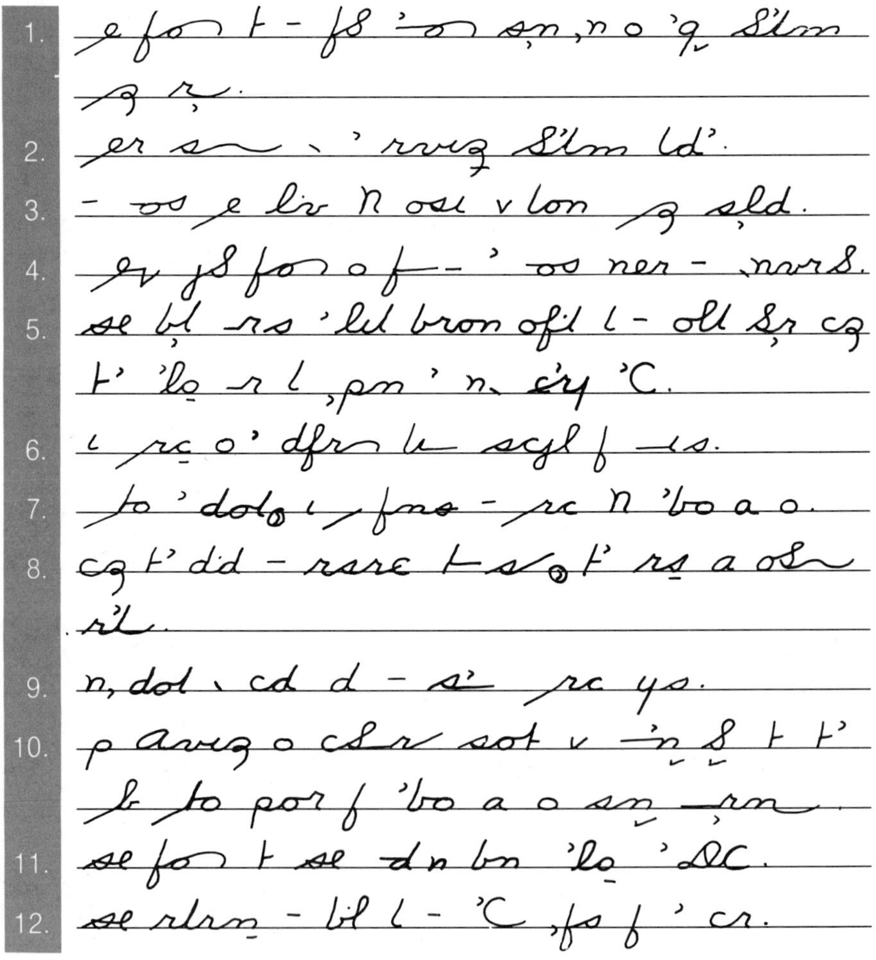

13.
14.
15.
16.

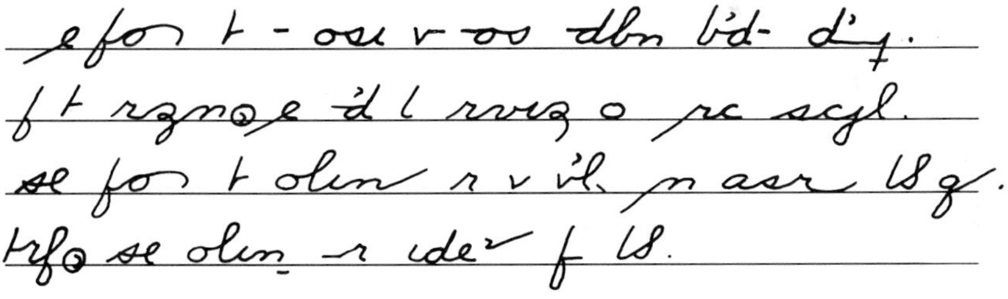

BUILDING TRANSCRIPTION SKILLS

Assignment 4 — **Capitalizing names of states, towns, streets, avenues, boulevards, and routes.** Because these are proper nouns, they are capitalized. Study the examples below and remember to capitalize such proper nouns when transcribing.

1. We live two blocks south of Main Street.
2. Many large companies have offices on Park Avenue.
3. Sunset Boulevard runs through Hollywood, California.
4. To go from Portland to Seattle, you go north on Route 5.

BUILDING SHORTHAND SPEED AND TRANSCRIPTION ACCURACY

Assignment 5 — **Self-testing.** Complete Unit 18 in your *Study Guide* before you proceed with the rest of this chapter.

Assignment 6 — **Taking tape dictation.** To write from dictation the new words and sentences in this chapter, use Cassette 2 Side B from *Theory and Speed-Building Tapes*.

Assignment 7 — **Taking live dictation.** Write from dictation the sentences which are printed at the end of this chapter. Your instructor will dictate each group of 20 words to you at various speeds.

Assignment 8 — **Own-note transcription.** After you have taken the sentences in shorthand, select your best set of notes and transcribe them at your best typing rate. Do not number the sentences.

Assignment 9 — **Supplemental business letters.** If instructed to do so, read and write the additional business letter for this chapter found in "Supplemental Letters for Dictation" in Appendix A.

TRANSCRIPT OF SHORTHAND SENTENCES

1. We found that the first amount shown on our August statement was wrong.
2. We are sending you a revised statement today. (20)
3. The house we live in outside of town was sold.
4. We have just found our family a house near the university. (40)
5. She bought herself a light brown outfit at the outlet store because they allowed her to open a new charge account. (60)
6. I worked out a different time schedule for myself.
7. Without a doubt, I will finish the work in about an hour. (80)
8. Because they did the research themselves, they received an outstanding rating.
9. No doubt you could do the same work yourself. (100)
10. Please advise our customers south of Main Street that they will be without power for about an hour Sunday morning. (120)
11. She found that she had not been allowed a discount.
12. She returned the bill to the accounting office for a credit. (140)
13. We found that the outside of the house had been badly damaged.
14. For that reason, we had to revise our work schedule. (160)
15. She found that outlines are of value when answering test questions.
16. Therefore, she outlined her ideas for the test. (180)

CHAPTER 19

WRITING THE SOUND OF **SHUN**

Assignment 1 — **Rule discovery**. Follow the three-step plan to learn the new writing principles: (1) Discover the rule for each group of words. (2) Read the shorthand outlines until you can read them rapidly. (3) Cover the shorthand and write each word until you can do so rapidly and accurately.

SOUND OF **SHUN**

condition   edition   education   attention   information

addition   decision   cooperation   association   division

communication   mentioned   occasion   national

operation   competition   demonstration   recommendations

application   applications   commissioner   discussion

consideration   foundation   invitation   reputation

stations   divisions   conditional

WRITING PRINCIPLES

SHUN Write a short, vertical, downward stroke under the last letter or symbol of a word to express the *shun* sound and the preceding vowel. Note how additional endings are added to the *shun* symbol.

Assignment 2 — **New vocabulary.** Read and write the following words and phrases until you can read and write them rapidly. Memorize the abbreviated words.

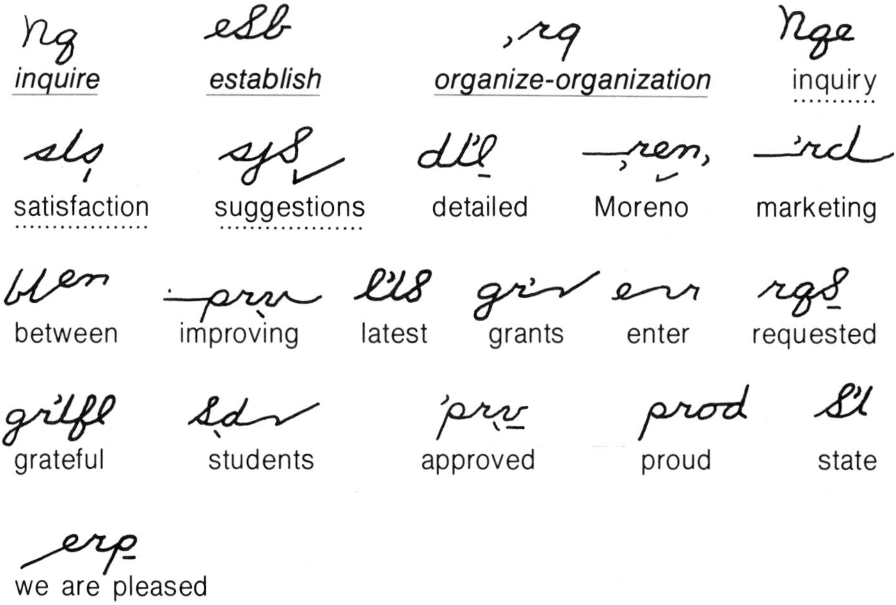
inquire
establish
organize-organization
inquiry
satisfaction
suggestions
detailed
Moreno
marketing
between
improving
latest
grants
enter
requested
grateful
students
approved
proud
state
we are pleased

Assignment 3 — **Reading and writing shorthand.** Read each sentence from shorthand until you can read it as rapidly as you can read from print. Write each sentence in shorthand until you can write each one rapidly and accurately.

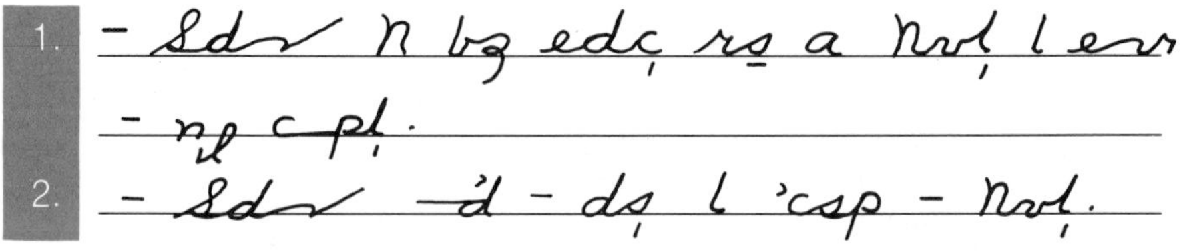
1.
2.

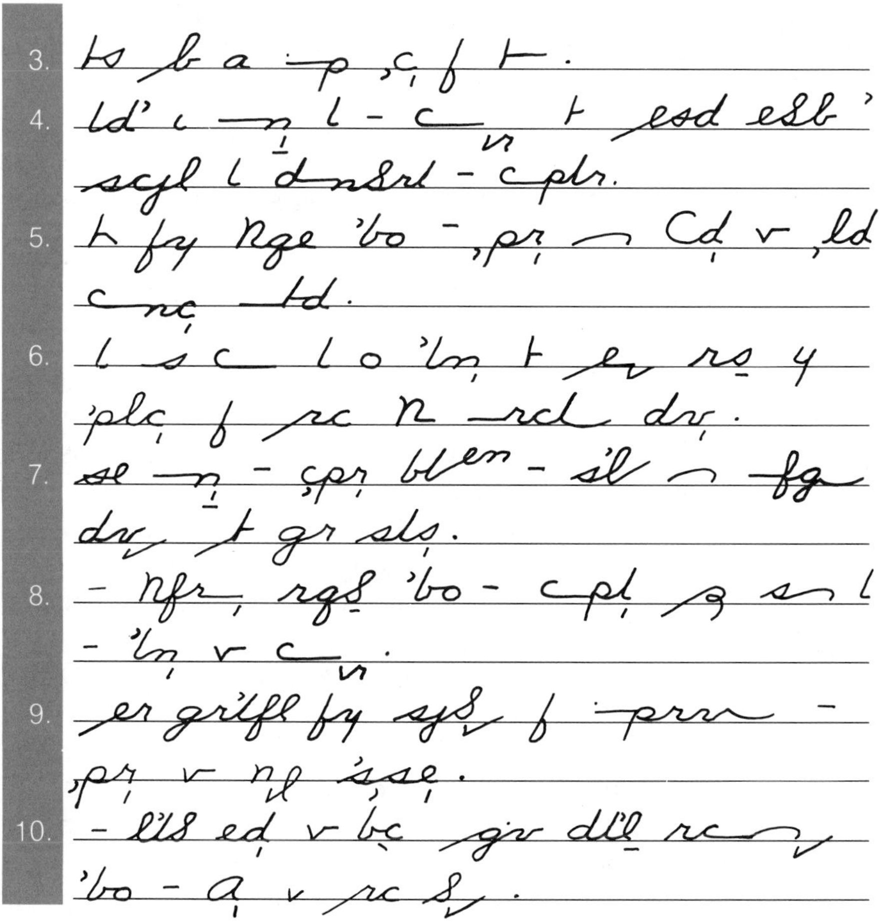

BUILDING SHORTHAND SPEED AND TRANSCRIPTION ACCURACY

Assignment 4 — **Self-testing**. Complete Unit 19 in your *Study Guide* before you proceed with the rest of this chapter.

Assignment 5 — **Taking tape dictation**. To write from dictation the new words and sentences in this chapter, use Cassette 3 Side B from *Theory and Speed-Building Tapes*.

Assignment 6 — **Taking live dictation**. Write from dictation the sentences which are printed at the end of this chapter. Your instructor will dictate each group of 20 words to you at various speeds.

Assignment 7 — **Own-note transcription**. After you have taken the sentences in shorthand, select your best set of notes and transcribe them at your best typing rate. Do not number the sentences.

Assignment 8 — **Supplemental business letters**. If instructed to do so, read and write the additional business letter for this chapter found in "Supplemental Letters for Dictation" in Appendix A.

TRANSCRIPT OF SHORTHAND SENTENCES

1. The students in business education received an invitation to enter the national competition. (20)
2. The students made the decision to accept the invitation.
3. This will be an important occasion for them. (40)
4. Today I mentioned to the commissioner that we should establish a schedule to demonstrate the computer. (60)
5. Thank you for your inquiry about the operation and condition of the old communication method. (80)
6. It has come to our attention that we have received your application for work in the marketing division. (100)
7. She mentioned the cooperation between the sales and manufacturing divisions with great satisfaction. (120)
8. The information requested about the competition was sent to the attention of the commissioner. (140)
9. We are grateful for your suggestions for improving the operation of the national association. (160)
10. The latest edition of the book will give detailed recommendations about the addition of work stations. (180)

CHAPTER 20

BUSINESS LETTER DICTATION AND TRANSCRIPTION

BUILDING TRANSCRIPTION SKILLS

Assignment 1 — **Capitalization**. Names of businesses, organizations, associations, governmental agencies, schools, and colleges are proper nouns. They should be capitalized when transcribing. Study the examples that follow and remember to capitalize such proper nouns when transcribing.

1. I have a savings account at the Dollar Savings Bank.
2. Our football team at Northern High School is known as the Tigers.
3. The Dominion Insurance Company has its home office in our town.
4. We attended the convention of the Future Business Leaders last summer.
5. We belong to the North American Association of Insurance Agencies.

Assignment 2 – **Spelling review**. Follow the steps outlined in Chapter 12 to check your ability to spell the following words correctly:

1. acknowledge
2. again
3. association
4. attention
5. appear
6. benefit
7. between
8. condition
9. cooperation
10. discussion
11. division
12. double
13. doubt
14. estimate
15. grateful
16. history
17. install
18. occasion
19. request
20. shop
21. shopping
22. suggest

BUSINESS LETTERS

Assignment 3 — **Letter 1**. Read and write each of the new words and phrases until you can read and write each one rapidly and accurately. Then read and write the shorthand for Letter 1 to build your writing speed.

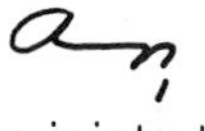

administration

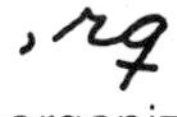

organized

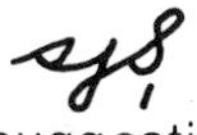

suggestion

hours-ours

classes maintain committees visits members

methods helps conditions superior various

teaching introduction courses inviting similar

world skills valuable bond advisory matters

off sometimes times used vocational black

to serve to get at this

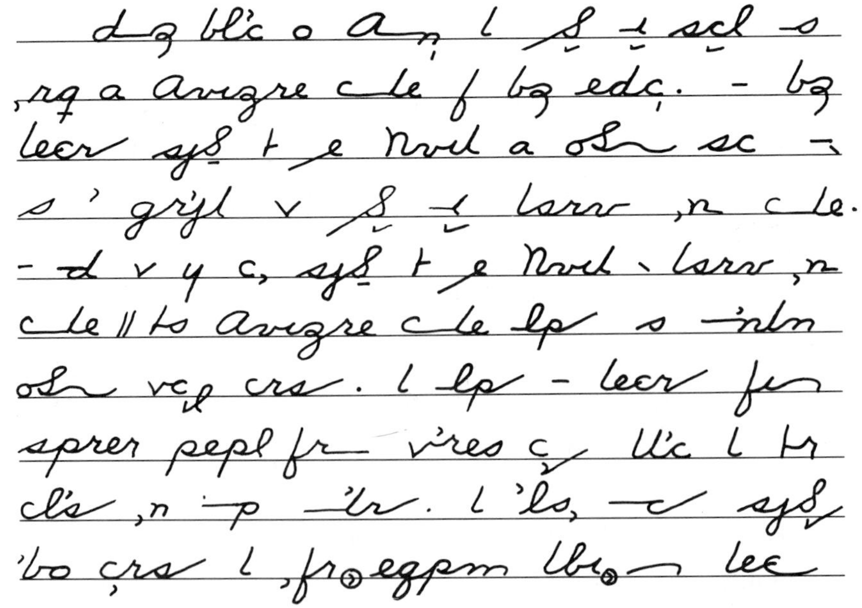

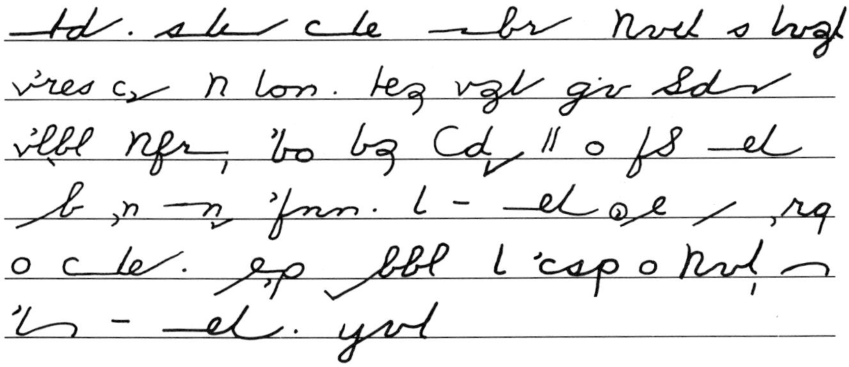

Assignment 4 — **Letter 2.** Read and write each of the new words and phrases for Letter 2 until you can read and write each one rapidly and accurately. Then read and write the shorthand for Letter 2 to build your writing speed.

December .... represented .... states associations

undoubtedly someone entire conservation phone

met use (n) federal hearings hearing reduction

recommendations involved revising session sessions

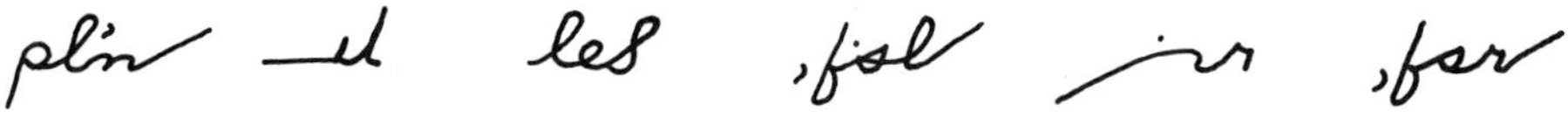

plans might least officials winter officers

users series to this this is let us know at least

there are

Learning tip:: The (n) after the word *use* means the word is a noun.

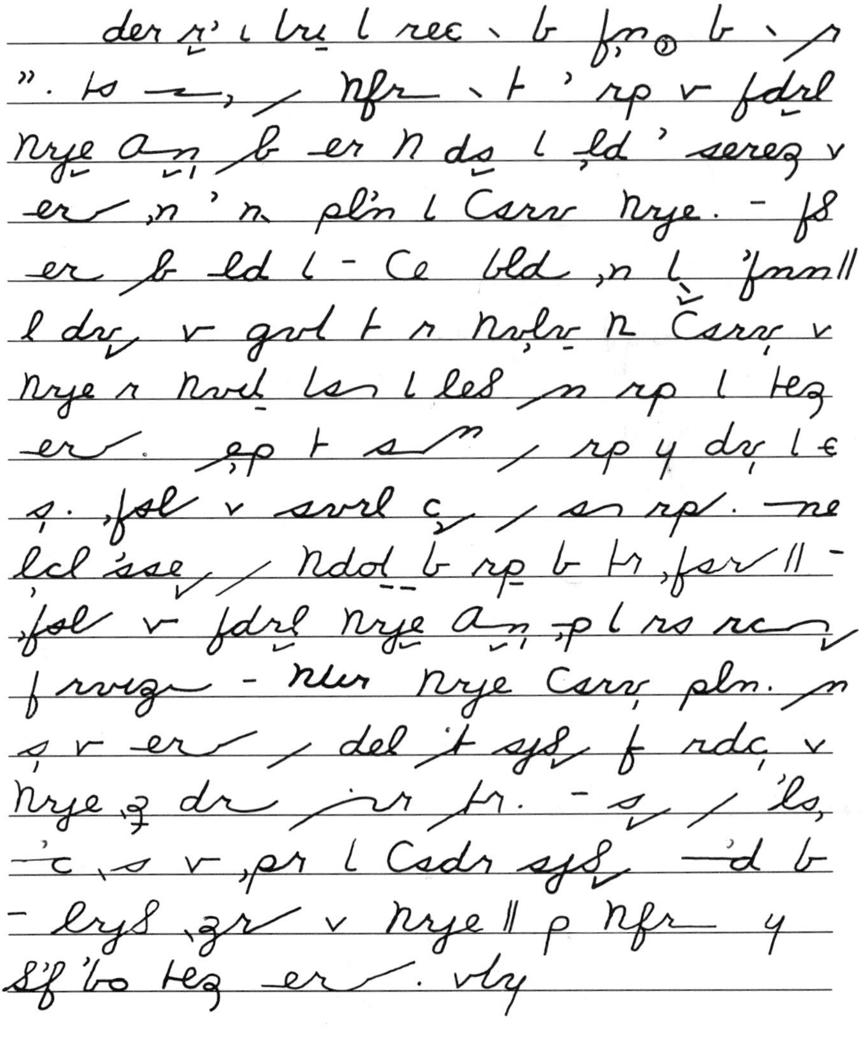

Assignment 5 — **Supplemental business letters**. If instructed to do so, read and write the additional business letters for this chapter found in "Supplemental Letters for Dictation" in Appendix A.

BUILDING SHORTHAND SPEED AND TRANSCRIPTION ACCURACY

Assignment 6 — **Self-testing**. Complete Unit 20 in your *Study Guide* before you proceed with the rest of this chapter.

Assignment 7 — **Taking tape dictation**. To write from dictation the new words and letters in this chapter, use Cassette 4 Side B from *Theory and Speed-Building Tapes*.

Assignment 8 — **Taking live dictation**. Write from dictation the letters which are printed at the end of this chapter. Your instructor will dictate to you from these transcripts at various speeds.

Assignment 9 — **Own-note transcription**. Transcribe at your best typing rate an accurate copy of at least one of the letters you took in shorthand in Assignment 8. Type the letter in the form requested by your instructor.

TRANSCRIPTS OF LETTERS 1 AND 2

Letter 1 Dear Ms. Black: Our administration at West High School has organized an advisory committee for business (20) education. The business teachers suggested that we invite an outstanding secretary who is a (40) graduate of West High to serve on the committee. The head of your company suggested that we invite you to (60) serve on the committee.

This advisory committee helps us maintain outstanding vocational courses. It (80) helps the teachers find superior people from various companies to talk to their classes on important matters. (100) It also makes suggestions about courses to offer, equipment to buy, and teaching methods. Sometimes (120) committee members invite us to visit various companies in town. These visits give students valuable (140) information about business conditions.

Our first meeting will be on Monday afternoon. At the meeting, we (160) will organize our committees. We hope you will be able to accept our invitation and attend the meeting. (180) Yours very truly, (184)

Letter 2 Dear Ray: I tried to reach you by phone, but you were away. This memo will inform you that a representative (20) of the Federal Energy Administration will be here in December to hold a series of hearings (40) on a new plan to conserve energy. The first hearing will be held at the county building on Tuesday afternoon. (60)

All divisions of the government that are involved in the conservation of energy are invited (80) to send at least one representative to these hearings. We hope that someone will represent your division (100) at each session. Officials of several companies will send representatives. Many local associations (120) will undoubtedly be represented by their officers.

The officials of the Federal Energy (140) Administration hope to receive recommendations for revising the entire energy conservation (160) plan. One session of the hearings will deal with suggestions for the reduction of energy used during winter (180) weather. The sessions will also make use of the opportunity to consider suggestions made by the largest (200) users of energy.

Please inform your staff about these hearings. Very truly yours, (215)

EXAMINATION 5

- Remove and complete Examination 5, which follows Unit 20 in your *Study Guide*, before proceeding to Chapter 21 of your textbook.
- Self-check with the Key to Examination 5 which appears at the back of the *Study Guide*.

CHAPTER 21

WRITING **SP**, **CT**, AND **INSTR**

Assignment 1 — **Rule discovery**. Follow the three-step plan to learn the new writing principles: (1) Discover the rule for each group of words. (2) Read the shorthand outlines until you can read them rapidly. (3) Cover the shorthand and write each word until you can do so rapidly and accurately.

SP

special especially spring space splendid spoke

specifications hospital speak specific specify

CT

subject correct collect direct district act

construct inspect effective director directed

active facts deduct inspects directs

INSTR

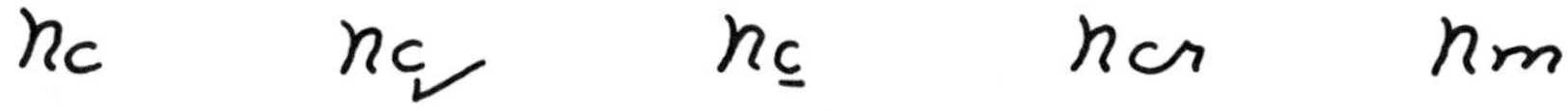

instruct instructions instructed instructor instrument

WRITING PRINCIPLES

SP Write a small printed *s* thus s to express the *sp* combination when no vowel occurs between the *s* and *p*.

CT Omit *t* in the combination *ct* when *ct* ends a word because the *t* is lightly sounded. The *t* is also omitted when *ct* is followed by a common word ending such as *ed*, *ly*, *ing*, *ive*, etc.

INSTR Write a disjoined capital *N* thus n to express the combination *instr* and the following vowel. Write the disjoined capital *N* close to the word to which it belongs.

Assignment 2 — **New Vocabulary**. Read and write the following words and phrases until you can read and write them rapidly. Memorize the abbreviated words.

correspond-correspondence		March	established	willing	
achievement	associates	section	situation	attorney	
believes	collection	construction	deductions		
inspection	activity	however	band	student	
son's	sons-suns	friends	submit	patient	fire
rest	operating	to try	let us	Dear Dr.	

Assignment 3 — **Reading and writing shorthand**. Read each sentence from shorthand until you can read it as rapidly as you can read from print. Write each sentence in shorthand until you can write each one rapidly and accurately.

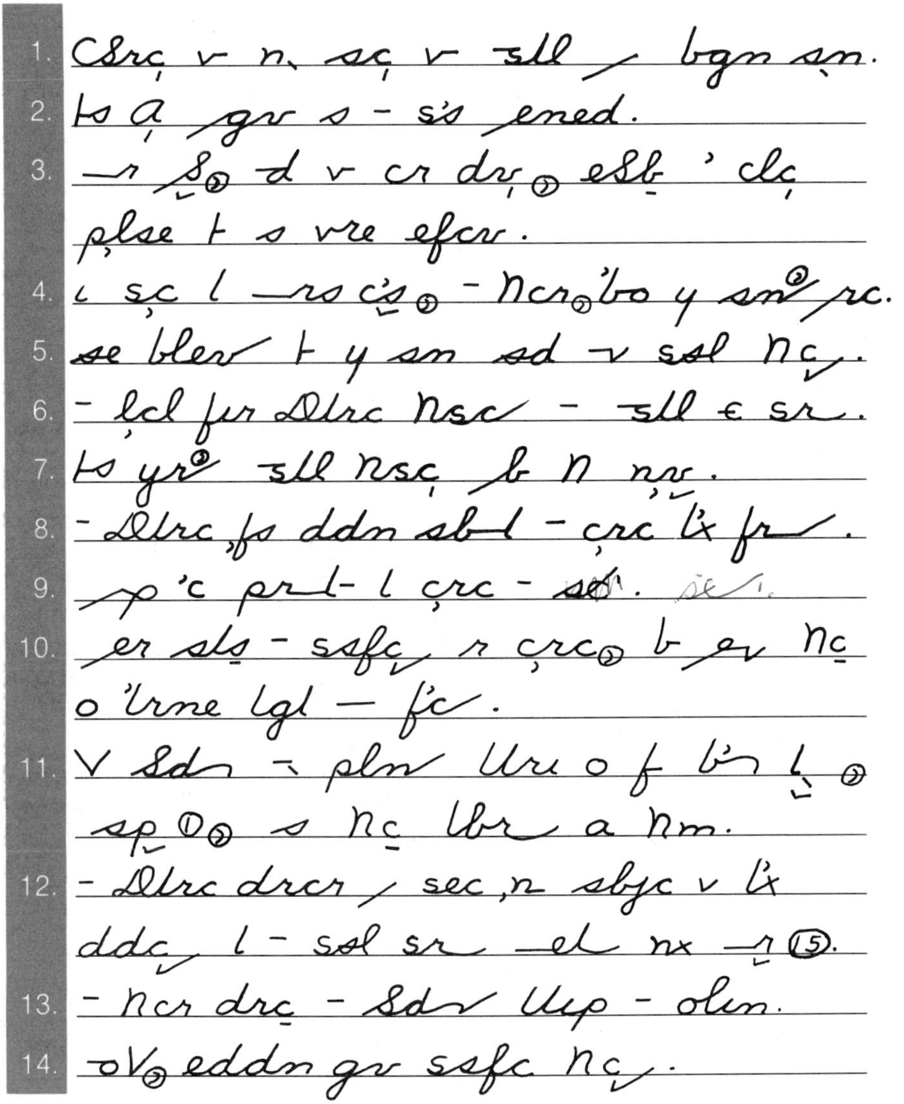

Learning tip: Note that the numbers in sentences 11 and 12 are circled in the shorthand notes above. When writing numbers in shorthand, circle them so that you can transcribe them easily.

BUILDING TRANSCRIPTION SKILLS

Assignment 4 — **Punctuating appositives**. Words and phrases that describe or explain a preceding word or expression are called *appositives*. *Place a comma before and after appositives*.

1. Mr. Jones, our shorthand teacher, gave us an easy test. (The phrase, *our shorthand teacher*, describes Mr. Jones.)
2. One of the secretaries, a graduate of our college, can type 80 words a minute.
3. The meeting will be held Tuesday, May 21, at the new hotel.

BUILDING SHORTHAND SPEED AND TRANSCRIPTION ACCURACY

Assignment 5 — **Self-testing.** Complete Unit 21 in your *Study Guide* before you proceed with the rest of this chapter.

Assignment 6 — **Taking tape dictation.** To write from dictation the new words and sentences in this chapter, use Cassette 5 Side B from *Theory and Speed-Building Tapes*.

Assignment 7 — **Taking live dictation.** Write from dictation the sentences which are printed at the end of this chapter. Your instructor will dictate each group of 20 words to you at various speeds.

Assignment 8 — **Own-note transcription.** After you have taken the sentences in shorthand, select your best set of notes and transcribe them at your best typing rate. Do not number the sentences.

Assignment 9 — **Supplemental business letters.** If instructed to do so, read and write the additional business letter for this chapter found in "Supplemental Letters for Dictation" in Appendix A.

TRANSCRIPT OF SHORTHAND SENTENCES

1. Construction of the new section of the hospital will begin soon.
2. This addition will give us the space we need. (20)
3. Mr. West, head of the credit division, established a collection policy that is very effective. (40)
4. I spoke to Mrs. Case, the instructor, about your son's work.
5. She believes that your son should have special instructions. (60)
6. The local fire district inspects the hospital each spring.
7. This year's hospital inspection will be in November. (80)
8. The district office did not submit the correct tax forms.
9. Will you please act promptly to correct the situation. (100)

10. We are satisfied the specifications are correct, but we have instructed our attorney to get more facts. (120)
11. Every student who plans to try out for the band Tuesday, September 1, is instructed to bring an instrument. (140)
12. The district director will speak on the subject of tax deductions at the special spring meeting next March 15. (160)
13. The instructor directed the students to type the outline.
14. However, he did not give specific instructions. (180)

CHAPTER 22

WRITING **RT-RD** AND **RITY**

Assignment 1 — **Rule discovery**. Follow the three-step plan to learn the new writing principles: (1) Discover the rule for each group of words. (2) Read the shorthand outlines until you can read them rapidly. (3) Cover the shorthand and write each word until you can do so rapidly and accurately.

RT-RD

record report according records board third

transportation standard article ordinary cards

heard-herd hard effort part reports support

card start quarter started quarterly guards

RITY

authority authorities security majority securities

WRITING PRINCIPLES

RT-RD Write a capital *R* thus to express *rt-rd* when no vowel occurs between the letters. When writing the capital *R*, begin the letter on the line and write upward thus

RITY Write a disjoined capital *R* to express the combination *rity* and the preceding vowel. Write the disjoined capital *R* close to the word to which it belongs.

Assignment 2 — **New vocabulary**. Read and write the following words and phrases until you can read and write them rapidly. Memorize the abbreviated words.

certificate
order
particular
distribute
January
organizations-organizes
particularly
orders
quantities
model
anxious
needed
central
recognize
sufficient
cold
envelopes
spend-spent
written
develop
certainly
directors
cities
city's
in this
in order to
will not be
we have had

Assignment 3 — **Reading and writing shorthand**. Read each sentence from shorthand until you can read it as rapidly as you can read from print. Write each sentence in shorthand until you can write each one rapidly and accurately.

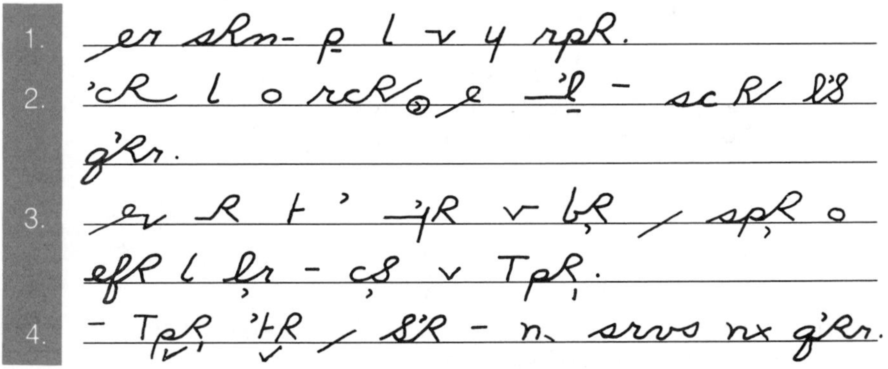
1.
2.
3.
4.

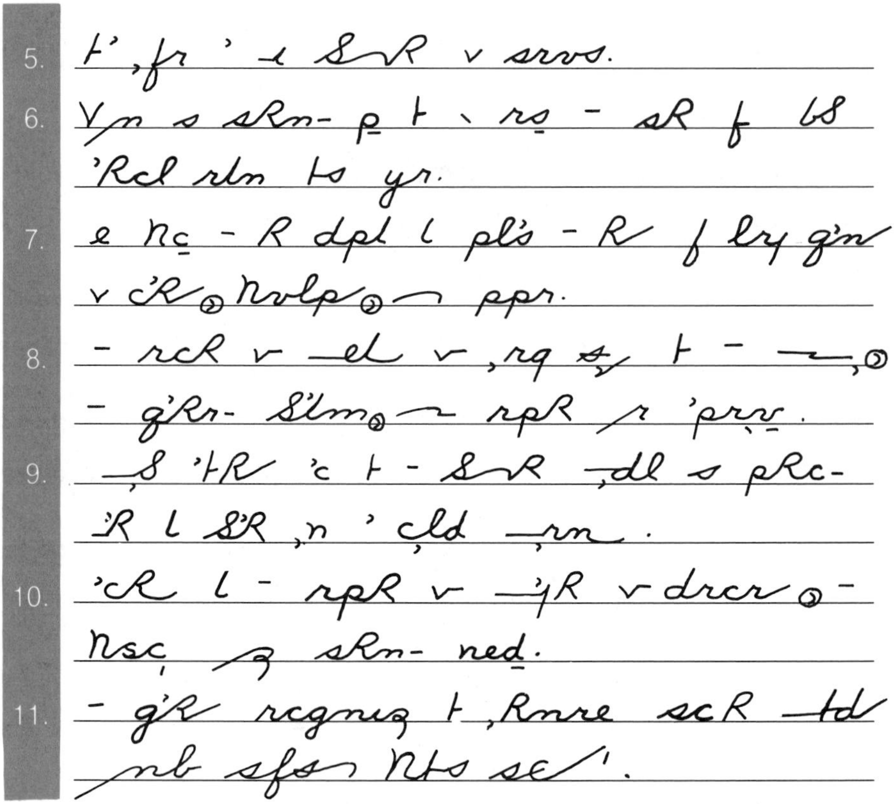

BUILDING TRANSCRIPTION SKILLS

Assignment 4 — **Punctuating a series.** Study the following rule and examples. Apply this rule when transcribing.

When two or more words, phrases, or clauses appear in a series (one after the other), they are separated by commas.

1. I will buy paper, ink, and a pen to do the assignment.
2. You may pay by cash, by cheque, or by credit card.
3. He helped to prepare the meal, clear the table, and wash the dishes.

BUILDING SHORTHAND SPEED AND TRANSCRIPTION ACCURACY

Assignment 5 — **Self-testing.** Complete Unit 22 in your *Study Guide* before you proceed with the rest of this chapter.

Assignment 6 — **Taking tape dictation.** To write from dictation the new words and sentences in this chapter, use Cassette 6 Side B from *Theory and Speed-Building Tapes*.

Assignment 7 — **Taking live dictation.** Write from dictation the sentences which are printed at the end of this chapter. Your instructor will dictate each group of 20 words to you at various speeds.

Assignment 8 — **Own-note transcription.** After you have taken the sentences in shorthand, select your best set of notes and transcribe them at your best typing rate. Do not number the sentences.

Assignment 9 — **Supplemental business letters.** If instructed to do so, read and write the additional business letter for this chapter found in "Supplemental Letters for Dictation" in Appendix A.

TRANSCRIPT OF SHORTHAND SENTENCES

1. We are certainly pleased to have your report.
2. According to our records, we mailed the securities last quarter. (20)
3. We have heard that a majority of the board will support our effort to lower the cost of transportation. (40)
4. The Transportation Authority will start the new service next quarter.
5. They offer a high standard of service. (60)
6. Everyone is certainly pleased that you received the certificate for the best article written this year. (80)
7. He instructed the order department to place the orders for large quantities of cards, envelopes, and paper. (100)
8. The record of the meeting of the organization shows that the memo, the quarterly statement, and the report were approved. (120)
9. Most authorities acknowledge that the standard model is particularly hard to start on a cold morning. (140)
10. According to the report of the majority of the directors, the inspection was certainly needed. (160)
11. The guards recognize that ordinary security methods will not be sufficient in this situation. (180)

CHAPTER 23

WRITING SOUNDS OF **OI-OY**, **NCE-NSE**, AND **POST** AND **POSITION**

Assignment 1 — **Rule discovery**. Follow the three-step plan to learn the new writing principles: (1) Discover the rule for each group of words. (2) Read the shorthand outlines until you can read them rapidly. (3) Cover the shorthand and write each word until you can do so rapidly and accurately.

SOUND OF **OI-OY**

boys   boy's   oil   employees   appointment

employment   choice   employer   unemployment   point

avoid   boiler   royal

NCE-NSE

accordance   balance   remittance   since   responsible

agency   insurance   conference   announcement

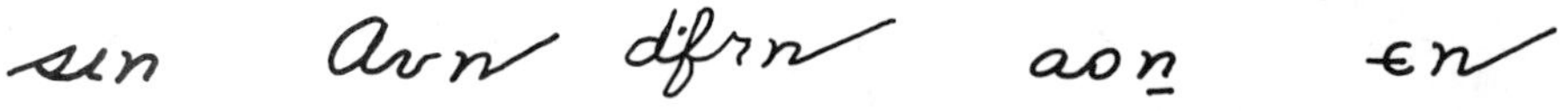

science   advances   differences   announced   chances

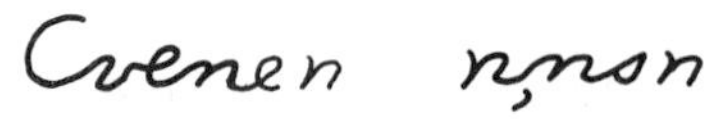

convenience   nonsense

POST AND POSITION

post-position
disposition
postponed
postage
posted

WRITING PRINCIPLES

OI-OY Write a dotted *i* to express the sound *oi-oy*.

NCE-NSE Write a small, disjoined *n* to express the combinations *nce-nse* and the preceding vowel. Write the disjoined *n* close to the word to which it belongs.

POST-POSITION Write a capital *P* to express the prefix and suffix *post* and *position*. Start the first stroke of *P* on the line and write upward.

Assignment 2 — **New vocabulary**.. Read and write the following words and phrases until you can read and write them rapidly. Memorize the abbreviated words.

sincere-sincerely
remember
purchase order
invoice
October
regard
February
regarding
post office
correction
cases
remaining
efforts
warns
answered
deducted
securing
charged
decrease
despite
known
error
making
gas
claims
suit
ladies
mistake
has been

Assignment 3 — **Reading and writing shorthand**. Read each sentence from shorthand until you can read it as rapidly as you can read from print. Write each sentence in shorthand until you can write each one rapidly and accurately.

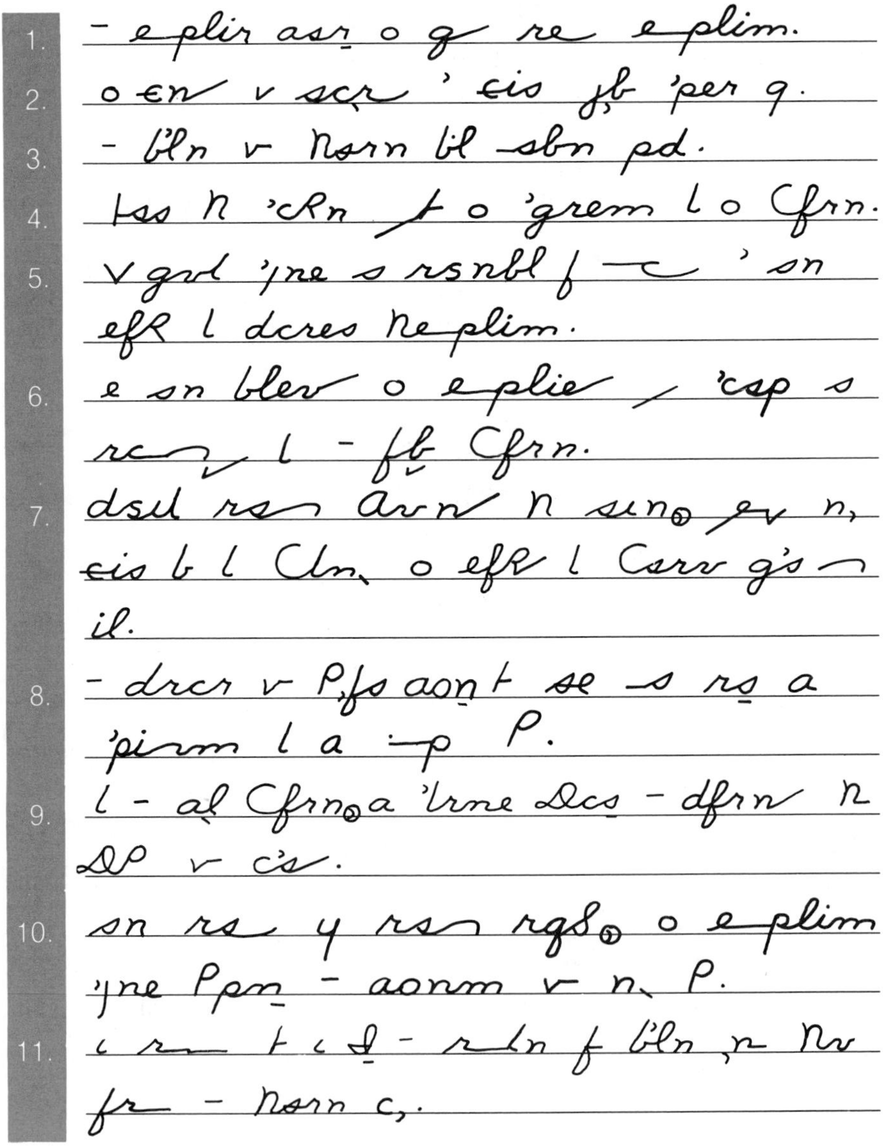

BUILDING SHORTHAND SPEED AND TRANSCRIPTION ACCURACY

Assignment 4 — **Self-testing.** Complete Unit 23 in your *Study Guide* before you proceed with the rest of this chapter.

Assignment 5 — **Taking tape dictation.** To write from dictation the new words and sentences in this chapter, use Cassette 7 Side B from *Theory and Speed-Building Tapes*.

Assignment 6 — **Taking live dictation.** Write from dictation the sentences which are printed at the end of this chapter. Your instructor will dictate each group of 20 words to you at various speeds.

Assignment 7 — **Own-note transcription.** After you have taken the sentences in shorthand, select your best set of notes and transcribe them at your best typing rate. Do not number the sentences.

Assignment 8 — **Supplemental business letters.** If instructed to do so, read and write the additional business letter for this chapter found in "Supplemental Letters for Dictation" in Appendix A.

TRANSCRIPT OF SHORTHAND SENTENCES

1. The employer answered our questions regarding employment.
2. Our chances of securing a choice job appear good. (20)
3. The balance of the insurance bill has been paid.
4. This is in accordance with our agreement at our conference. (40)
5. Every government agency is responsible for making a sincere effort to decrease unemployment. (60)
6. He sincerely believes our employees will accept his recommendations at the February conference. (80)
7. Despite recent advances in science, we have no choice but to continue our efforts to conserve gas and oil. (100)
8. The director of the post office announced that she has received an appointment to an important position. (120)
9. At the annual conference, an attorney discussed the differences in the disposition of the cases. (140)
10. Since receiving your recent request, our employment agency postponed the announcement of the new position. (160)
11. I remember that I enclosed the remittance for the balance on the invoice from the insurance company. (180)

CHAPTER 24

BUSINESS LETTER DICTATION AND TRANSCRIPTION

BUILDING TRANSCRIPTION SKILLS

Assignment 1 — **Hyphenating words.** In the letters that follow are some words that require a hyphen. Study the rule and the examples and apply the rule when you transcribe.

Two or more words that are used as a single descriptive word should be hyphenated when they come before the word they describe.

1. Fred will take a full-time job. (Note that *full-time* describes the kind of job Fred will take.)
2. I can take a part-time job, but I cannot work full time. (In this case, *full time* does not have a hyphen because the words do not come before a noun they describe.)
3. She is a well-known actress, but the leading man is not well known.
4. The dance will be our main fund-raising event this year.

Assignment 2 — **Setting up business letters.** Names and addresses are given for each of the remaining letters in this text. Unless your instructor tells you otherwise, you should transcribe the business letters in this and the remaining chapters in business-letter form.

Examine the example of a business letter in *full-block style* on page 154 of your text. This style is used in many offices. Use this style when transcribing the letters in this text unless your instructor asks you to use a different letter style.

For each letter, your instructor will give you the name of the person signing the letter.

Names and addresses are seldom dictated in offices. The secretary gets this information from previous correspondence. Therefore, names and addresses are not included in the word count of the letters. Your instructor will start timing the dictation with the salutation.

Assignment 3 — **Spelling review.** Follow the steps outlined in Chapter 12 to check your ability to spell the following words correctly:

1. according	9. federal	17. quantity
2. achievement	10. hospital	18. quantities
~~3. assistance~~	11. insurance	19. remittance
4. balance	12. least	20. special
5. classes	13. maintain	21. specific
6. collection	14. model	22. valuable
7. conference	15. organization	23. various
8. February	16. particularly	24. written

BUSINESS LETTERS

Assignment 4 — **Letter 1.** Read and write each of the new words and phrases until you can read and write each one rapidly and accurately. Then read and write the shorthand for Letter 1 to build your writing speed.

avenue	opportunities	buyer	fuel-fool	qualify	
employers	sportswear	positions	reference	library	
welcome	training	collect	contact	certain	began
heads	employ	months	assume	learn	career
full	vocational	Montreal	Alice	Sincerely yours	

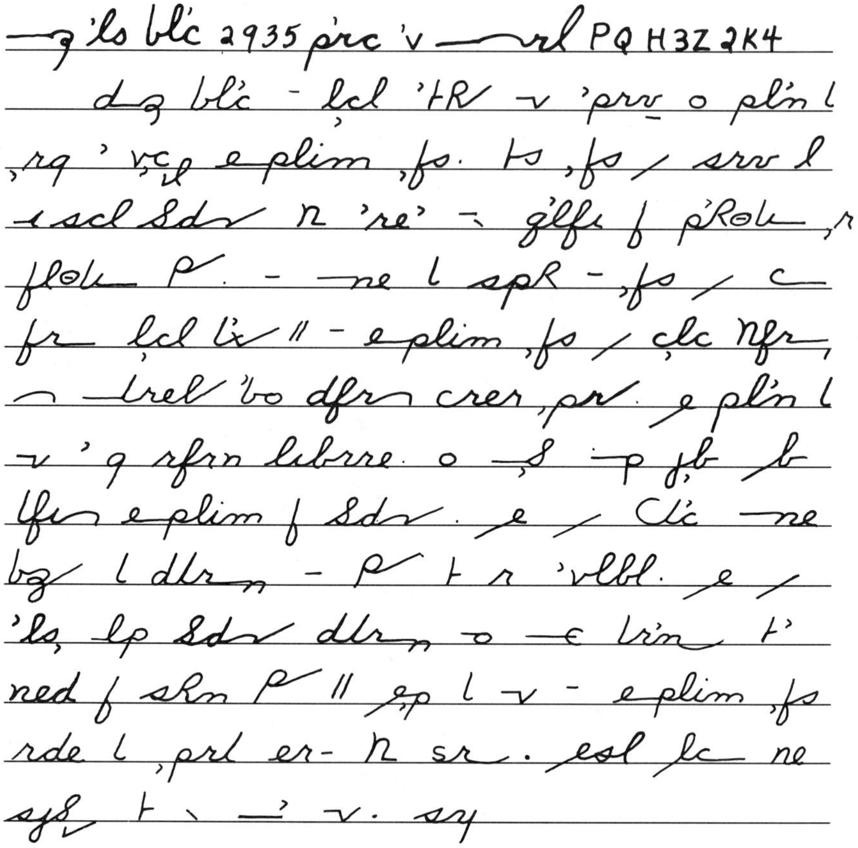

Assignment 5 — **Letter 2**. Read and write each new word and phrase for Letter 2 until you can read and write each one rapidly and accurately. Then read and write the shorthand for Letter 2 to build your writing speed.

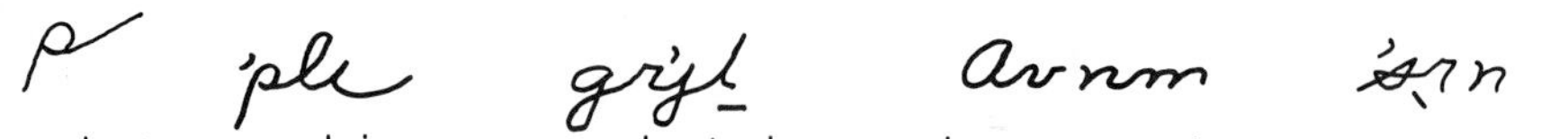

posts applying graduated advancement assurance

Eve assure fund raising chance often rapid

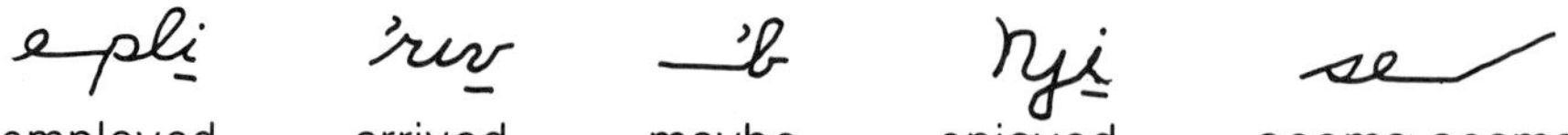

employed arrived maybe enjoyed seems-seams

alumni | offers | Martin | wise | Vancouver | to do so

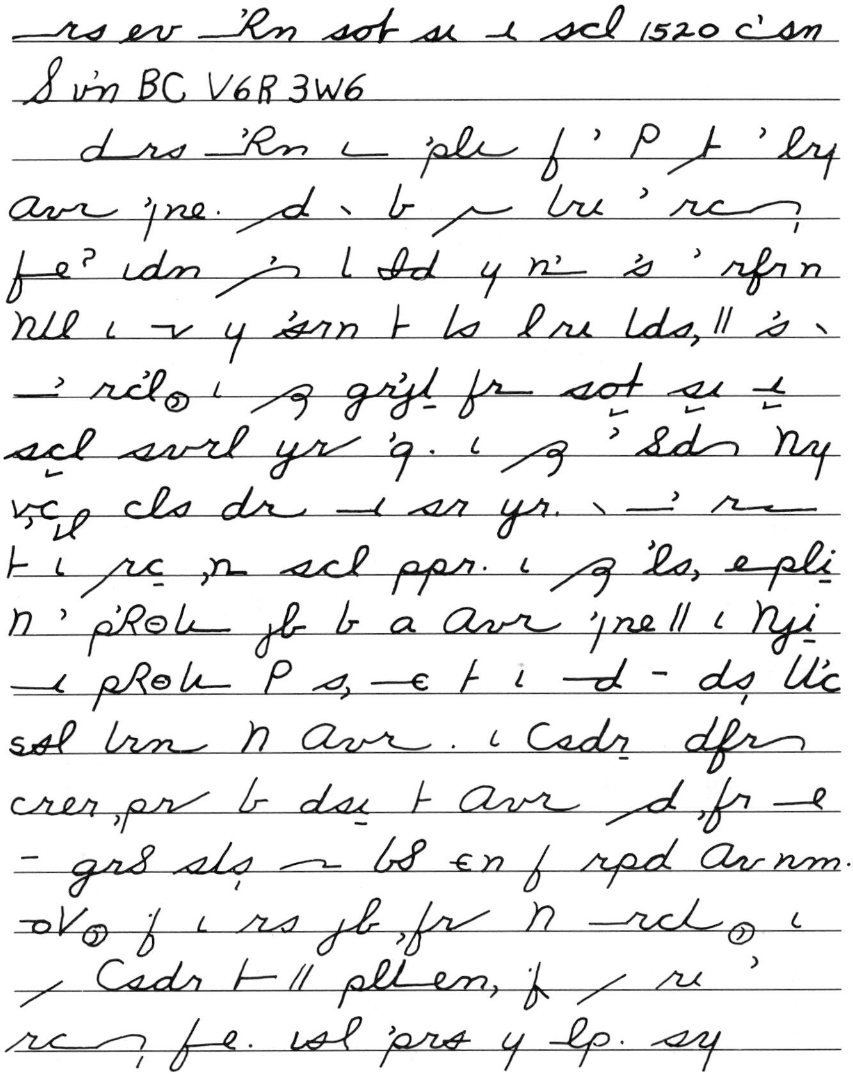

Assignment 6 — **Supplemental business letters**. If instructed to do so, read and write the additional business letters for this chapter found in "Supplemental Letters for Dictation" in Appendix A.

BUILDING SHORTHAND SPEED AND TRANSCRIPTION ACCURACY

Assignment 7 — **Self-testing**. Complete Unit 24 in your *Study Guide* before you proceed with the rest of this chapter.

Assignment 8 — **Taking tape dictation**. To write from dictation the new words and letters in this chapter, use Cassette 8 Side B from *Theory and Speed-Building Tapes*.

Assignment 9 — **Taking live dictation**. Write from dictation the letters which are printed at the end of this chapter. Your instructor will dictate to you from these transcripts at various speeds.

Assignment 10 — **Own-note transcription**. Transcribe at your best typing rate an accurate copy of at least one of the letters you took in shorthand in Assignment 9. Type the letter in the form requested by your instructor.

TRANSCRIPTS OF LETTERS 1 AND 2

Letter 1 Ms. Alice Black, 2935 Park Avenue, Montreal, PQ H3Z 2K4

Dear Ms. Black: The local authorities have approved our plan to organize a vocational employment (20) office. This office will serve all high school students in the area who qualify for part-time or full-time positions. (40) The money to support the office will come from local taxes.

The employment office will collect information (60) and materials about different career opportunities. We plan to have a good reference (80) library. Our most important job will be to find employment for students. We will contact many businesses (100) to determine the positions that are available. We will also help students determine how much training (120) they need for certain positions.

We hope to have the employment office ready to operate early in (140) the spring. We shall welcome any suggestions that you may have. Sincerely yours, (154)

Letter 2 Mrs. Eve Martin, South Side High School, 1520 Camosun Street, Vancouver, BC V6R 3W6

Dear Mrs. Martin: I am applying for a position with a large advertising agency. Would you be (20) willing to write a recommendation for me? I do not want to include your name as a reference until (40) I have your assurance that it is all right to do so.

As you may recall, I was graduated from South Side (60) High School several years ago. I was a student in your vocational class during my senior year. You may (80) remember that I worked on the school paper. I was also employed in a part-time job by an advertising (100) agency.

I enjoyed my part-time position so much that I made the decision to take special training in (120) advertising. I considered different career opportunities but decided that advertising would (140) offer me the greatest satisfaction and the best chance for rapid advancement. However, if I receive job (160) offers in marketing, I will consider them.

Please let me know if you will write a recommendation for me. (180) I shall appreciate your help. Sincerely yours, (189)

REVIEWING THE WRITING PRINCIPLES

All the writing principles, abbreviated words, and standard abbreviations you have learned in Chapters 17 through 24 are reviewed on Tape 17 Side B of the *Theory and Speed-Building Tapes*. Take dictation from this tape before completing Examination 6.

EXAMINATION 6

- Remove and complete Examination 6, which follows Unit 24 in your *Study Guide*, before proceeding to Chapter 25 of your textbook.
- Self-check with the Key to Examination 6 which appears at the back of the *Study Guide*.

CHAPTER 25

WRITING **FOR-FORE-FER-FUR**,

BILITY, AND **LETTER-LITER**

Assignment 1 — **Rule discovery**. Follow the three-step plan to learn the new writing principles: (1) Discover the rule for each group of words. (2) Read the shorthand outlines until you can read them rapidly. (3) Cover the shorthand and write each word until you can do so rapidly and accurately.

PREFIXES **FOR-FORE-FER-FUR**

furnace furnish further formerly formal former

foreign forests forget forecast foremost formula

fortunate furniture forgot fertilizer furnished

BILITY

ability eligibility liability possibility flexibility

responsibilities advisability desirability responsibility

LETTER-LITER

letter letters literary literature literally

WRITING PRINCIPLES

FOR-FORE FER-FUR Write a disjoined *f* for the prefixes *for-fore-fer-fur*. The disjoined *f* is used *only* when it represents a syllable. Note the following example: *form* [shorthand] *formal* [shorthand]. The *f* is joined in the word *form* because the *for* is not a syllable.

BILITY Write a capital *B* to express the combination *bility* and the preceding vowel. When writing the capital *B*, begin on the line and write upward thus [shorthand].

LETTER-LITER Write a capital *L* thus [shorthand] to express the combinations *letter-liter*. Do not write a printed *L* for the combinations *letter* and *liter* because the printed *L* could be taken for the shorthand *t-m*.

Assignment 2 — **New vocabulary**. Read and write the following words and phrases until you can read and write them rapidly.

furthermore
shipments
conserving
difference
quotation
American
requesting
typing
turn
warranty
western
applicants
sports
Gonzales
helped
wants
wrote
north
Alfredo
publication
countries
Winnipeg
to call
there is

Assignment 3 — **Reading and writing shorthand**. Read each sentence from shorthand until you can read it as rapidly as you can read from print. Write each sentence in shorthand until you can write each one rapidly and accurately.

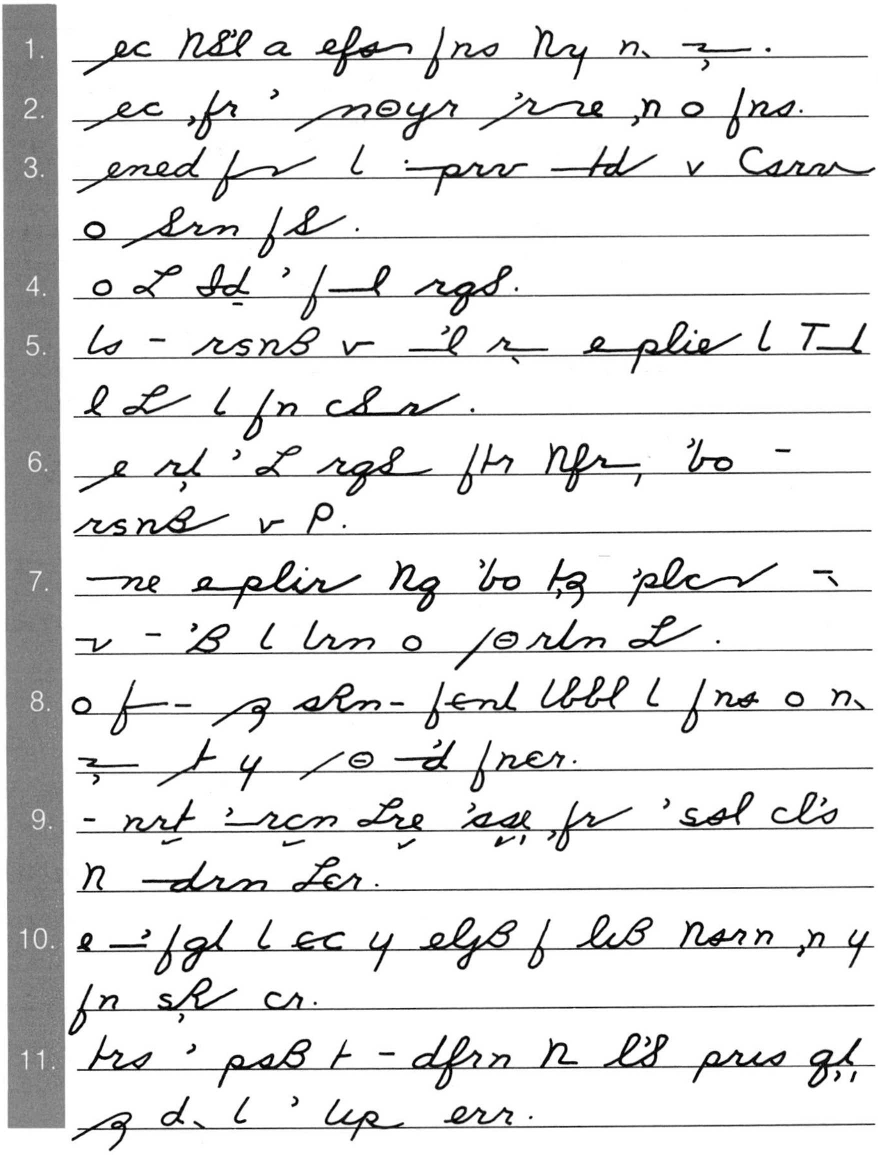

BUILDING SHORTHAND SPEED AND TRANSCRIPTION ACCURACY

Assignment 4 — **Self-testing**. Complete Unit 25 in your *Study Guide* before you proceed with the rest of this chapter.

Assignment 5 — **Taking tape dictation**. To write from dictation the new words and sentences in this chapter, use Cassette 9 Side B from *Theory and Speed-Building Tapes*.

Assignment 6 — **Taking live dictation**. Write from dictation the sentences which are printed at the end of this chapter. Your instructor will dictate each group of 20 words to you at various speeds.

Assignment 7 — **Own-note transcription**. After you have taken the sentences in shorthand, select your best set of notes and transcribe them at your best typing rate. Do not number the sentences.

Assignment 8 — **Supplemental business letters**. If instructed to do so, read and write the additional business letter for this chapter found in ''Supplemental Letters for Dictation'' in Appendix A.

TRANSCRIPT OF SHORTHAND SENTENCES

1. We can install an efficient furnace in your new home.
2. We can offer a one-year warranty on our furnace. (20)
3. We need funds to improve methods of conserving our western forests.
4. Our letter included a formal request. (40)
5. It is the responsibility of the mail room employees to transmit all letters to foreign customers. (60)
6. We wrote a letter requesting further information about the responsibilities of the position. (80)
7. Many employers inquire about those applicants who have the ability to turn out well-written letters. (100)
8. Our family was certainly fortunate to be able to furnish our new home with your well-made furniture. (120)
9. The North American Literary Association offers a special class in modern literature. (140)
10. He may forget to check your eligibility for liability insurance on your foreign sports car. (160)
11. There is a possibility that the difference in the last price quotation was due to a typing error. (180)

CHAPTER 26

WRITING PRE-PRI-PRO-PER-PUR

Assignment 1 — **Rule discovery**. Follow the three-step plan to learn the new writing principles: (1) Discover the rule for each group of words. (2) Read the shorthand outlines until you can read them rapidly. (3) Cover the shorthand and write each word until you can do so rapidly and accurately.

PRE-PRI-PRO-PER-PUR

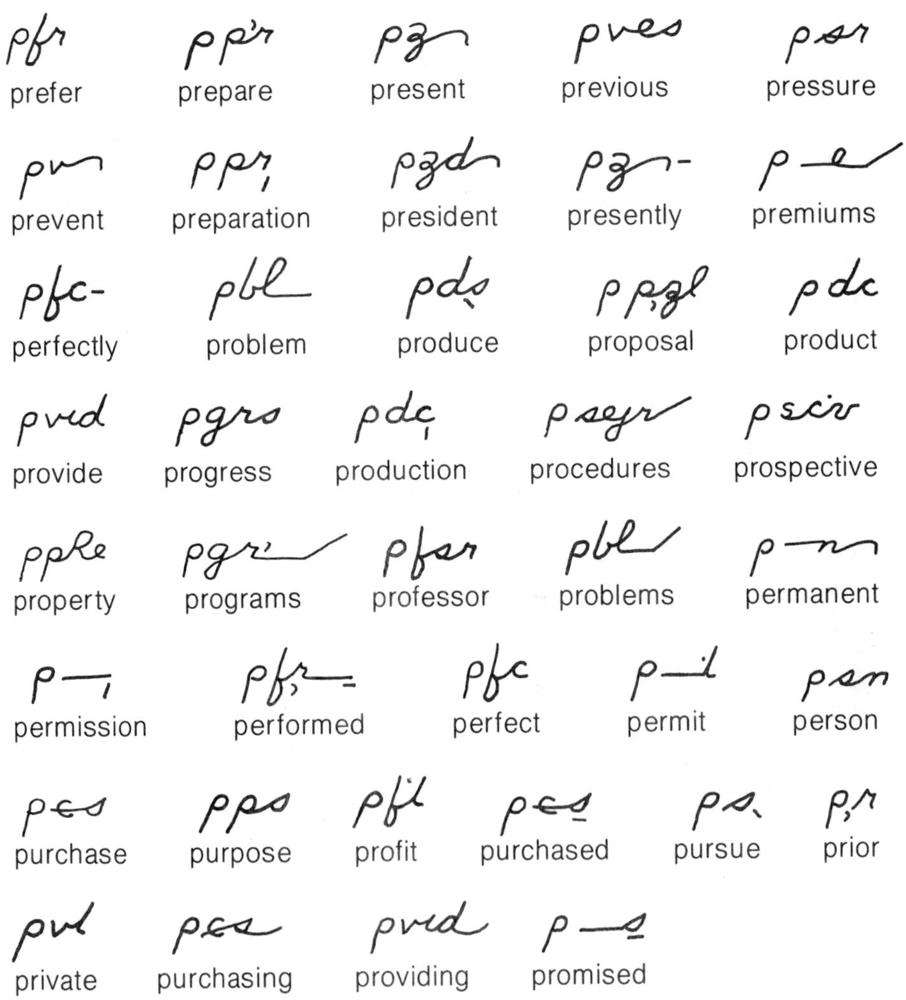
prefer
prepare
present
previous
pressure
prevent
preparation
president
presently
premiums
perfectly
problem
produce
proposal
product
provide
progress
production
procedures
prospective
property
programs
professor
problems
permanent
permission
performed
perfect
permit
person
purchase
purpose
profit
purchased
pursue
prior
private
purchasing
providing
promised

WRITING PRINCIPLES

PRE-PRI-PRO-PER-PUR Write a small disjoined *p* to express the combinations *pre-pri-pro-per-pur* when they begin a word containing more than one syllable. Write the disjoined *p* close to the remainder of the word. Note the following examples:

press preside prove provide price priority

Assignment 2 — **New vocabulary**. Read and write the following words and phrases until you can read and write them rapidly.

appreciated manufacturer attendance supervisor

stereo telephoned increases almost commission

against Rita appointed demonstrated additional

studying continued trouble complaint refused

Lethbridge Jones to follow

Assignment 3 — **Reading and writing shorthand**. Read each sentence from shorthand until you can read it as rapidly as you can read from print. Write each sentence in shorthand until you can write each one rapidly and accurately.

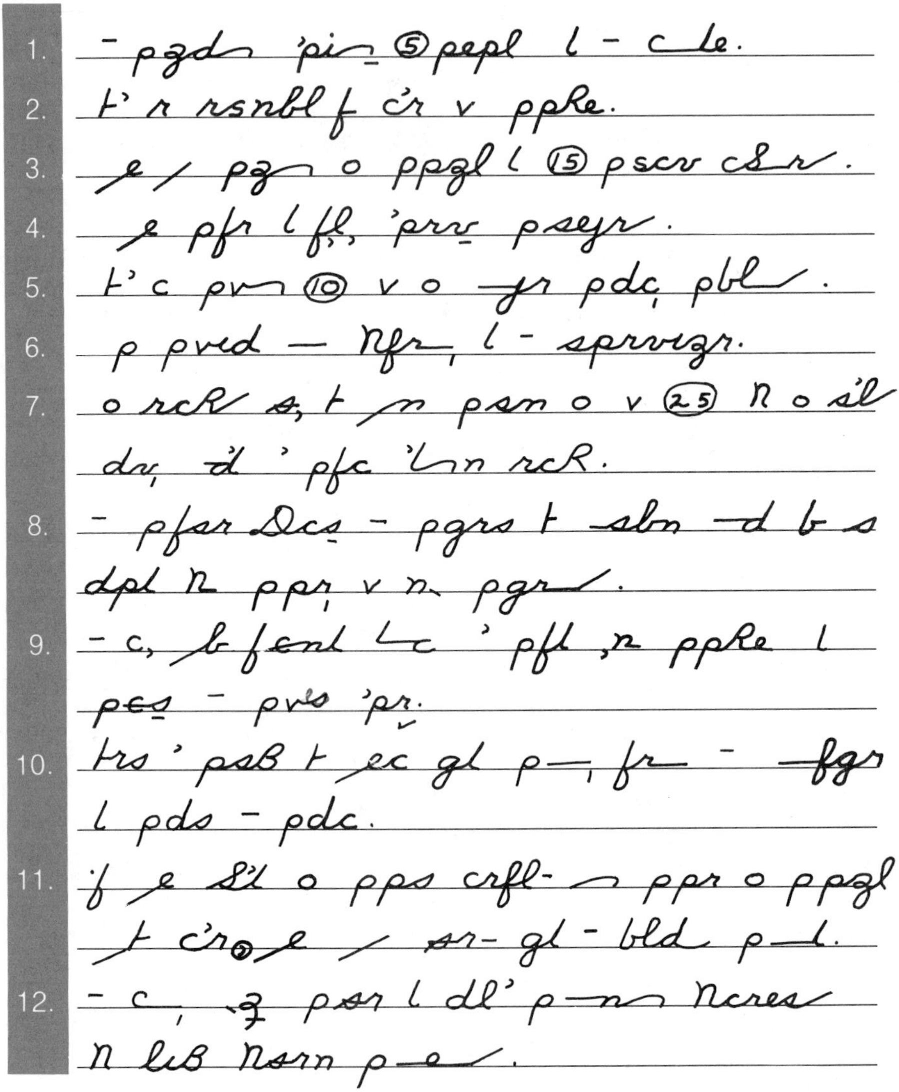

BUILDING TRANSCRIPTION SKILLS

Assignment 4 — **Transcribing numbers**.

1. Spell out numbers that begin a sentence.
   - Thirty-five students from our class will attend the game.
2. Spell out isolated numbers from one to ten.
   - I went to the library two times today.
   - There are five books and three magazines in my bag.

3. Use figures for other numbers (numbers of 11 and over, amounts of money, dates, percentages, and figures to denote time).
   - All 35 students in our class will attend the game.
   - Tomorrow's assignment begins on page 64.
   - Each ticket sells for $2.50, and we paid $45 to rent the bus.
   - We will return on November 5 at 2 p.m.
   - Our sales have increased 25 per cent this year.
4. Use the same style to express related numbers above and below 10. (If any of the numbers are above 10, place all numbers in figures).
   - There are 5 books and 14 magazines in my bag.

BUILDING SHORTHAND SPEED AND TRANSCRIPTION ACCURACY

Assignment 5 — **Self-testing**. Complete Unit 26 in your *Study Guide* before you proceed with the rest of this chapter.

Assignment 6 — **Taking tape dictation**. To write from dictation the new words and sentences in this chapter, use Cassette 10 Side B from *Theory and Speed-Building Tapes*.

Assignment 7 — **Taking live dictation**. Write from dictation the sentences which are printed at the end of this chapter. Your instructor will dictate each group of 20 words to you at various speeds.

Assignment 8 — **Own-note transcription**. After you have taken the sentences in shorthand, select your best set of notes and transcribe them at your best typing rate. Do not number the sentences.

Assignment 9 — **Supplemental business letters**. If instructed to do so, read and write the additional business letter for this chapter found in "Supplemental Letters for Dictation" in Appendix A.

TRANSCRIPT OF SHORTHAND SENTENCES

1. The president appointed five people to the committee.
2. They are responsible for the care of property. (20)
3. We will present our proposal to 15 prospective customers.
4. We prefer to follow approved procedures. (40)
5. They can prevent ten of our major production problems.
6. Please provide more information to the supervisor. (60)
7. Our records show that 1 person out of 25 in our sales division had a perfect attendance record. (80)

8. The professor discussed the progress that has been made by his department in the preparation of new programs. (100)
9. The company will be fortunate to make a profit on the property it purchased the previous April. (120)
10. There is a possibility that we can get permission from the manufacturer to produce the product. (140)
11. If we state our purpose carefully and prepare our proposal with care, we will surely get the building permit. (160)
12. The commission used pressure to delay permanent increases in liability insurance premiums. (180)

CHAPTER 27

WRITING **AX-EX-OX** AND **NGE**

Assignment 1 — **Rule discovery**. Follow the three-step plan to learn the new writing principles: (1) Discover the rule for each group of words. (2) Read the shorthand outlines until you can read them rapidly. (3) Cover the shorthand and write each word until you can do so rapidly and accurately.

PREFIXES **AX-EX-OX**

expense except expect examples examine exact

expected excellent export explain extend-extent

expects extension experience exceptionally

explained expensive extending examination

examined expressed explanation exactly axle-excel

oxygen express

NGE

arrange change passengers changes arrangements

WRITING PRINCIPLES

AX-EX-OX Write a long, straight slanted, downward stroke to express the prefixes *ax*, *ex*, and *ox*. Be sure to slant the stroke so you will not confuse it with the letter *t*.

NGE Write a dotted *j* to express the combination *nge*.

Assignment 2 — **New vocabulary**. Read and write the following words and phrases until you can read and write them rapidly. Memorize the abbreviated words.

extra *extreme* executive metre substitute

metres extremely chairperson knows articles

speaker project unit green provided exchange

convince items preparing permitted probably

Fredericton brochure employee gift stewardess

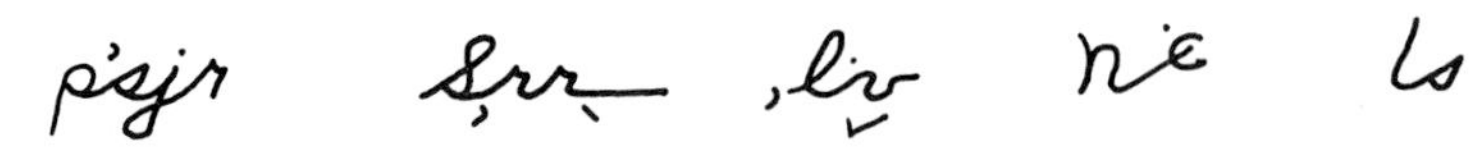

passenger storeroom Olive in which to us

Assignment 3 — **Reading and writing shorthand**. Read each sentence from shorthand until you can read it as rapidly as you can read from print. Write each sentence in shorthand until you can write each one rapidly and accurately.

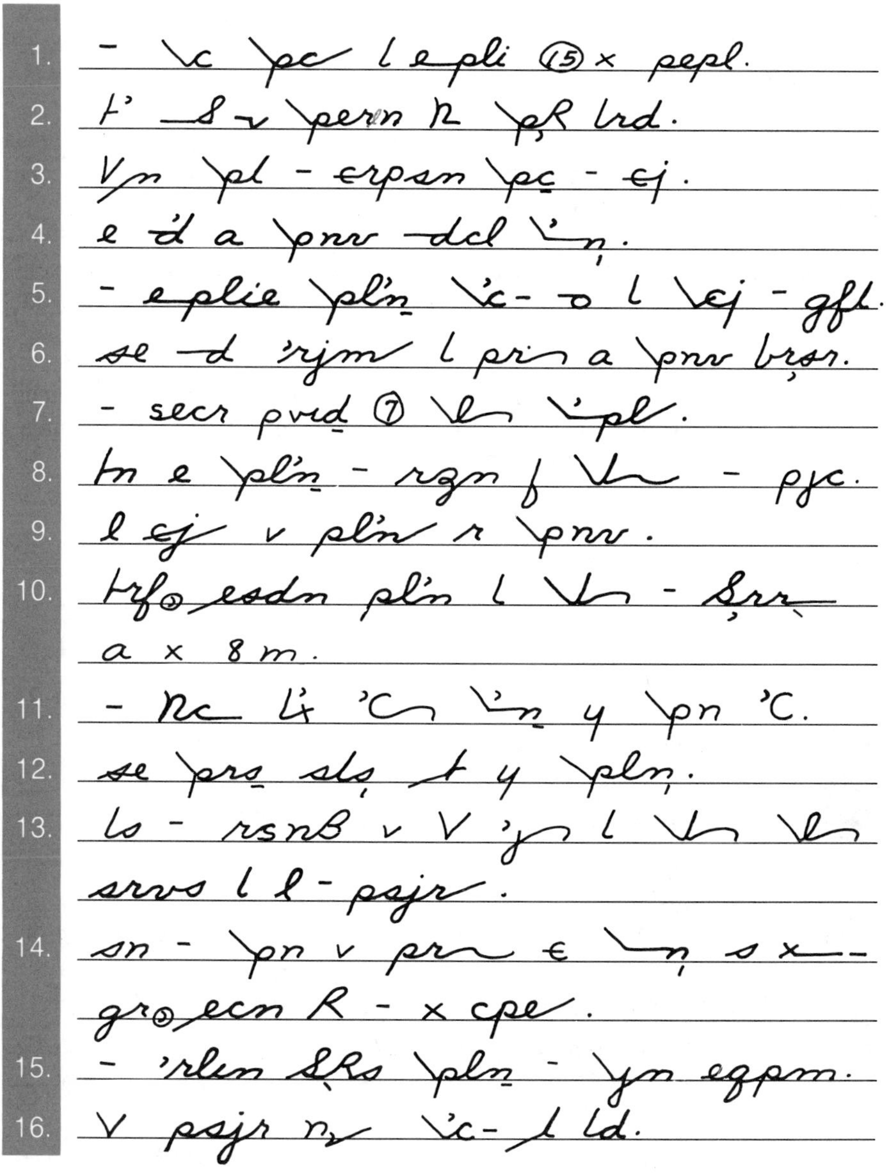

BUILDING SHORTHAND SPEED AND TRANSCRIPTION ACCURACY

Assignment 4 — **Self-testing**. Complete Unit 27 in your *Study Guide* before you proceed with the rest of this chapter.

Assignment 5 — **Taking tape dictation**. To write from dictation the new words and sentences in this chapter, use Cassette 11 Side B from *Theory and Speed-Building Tapes*.

Assignment 6 — **Taking live dictation**. Write from dictation the sentences which are printed at the end of this chapter. Your instructor will dictate each group of 20 words to you at various speeds.

Assignment 7 — **Own-note transcription**. After you have taken the sentences in shorthand, select your best set of notes and transcribe them at your best typing rate. Do not number the sentences.

Assignment 8 — **Supplemental business letters**. If instructed to do so, read and write the additional business letter for this chapter found in "Supplemental Letters for Dictation" in Appendix A.

TRANSCRIPT OF SHORTHAND SENTENCES

1. The executive expects to employ 15 extra people.
2. They must have experience in the export trade. (20)
3. Everyone except the chairperson expected the change.
4. He had an expensive medical examination. (40)
5. The employee explained exactly how to exchange the gift.
6. She made arrangements to print an expensive brochure. (60)
7. The speaker provided seven excellent examples.
8. Then he explained the reason for extending the project. (80)
9. All changes of plans are expensive.
10. Therefore, we should not plan to extend the storeroom an extra 8 m. (100)
11. The income tax accountant examined your expense account.
12. She expressed satisfaction with your explanation. (120)
13. It is the responsibility of every agent to extend excellent service to all the passengers. (140)
14. Since the expense of printing each examination is extremely great, we cannot order the extra copies. (160)
15. The airline stewardess explained the oxygen equipment.
16. Every passenger knows exactly what to do. (180)

CHAPTER 28

BUSINESS LETTER DICTATION AND TRANSCRIPTION

BUILDING TRANSCRIPTION SKILLS

Assignment 1 — **Spelling review.** Follow the steps outlined in Chapter 12 to check your ability to spell the following words correctly:

1.	attendance	10.	experience	19.	quotation
2.	almost	11.	extremely	20.	reference
3.	buyer	12.	foreign	21.	responsibilities
4.	career	13.	library	22.	responsible
5.	employee	14.	literature	23.	supervisor
6.	errors	15.	permit	24.	type
7.	excellent	16.	permitted	25.	typing
8.	exceptionally	17.	president	26.	welcome
9.	expense	18.	previous		

BUSINESS LETTERS

Assignment 2 — **Letter 1.** Read and write each of the new words and phrases until you can read and write each one rapidly and accurately. Then read and write the shorthand for Letter 1 to build your writing speed. Memorize the standard abbreviation.

television	departments	forest	educational	occasions
proposed	program	includes	period	arranged
topics	classroom	music	agrees	instruction
material	communicate	events	interesting	

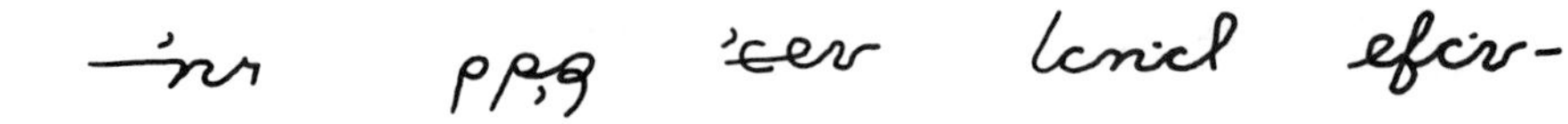

manner-manor propose achieve technical effectively

art mind skill level Regina working

station Edmonton we plan Cordially yours

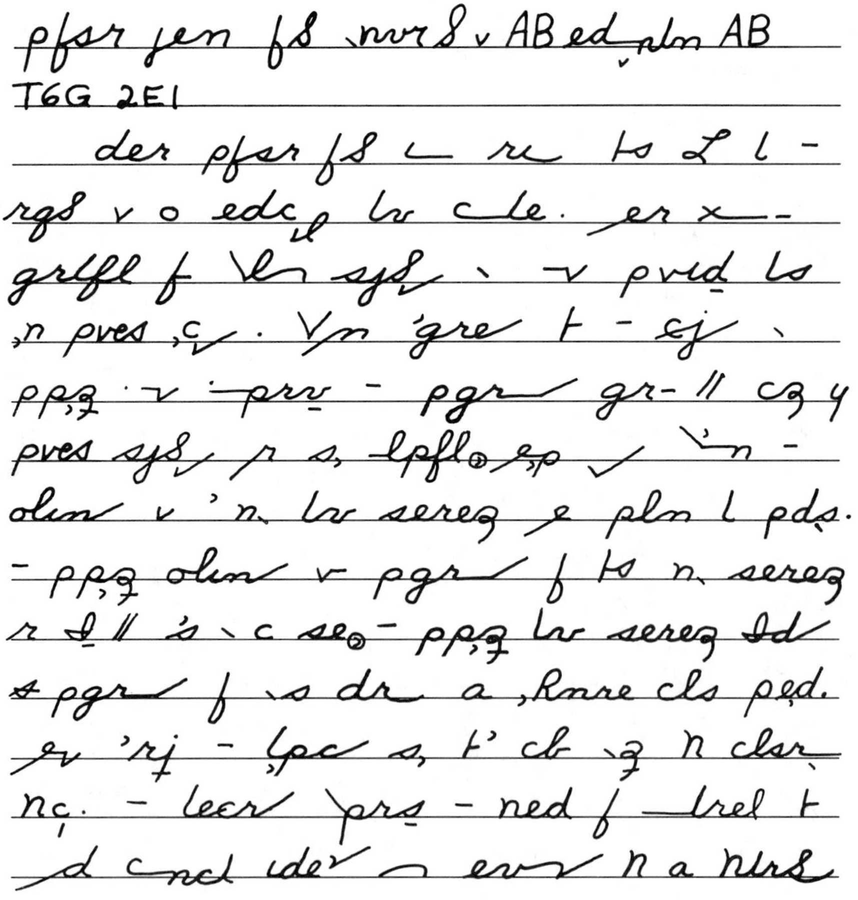

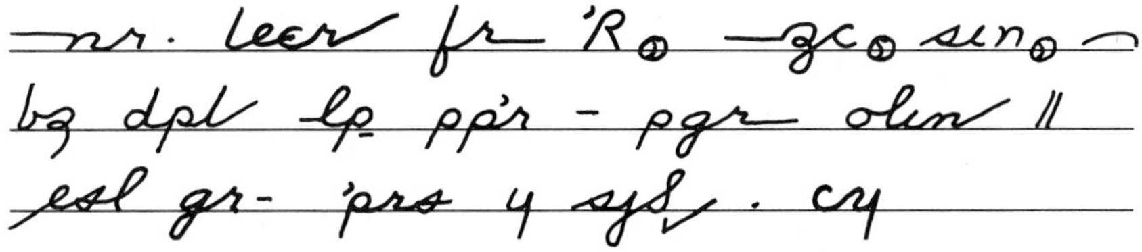

Assignment 3 — **Letter 2**. Read and write each new word and phrase for Letter 2 until you can read and write each one rapidly and accurately. Then read and write the shorthand for Letter 2 to build your writing speed.

copyright · writers · distribution · economics · textbook

published · consumer · produced · title · workbook

basic · unfortunately · Chicago · actual · workbooks

textbooks · mimeograph · photocopies · favorable · reply

informative · text · magazines · protection · deals

Rosa · printed · schools · books · Halifax · editor

law-lay · producer · we may not be able · Yours sincerely

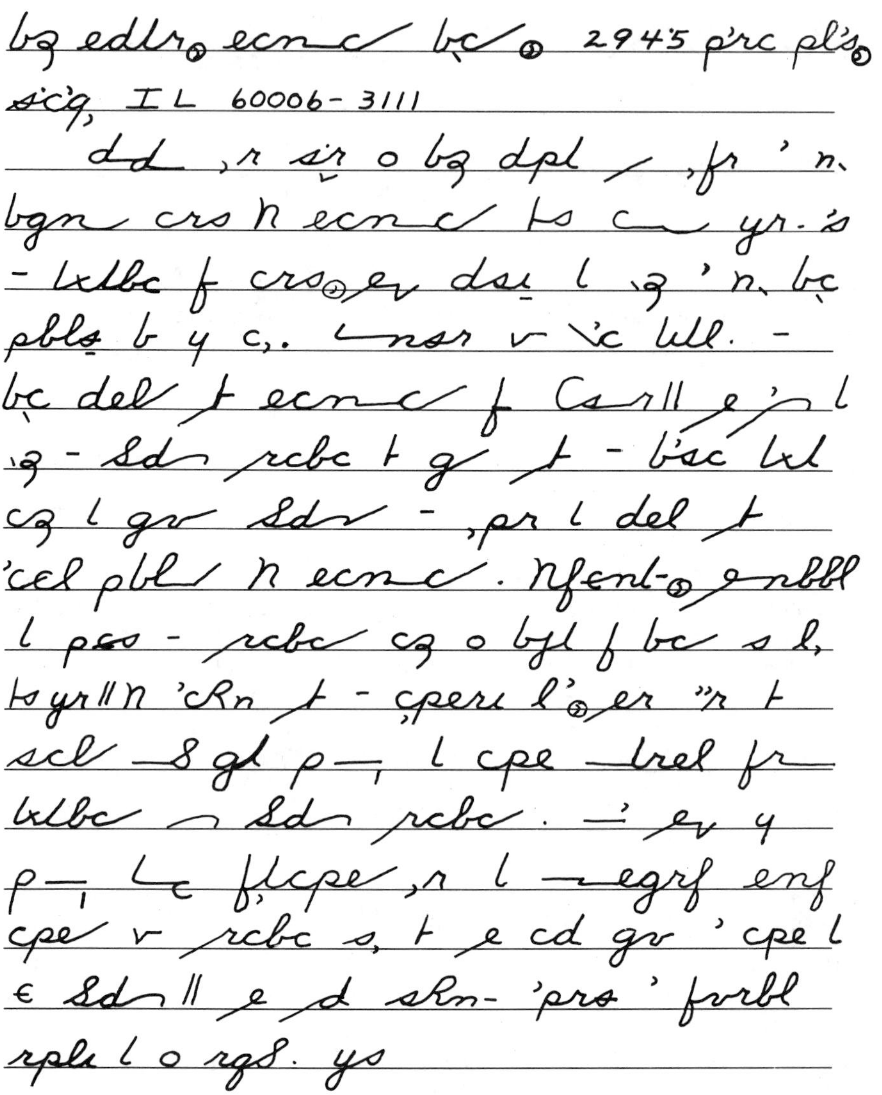

Assignment 4 — **Supplemental business letters**. If instructed to do so, read and write the additional business letter for this chapter found in ''Supplemental Letters for Dictation'' in Appendix A.

BUILDING SHORTHAND SPEED AND TRANSCRIPTION ACCURACY

Assignment 5 — **Self-testing**. Complete Unit 28 in your *Study Guide* before you proceed with the rest of this chapter.

Assignment 6 — **Taking tape dictation**. To write from dictation the new words and letters in this chapter, use Cassette 12 Side B from *Theory and Speed-Building Tapes*.

Assignment 7 — **Taking live dictation**. Write from dictation the letters printed at the end of this chapter. Your instructor will dictate to you from these transcripts at various speeds.

Assignment 8 — **Own-note transcription**. Transcribe at your best typing rate an accurate copy of at least one of the letters you took in shorthand in Assignment 7. Type the letter in the form requested by your instructor.

TRANSCRIPTS OF LETTERS 1 AND 2

Letter 1 Professor Jean Forest, University of Alberta, Edmonton, AB T6G 2E1

Dear Professor Forest: I am writing this letter at the request of our educational television (20) committee. We are extremely grateful for the excellent suggestions you have provided to us on previous (40) occasions. Everyone agrees that the changes you proposed have improved the programs greatly.

Because your (60) previous suggestions were so helpful, we hope you will examine the outlines of a new television series (80) we plan to produce. The proposed outlines of the programs for this new series are enclosed.

As you can see, the proposed (100) television series includes short programs for use during an ordinary class period. We have arranged (120) the topics so they can be used in classroom instruction. The teachers expressed the need for material that would (140) communicate ideas and events in an interesting manner. Teachers from art, music, science, and (160) business departments helped prepare the program outlines.

We shall greatly appreciate your suggestions. Cordially yours, (180)

Letter 2 Business Editor, Economics Books, 2945 Park Place, Chicago, IL 60006-3111

Dear Madam or Sir: Our business department will offer a new beginning course in economics this coming (20) year. As the textbook for the course, we have decided to use a new book published by your company. I am not (40) sure of the exact title. The book deals with economics for the consumer.

We want to use the student workbook (60) that goes with the basic text because it gives students the opportunity to deal with actual problems in (80) economics. Unfortunately, we may not be able to purchase the workbooks because our budget for books (100) is low this year.

In accordance with the copyright law, we are aware that schools must get permission to copy (120) material from textbooks and student workbooks. May we have your permission to make photocopies or to (140) mimeograph enough copies of the workbook so that we could give a copy to each student.

We would certainly (160) appreciate a favorable reply to our request. Yours sincerely, (174)

EXAMINATION 7

- Remove and complete Examination 7, which follows Unit 28 in your *Study Guide*, before proceeding to Chapter 29 of your textbook.
- Self-check with the Key to Examination 7 which appears at the back of the *Study Guide*.

CHAPTER 29

WRITING **SYS-SESS-SUS-SIS-CESS-CIS**, **ULATE**, AND **SCRIBE-SCRIPT**

Assignment 1 — **Rule discovery**. Follow the three-step plan to learn the new writing principles: (1) Discover the rule for each group of words. (2) Read the shorthand outlines until you can read them rapidly. (3) Cover the shorthand and write each word until you can do so rapidly and accurately.

SYS-SESS-SUS-SIS-CESS-CIS

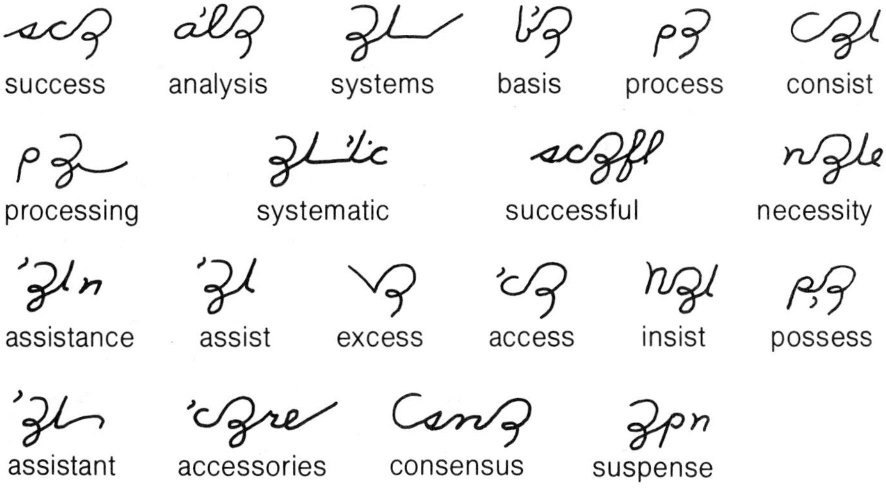
success
analysis
systems
basis
process
consist
processing
systematic
successful
necessity
assistance
assist
excess
access
insist
possess
assistant
accessories
consensus
suspense

ULATE

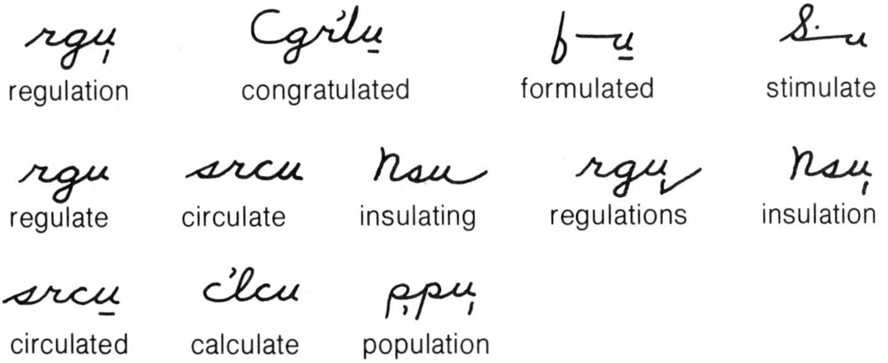
regulation
congratulated
formulated
stimulate
regulate
circulate
insulating
regulations
insulation
circulated
calculate
population

SCRIBE-SCRIPT

subscribe description subscription transcription

describes inscribe prescribe prescription

WRITING PRINCIPLES

SYS-SESS-SUS-SIS-CESS-CIS Write a capital *Z* thus for the combinations *sys-sess-sus-sis-cèss-cis*.

ULATE Write a small longhand *u* to express the combination *ulate*.

SCRIBE-SCRIPT Write a printed capital *S* to express the combinations *scribe-script*. The *S* may be joined or disjoined.

Assignment 2 — **New vocabulary**. Read and write the following words and phrases until you can read and write them rapidly. Memorize the abbreviated words.

necessary debit junior administrative railroad

Roger booklet promoted filing corporation profits

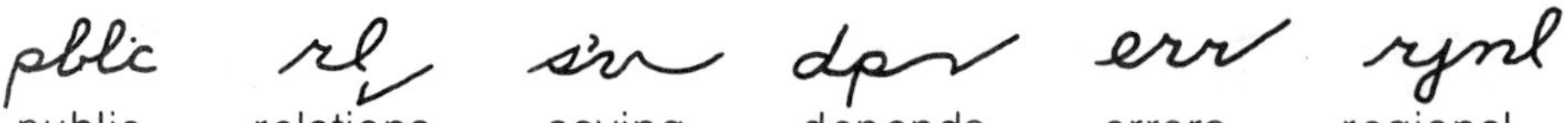

public relations saving depends errors regional

word proper example expert Calgary products

allowing

Assignment 3 — **Reading and writing shorthand**. Read each sentence from shorthand until you can read it as rapidly as you can read from print. Write each sentence in shorthand until you can write each one rapidly and accurately.

1. The secretary was promoted to Administrative Assistant.
2. Then all of us congratulated her.
3. The booklet gives regulations for insulating buildings.
4. Send a copy promptly to each representative.
5. I thought a subscription to a magazine would be a nice gift.
6. Is it necessary to send a cheque today?
7. Did the corporation earn excess profit last year?
8. The regulations give the basis for computing the tax.
9. I can give expert assistance with Public Relations.
10. We may be able to stimulate my friend to assist.
11. We need a systematic description of word processing systems.
12. Can you assist with the transcription process?
13. Success in saving energy depends on good insulation.
14. The enclosed brochure describes the proper process.
15. The instructor had an analysis of transcription errors.
16. The students have access to the analysis.
17. Do you possess the experience and desire necessary to be a successful regional manager?
18. You debit the cash account when making a bank deposit.
19. She is a junior executive with the railroad.

BUILDING SHORTHAND SPEED AND TRANSCRIPTION ACCURACY

Assignment 4 — **Self-testing**. Complete Unit 29 in your *Study Guide* before you proceed with the rest of this chapter.

Assignment 5 — **Taking tape dictation**. To write from dictation the new words and sentences in this chapter, use Cassette 13 Side B from *Theory and Speed-Building Tapes*.

Assignment 6 — **Taking live dictation**. Write from dictation the sentences which are printed at the end of this chapter. Your instructor will dictate each group of 20 words to you at various speeds.

Assignment 7 — **Own-note transcription**. After you have taken the sentences in shorthand, select your best set of notes and transcribe them at your best typing rate. Do not number the sentences.

Assignment 8 — **Supplemental business letters**. If instructed to do so, read and write the additional business letter for this chapter found in "Supplemental Letters for Dictation" in Appendix A.

TRANSCRIPT OF SHORTHAND SENTENCES

1. The secretary was promoted to administrative assistant.
2. Then all of us congratulated her. (20)
3. The booklet gives regulations for insulating buildings.
4. Send a copy promptly to each representative. (40)
5. I thought a subscription to a magazine would be a nice gift.
6. Is it necessary to send a cheque today? (60)
7. Did the corporation earn excess profits last year?
8. The regulations give the basis for computing the tax. (80)
9. I can give expert assistance with public relations.
10. We may be able to stimulate my friend to assist. (100)
11. We need a systematic description of word processing systems.
12. Can you assist with the transcription process? (120)
13. Success in saving energy depends on good insulation.
14. The enclosed brochure describes the proper process. (140)
15. The instructor made an analysis of transcription errors.
16. The students have access to the analysis. (160)

17. Do you possess the experience and desire necessary to be a successful regional manager? (180)
18. You debit the cash account when making a bank deposit.
19. She is a junior executive with the railroad. (200)

CHAPTER 30

WRITING **CONTR**, **OVER-OTHER**, AND **UNDER**

Assignment 1 — **Rule discovery**. Follow the three-step plan to learn the new writing principles: (1) Discover the rule for each group of words. (2) Read the shorthand outlines until you can read them rapidly. (3) Cover the shorthand and write each word until you can do so rapidly and accurately.

CONTR

contract | contribute | control | contracts | contributions

contributed | controls | contribution | contrast | controller

OVER-OTHER

over-other | another | overseas | otherwise | overcharged

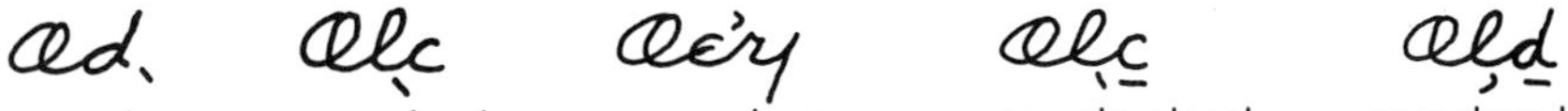

overdue | overlook | overcharge | overlooked | overloaded

overtime | oversight | overnight | overcome | others

UNDER

under | understand | understanding | understood

ul'c	-sus'n	-sus'n
undertake	misunderstand	misunderstanding
-susd	ugron	
misunderstood	underground	

WRITING PRINCIPLES

CONTR Write a small longhand *k* to express the combination *contr* and the following vowel. Avoid writing extra strokes when writing the longhand *k*.

OVER-OTHER Write a joined or disjoined capital *O* to express *over* and *other*.

UNDER Write a small longhand *u* to express the combination *under*.

Assignment 2 — **New vocabulary**. Read and write the following words and phrases until you can read and write them rapidly. Memorize the abbreviated words.

pr'c	$	spl	'cspbl	c
practical	dollar	superintendent	acceptable	company's
p'p	,pr	Csqn-	pp'r	rfn
perhaps	operations	consequently	prepared	refund
ddc	psnl	Hlln	evn	
deduct	personal-personnel	Hamilton	we have not	
zn				
was not				

Assignment 3 Read each sentence from shorthand until you can read it as rapidly as you can read from print. Write each sentence in shorthand until you can write each one rapidly and accurately.

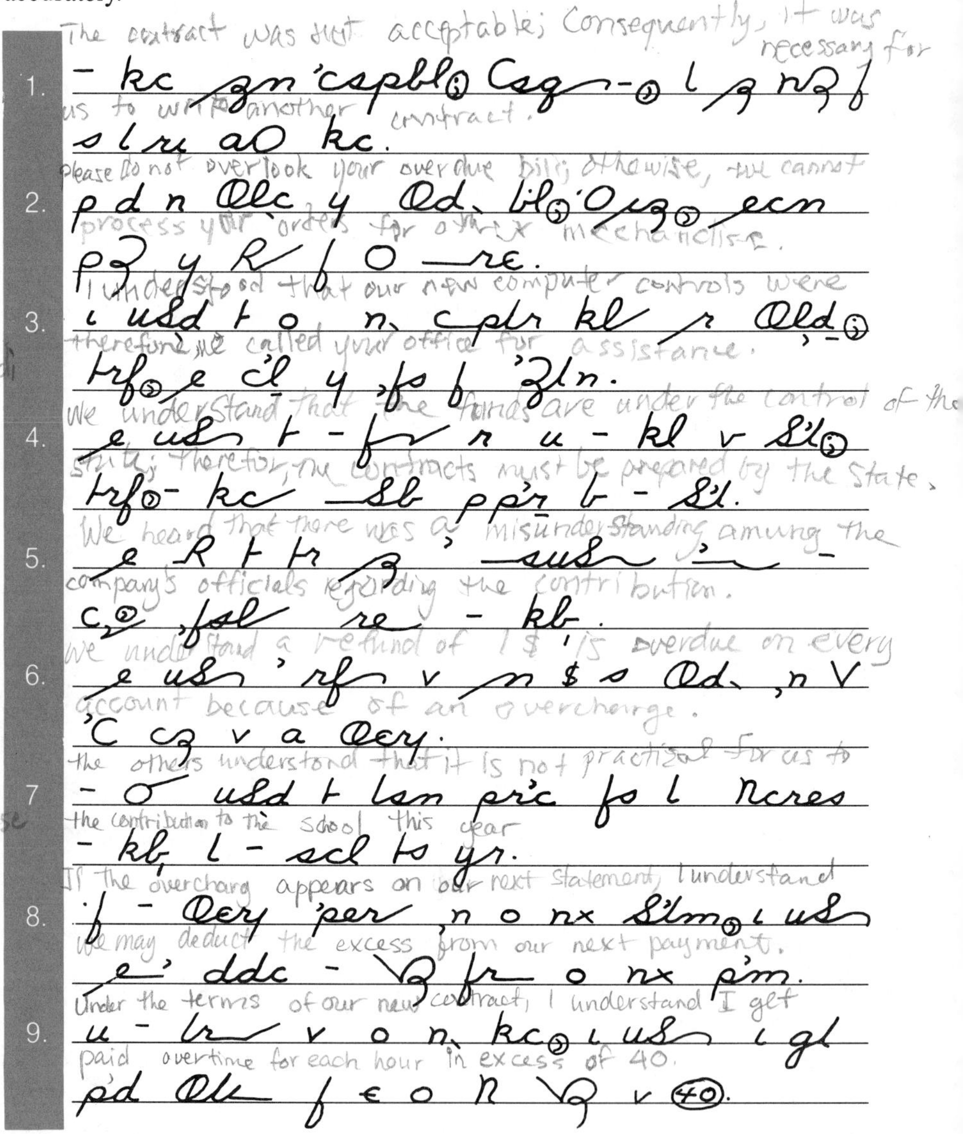

BUILDING TRANSCRIPTION SKILLS

Assignment 4 — **Punctuating sentences joined by a transitional word**. Place a semicolon before and a comma after a transitional word or phrase that joins two sentences. Common transitional words and phrases include: *therefore*, *however*, *accordingly*, *consequently*, *in fact*, *as a result*. Study the examples that follow and apply this rule when transcribing.

1. Our sales are up; therefore, we have hired several new sales clerks. (Note that the transitional word, *therefore*, joins the two sentences.)
2. We have not received your cheque; consequently, we cannot ship the merchandise to you.
3. We can ship the present model; however, you should know that next year's model will be available in one month.
4. We are in first place in our baseball league; in fact, our team is having its best year yet.

BUILDING SHORTHAND SPEED AND TRANSCRIPTION ACCURACY

Assignment 5 — **Self-testing**. Complete Unit 30 in your *Study Guide* before you proceed with the rest of this chapter.

Assignment 6 — **Taking tape dictation**. To write from dictation the new words and sentences in this chapter, use Cassette 14 Side B from *Theory and Speed-Building Tapes*.

Assignment 7 — **Taking live dictation**. Write from dictation the sentences which are printed at the end of this chapter. Your instructor will dictate each group of 20 words to you at various speeds.

Assignment 8 — **Own-note transcription**. After you have taken the sentences in shorthand, select your best set of notes and transcribe them at your best typing rate. Do not number the sentences.

Assignment 9 — **Supplemental business letters**. If instructed to do so, read and write the additional business letter for this chapter found in "Supplemental Letters for Dictation" in Appendix A.

TRANSCRIPT OF SHORTHAND SENTENCES

1. The contract was not acceptable; consequently, it was necessary for us to write another contract. (20)
2. Please do not overlook your overdue bill; otherwise, we cannot process your orders for other merchandise. (40)

3. I understood that our new computer controls were overloaded; therefore, we called your office for assistance. (60)
4. We understand that the funds are under the control of the state; therefore, the contracts must be prepared by the state. (80)
5. We heard that there was a misunderstanding among the company's officials regarding the contribution. (100)
6. We understand a refund of one dollar is overdue on every account because of an overcharge. (120)
7. The others understood that it is not practical for us to increase the contribution to the school this year. (140)
8. If the overcharge appears on our next statement, I understand we may deduct the excess from our next payment. (160)
9. Under the terms of our new contract, I understand I get paid overtime for each hour in excess of 40. (180)

CHAPTER 31

WRITING **ELECTR**, **OLOGY**, AND **ITIS-ICITIS**

Assignment 1 — **Rule discovery**. Follow the three-step plan to learn the new writing principles: (1) Discover the rule for each group of words. (2) Read the shorthand outlines until you can read them rapidly. (3) Cover the shorthand and write each word until you can do so rapidly and accurately.

ELECTR

electric electrical electrician electricity electronic

OLOGY

biology geology psychology psychological sociology

ITIS-ICITIS

appendicitis arthritis bursitis tonsillitis bronchitis

WRITING PRINCIPLES

ELECTR	Write a capital *E* thus Ɛ to express the combination *electr* and the following vowel.
OLOGY	Write a small disjoined *l* to express the combination *ology.*
ITIS-ICITIS	Write a disjoined capital *I* thus *I* to express the combinations *itis-icitis*. Write it close to the word to which it belongs.

Assignment 2 — **New vocabulary**. Read and write the words and phrases on page 144 until you can read and write them rapidly. Memorize the standard symbols.

kilometres · kilograms · litres · degrees Celsius · aren't

it's · stops · living · things · geologists · minerals

industrial · rocks · connection · soil · currently

calculator · gold · suffix · means · weather · plant

current · reported · covered · formulate · absent

painful · models · I'd · I'm · we'll · we've · engineers

costs · birthday · ways-weighs · France · metric

system · tank · holds · race · running · lost

degree · "ology"

Learning tip: Note that special symbols are used to express metric measures. They represent both the singular and plural. These symbols are used throughout the world.

Assignment 3 — **Reading and writing shorthand**. Read each sentence from shorthand until you can read it as rapidly as you can read from print. Write each sentence in shorthand until you can write each one rapidly and accurately.

1. L° — i plin l Sde bt bil — jel.
2. bil s - Sde v lv —.
3. jel del t - Sre v rç — sil.
4. jelS lp fu il gld — O —rl.
5. - sfx "l" —en "sin v."
6. - sin v ssile — pepl s cl ssel.
7. - Ec ç c pvid ES l - ndSrel pl l
rznbl pris.
8. - E c pvid a Ecl Cç.
9. U i — o —E cr \ ned l E kl.
10. a eplie g 'bs fr —rc cg v 'prd.
11. aO eplie 'd lnsld.
12. - c, dr 'n t.
13. e rpk t' r cr- cvr b —dcl nsrn.
14. d \ v 'rtrd, r brsd?
15. i uS t 'rtrd çb vre pinfl n - tr s bid.
16. Od 'prs a Enc clcur f — i brtd'
17. Vr —dl r vre 'prv.
18. frn Apl - —lrc zt n 1940.
19. sntn —S Cre —v Apl - —lrc zt.
20. - g's l'c n — i cr ld 50 L.
21. i driv 650 km bl en Sp f g's.
22. l g 24°C dr - r's.
23. il rn 5000 m se lS 3 kg.

BUILDING TRANSCRIPTION SKILLS

Assignment 4 — **Forming contractions**. In the sentences that follow, you will find words that are *contractions*. Study the rule for forming contractions and apply the rule when you transcribe.

A *contraction* is a shortened form of a word or a group of words. Here are some examples: *can't* for *cannot*, *we've* for *we have*. Note that you insert an apostrophe in a contraction to show that one or more letters have been omitted. The sentences that follow include contracted words. The words that have been contracted are given at the end of each sentence.

1. It's the first time I've been asked. (*it is*, *I have*)
2. Don't worry if you've lost your ticket because I've another one in my wallet. (*do not*, *you have*, *I have*)
3. Everybody's coming to the picnic. (*everybody is*)
4. It's important to use the original carton to return the merchandise to its manufacturer. (*it is*)

Learning tip: Note that both *its* and *it's* appear in the last sentence above. The word *its* is already in the possessive case, as in *his, hers*. How can you tell when to add or omit the apostrophe? Apply this test: If you can substitute *it is* for the word in question, add the apostrophe. In the last sentence, *it is* can be substituted for *it's*; therefore, you add the apostrophe. You cannot substitute *it is* for *its*.

BUILDING SHORTHAND SPEED AND TRANSCRIPTION ACCURACY

Assignment 5 — **Self-testing**. Complete Unit 31 in your *Study Guide* before you proceed with the rest of this chapter.

Assignment 6 — **Taking tape dictation**. To write from dictation the words and sentences in this chapter, use Cassette 15 Side B from *Theory and Speed-Building Tapes*.

Assignment 7 — **Taking live dictation**. Write from dictation the sentences which are printed at the end of this chapter. Your instructor will dictate each group of 20 words to you at various speeds.

Assignment 8 — **Own-note transcription**. After you have taken the sentences in shorthand, select your best set of notes and transcribe them at your best typing rate. Do not number the sentences.

Assignment 9 — **Supplemental business letters**. If instructed to do so, read and write the additional business letter for this chapter found in "Supplemental Letters for Dictation" in Appendix A.

TRANSCRIPT OF SHORTHAND SENTENCES

1. It's my plan to study both biology and geology.
2. Biology is the study of living things. (20)
3. Geology deals with the history of rocks and soil.
4. Geologists help find oil, gold, and other minerals. (40)
5. The suffix "ology" means "science of."
6. The science of society and people is called sociology. (60)
7. The electric company can provide electricity at the industrial plant at reasonable prices. (80)
8. The electrician can provide an electrical connection.
9. Tell him how much current you need at each control. (100)
10. An employee was absent from work because of appendicitis.
11. Another employee had tonsillitis. (120)
12. The company doctor examined them.
13. He reported they are currently covered by medical insurance. (140)
14. Do you have arthritis or bursitis?
15. I understand that arthritis can be very painful when the weather is bad. (160)
16. I'd appreciate an electronic calculator for my birthday.
17. Excellent models aren't very expensive. (180)
18. France adopted the metric system in 1940.
19. Since then, most countries have adopted the metric system. (200)
20. The gas tank in my car holds 50 L.
21. I drive 650 km between stops for gas. (220)
22. It was 24°C during the race.
23. While running 5 000 m, she lost 3 kg. (240)

CHAPTER 32

BUSINESS LETTER DICTATION AND TRANSCRIPTION

BUILDING TRANSCRIPTION SKILLS

Assignment 1 — **Spelling review**. Follow the steps outlined in Chapter 12 to check your ability to spell the following words correctly:

1. benefits
2. brief
3. completion
4. connection
5. currently
6. educational
7. effectively
8. electrical
9. expenses
10. filing
11. interested
12. material
13. models
14. necessary
15. nuclear
16. operations
17. regulations
18. system

BUSINESS LETTERS

Assignment 2 — **Letter 1**. Read and write each of the new words and phrases until you can read and write each one rapidly and accurately. Then read and write the shorthand for Letter 1 to build your writing speed.

accepted
don't
forward
Franco
covering
edit
detail
look
concerning
zoology
hesitate
social
comments
Gary
herewith
Miami
texts
dated
subjects
press
brief
Costa
St. John's
I'll
we should not
you will be

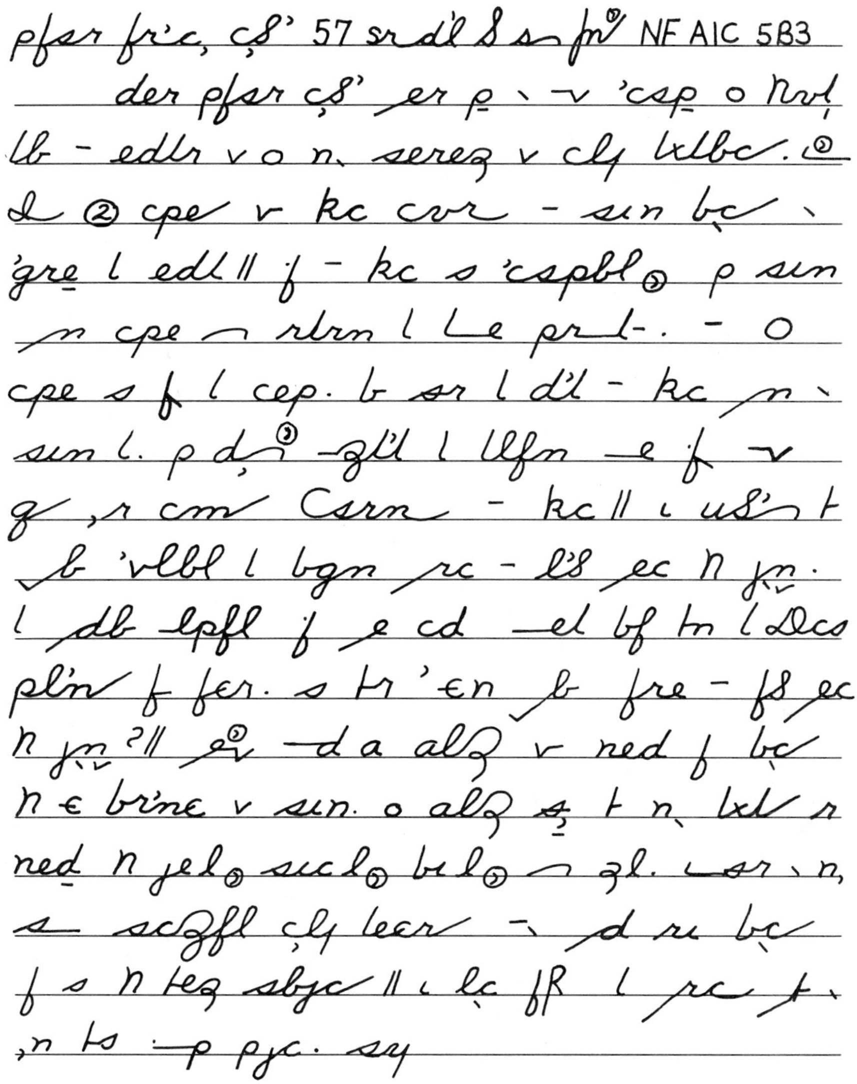

Assignment 3 — Letter 2. Read and write each new word for Letter 2 until you can read and write each one rapidly and accurately. Then read and write the shorthand for Letter 2 to build your writing speed.

July signature executives governmental financial

subscribers · interest · Red Deer · completion · reducing

James · expenses · benefits · supervised

congratulations · experts · editors · advantage · Paula

simply · agencies · rush · upon · coal · nuclear

fuels · interested · Detroit · describe · won't · issues

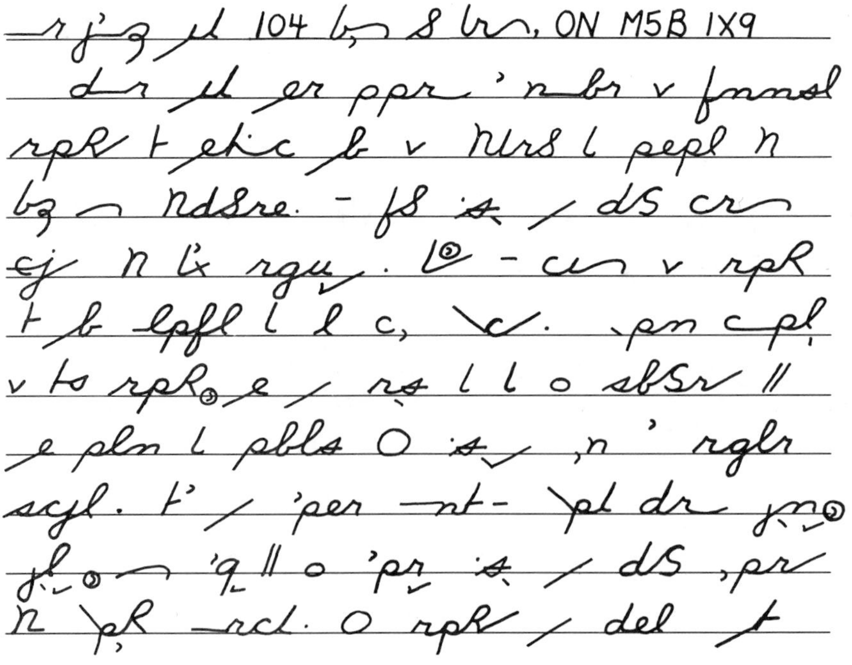
104
ON M5B 1X9

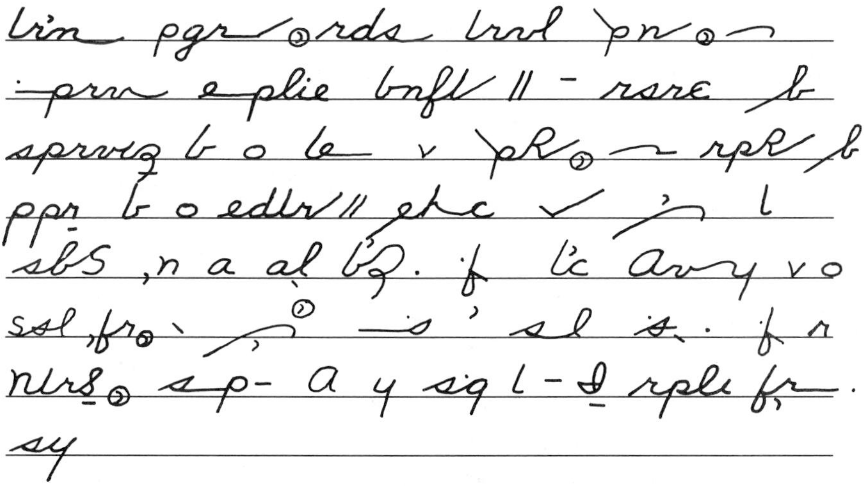

Assignment 4 — **Supplemental business letters**. If instructed to do so, read and write the additional business letters for this chapter found in ''Supplemental Letters for Dictation'' in Appendix A.

BUILDING SHORTHAND SPEED AND TRANSCRIPTION ACCURACY

Assignment 5 — **Self-testing**. Complete Unit 32 in your *Study Guide* before you proceed with the rest of this chapter.

Assignment 6 — **Taking tape dictation**. To write from dictation the new words and letters in this chapter, use Cassette 16 Side B from *Theory and Speed-Building Tapes*

Assignment 7 — **Taking live dictation**. Write from dictation the letters which are printed at the end of this chapter. Your instructor will dictate to you from these transcripts at various speeds.

Assignment 8 — **Own-note transcription**. Transcribe at your best typing rate an accurate copy of at least one of the letters you took in shorthand in Assignment 7. Type the letter in the form requested by your instructor.

TRANSCRIPTS OF LETTERS 1 AND 2

Letter 1 Professor Franco Costa, 57 Springdale Street, St. John's NF A1C 5B3

Dear Professor Costa: We are pleased you have accepted our invitation to be the editor of our new (20) series of college textbooks. I'm enclosing two copies of the contract covering the science books you agreed (40) to edit.

If the contract is acceptable, please sign one copy and return it to me promptly. The other (60) copy is for you to keep. Be sure to date the contract when you sign it. Please don't hesitate to telephone me (80) if you have questions or comments concerning the contract.

I understand that you will be available to (100) begin work the last week in June. It would be helpful if we could meet before then to discuss plans for the future. Is (120) there a chance you will be free the first week in June?

We've made an analysis of the need for books in each branch of (140) science. Our analysis showed that new texts are needed in geology, psychology, biology, and (160) zoology. I am sure you know some successful college teachers who would write books for us in these subjects.

I (180) look forward to working with you on this important project. Sincerely yours, (194)

Letter 2 Mr. James White, 104 Bond Street, Toronto, ON M5B 1X9

Dear Mr. White: We are preparing a number of financial reports that we think will be of interest to (20) people in business and industry. The first issue will describe current changes in tax regulations. It's the (40) kind of report that will be helpful to all company executives. Upon completion of this report, we (60) will rush it to our subscribers.

We plan to publish other issues on a regular schedule. They will appear (80) monthly except during June, July, and August.

Our April issue will describe opportunities in the export (100) mar-ket. Other reports will deal with training programs, reducing travel expenses, and improving employee (120) benefits.

The research will be supervised by our team of experts, and the reports will be prepared by our (140) editors.

We think you will want to subscribe on an annual basis. If you take advantage of our special (160) offer, you won't miss a single issue. If you are interested, simply add your signature to the enclosed reply (180) form. Sincerely yours, (184)

REVIEWING THE WRITING PRINCIPLES

All the writing principles, abbreviated words, and standard abbreviations you have learned in Chapters 25 through 32 are reviewed on Tape 18 Side B of the *Theory and Speed-Building Tapes*. Take dictation from this tape before completing the Final Examination.

EXAMINATION 8

- Remove and complete Examination 8 which follows Unit 32 in your *Study Guide*, before proceeding to the Final Examination on theory.
- Self-check with the Key to Examination 8 which appears at the back of the *Study Guide*.

FINAL EXAMINATION-PART A

- Remove and complete the Final Examination which follows Examination 8 in your *Study Guide*.
- Self-check with the Key to Final Examination which appears at the back of the *Study Guide*.

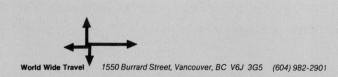

World Wide Travel *1550 Burrard Street, Vancouver, BC V6J 3G5 (604) 982-2901*

(Current date)

Mr. John Seagram
7120 Ada Boulevard
Edmonton, AB T5B 4E4

Dear John

There are many acceptable styles for setting up business letters. This is an example of the full-block style.

Punctuation styles also vary in business letters. In this letter we use open punctuation. With this style, punctuation is omitted at the end of each line in the inside address, following the salutation, and following the complimentary close.

The date is placed on the left margin two line spaces below the last line of the printed letterhead. The inside address is placed at least four line spaces below the date. For short letters, more space may be placed between the date and the inside address so that the letter is well centred.

The salutation is positioned on the left margin two line spaces below the inside address. The first paragraph begins at the left margin two line spaces below the salutation. Leave a double space between each paragraph.

The complimentary close is placed at the left margin, two line spaces below the last paragraph. The typed signature of the dictator is placed four line spaces below the complimentary close. The title of the dictator, if any, is placed on the line immediately following the typed signature.

The identifying initials of the typist are typed two line spaces below the typed signature (or title of the dictator). If the dictator's initials are included, they appear first, on the left margin, separated from the secretary's initials by the colon.

Yours sincerely

Keith Murray

N. Keith Murray
General Manager

js

Tokyo • Sao Paulo • London • New York • Vancouver

Model letter—Full-block style; open punctuation

PART A

APPENDIX A

SUPPLEMENTAL LETTERS FOR DICTATION

This appendix provides 34 supplemental letters for dictation practice, consisting of the following: one letter for each theory chapter beginning with Chapter 6; two letters for each of seven consolidation chapters, beginning with Chapter 8. Each piece of dictation contains only the writing principles introduced up to that chapter. This supplemental dictation material is included on the cassettes with the chapter dictation to which each is appended. It is also recorded, for sustained dictation, on Cassette 23 of *Theory and Speed-Building Tapes*.

They may be used as follows:

- As additional class assignments.
- As new material dictation.
- As test letters.

INSTRUCTIONS

1. **Dictation** — Have each letter dictated to you until you can write each letter in shorthand at your best dictation rate.

2. **Transcription** — Transcribe from your own notes in a style directed by your instructor.

Chapter 6 — Supplemental Letter

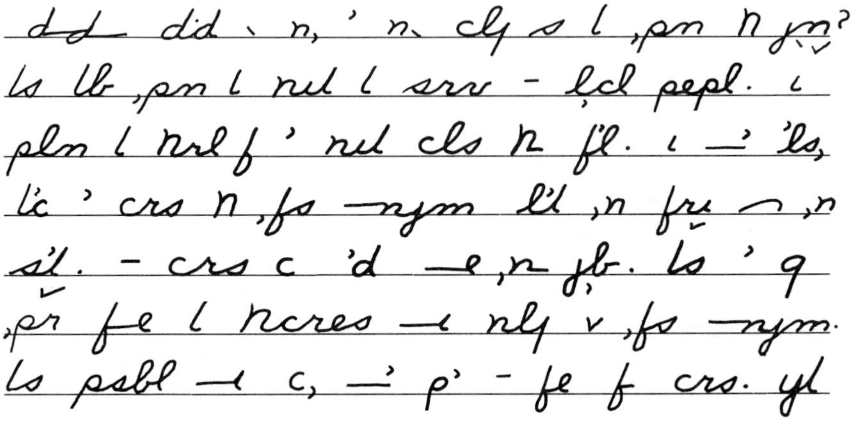

Dear Madam: Did you know a new college is to open in June? It is to be open at night to serve the (20) local people. I plan to enrol for a night class in the fall. I may also take a course in office management (40) late on Friday and on Saturday. The course can aid me on the job. It is a good opportunity for me (60) to increase my knowledge of office management. It is possible my company may pay the fee for the course. (80) Yours truly, (82)

Chapter 7 — Supplemental Letter

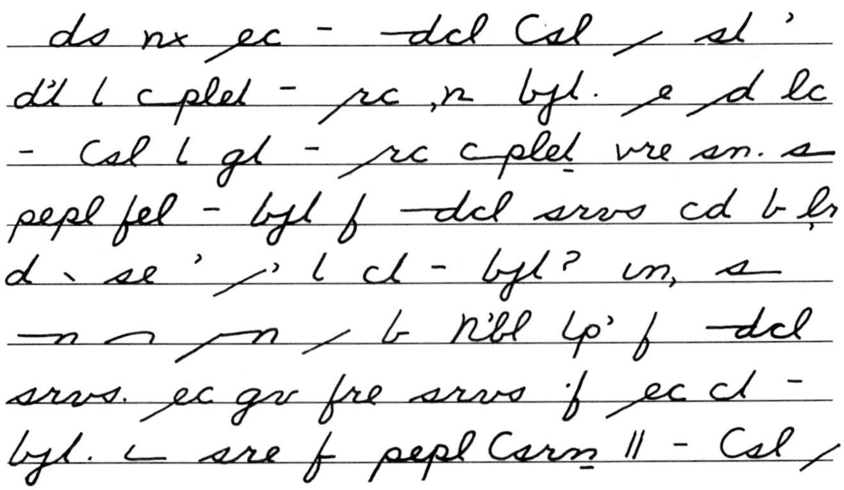

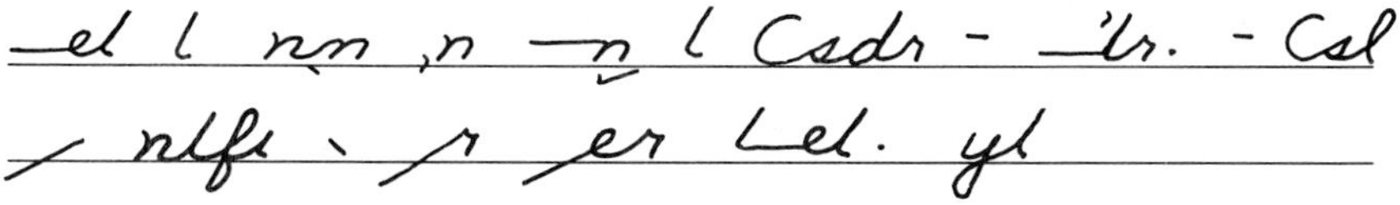

Dear Sir: Next week the medical council will set a date to complete the work on the budget. We would like the council (20) to get the work completed very soon. Some people feel the budget for medical service could be lower. (40) Do you see a way to cut the budget? I know some men and women will be unable to pay for medical (60) service. We can give free service if we can cut the budget. I am sorry for the people concerned.

The council (80) will meet at noon on Monday to consider the matter. The council will notify you where we are to meet. Yours (100) truly, (101)

Chapter 8 — Supplemental Letter 3

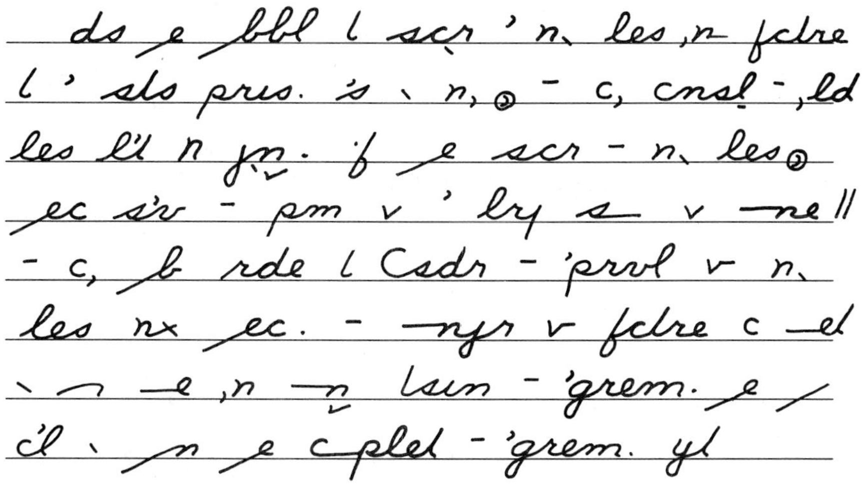

Dear Sir: We will be able to secure a new lease on the factory at a satisfactory price. As you (20) know, the company cancelled the old lease late in June. If we secure the new lease, we can save the payment of a (40) large sum of money.

The company will be ready to consider the approval of the new lease next week. The (60) manager of the factory can meet you and me on Monday to sign the agreement. We will call you when we (80) complete the agreement. Yours truly, (87)

Chapter 8 — Supplemental Letter 4

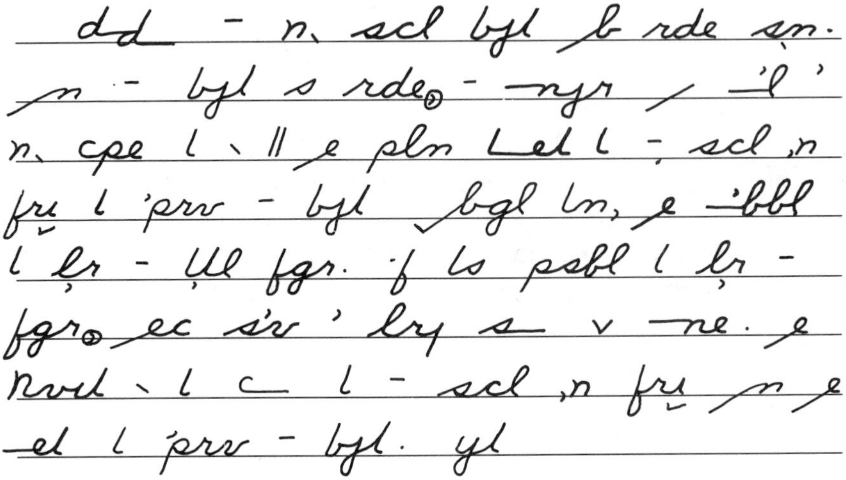

Dear Madam: The new school budget will be ready soon. When the budget is ready, the manager will mail a new (20) copy to you.

We plan to meet at the school on Friday to approve the budget. You will be glad to know we may (40) be able to lower the total figure. If it is possible to lower the figure, we can save a large (60) sum of money. We invite you to come to the school on Friday when we meet to approve the budget. Yours truly, (80)

Chapter 9 — Supplemental Letter

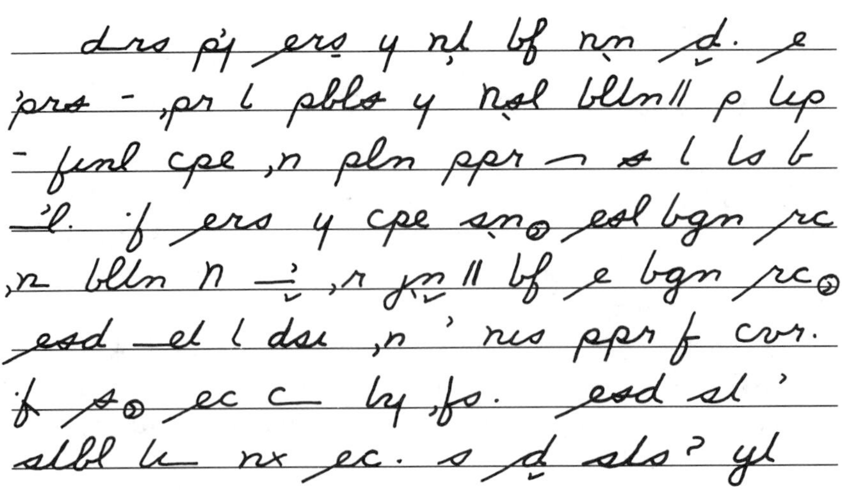

Dear Mrs. Page: We received your note before noon Wednesday. We appreciate the opportunity to publish (20) your unusual bulletin.

Please type the final copy on plain paper and ship it to us by mail. If we (40) receive your copy soon, we shall begin work on the bulletin in May or June.

Before we begin work, we should (60) meet to decide on a nice paper for the cover. If you wish, we can come to your office. We should set a (80) suitable time next week. Is Wednesday satisfactory? Yours truly, (91)

Chapter 10 — Supplemental Letter

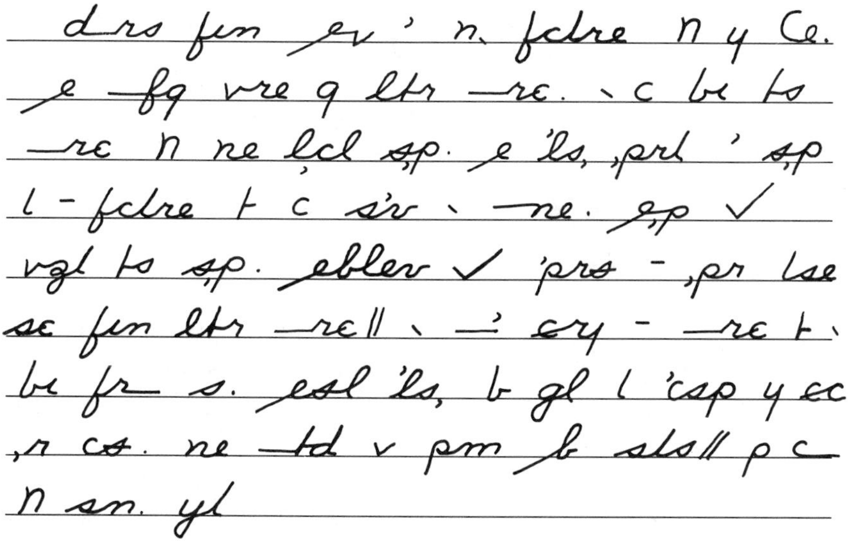

Dear Mrs. Fine: We have a new factory in your county. We manufacture very good leather merchandise. (20) You can buy this merchandise in any local shop. We also operate a shop at the factory that can (40) save you money. We hope you will visit this shop. We believe you will appreciate the opportunity to (60) see such fine leather merchandise.

You may charge the merchandise that you buy from us. We shall also be glad to accept (80) your cheque or cash. Any method of payment will be satisfactory.

Please come in soon. Yours truly, (99)

Chapter 11 — Supplemental Letter

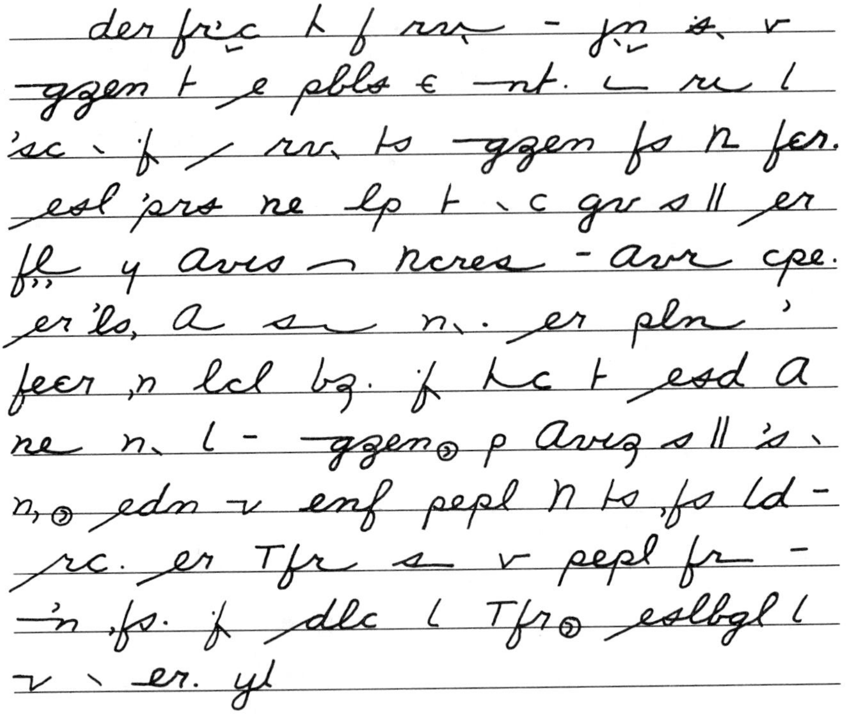

Dear Frank: Thank you for reviewing the June issue of the magazine that we publish each month. I am writing to (20) ask you if you will review this magazine for us in the future. We shall appreciate any help that you (40) can give us.

We are following your advice and increasing the advertising copy. We are also adding (60) something new. We are planning a feature on local business. If you think that we should add anything new to the (80) magazine, please advise us.

As you know, we do not have enough people in this office to do the work. We are (100) transferring some of the people from the main office. If you would like to transfer, we shall be glad to have you here. (120) Yours truly, (122)

Chapter 12 — Supplemental Letter 3

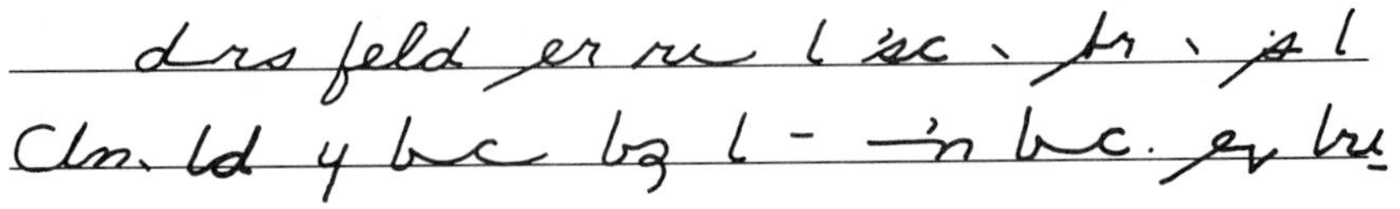

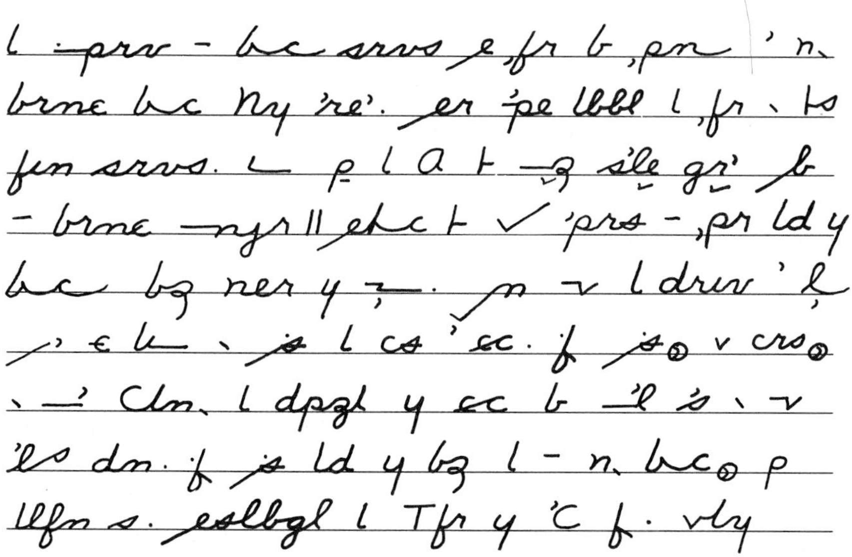

Dear Mrs. Field: We are writing to ask you whether you wish to continue to do your banking business at the (20) main bank. We have tried to improve the banking service we offer by opening a new branch bank in your area (40). We are happy to be able to offer you this fine service. I am pleased to add that Ms. Sally Gray will (60) be the branch manager.

We think that you will appreciate the opportunity to do your banking business (80) near your home. You will not have to drive a long way each time you wish to cash a cheque. If you wish, of course, you may (100) continue to deposit your cheque by mail as you have always done. If you wish to do your business at the new bank, (120) please telephone us. We shall be glad to transfer your account for you. Very truly yours, (136)

Chapter 12 — Supplemental Letter 4

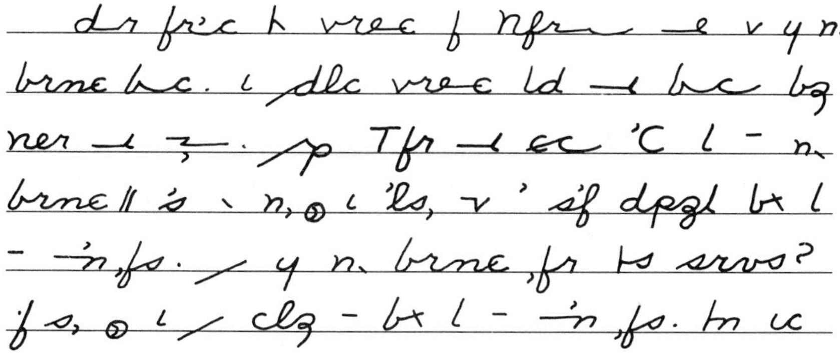

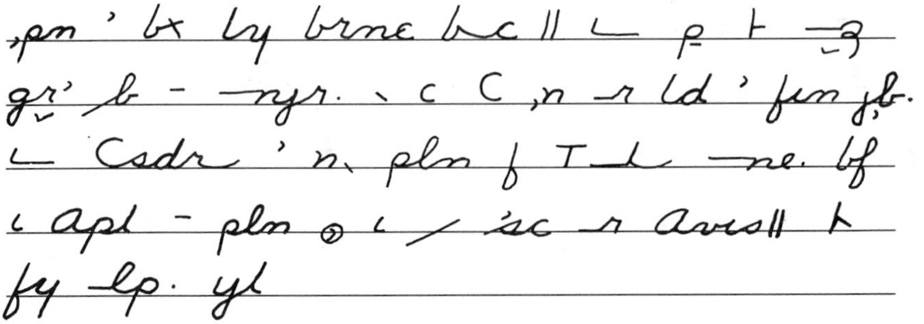

Dear Mr. Frank: Thank you very much for informing me of your new branch bank. I would like very much to do my (20) banking business near my home. Will you please transfer my chequing account to the new branch.

As you know, I also have (40) a safe deposit box at the main office. Will your new branch offer this service? If so, I will close the box at (60) the main office. Then I can open a box at your branch bank.

I am pleased that Ms. Gray will be the manager. You (80) can count on her to do a fine job. I am considering a new plan for transmitting money. Before I adopt (100) the plan, I will ask her advice.

Thank you for your help. Yours truly, (112)

Chapter 13 — Supplemental Letter

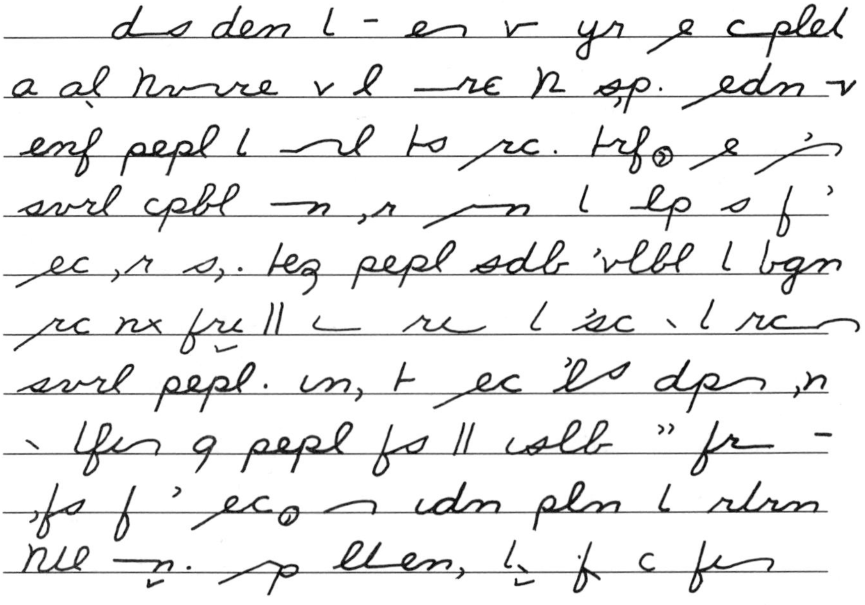

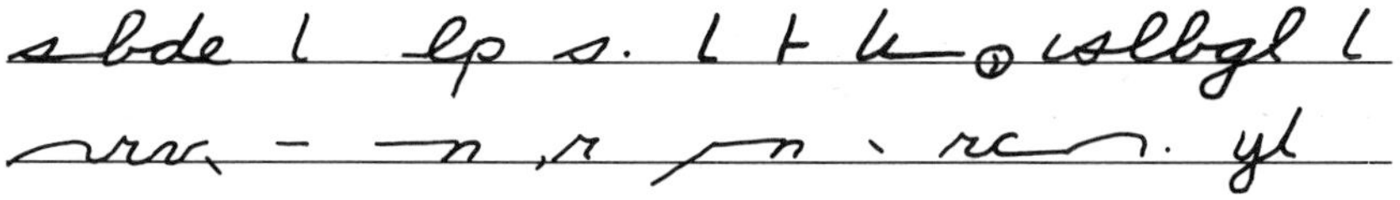

Dear Miss Dean: At the end of the year we complete an annual inventory of all merchandise in the shop. (20) We do not have enough people to handle this work. Therefore, we want several capable men or women to (40) help us for a week or so. These people should be available to begin work next Friday.

I am writing to (60) ask you to recommend several people. I know that we can always depend on you to find good people for (80) us.

I shall be away from the office for a week, and I do not plan to return until Monday. Will you please (100) let me know Tuesday if you can find somebody to help us. At that time, I shall be glad to interview the men (120) or women you recommend. Yours truly, (127)

Chapter 14 — Supplemental Letter

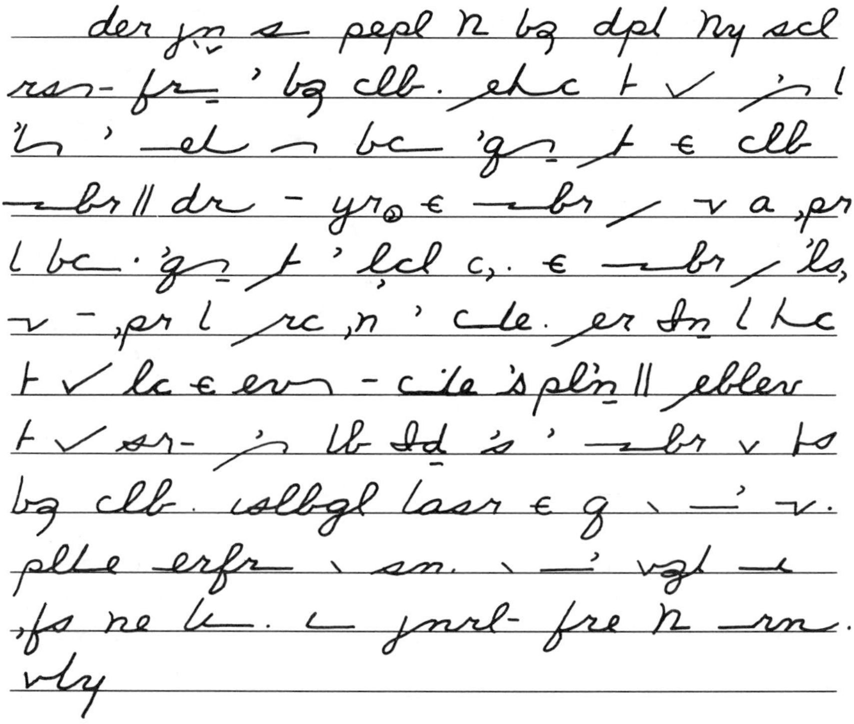

Dear June: Some people in the business department in your school recently formed a business club. We think that you will (20) want to attend a meeting and become acquainted with each club member.

During the year, each member will have an (40) opportunity to become acquainted with a local company. Each member will also have the (60) opportunity to work on a committee. We are inclined to think that you will like each event the committee has (80) planned.

We believe that you will surely want to be included as a member of this business club. I shall be glad (100) to answer each question you may have. Please let me hear from you soon. You may visit my office any time. I am (120) generally free in the morning. Very truly yours, (128)

Chapter 15 — Supplemental Letter

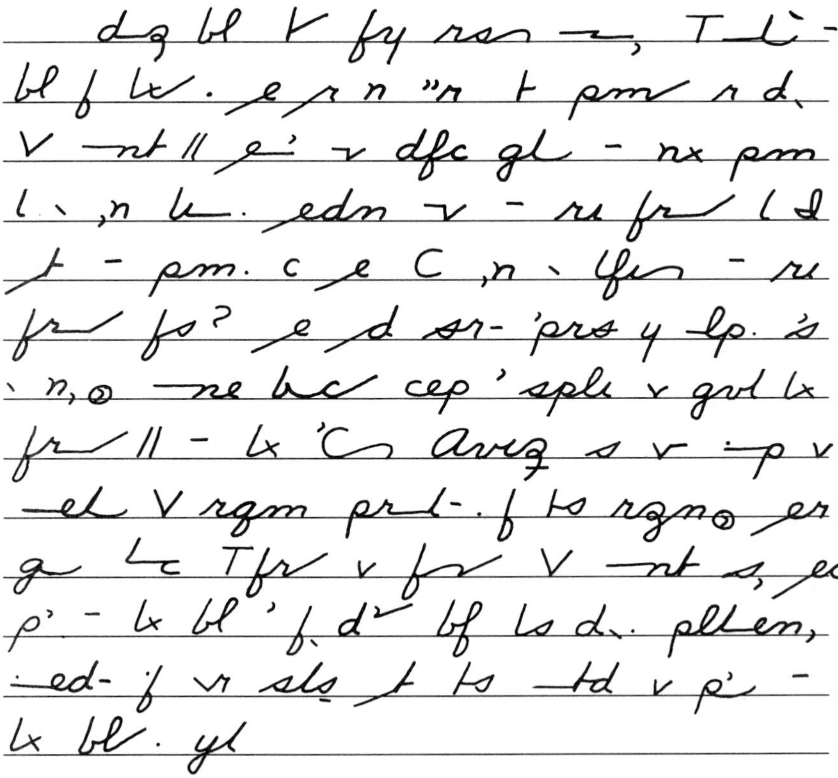

Dear Ms. Bell: Thanks for your recent memo transmitting the bill for taxes. We were not aware that payments are due (20) every month.

We may have difficulty getting the next payment to you on time. We do not have the right forms (40) to enclose with the payment. Can we count on you to find the right forms for us? We would surely appreciate your (60) help. As you know, many banks keep a supply of government tax forms.

The tax accountant advised us of the (80) importance of meeting every requirement promptly. For this reason, we are going to make transfers of funds every (100) month so we can pay the tax bill a few days before it is due. Please let me know immediately if you (120) are satisfied with this method of paying the tax bills. Yours truly, (133)

Chapter 16 — Supplemental Letter 3

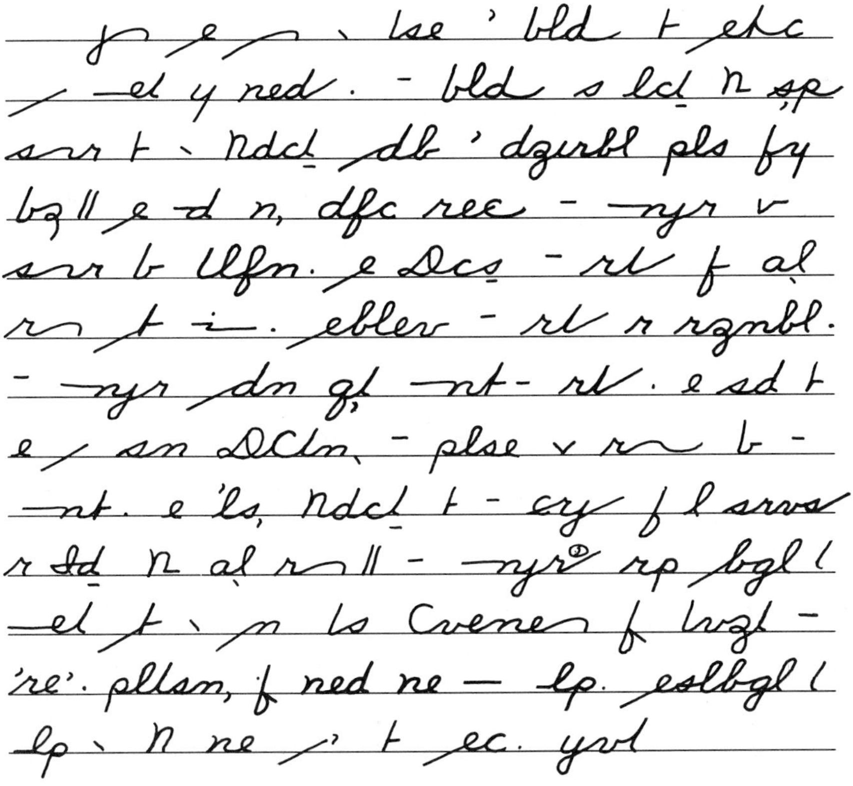

Gentlemen: We want you to see a building that we think will meet your needs. The building is located in the shopping (20) centre that you indicated would be a desirable place for your business.

We had no difficulty (40) reaching the manager of the centre by telephone. We discussed the rates for the annual rent with him. We (60) believe the rates are reasonable. The manager would not quote monthly rates. He said that he will soon discontinue (80) the policy of renting by the month. He also indicated that the charges for all services are (100) included in the annual rent.

The manager's representative will be glad to meet with you when it is (120) convenient for you to visit the area. Please let us know if you need any more help. We shall be glad to help (140) you in any way that we can. Yours very truly, (150)

Chapter 16 — Supplemental Letter 4

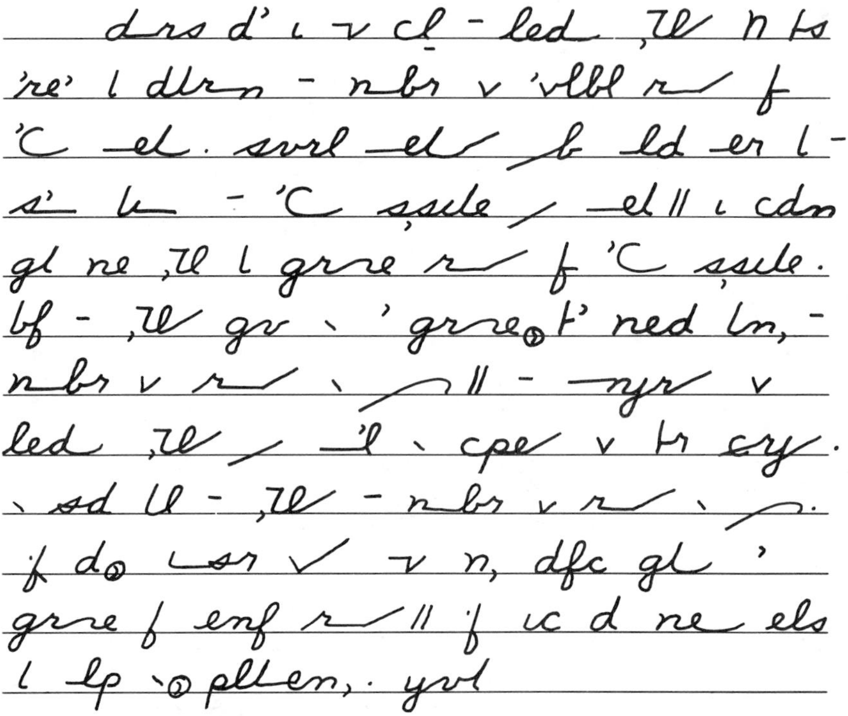

Dear Mrs. Day: I have called the leading hotels in this area to determine the number of available (20) rooms for the accounting meeting. Several meetings will be held here at the same time the accounting society (40) will meet.

I could not get any hotel to guarantee rooms for the accounting society. Before (60) the hotels give you a guarantee, they need to know the number of rooms you want.

The managers of leading hotels (80) will mail you copies of their charges. You should tell the hotels the number of rooms you want. If you do, I am (100) sure you will have no difficulty getting a guarantee for enough rooms.

If I can do anything else to (120) help you, please let me know. Yours very truly, (128)

Chapter 17 — Supplemental Letter

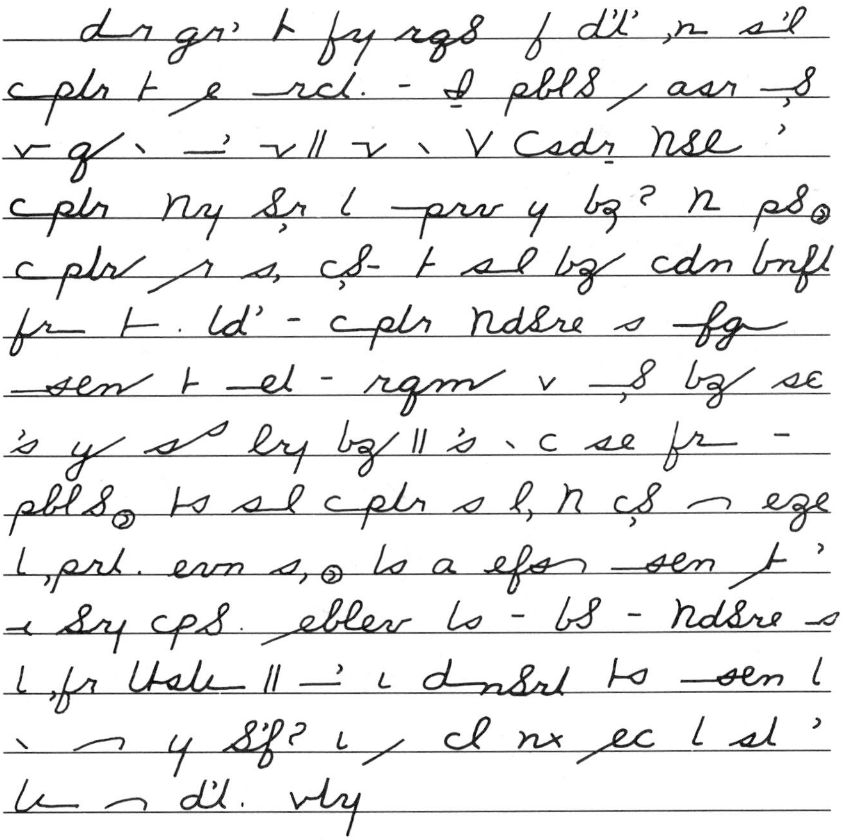

Dear Mr. Gray: Thank you for your request for data on the small computer that we market. The enclosed publicity (20) will answer most of the questions you may have.

Have you ever considered installing a computer (40) in your store to improve your business? In the past, computers were so costly that small businesses could not (60) benefit from them. Today the computer industry is manufacturing machines that meet the requirements (80) of most businesses such as yours as well as large businesses.

As you can see from the publicity, this small (100) computer is low in cost and easy to operate. Even so, it is an efficient machine with a high (120) storage capacity. We believe it is the best the industry has to offer at this time.

May I demonstrate (140) this machine to you and your staff? I will call next week to set a time and a date. Very truly yours, (160)

Chapter 18 — Supplemental Letter

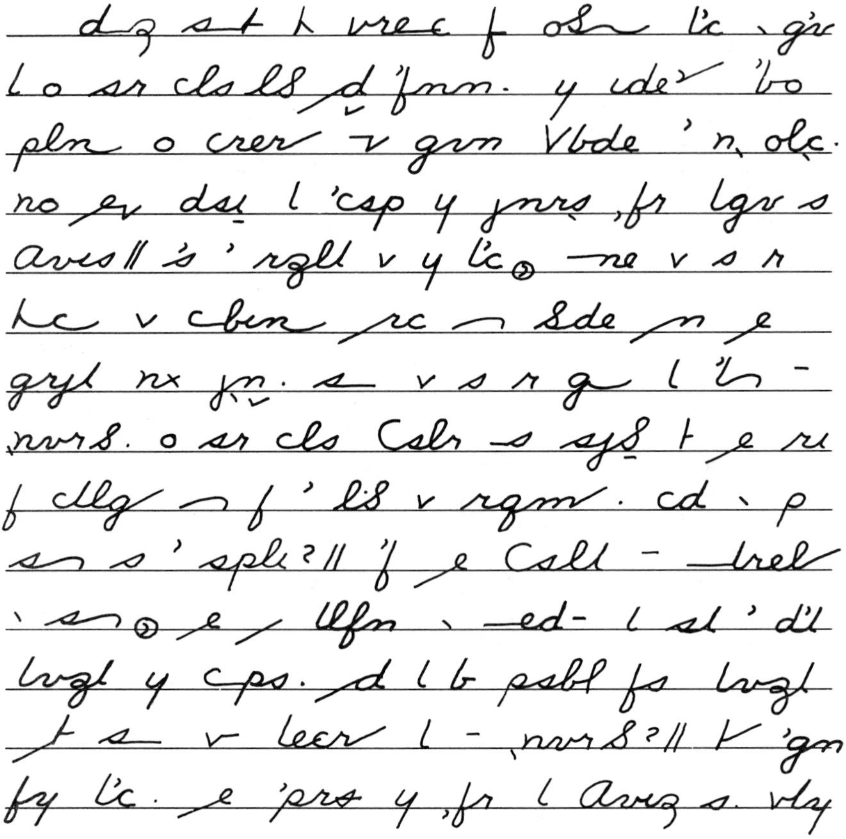

Dear Ms. Smith: Thank you very much for the outstanding talk you gave to our senior class last Wednesday afternoon. Your (20) ideas about planning our careers have given everybody a new outlook. Now we have decided to (40) accept your generous offer to give us advice.

As a result of your talk, many of us are thinking of (60) combining work and study when we graduate next June. Some of us are going to attend the university. (80) Our senior class counsellor has suggested that we write for catalogues and for a list of requirements. Could you (100) please send us a supply?

After we consult the materials you send, we will telephone you immediately (120) to set a date to visit your campus. Would it be possible for us to visit with some of the teachers at (140) the university?

Thanks again for your talk. We appreciate your offer to advise us. Very truly yours, (161)

Chapter 19 — Supplemental Letter

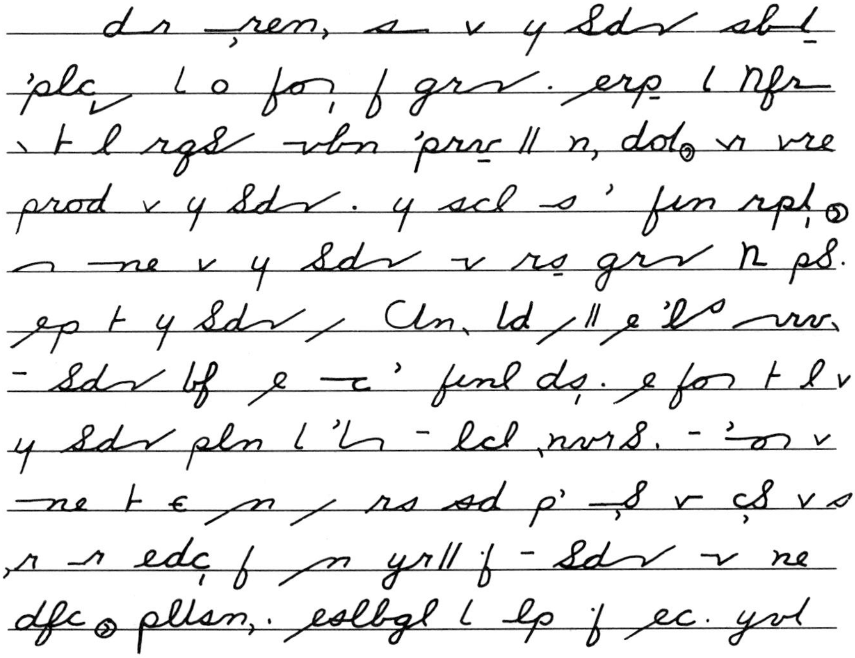

Dear Mr. Moreno: Some of your students submitted applications to our foundation for grants. We are pleased (20) to inform you that all requests have been approved.

No doubt, you are very proud of your students. Your school has a fine (40) reputation, and many of your students have received grants in the past. We hope that your students will continue to (60) do well.

We always interview the students before we make a final decision. We found that all of your (80) students plan to attend the local university. The amount of money that each one will receive should pay most (100) of the cost of his or her education for one year.

If the students have any difficulty, please let us (120) know. We shall be glad to help if we can. Yours very truly, (131)

Chapter 20 — Supplemental Letter 3

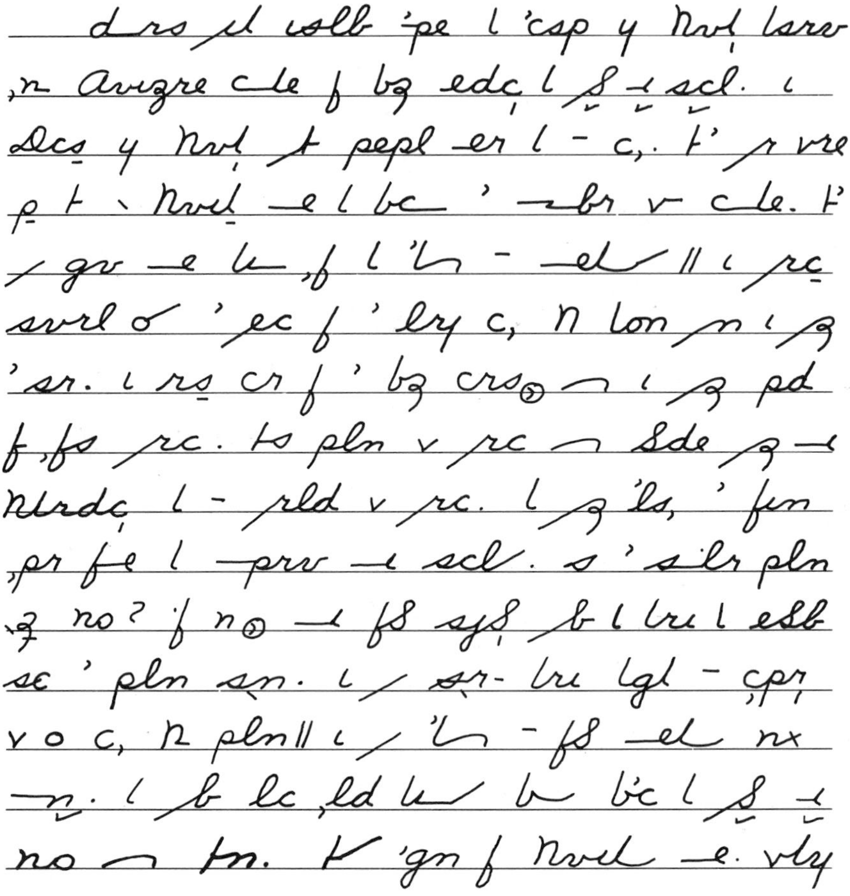

Dear Mrs. White: I shall be happy to accept your invitation to serve on the advisory committee (20) for business education at West High School. I discussed your invitation with people here at the company (40). They were very pleased that you invited me to become a member of the committee. They will give me time off (60) to attend the meetings.

I worked several hours a week for a large company in town when I was a senior (80). I received credit for a business course, and I was paid for the office work. This plan of work and study was my (100) introduction to the world of work. It was also a fine opportunity for me to improve my skills. Is (120) a similar plan used now? If not, my first suggestion will be to try to establish such a plan soon. I will (140) surely try to get the cooperation of our company in the plan.

I will attend the first meeting next (160) Monday. It will be like old times being back to West High now and then. Thanks again for inviting me. Very truly (180) yours, (181)

Chapter 20 — Supplemental Letter 4

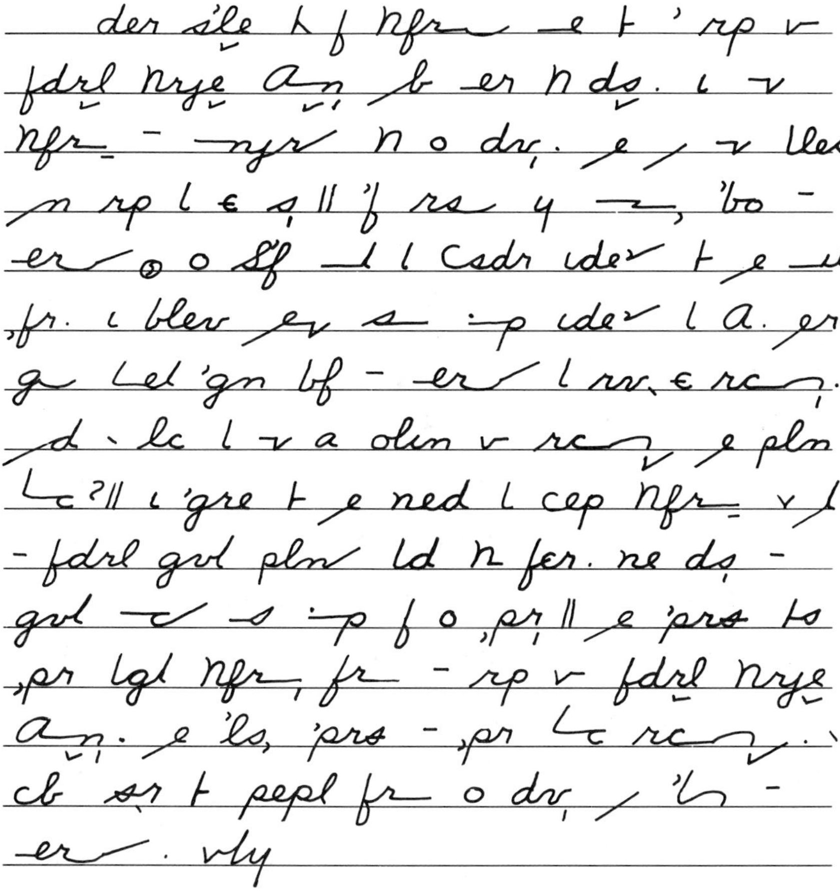

Dear Sally: Thank you for informing me that a representative of the Federal Energy Administration (20) will be here in December. I have informed the managers in our division. We will have at least one (40) representative at each session.

After receiving your memo about the hearings, our staff met to consider (60) ideas that we might offer. I believe we have some important ideas to add. We are going (80) to meet again before the hearings to review each recommendation. Would you like to have an outline of (100) the recommendations we plan to make?

I agree that we need to keep informed of what the federal government (120) plans to do in the future. Any decision the government makes has importance for our operation.

We (140) appreciate this opportunity to get information from the representative of the Federal (160) Energy Administration. We also appreciate the opportunity to make recommendations. (180) You can be sure that people from our division will attend the hearings. Very truly yours, (197)

Chapter 21 — Supplemental Letter

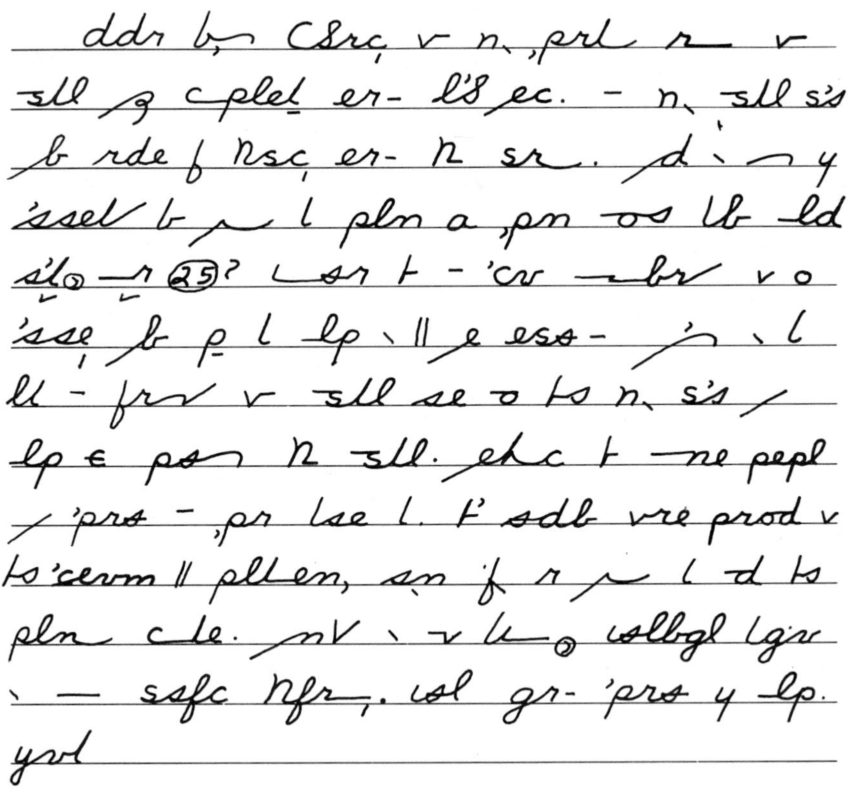

Dear Dr. Bond: Construction of the new operating room of the hospital was completed early last week. (20) The new hospital space will be ready for inspection early in the spring. Would you and your associates be (40) willing to plan an open house to be held Saturday, March 25? I am sure that the active members of (60) our association will be pleased to help you.

We especially want you to let the friends of the hospital (80) see how this new space will help each patient in the hospital. We think that many people will appreciate the (100) opportunity to see it. They should be very proud of this achievement.

Please let me know soon if you are willing (120) to head this planning committee. Whenever you have time, I shall be glad to give you more specific information. (140) I shall greatly appreciate your help. Yours very truly, (152)

Chapter 22 — Supplemental Letter

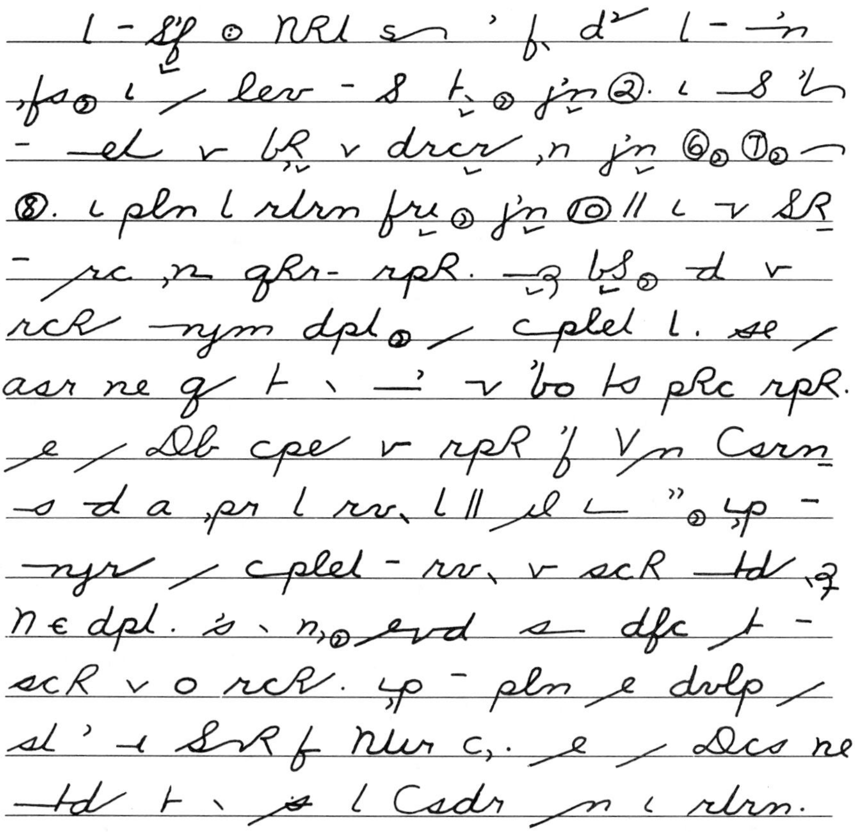

To the Staff: In order to spend a few days at the main office, I will leave the city Thursday, January 2. I (20) must attend the meeting of the Board of Directors on January 6, 7, and 8. I plan to return (40) Friday, January 10.

I have started the work on the quarterly report. Ms. Best, head of the Records Management (60) Department, will complete it. She will answer any questions that you may have about this particular (80) report. We will distribute copies of the report after everyone concerned has had an opportunity to (100) review it.

While I am away, I hope the managers will complete the review of the security methods (120) used in each department. As you know, we have had some difficulty with the security of our records. I (140) hope the plan we develop will set a high standard for the entire company. We will discuss any methods that (160) you wish to consider when I return. (170)

Chapter 23 — Supplemental Letter

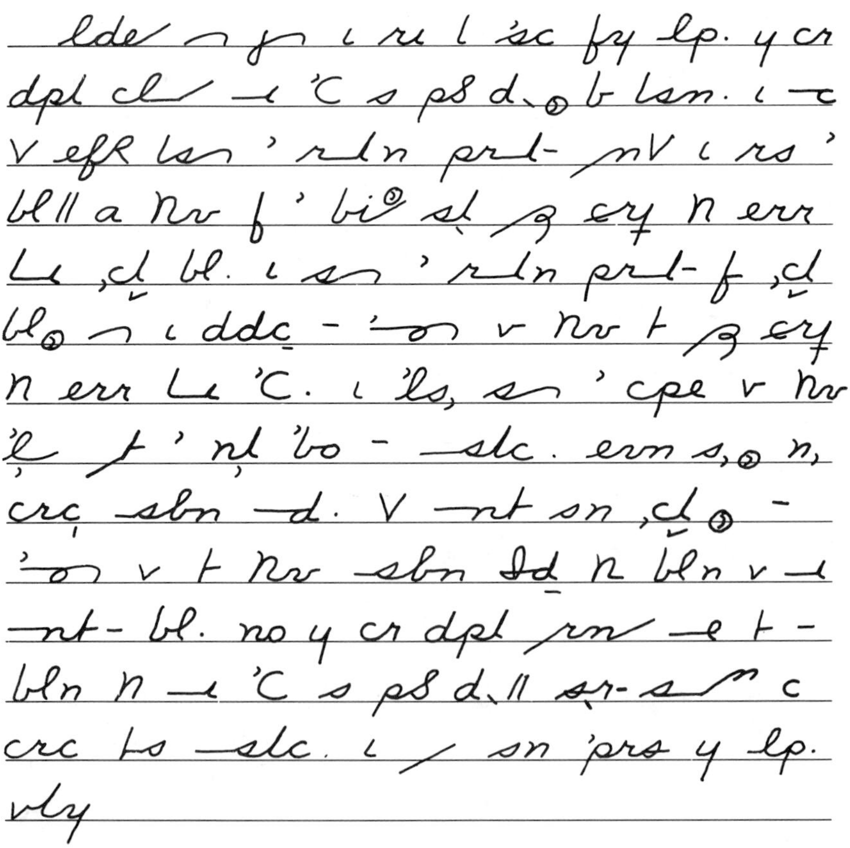

Ladies and Gentlemen: I write to ask for your help. Your credit department claims my account is past due, but it (20) is not. I make every effort to send a remittance promptly whenever I receive a bill.

An invoice for (40) a boy's suit was charged in error to my October bill. I sent a remittance promptly for the October bill, (60) and I deducted the amount of the invoice that was charged in error to my account. I also sent a (80) copy of the invoice along with a note about the mistake. Even so, no correction has been made. Every month (100) since October, the amount of that invoice has been included in the balance of my monthly bill. Now your (120) credit department warns me that the balance in my account is past due.

Surely someone can correct this mistake. I (140) will sincerely appreciate your help. Very truly yours, (151)

Chapter 24 —Supplemental Letter 3

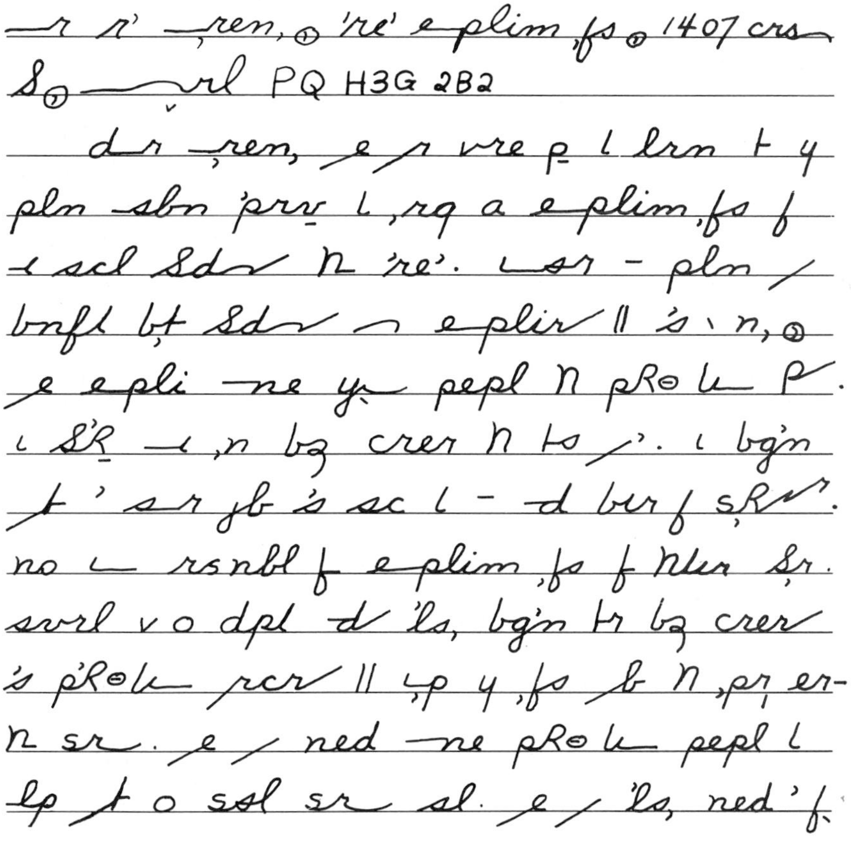

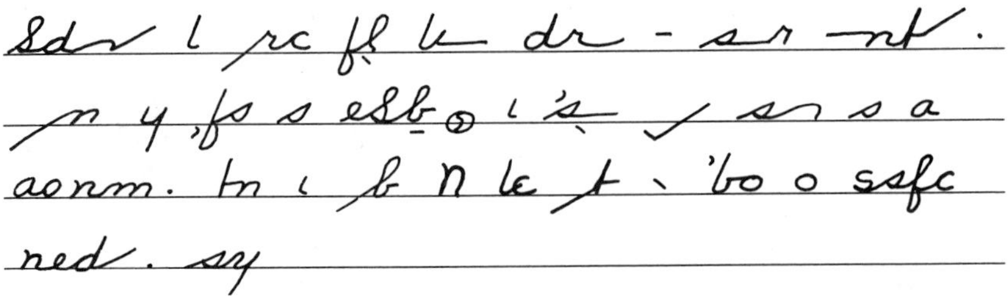

Mr. Ray Moreno, Area Employment Office, 1407 Crescent Street, Montreal, PQ H3G 2B2

Dear Mr. Moreno: We were very pleased to learn that your plan has been approved to organize an employment (20) office for high school students in the area. I am sure the plan will benefit both students and employers. (40)

As you know, we employ many young people in part-time positions. I started my own business career in this (60) way. I began with a summer job as secretary to the head buyer for sportswear. Now I am responsible (80) for the employment office for the entire store. Several of our department heads also began their (100) business careers as part-time workers.

I hope your office will be in operation early in the spring. We will need (120) many part-time people to help with our special spring sale. We will also need a few students to work full time (140) during the summer months. When your office is established, I assume you will send us an announcement. Then I will be (160) in touch with you about our specific needs. Sincerely yours, (170)

Chapter 24 — Supplemental Letter 4

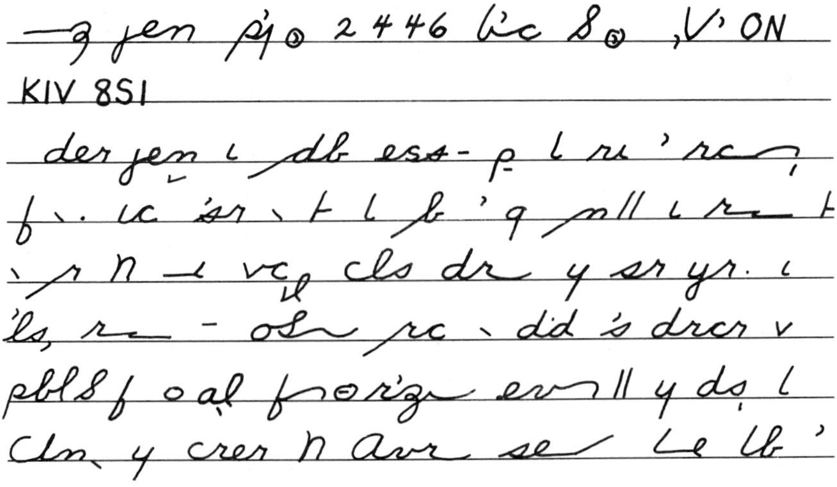
KIV 8SI

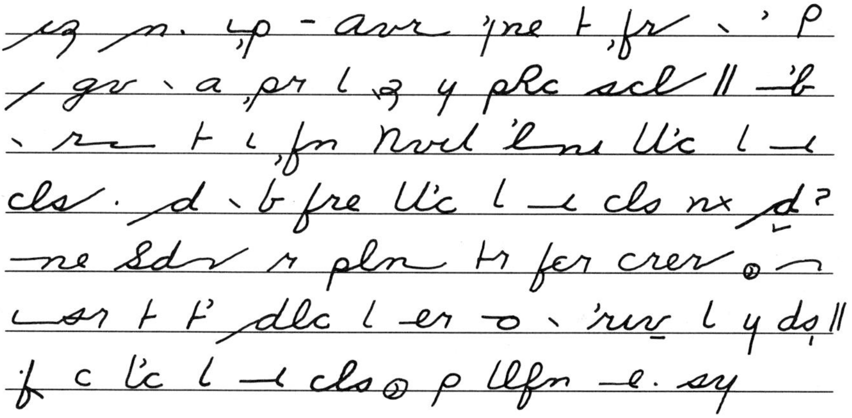

Ms. Jean Page, 2446 Bank Street, Ottawa, ON K1V 8S1

Dear Jean: I would be especially pleased to write a recommendation for you. I can assure you that it will (20) be a good one.

I remember that you were in my vocational class during your senior year. I also (40) remember the outstanding work you did as director of publicity for our annual fund-raising event. (60)

Your decision to continue your career in advertising seems to me to be a wise one. I hope the (80) advertising agency that offers you a position will give you an opportunity to use your (100) particular skills.

Maybe you remember that I often invite alumni to talk to my classes. Would you be (120) free to talk to my class next Wednesday? Many students are planning their future careers, and I am sure that they would (140) like to hear how you arrived at your decision.

If you can talk to my class, please telephone me. Sincerely yours, (160)

Chapter 25 — Supplemental Letter

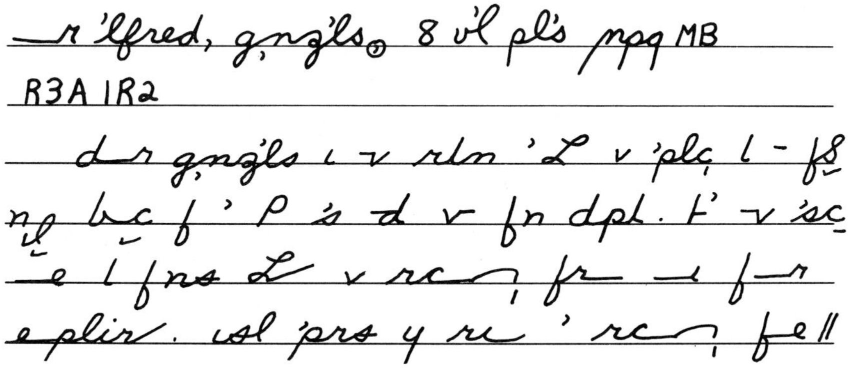

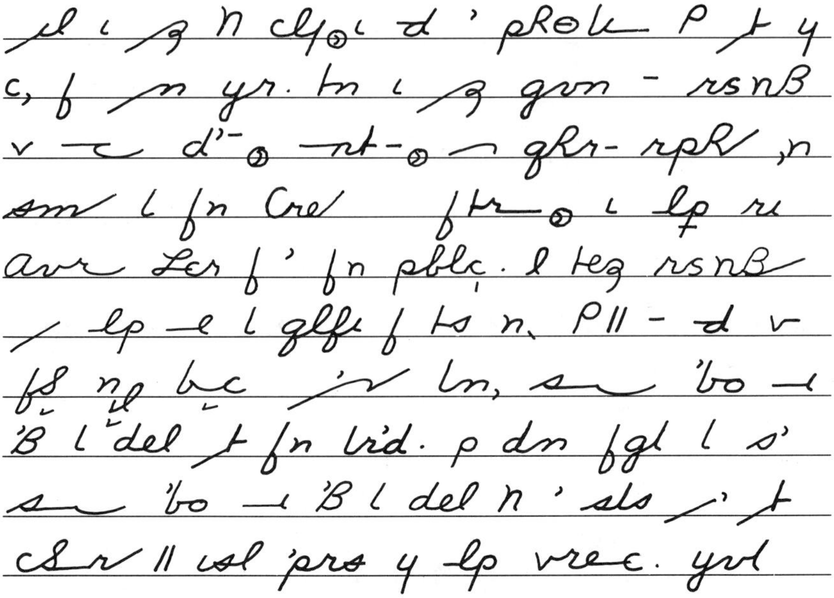

Mr. Alfredo Gonzales, 8 Vale Place, Winnipeg, MB R2J 3N8

Dear Mr. Gonzales: I have written a letter of application to the First National Bank for a (20) position as head of the foreign department. They have asked me to furnish letters of recommendation from my (40) former employers. I shall appreciate your writing a recommendation for me.

While I was in college, (60) I had a part-time position with your company for one year. Then I was given the responsibility (80) of making daily, monthly, and quarterly reports on shipments to foreign countries. Furthermore, I helped write advertising (100) literature for a foreign publication. All these responsibilities will help me to qualify for (120) this new position.

The head of the First National Bank wants to know something about my ability (140) to deal with foreign trade. Please do not forget to say something about my ability to deal in a (160) satisfactory way with customers.

I shall appreciate your help very much. Yours very truly, (178)

Chapter 26 — Supplemental Letter

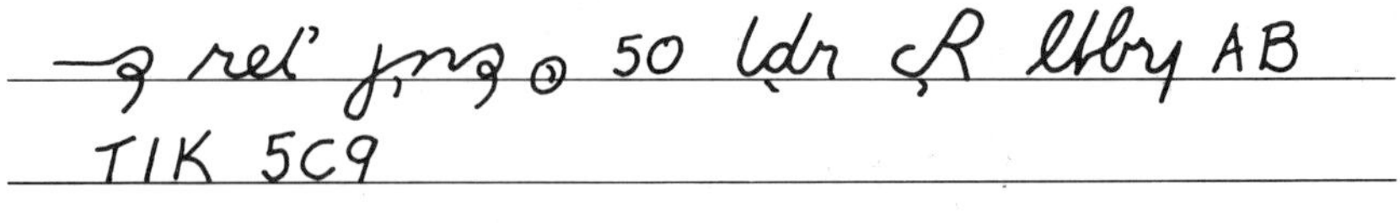

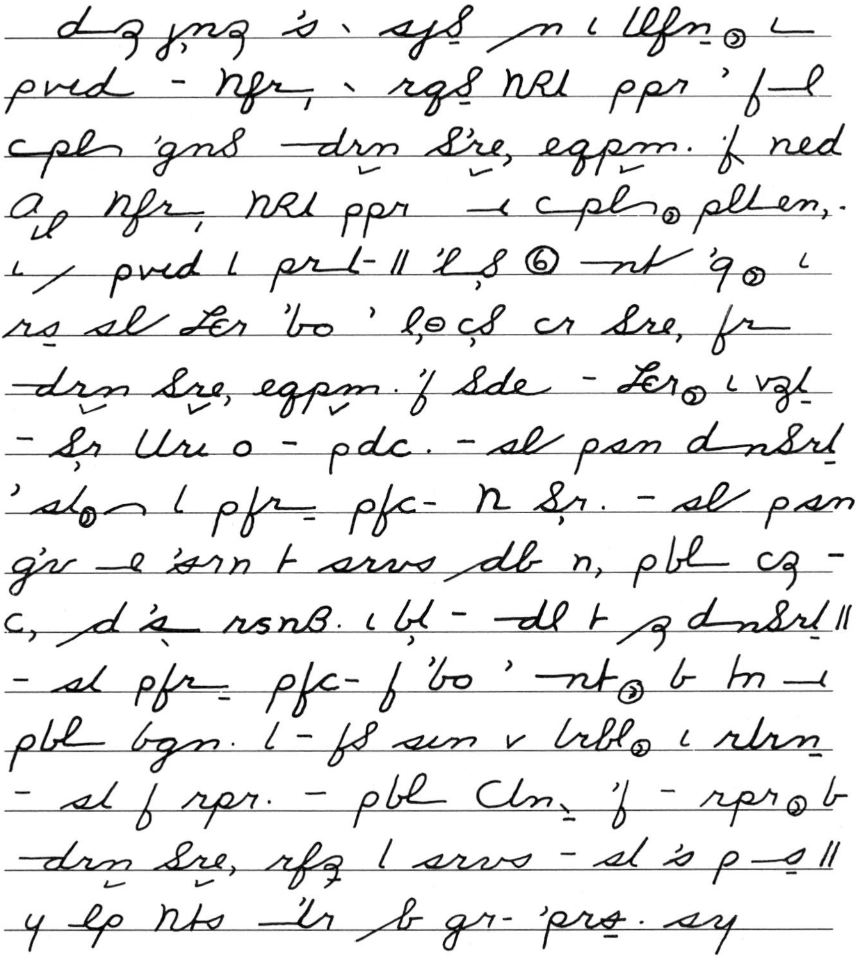

Ms. Rita Jones, 50 Tudor Court, Lethbridge, AB T1K 5C9

Dear Ms. Jones: As you suggested when I telephoned, I am providing the information you requested in (20) order to prepare a formal complaint against Modern Stereo Equipment. If you need additional (40) information in order to prepare my complaint, please let me know. I will provide it promptly.

Almost six months ago, (60) I received sales literature about a low-cost car stereo from Modern Stereo Equipment. After (80) studying the literature, I visited the store to try out the product. The sales person demonstrated (100) a set, and it performed perfectly in the store. The sales person gave me assurance that service would be no problem (120) because the company would assume responsibility. I bought the model that was demonstrated.

The (140) set performed perfectly for about a month, but then my problem began. At the first sign of trouble, I returned (160) the set for repair. The problem continued after the repair, but Modern Stereo refused to service the (180) set as promised.

Your help in this matter will be greatly appreciated. Sincerely yours, (196)

Chapter 27 — Supplemental Letter

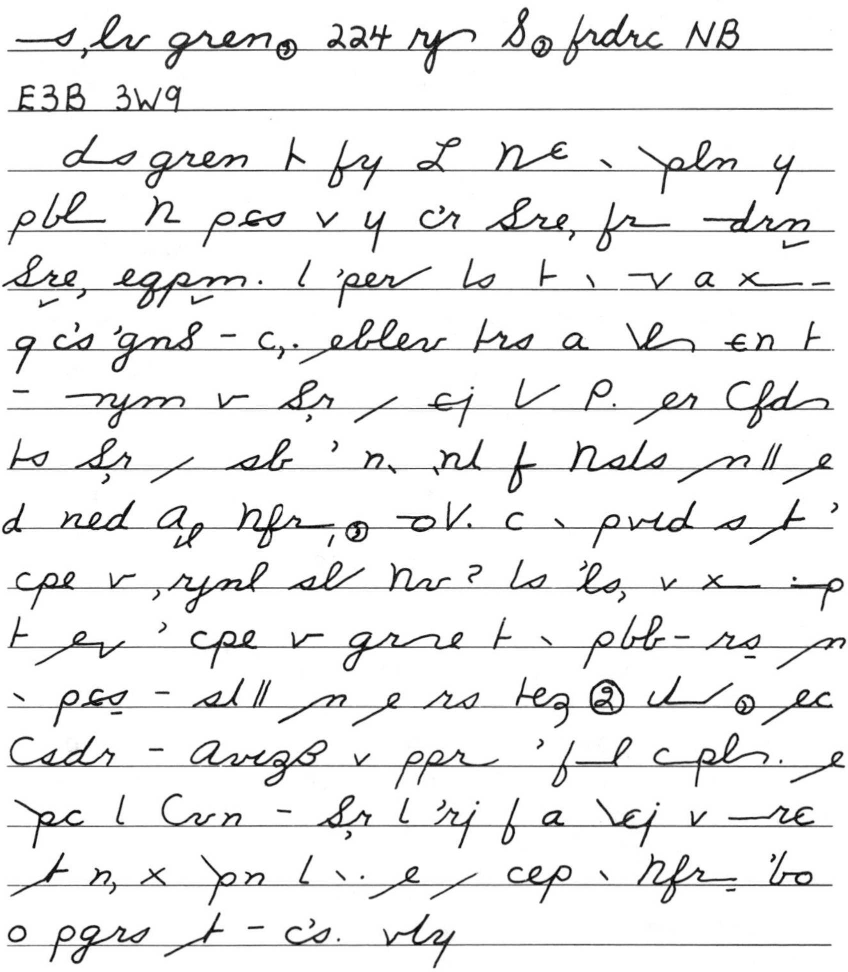

Miss Olive Green, 224 Regent Street, Fredericton, NB E3B 3W9

Dear Miss Green: Thank you for your letter in which you explain your problem in the purchase of your car stereo from (20) Modern Stereo Equipment. It appears to us that you have an extremely good case against the company. (40) We believe there is an excellent chance that the management of the store will change its position. We are confident (60) this store will substitute a new unit for the unsatisfactory one.

We do need additional (80) information, however. Can you provide us with a copy of the original sales invoice? It is also (100) of extreme importance that we have a copy of the guarantee that you probably received when you purchased (120) the set.

When we receive these two items, we can consider the advisability of preparing a formal (140) complaint. We expect to convince the store to arrange for an exchange of merchandise with no extra expense (160) to you. We will keep you informed about our progress with the case. Very truly yours, (175)

Chapter 28 —Supplemental Letter 3

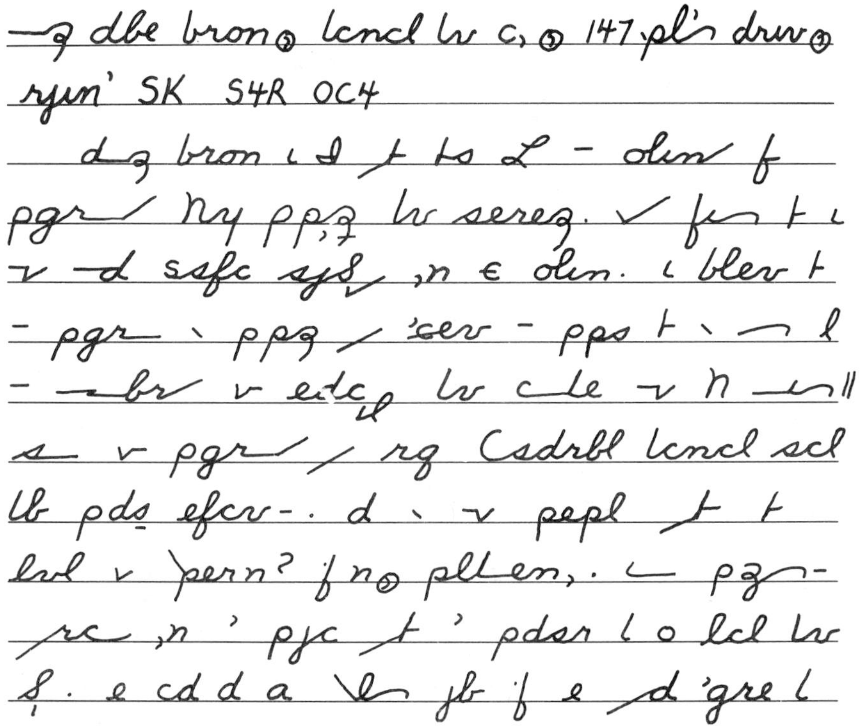

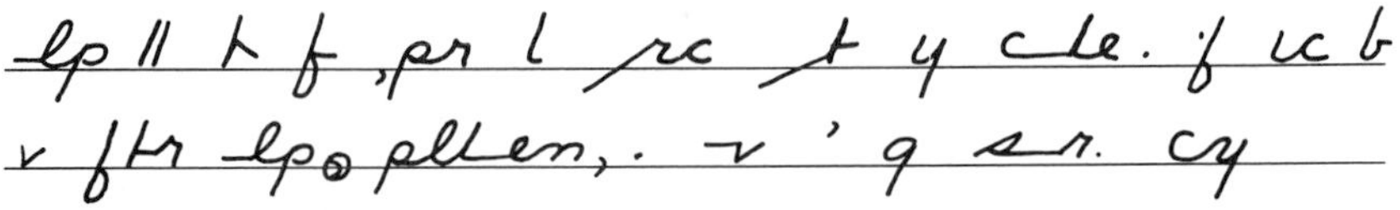

Ms. Debby Brown, Technical Television Company, 147 Upland Drive, Regina, SK S4R 0C4

Dear Ms. Brown: I enclose with this letter the outlines for the programs in your proposed television series. You (20) will find that I have made specific suggestions on each outline. I believe that the program you propose will (40) achieve the purpose that you and all the members of the educational television committee have in mind. (60)

Some of the programs will require considerable technical skill to be produced effectively. Do you have (80) people with that level of experience? If not, please let me know. I am presently working on a project (100) with a producer at our local television station. He could do an excellent job if he would agree (120) to help.

Thank you for the opportunity to work with your committee. If I can be of further help, please let (140) me know. Have a good summer. Cordially yours, (148)

Chapter 28 — Supplemental Letter 4

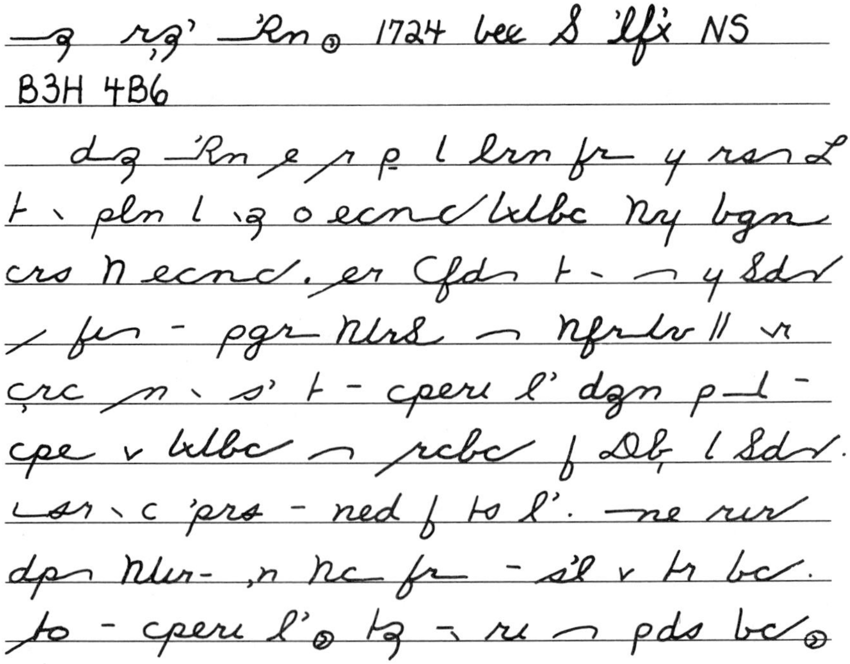
1724
NS
B3H 4B6

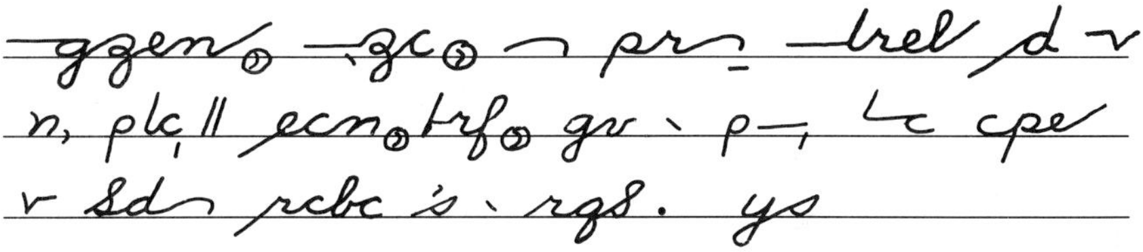

Ms. Rosa Martin, 1724 Beech Street, Halifax, NS B3H 4B6

Dear Ms. Martin: We were pleased to learn from your recent letter that you plan to use our economics textbook in (20) your beginning course in economics. We are confident that you and your students will find the program interesting (40) and informative.

You are correct when you say that the copyright law does not permit the copying of (60) textbooks and workbooks for distribution to students. I am sure you can appreciate the need for this law. Many (80) writers depend entirely on income from the sale of their books. Without the copyright law, those who write and (100) produce books, magazines, music, and printed materials would have no protection.

We cannot, therefore, give you (120) permission to make copies of the student workbook as you request. Yours sincerely, (135)

Chapter 29 — Supplemental Letter

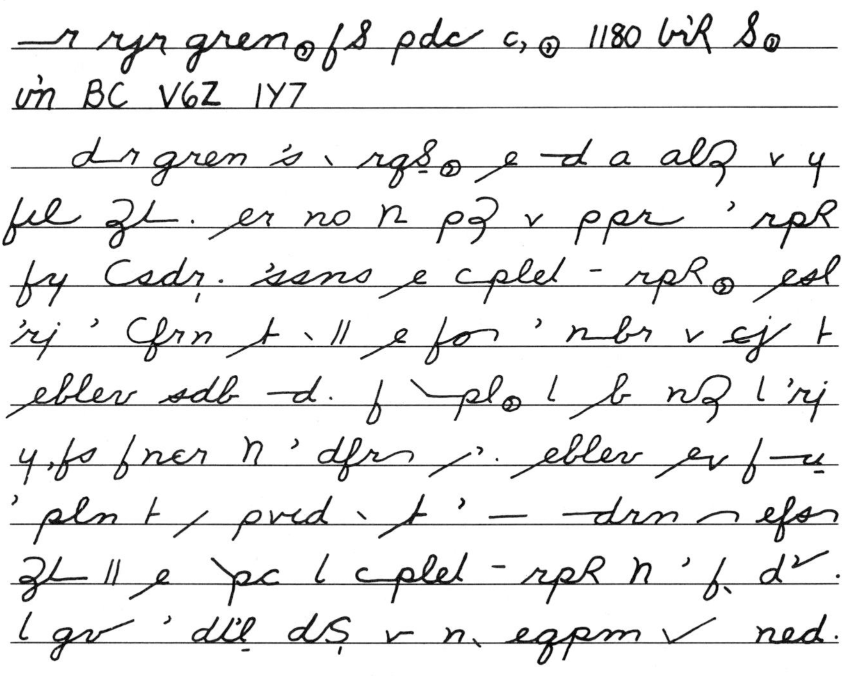

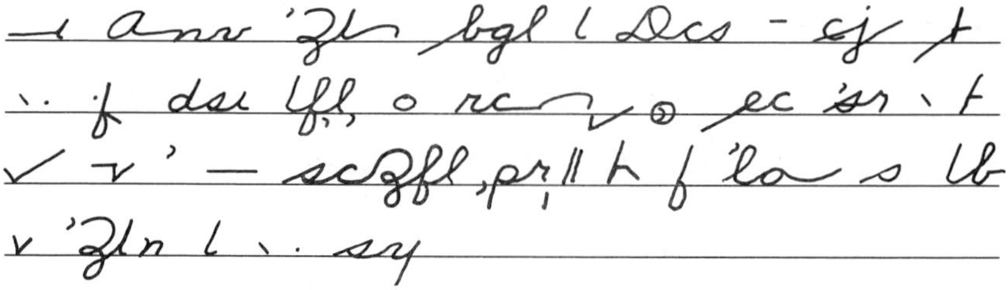

Mr. Roger Green, Forest Products Company, 1180 Burrard Street, Vancouver, BC V6Z 1Y7

Dear Mr. Green: As you requested, we made an analysis of your filing system. We are now in the process (20) of preparing a report for your consideration. As soon as we complete the report, we shall arrange (40) a conference with you.

We found a number of changes that we believe should be made. For example, it will be (60) necessary to arrange your office furniture in a different way. We believe we have formulated (80) a plan that will provide you with a more modern and efficient system.

We expect to complete the report in a (100) few days. It gives a detailed description of the new equipment you will need. My administrative (120) assistant will be glad to discuss the changes with you. If you decide to follow our recommendations, we can assure (140) you that you will have a more successful operation.

Thank you for allowing us to be of assistance to (160) you. Sincerely yours, (164)

Chapter 30 — Supplemental Letter

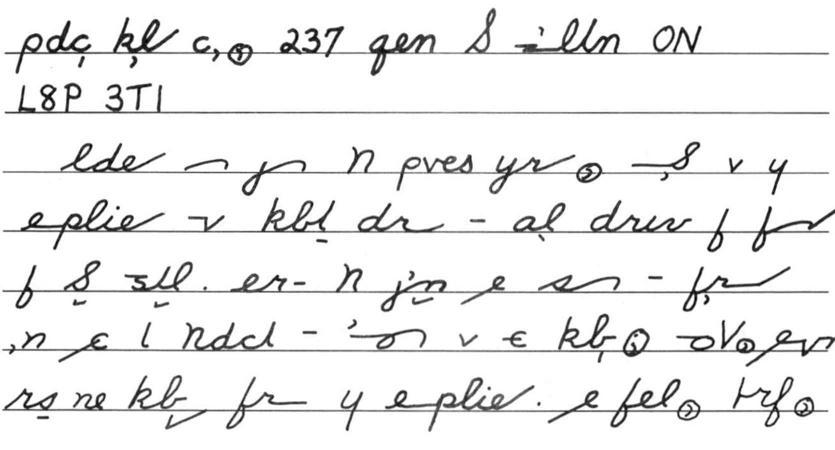

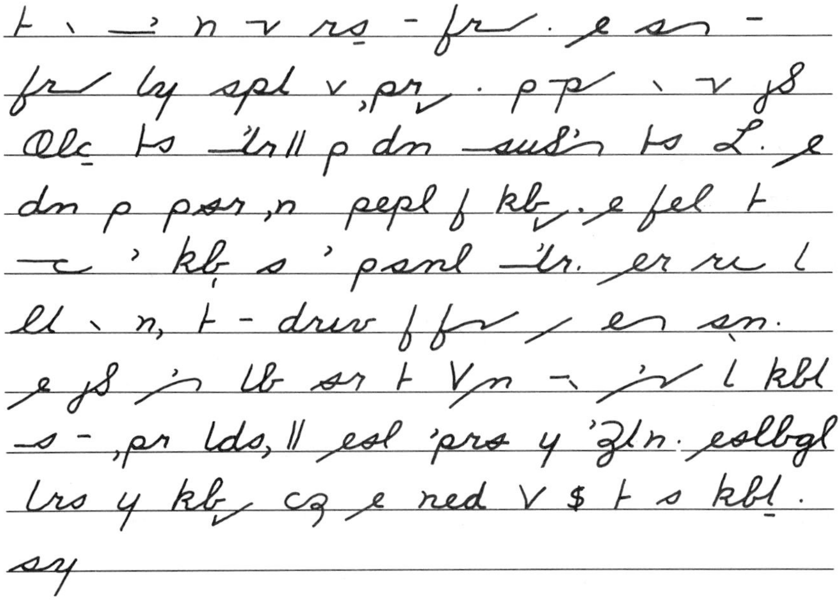

Production Controls Company, 237 Queen Street, Hamilton, ON L8P 3T1

Ladies and Gentlemen: In previous years, most of your employees have contributed during the annual (20) drive for funds for City Hospital. Early in January we sent the forms on which to indicate the amount (40) of each contribution; however, we have not received any contributions from your employees. We feel, (60) therefore, that you may not have received the forms. We sent the forms to your superintendent of operations. Perhaps (80) you have just overlooked this matter.

Please do not misunderstand this letter. We do not put pressure on people (100) for contributions. We feel that making a contribution is a personal matter. We are writing to (120) let you know that the drive for funds will end soon. We just want to be sure that everyone who wants to contribute has (140) the opportunity to do so.

We shall appreciate your assistance. We shall be glad to receive your (160) contributions because we need every dollar that is contributed. Sincerely yours, (175)

Chapter 31—Supplemental Memorandum

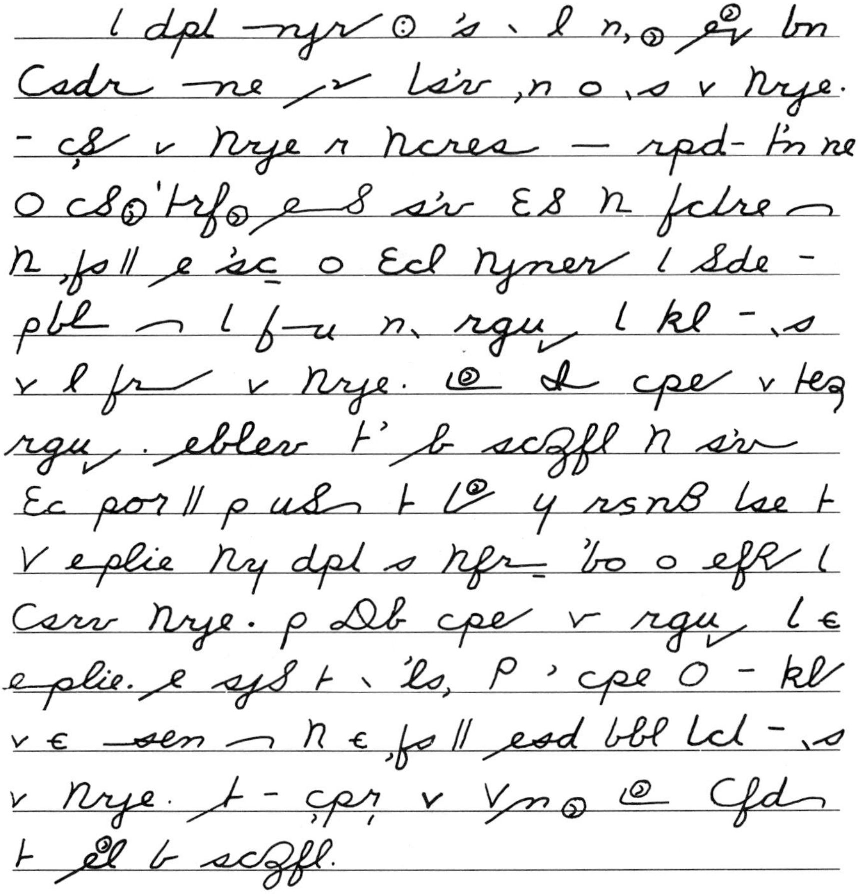

To Department Managers: As you all know, we've been considering many ways to save on our use of energy. (20) The costs of energy are increasing more rapidly than any other cost; therefore, we must save electricity (40) in the factory and in the office.

We asked our electrical engineers to study the problem (60) and to formulate new regulations to control the use of all forms of energy. I'm enclosing copies (80) of these regulations. We believe they will be successful in saving electric power.

Please understand that (100) it's your responsibility to see that every employee in your department is informed about our efforts (120) to conserve energy. Please distribute copies of the regulations to each employee. We suggest that (140) you also post a copy over the controls of each machine and in each office.

We should be able to cut (160) the use of energy. With the cooperation of everyone, I'm confident that we'll be successful. (179)

Chapter 32 — Supplemental Letter 3

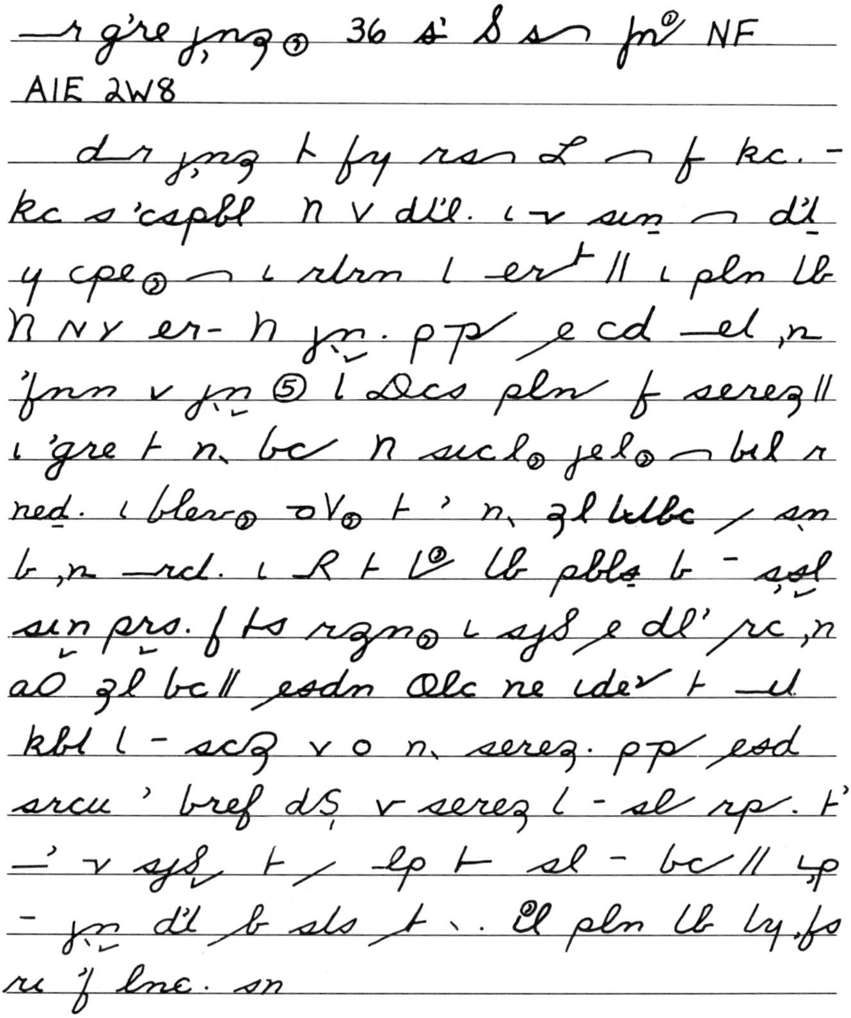

Mr. Gary Jones, 36 Shaw Street, St. John's NF A1E 2W8

Dear Mr. Jones: Thank you for your recent letter and for the contract. The contract is acceptable in every (20) detail. I have signed and dated your copy, and I return it herewith.

I plan to be in New York early in (40) June. Perhaps we could meet on the afternoon of June 5 to discuss plans for the series.

I agree that new books (60) in psychology, geology, and biology are needed. I believe, however, that a new zoology (80) textbook will soon be on the market. I heard that it's to be published by the Social Science Press. For this (100) reason, I suggest we delay work on another zoology book.

We should not overlook any ideas (120) that might contribute to the success of our new series. Perhaps we should circulate a brief description of the (140) series to the sales representatives. They may have suggestions that will help them sell the books.

I hope the June date (160) will be satisfactory with you. I'll plan to be at your office right after lunch. Sincerely, (178)

Chapter 32 —Supplemental Letter 4

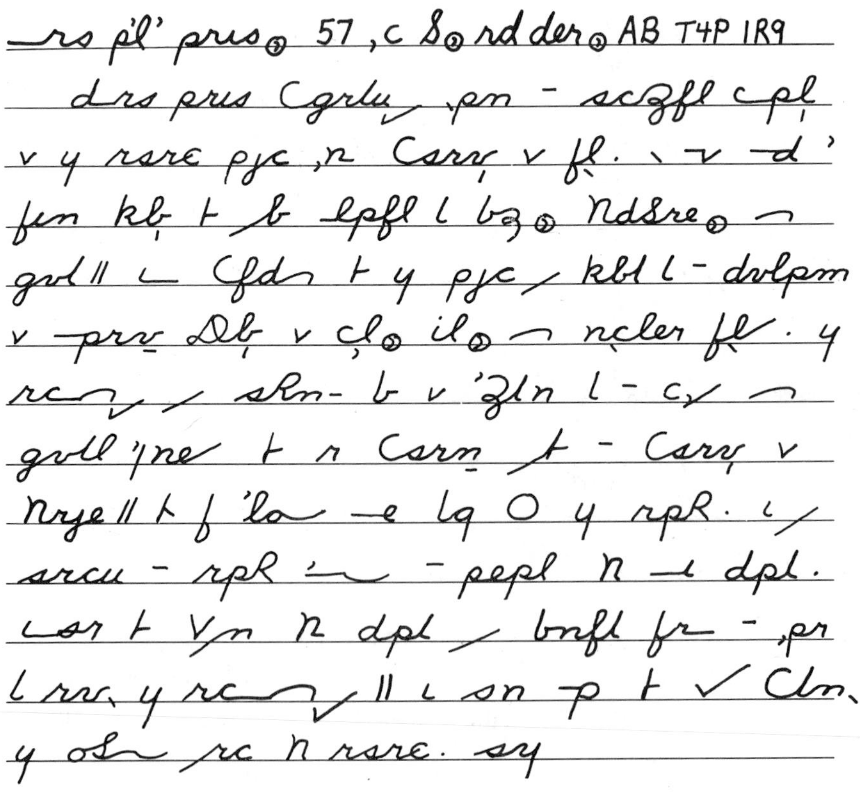

Mrs. Paula Price, 57 Oak Street, Red Deer, AB T4P 1R9

Dear Mrs. Price: Congratulations upon the successful completion of your research project on the (20) conservation of fuel. You have made a fine contribution that will be helpful to business, industry, and government. (40)

I am confident that your project will contribute to the development of improved distribution of (60) coal, oil, and nuclear fuels. Your recommendations will certainly be of assistance to the companies (80) and governmental agencies that are concerned with the conservation of energy.

Thank you for allowing (100) me to go over your report. I will circulate the report among the people in my department. I am (120) sure that everyone in the department will benefit from the opportunity to review your recommendations (140).

I sincerely hope that you will continue your outstanding work in research. Sincerely yours, (157)

M E M O R A N D U M

DATE: (current date)

TO: Department Managers

FROM: Marketing Manager

SUBJECT: Energy Conservation

As you all know, we've been considering many ways to save on our use of energy. The costs of energy are increasing more rapidly than any other cost; therefore, we must save electricity in the factory and in the office.

We asked our electrical engineers to study the problem and to formulate new regulations to control the use of all forms of energy. I'm enclosing copies of these regulations. We believe they will be successful in saving electric power.

Please understand that it's your responsibility to see that every employee in your department is informed about our efforts to conserve energy. Please distribute copies of the regulations to each employee. We suggest that you also post a copy over the controls of each machine and in each office.

We should be able to cut the use of energy. With the cooperation of everyone, I'm confident that we'll be successful.

R. K. M.

Model Memorandum

PART B

CHAPTER 33

THEORY REVIEW OF CHAPTERS 1 THROUGH 4

Asssignment 1 — **Theory Review**. The following sentence contains all the writing principles presented in Chapters 1 through 4. Study the writing principles and practise reading and writing this sentence until you can do so without hesitation and can quickly identify each writing principle.

Eve gave the press a big photo of the bike race.

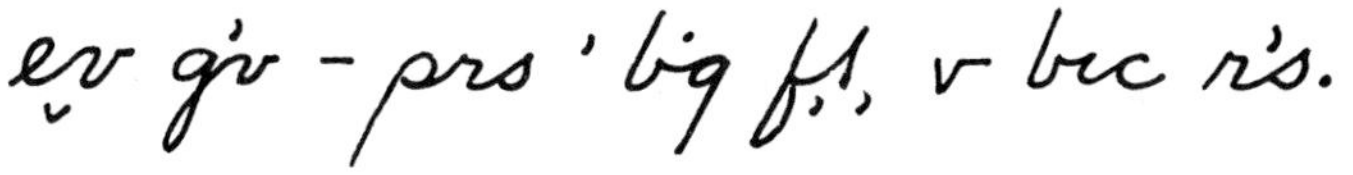

SUMMARY OF WRITING PRINCIPLES

LONG AND SHORT **E**	Write *e* for long *e* sounds. Omit *e* when the short sound of *e* occurs in the body of a word.
Long **I**	Write an undotted *i* for all long sounds of *i*.
A	Write a stroke like an apostrophe for all sounds of *a*.
T	Write the *t* without a cross.
SHORT **I**	Where the sound of short *i* occurs, write a dot above the line.
HARD **C &** **K**	Write the longhand *c* to express the sound of hard *c* and *k*.
O	Write a small curved stroke like a comma on or below the line of writing for all sounds of *o*.
SOFT **C**	Write a longhand *s* when *c* has an *s* sound.

Assignment 2 — **Abbreviations and phrasing review.** Read and write the following sentences containing abbreviations and phrases until you can write them quickly and easily and without hesitation.

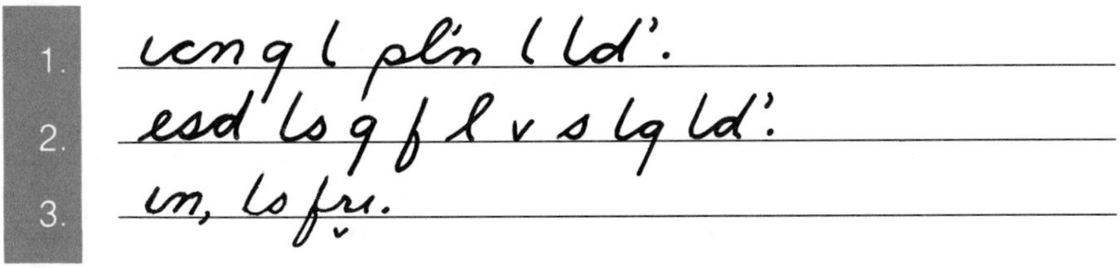

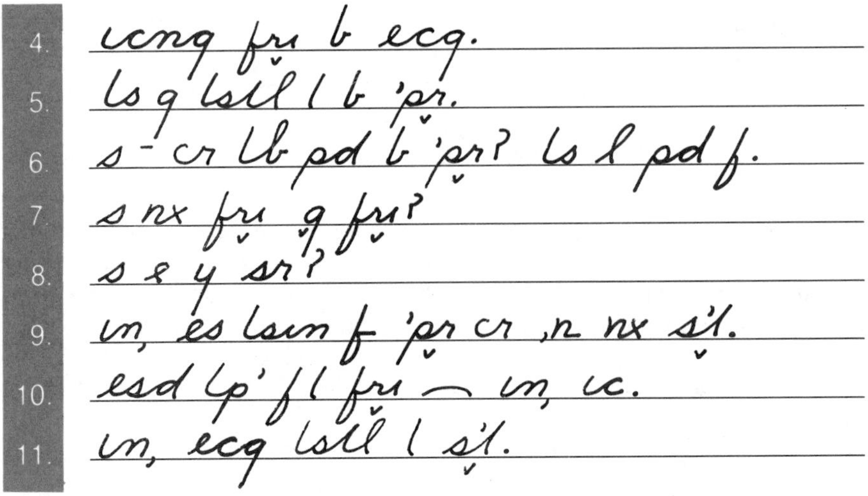

BUILDING TRANSCRIPTION SKILLS

Assignment 3 — **Transcription skills review—the comma**. Review the following rules governing the use of the comma, and then transcribe the sentences inserting the correct punctuation. The key to these sentences appears on page 196.

1. **Punctuating introductory words, phrases, and clauses**. Introductory words or expressions introduce the reader to the rest of the sentence. Place a comma after an introductory word, phrase, or clause. The most common introductory words and expressions include: *therefore*, *however*, *nevertheless*, *even so*, *furthermore*, *for example*. Introductory phrases and clauses usually begin with one of the following words: *if*, *since*, *when*, *after*, *although*, *as*, *because*, *in*, *unless*, *upon*, *whenever*, *while*.

2. **Punctuating parenthetical words and expressions**. Parenthetical words and expressions are those that can be omitted without changing the meaning of a sentence. Place a comma before and after parenthetical words or expressions. Common parenthetical words and expressions include: *indeed*, *also*, *however*, *therefore*, *perhaps*, *as you know*, *at any rate*, *I believe*, *I think*, *no doubt*, *of course*.

3. **Punctuating compound sentences**. A compound sentence is two sentences joined together. The two sentences are usually joined by a connecting word (conjunction). Common connecting words are: *and*, *but*, *for*, *either*, *or*, *nor*, *neither*. Place a comma before the connecting word in a compound sentence.

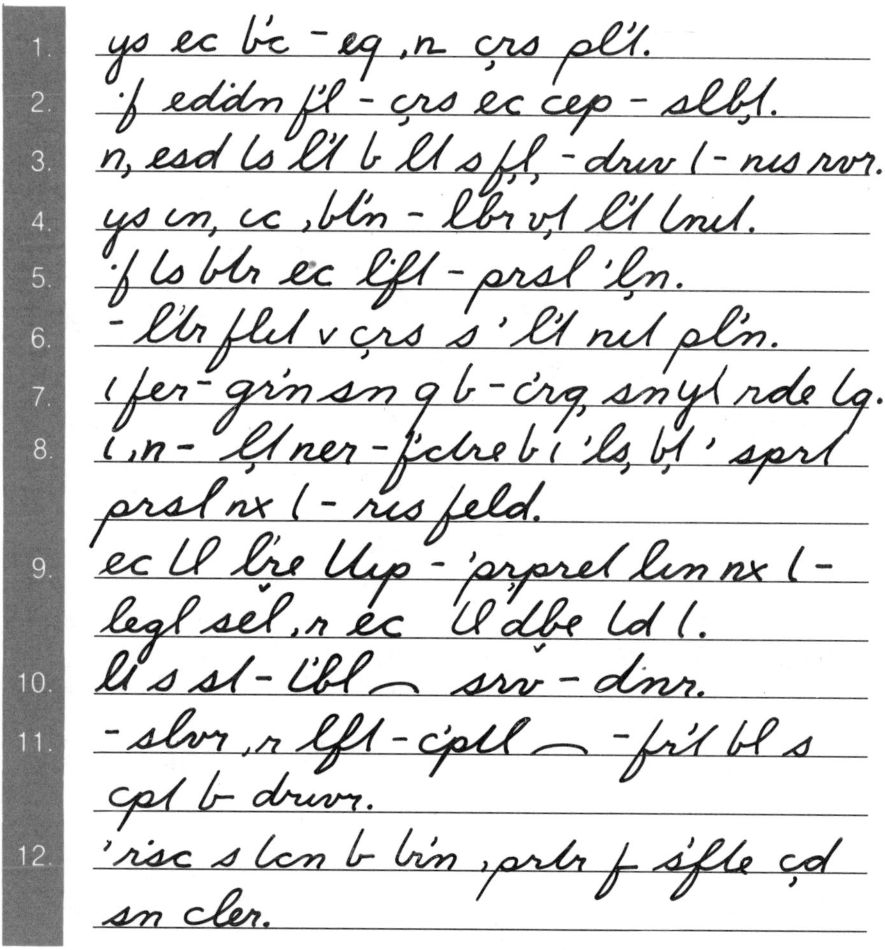

READING AND WRITING SHORTHAND

Assignments 4 and 5, except for those previewed, contain only words presented in Chapters and Units 1 through 4 of the text and *Study Guide*. Assignments 6 and 11 include vocabulary from Chapters and Units 1 through 32.

Assignment 4 — **Letter 1**. Read and write each of the preview phrases for Letter 1 until you can read and write each one rapidly and accurately. Then read and write the shorthand for Letter 1 to build your writing speed.

to serve	to set	to see	if the	to sign	I can go

of the

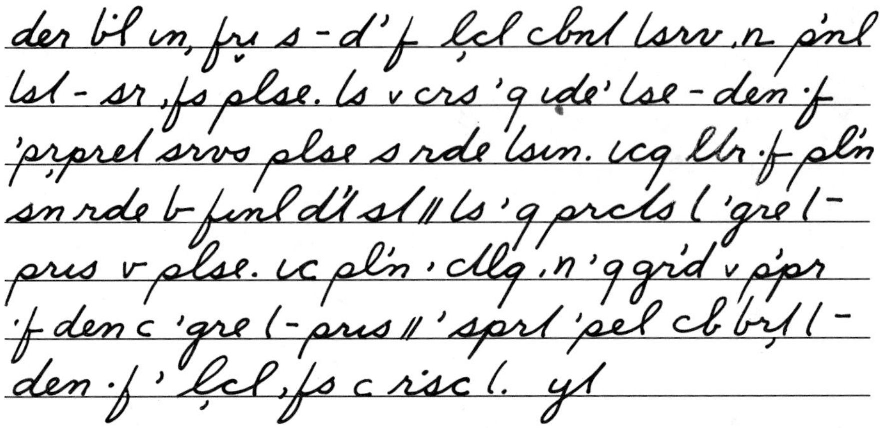

Assignment 5 — **Letter 2**. Read and write each preview word and phrase for Letter 2 until you can read and write each one rapidly and accurately. Then read and write the shorthand for Letter 2 to build your writing speed.

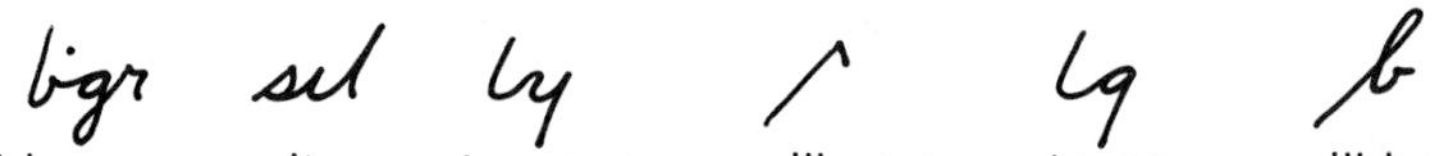
bigger site to your will you to go will be

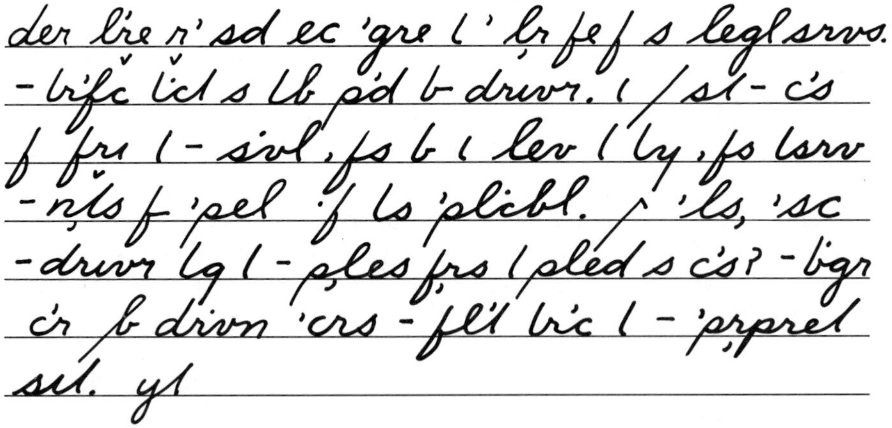

Assignment 6 — **Memorandum 1**. Read and write each of the preview words and phrases for Memorandum 1 until you can read and write each one rapidly and accurately. Then read and write the shorthand for Memorandum 1 to build your writing speed.

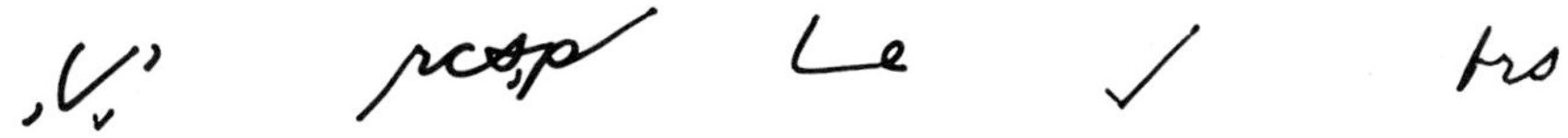

Ottawa workshops to me you will there is

you will be able if you to stay let me know

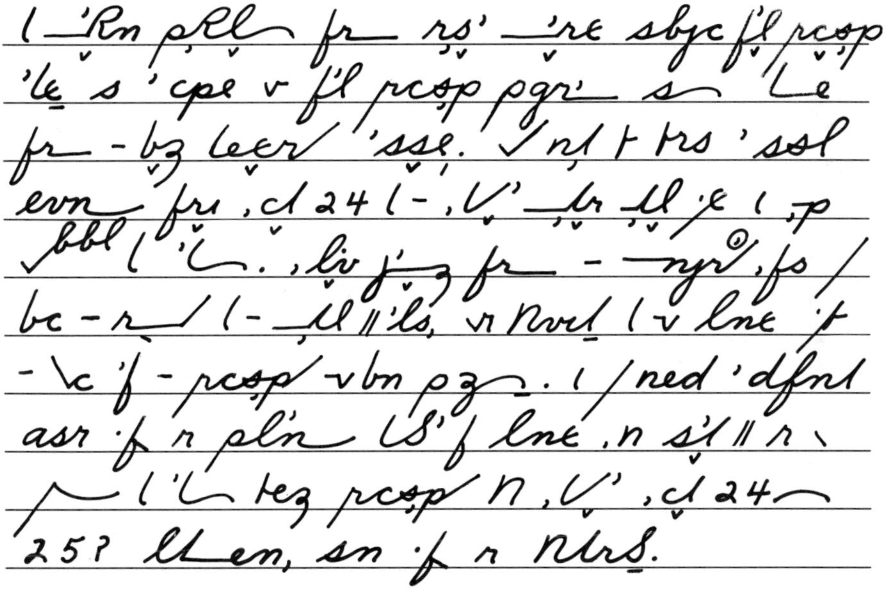

BUILDING SHORTHAND SPEED AND TRANSCRIPTION ACCURACY

Assignment 7 — **Self-testing**. Complete Unit 33 in your *Study Guide* before you proceed with the rest of this chapter.

Assignment 8 — **Taking tape dictation**. To write from dictation the sentences, letters, and memorandum in this chapter, use Cassette 19, Side A from *Theory and Speed-Building Tapes*.

Assignment 9 — **Taking live dictation**. Write from dictation the material which is printed at the end of this chapter. Your instructor will dictate to you at various speeds.

Assignment 10 — **Own-note transcription**. Transcribe at your best typing rate an accurate copy of at least one of the pieces of correspondence you took in shorthand in Assignment 9. Type the assignment in the style requested by your instructor.

Assignment 11 — **Supplementary dictation**. If instructed to do so, read and write the additional material for this chapter found in Appendix B, "Supplementary Correspondence for Dictation."

TRANSCRIPT OF SHORTHAND—ASSIGNMENT 2

1. I cannot go to plan it today.
2. He said it is good for all of us to go today.
3. I know it is Friday. (20)
4. I cannot go Friday, but he can go.
5. It is good to settle it by April.
6. Is the credit to be paid by (40) April? It is all paid for.
7. Is next Friday Good Friday?
8. Is he your senior?
9. I know he is to sign for the (60) April credit on the next Saturday.
10. He said to pay for it Friday, and I know I can.
11. I know he can go to (80) settle it Saturday. (84)

TRANSCRIPT OF SHORTHAND—ASSIGNMENT 3

1. Yes, he can bake the egg on the coarse plate.
2. If he did not fail the course, he can keep the sailboat.
3. No, he said it is (20) late, but let us follow the drive to the nice river.
4. Yes, I know I can obtain the labor vote late tonight.
5. If (40) it is better, he can lift the parcel alone.
6. The latter flight, of course, is a late night plane.
7. I fear the grain is (60) not good, but the cargo is not yet ready to go.
8. I own the lot near the factory, but I also bought a (80) separate parcel next to the rice field.
9. He can tell Larry to type the appropriate line next to the legal (100) seal, or he can tell Debby to do it.
10. Let us set the table and serve the dinner.
11. The silver ore left the (120) capital, and the freight bill is kept by the driver.
12. A risk is taken by the train operator, for the safety (140) code is not clear. (143)

TRANSCRIPT OF SHORTHAND—ASSIGNMENT 4

Letter 1 Dear Bill: I know Friday is the day for the local cabinet to serve on the panel to set the senior (20) office policy. It is, of course, a good idea to see the dean if the appropriate service policy (40) is ready to sign. I can go later if the plan is not ready by the final date set.

It is a good (60) practice to agree to the price of the policy. I can plan a catalogue on a good grade of paper if the (80) dean can agree to the price.

A separate appeal can be brought to the dean if a local office can risk it. (100) Yours truly, (*AW 108; SW 102; SI 1.32*)

TRANSCRIPT OF SHORTHAND—ASSIGNMENT 5

Letter 2 Dear Larry: Ray said he can agree to a lower fee for his legal service. The traffic ticket is to be (20) paid by the driver. I will set the case for Friday at the civil office, but I leave it to your office to (40) serve the notice for the appeal if it is applicable. Will you also ask the driver to go to the (60) police force to plead his case? The bigger car will be driven across the flat track to the appropriate site. Yours (80) truly, (*AW 86: SW 81; SI 1.31*)

TRANSCRIPT OF SHORTHAND—ASSIGNMENT 6

Memorandum 1

TO: Martin Portland
FROM: Rosa March
SUBJECT: Fall Workshop

Attached is a copy of the fall workshop program sent to me from the Business Teachers' Association. You (20) will note that there is a social evening Friday, October 24, at the Ottawa Motor (40) Hotel, which I hope you will be able to attend. Olive James, from the manager's office, will book the (60) rooms at the motel.

Also, you are invited to have lunch with the executive after the workshops (80) have been presented. I will need a definite answer if you are planning to stay for lunch on Saturday.

Are (100) you willing to attend these workshops in Ottawa, October 24 and 25? Let me know (120) soon if you are interested. (*AW 112; SW 125; SI 1.49*)

CHAPTER 34

THEORY REVIEW OF CHAPTERS 5 THROUGH 8

Assignment 1 — **Theory Review**. The following sentence contains all the writing principles presented in Chapters 5 through 8. Study the writing principles, and practise reading and writing this sentence until you can do so without hesitation and can quickly identify each.

Are you aware the general may not approve the payment when due unless

he is consulted?

SUMMARY OF WRITING PRINCIPLES

AWA	Write two *a* symbols for the sound *awa*.
SOFT G-J	The sound of soft *g* and *j* is represented by an undotted *j*.
M	Write a long straight line to express *m*.
U-OO	Write a short slanted downward stroke on or below the line to express sounds of *u-oo*.
MENT	Write a longhand *m* for the syllable *ment*.
W-WH	Write a long, upward slanted stroke for the sounds *w* and *wh*.
IN-EN-UN	Write a longhand capital *N* to express the prefixes *in-en-un*.
CON-COUN-COUNT	Write a longhand capital *C* to express the prefixes *con*, *coun*, and *count*.
D-ED ADDED TO A ROOT WORD	Make a short dash under the last letter or symbol in a word to show that *d* or *ed* is added to a root word to form the past tense.

Assignment 2 — **Abbreviations and phrasing review**. Read and write the following sentences containing abbreviations and phrases until you can write them quickly and easily and without hesitation.

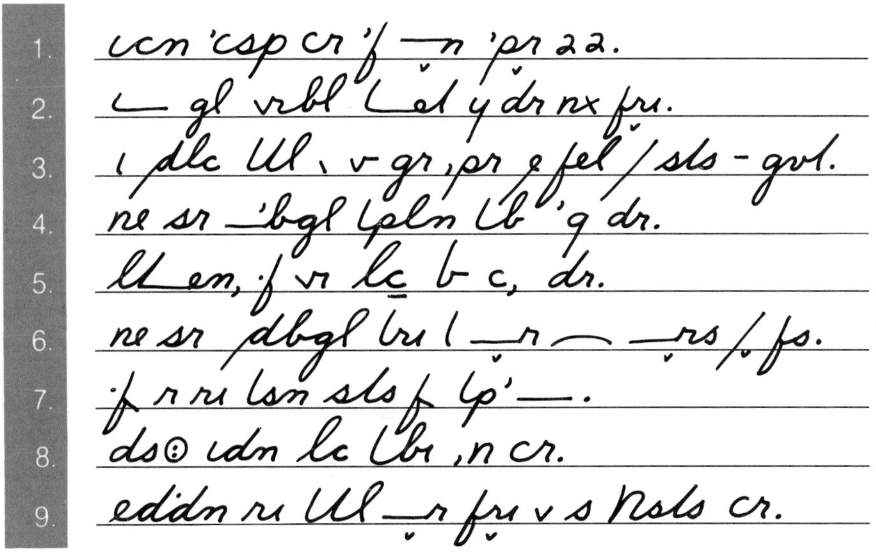

BUILDING TRANSCRIPTION SKILLS

Assignment 3 — **Transcription skills review—the comma.** Review the following rules governing the use of the comma, and then transcribe the sentences, inserting the correct punctuation. The key to these sentences appears on page 204.

1. **Punctuating appositives.** Words and phrases that describe or explain a preceding word or expression are called appositives. Place a comma before and after appositives.

2. **Punctuating a series.** When two or more words, phrases, or clauses appear in a series, they are separated by commas.

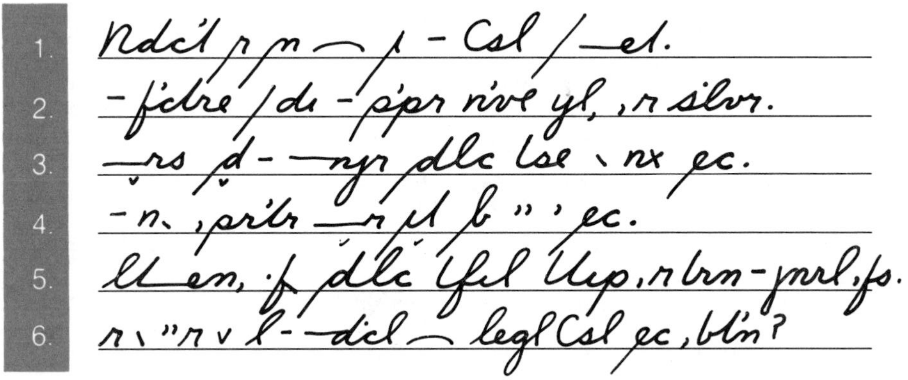

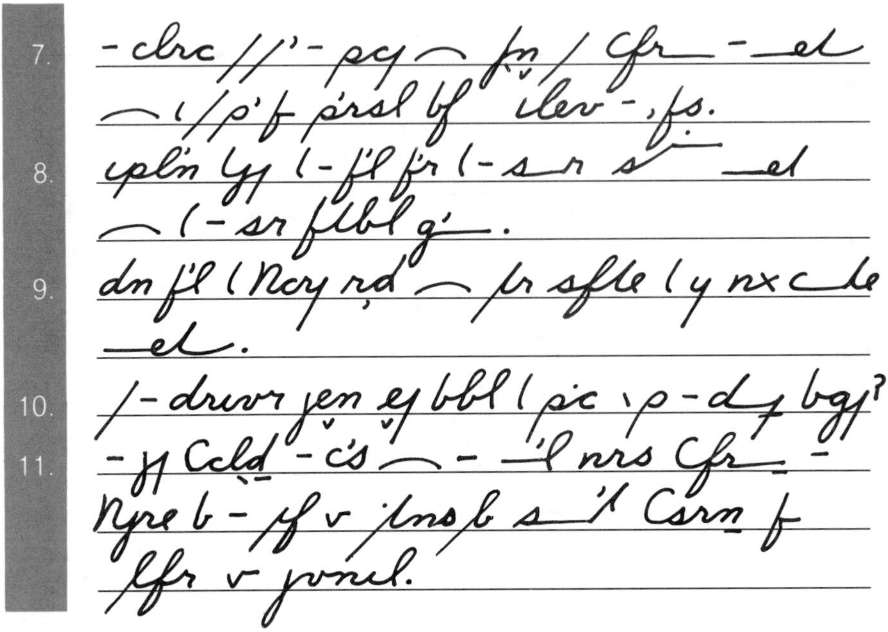
7.
8.
9.
10.
11.

READING AND WRITING SHORTHAND

Assignments 4 and 5, except for those previewed, contain only words presented in Chapters and Units 1 through 8 of the text and *Study Guide*. Assignments 6 and 11 include vocabulary from Chapters and Units 1 through 32.

Assignment 4 — **Memorandum 1**. Read and write each of the phrases for Memorandum 1 until you can read and write each one rapidly and accurately. Then read and write the shorthand for Memorandum 1 to build your writing speed.

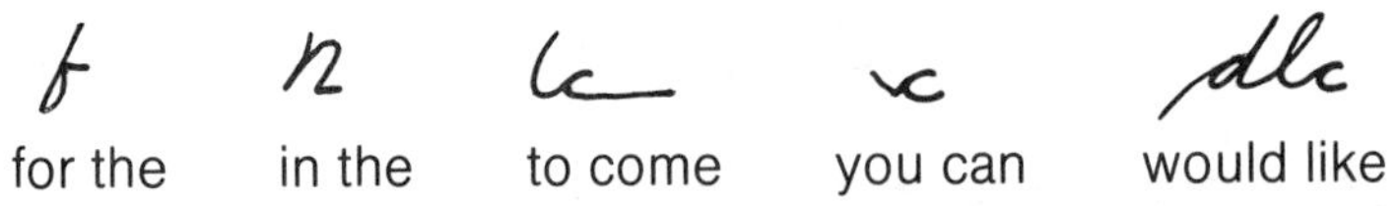
for the
in the
to come
you can
would like

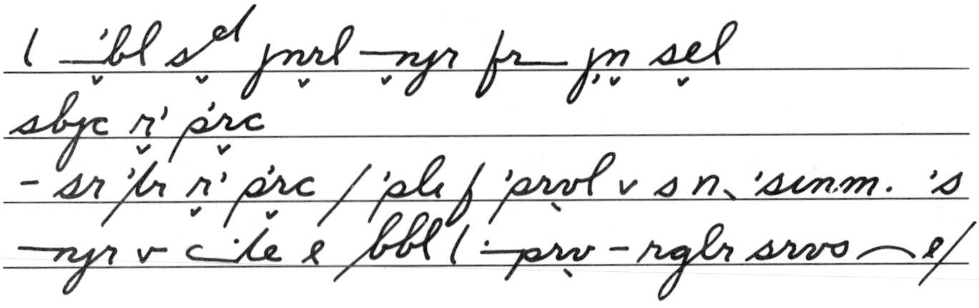

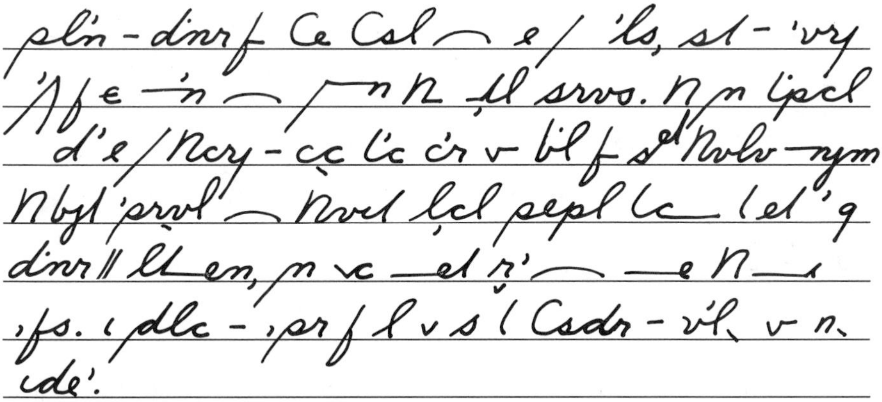

Assignment 5 — **Letter 1**. Read and write each of the preview words and phrases for Letter 1 until you can read and write each one rapidly and accurately. Then read and write the shorthand for Letter 1 to build your writing speed.

Winter York outline memorandums edition

preparing Murray reasonable should be has been

to receive I can be please let me know

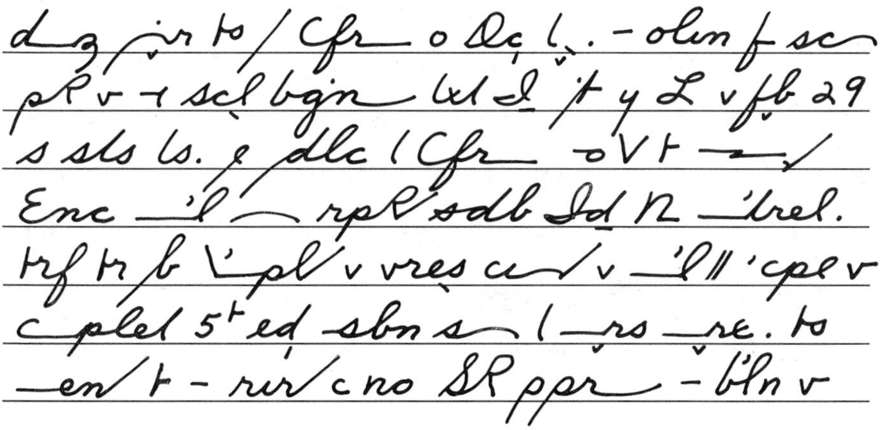

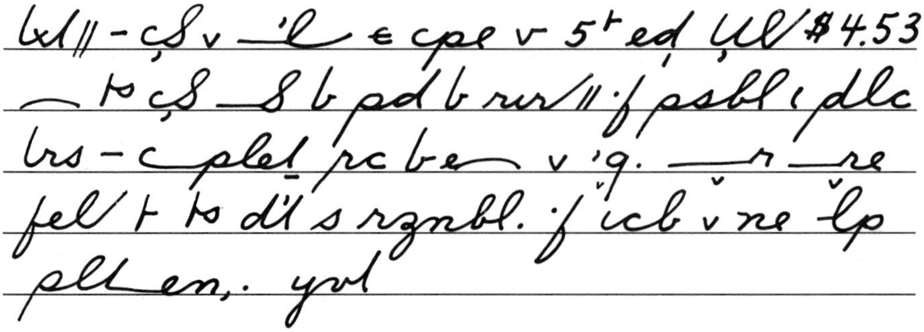

Assignment 6 — **Memorandum 2**. Read and write each preview word and phrase for Memorandum 2 until you can read and write each one rapidly and accurately. Then read and write the shorthand for memorandum 2 to build your writing speed.

Wood to be we can to meet

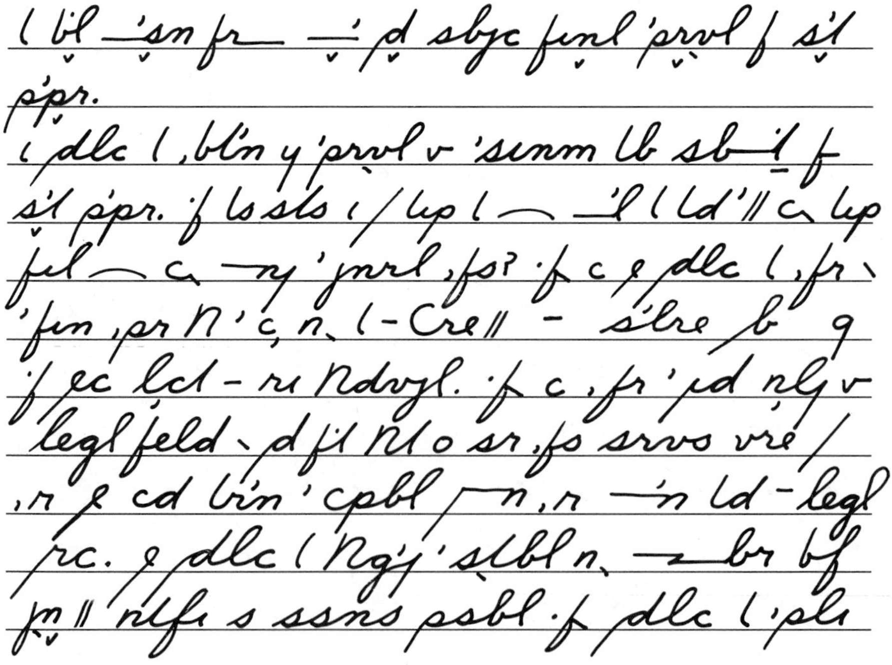

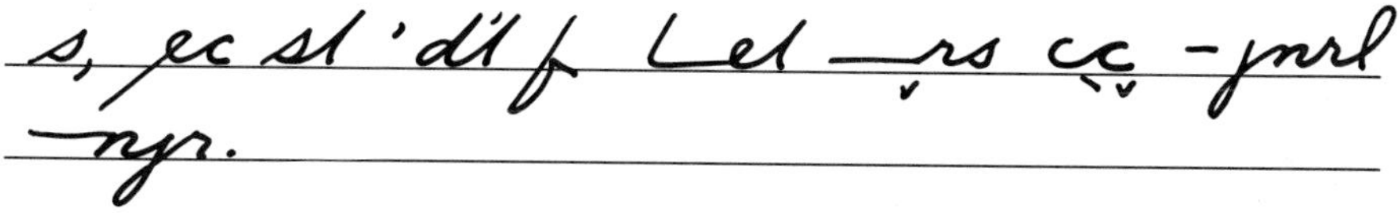

BUILDING SHORTHAND SPEED AND TRANSCRIPTION ACCURACY

Assignment 7 — **Self-testing**. Complete Unit 34 in your *Study Guide* before you proceed with the rest of this chapter.

Assignment 8 — **Taking tape dictation**. To write from dictation the sentences, letter, and memorandums in this chapter, use Cassette 19, Side A from *Theory and Speed-Building Tapes*.

Assignment 9 — **Taking live dictation**. Write from dictation the material which is printed at the end of this chapter. Your instructor will dictate to you at various speeds.

Assignment 10 — **Own-note transcription**. Transcribe at your best typing rate an accurate copy of at least one of the pieces of correspondence you took in shorthand in Assignment 9. Type the assignment in the style requested by your instructor.

Assignment 11 — **Supplementary dictation**. If instructed to do so, read and write the additional material for this chapter found in Appendix B, "Supplementary Correspondence for Dictation."

TRANSCRIPT OF SHORTHAND—ASSIGNMENT 2

1. I cannot accept credit after Monday, April 22.
2. I am glad you are able to meet your doctor (20) next Friday.
3. I would like to tell you of the great opportunity we feel will satisfy the government. (40)
4. Any senior may be glad to plan to be a good doctor.
5. Let me know if you are liked by the company doctor. (60)
6. Any senior would be glad to write to Mr. and Mrs. Well for us.
7. If you are right, it is not satisfactory (80) for you to pay more.
8. Dear Sir: I do not like to buy on credit.
9. He did not write to tell Mr. Friday of (100) his unsatisfactory credit. (106)

TRANSCRIPT OF SHORTHAND—ASSIGNMENT 3

1. Indicate where, when, and why the council will meet.
2. The factory will dye the paper navy, yellow, or silver. (20)
3. Mrs. Wood, the manager, would like to see you next week.
4. The new operator, Mr. White, will be away a week.
5. Let (40) me know if you would like to file, to type, or to run the general office.
6. Are you aware of all the medical and (60) legal counsel we can obtain?
7. The clerk will weigh the package, and June will confirm the meeting, and I will pay for (80) the parcel before I leave the office.
8. I plan to judge at the fall fair, at the summer swim meet, and at the senior (100) football game.
9. Do not fail to encourage road and water safety at your next committee meeting.
10. Will the driver, (120) Jean Edge, be able to pick up the damaged baggage?
11. The judge concluded the case, and the male nurse confirmed the (140) injury, but the wife of the witness will be somewhat concerned for the welfare of the juvenile. (158)

TRANSCRIPT OF SHORTHAND—ASSIGNMENT 4

Memorandum 1

TO: Mabel Sweet, General Manager
FROM: John Seal
SUBJECT: Ray Park

The senior waiter, Ray Park, will apply for approval of his new assignment. As manager of the committee, (20) he will be able to improve the regular service, and he will plan the dinner for the County Council, (40) and he will also set the average wage for each man and woman in the hotel service. In one typical (60) day he will encourage the cook, take care of the bill for the suite, involve management in budget approval, and (80) invite local people to come to eat a good dinner.

Let me know when you can meet Ray and me in my office. (100) I would like the opportunity for all of us to consider the value of the new idea. (*AW 117; SW 118; SI 1.41*)

TRANSCRIPT OF SHORTHAND—ASSIGNMENT 5

Letter 2 Dear Ms. Winter: This will confirm our discussion Tuesday. The outline for the second part of the high school beginning (20) text enclosed with your letter of February 29 is satisfactory to us. We would like to (40) confirm, however, that memorandums, electronic mail, and reports should be included in the material. (60) Therefore, there will be examples of various kinds of mail.

A copy of the complete Fifth edition has been sent to Mrs. March. This means that the writers can now start preparing the balance of the text.

The (100) cost of mailing each copy of the Fifth edition totals $4.53, and this cost must be paid (120) by the writers.

If possible, I would like to receive the completed work by the end of August. Mr. (140) Murray feels that this date is reasonable. If I can be of any help, please let me know. Yours very truly, (*AW 150; SW 159; SI 1.48*)

TRANSCRIPT OF SHORTHAND—ASSIGNMENT 6

Memorandum 2

TO: Bill Mason
FROM: May Wood
SUBJECT: Final Approval for Saturday Paper

I would like to obtain your approval of the assignment to be submitted for the Saturday paper. If (20) it is satisfactory, I will type it and mail it today.

Can you type, file, and can you manage a general (40) office? If you can, we would like to offer you a fine opportunity in a company new to the (60) country.

The salary will be good if we can locate the right individual. If you can offer a wide (80) knowledge of the legal field, you would fit into our senior office service very well, or we could train a (100) capable woman or man to do the legal work. We would like to engage a suitable new member before June. (120)

Notify us as soon as possible if you would like to apply, so we can set a date for you to meet (140) Mrs. Cook, the general manager. (*AW 144; SW 146; SI 1.42*)

CHAPTER 35

THEORY REVIEW OF CHAPTERS 9 THROUGH 12

Assignment 1 — **Theory Review**. The following sentence contains all the writing principles presented in Chapters 9 through 12. Study the writing principles and practise reading and writing this sentence until you can do so without hesitation and can quickly identify each writing principle.

She advised her children to transfer the deposit this evening.

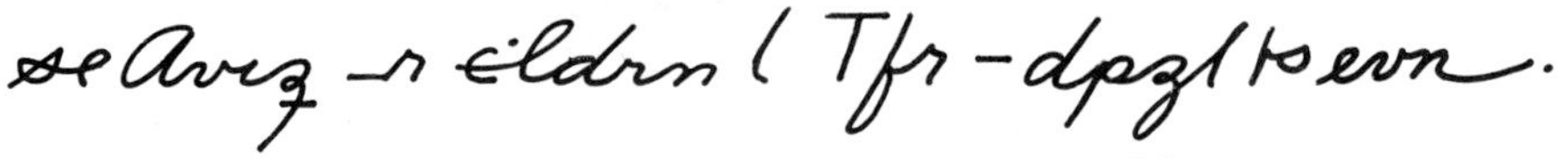

SUMMARY OF WRITING PRINCIPLES

H	Write a short dash thus — to express the sound of *h*.
SH	Write an *h* dash through the *s* to express *sh*.
BE-DE-RE	Omit the *e* in the prefixes *be*, *de*, and *re*.
CH	Write an *h* dash through the *c* to express *ch*.
TH	Join an *h* dash to the *t* to express *th*.
HARD S AND Z	Write a small longhand *z* to express the hard sound of *s*.
NG-ING-THING	Write a long, curved stroke thus ‿ to express the sounds of *ng-ing-thing*.
AD-ADD	Write a capital *a* to express the prefix *ad*.
TRANS	Write a capital *T* to express the prefix *trans*.

Assignment 2 — **Abbreviations and phrasing review**. Read and write the following sentences containing abbreviations and phrases until you can write them quickly and easily and without hesitation.

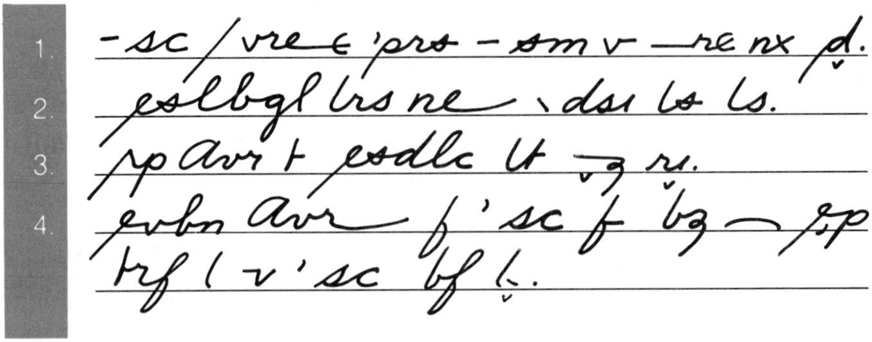
1.
2.
3.
4.

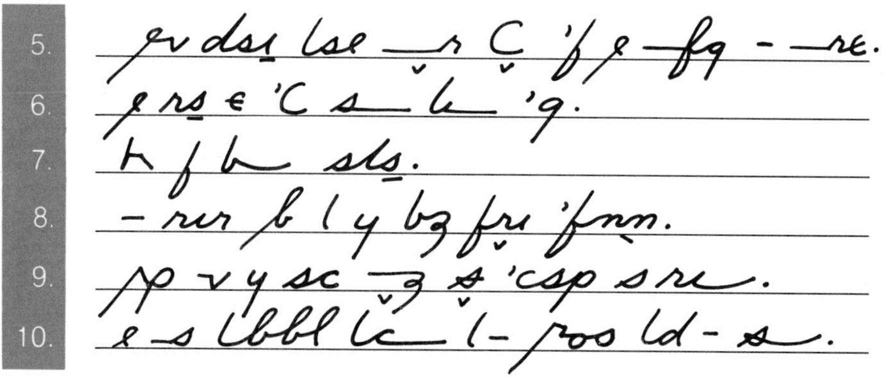

BUILDING TRANSCRIPTION SKILLS

Assignment 3 – **Transcription skills review—punctuating a polite request.** Review the following rules for punctuating the polite request and then transcribe the sentences inserting the correct punctuation. The key to these sentences appears on page 211.

1. A polite request asks for action rather than an answer.

2. Use a period after a polite request.

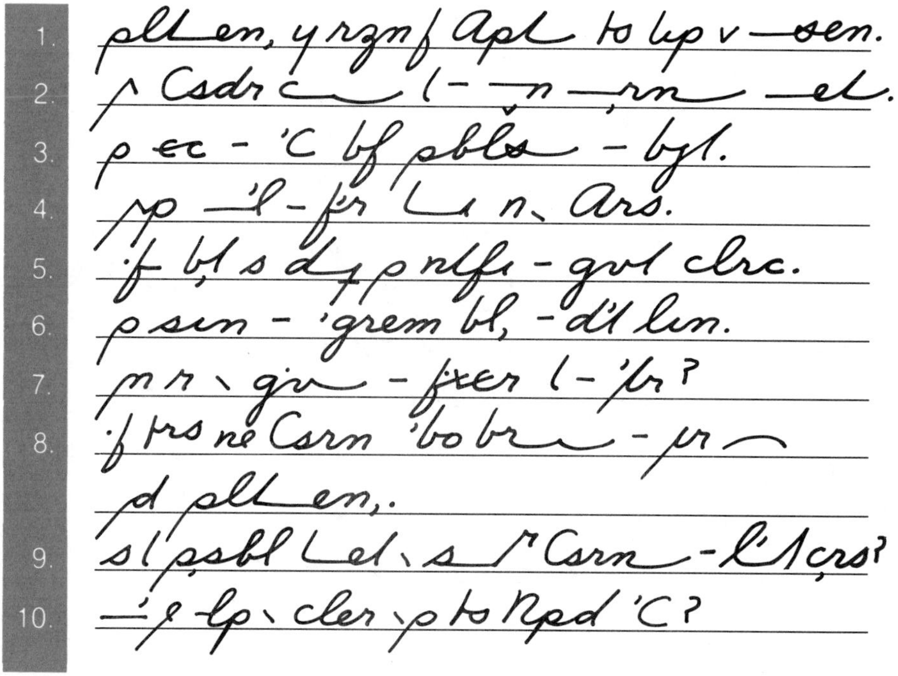

READING AND WRITING SHORTHAND

Assignments 4 and 5, except for those previewed, contain only words presented in Chapters and Units 1 through 12 of the text and *Study Guide*. Assignments 6 and 11 include vocabulary from Chapters and Units 1 through 32.

Assignment 4 — **Letter 1**. Read and write each of the preview words and phrases for Letter 1 until you can read and write each one rapidly and accurately. Then read and write the shorthand for Letter 1 to build your writing speed.

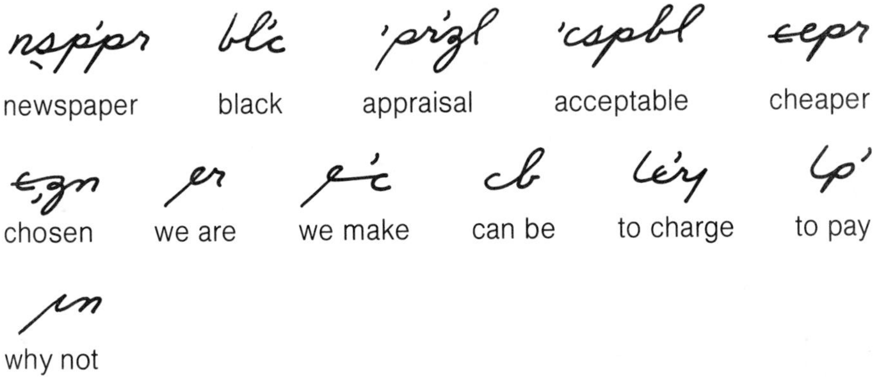
newspaper
black
appraisal
acceptable
cheaper
chosen
we are
we make
can be
to charge
to pay
why not

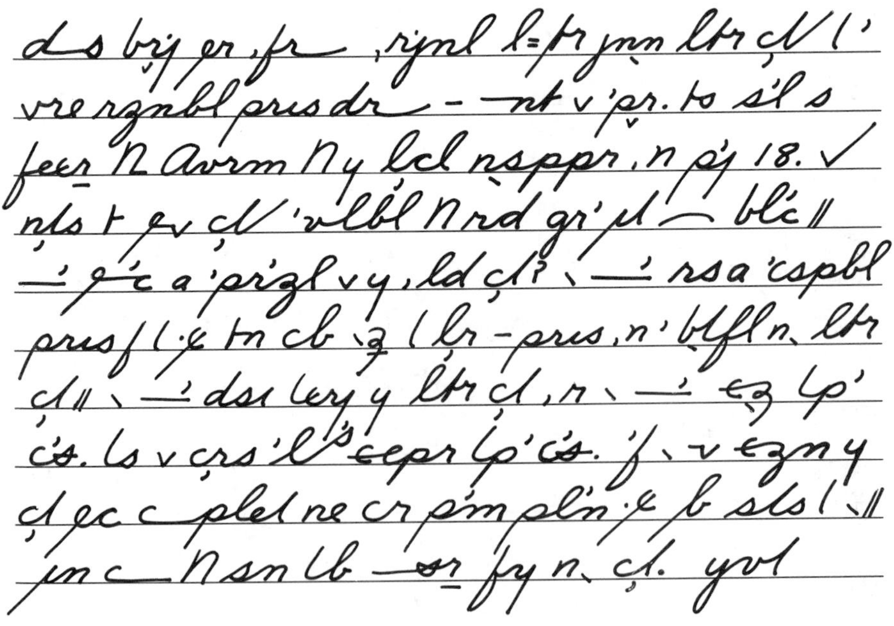

Assignment 5 — **Letter 2**. Read and write each preview word and phrase for Letter 2 until you can read and write each one rapidly and accurately. Then read and write the shorthand for Letter 2 to build your writing speed.

supplying for your to advertise should like to be able

to publish by return mail

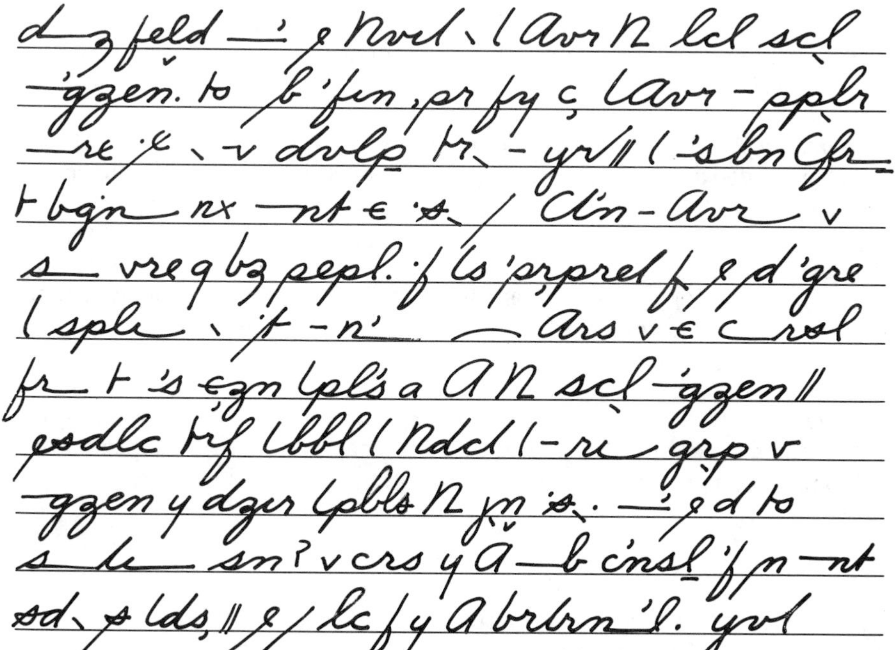

Assignment 6 — **Letter 3**. Read and write each phrase for Letter 3 until you can read and write each one rapidly and accurately. Then read and write the shorthand for Letter 3 to build your writing speed.

thank you I could not we have

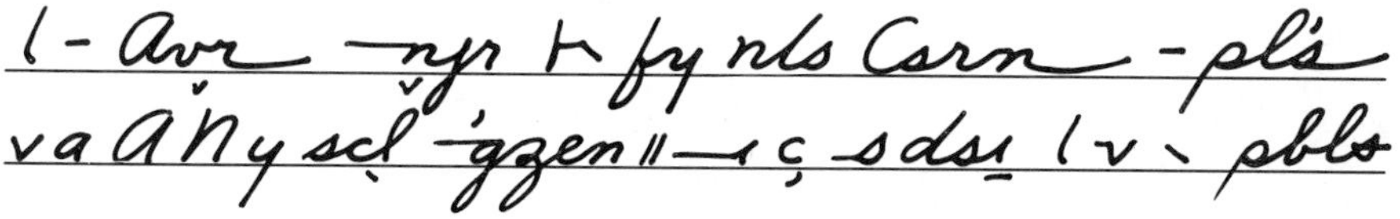

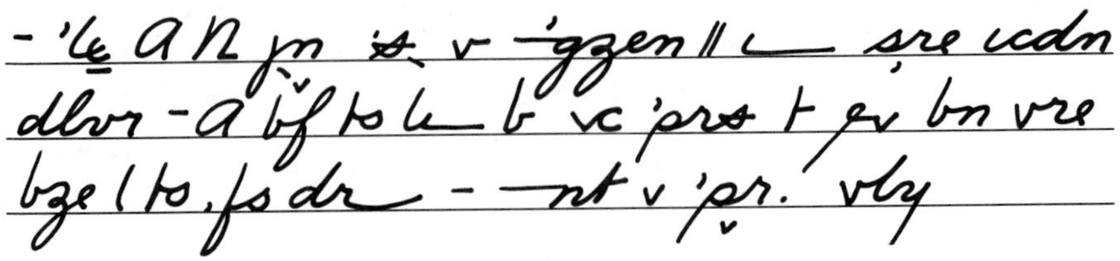

BUILDING SHORTHAND SPEED AND TRANSCRIPTION ACCURACY

Assignment 7 — **Self-testing**. Complete Unit 35 in your *Study Guide* before you proceed with the rest of this chapter.

Assignment 8 — **Taking tape dictation**. To write from dictation the sentences and letters in this chapter, use Cassette 20, Side A from *Theory and Speed-Building Tapes*.

Assignment 9 — **Taking live dictation**. Write from dictation the material which is printed at the end of this chapter. Your instructor will dictate to you at various speeds.

Assignment 10 — **Own-note transcription**. Transcribe at your best typing rate an accurate copy of at least one of the pieces of correspondence you took in shorthand in Assignment 9. Type the assignment in the style requested by your instructor.

Assignment 11 — **Supplementary dictation**. If instructed to do so, read and write the additional material for this chapter found in Appendix B, "Supplementary Correspondence for Dictation."

TRANSCRIPT OF SHORTHAND—ASSIGNMENT 2

1. The secretary will very much appreciate the shipment of the merchandise next Wednesday.
2. We shall be glad (20) to receive anything you decide to ship to us.
3. Will you please advertise that we should like to thank Ms. Wright.
4. We (40) have been advertising for a secretary for the business, and we hope, therefore, to have a secretary (60) before Tuesday.
5. We have decided to see Mr. Count after we manufacture the merchandise.
6. We received (80) each account some time ago.
7. Thank you for being satisfied.

8. The writer will be at your business Friday afternoon. (100)
9. Will you please have your secretary, Ms. Short, accept his writing.
10. He has to be able to come to the (120) warehouse to do the shipping. (125)

TRANSCRIPT OF SHORTHAND—ASSIGNMENT 3

1. Please let me know your reason for adopting this type of machine.
2. Will you consider coming to the Monday (20) morning meeting.
3. Please check the account before publishing the budget.
4. Will you please mail the fare to my new address.
5. If (40) the boat is damaged, please notify the government clerk.
6. Please sign the agreement below the date line.
7. When are (60) you giving the fixture to the waiter?
8. If there is any concern about bringing the wire and wood, please let me (80) know.
9. Is it possible to meet you somehwere concerning the language course?
10. May we help you clear up this unpaid (100) account? (101)

TRANSCRIPT OF SHORTHAND—ASSIGNMENT 4

Letter 1 Dear Miss Bridge: We are offering original, all-weather, genuine leather coats at a very reasonable (20) price during the month of April. This sale is featured in the advertisement in your local newspaper on page (40) 18. You will notice that we have coats available in red, gray, white, and black.

May we make an appraisal of your (60) old coat? You may receive an acceptable price for it which then can be used to lower the price on a beautiful, (80) new leather coat.

You may decide to charge your leather coat, or you may choose to pay cash. It is, of course, always (100) cheaper to pay cash. After you have chosen your coat, we can complete any credit payment plan which will be (120) satisfactory to you.

Why not come in soon to be measured for your new coat. Yours very truly, (*AW 139; SW 137; SI 1.38*)

TRANSCRIPT OF SHORTHAND—ASSIGNMENT 5

Letter 2 Dear Ms. Field: May we invite you to advertise in the local school magazine. This will be a fine opportunity (20) for your company to advertise the popular merchandise which you have developed through the years.

It (40) has been confirmed that beginning next month each issue will contain the advertising of some very good business (60) people. If it is appropriate for you, we would agree to supplying you with the name and address of (80) each commercial firm that has chosen to place an ad in the school magazine.

We should like, therefore, to be able (100) to indicate to the writing group of the magazine your desire to publish in the June issue. May we do (120) this sometime soon? Of course, your ad may be cancelled after one month, should you wish to do so.

We will look for your ad (140) by return mail. Yours very truly, (*AW 146; SW 146; SI 1.40*)

TRANSCRIPT OF SHORTHAND—ASSIGNMENT 6

Letter 3 To the Advertising Manager: Thank you for your notice concerning the placing of an ad in your school magazine. (20)

My company has decided to have you publish the attached ad in the June issue of the magazine. (40)

I am sorry I could not deliver the ad before this time, but you can appreciate that we have been very (60) busy at this office during the month of April. Very truly yours, (*AW 70; SW 74; SI 1.47*)

CHAPTER 36

BUSINESS LETTER DICTATION AND TRANSCRIPTION

Assignment 1 — **Review chart**. The chart below contains all the writing principles reviewed in Chapters 33 through 35. Transcribe each word quickly and accurately. The numbers in the left column indicate the chapter in which the writing principle was first introduced. If you have difficulty reading or writing any outline, review the writing principle and practise reading and writing other words incorporating that principle. The key to this chart appears at the end of this chapter.

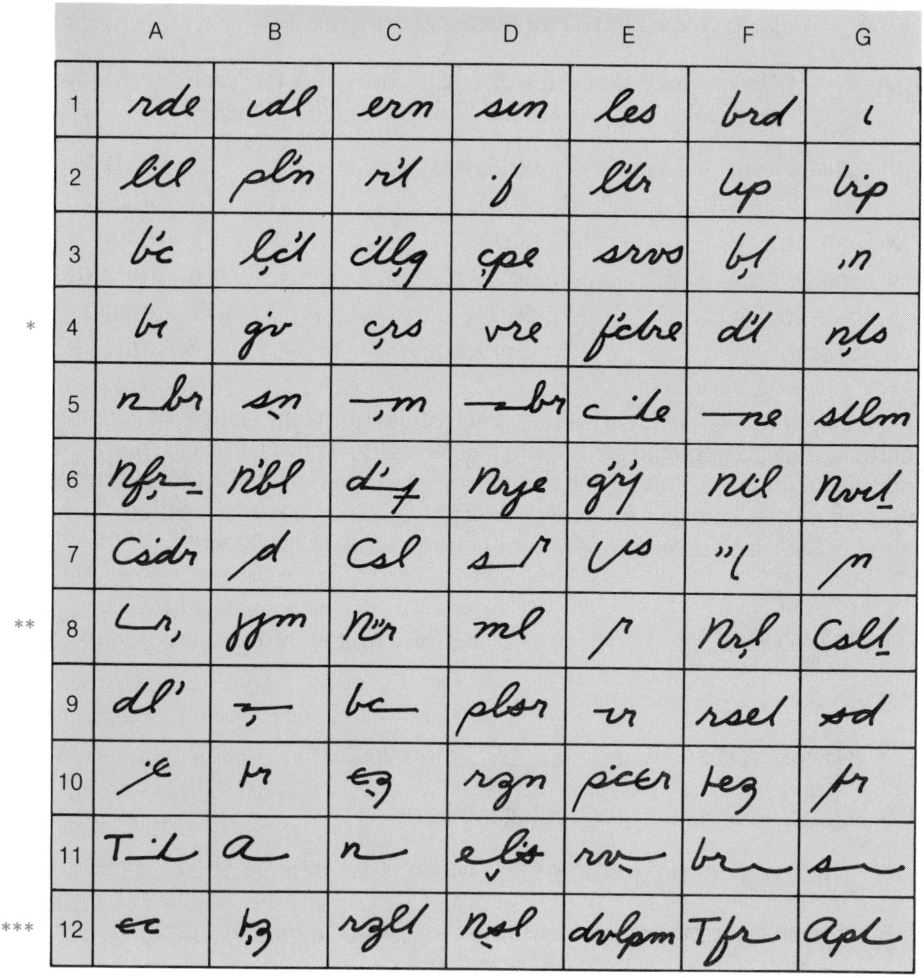

A
B
C
D
E
F
G
1
2
3
4
5
6
7
8
9
10
11
12

*Random review, Chapters 1–4
**Random review, Chapters 5–8
***Random review, Chapters 9–12

BUILDING TRANSCRIPTION SKILLS

Assignment 2 — **Spelling review**. Follow these steps to check your ability to spell the words below correctly:

Step 1. Pronounce each word slowly as you note how each word is spelled.

Step 2. Write the shorthand outline for each word in a column on the left side of your shorthand notebook.

Step 3. Close your textbook and write the transcript of each outline you have written in your notebook.

Step 4. Check your transcript of each word with the spelling in your textbook. Study any words you may have misspelled.

1. advice
2. advise
3. among
4. chequing
5. course
6. coarse
7. coming
8. council
9. counsel
10. development
11. enrol
12. mortgage
13. practice
14. practise
15. received
16. therefore
17. unpaid
18. urge

Assignment 3 — **Spelling review**. Each of the following sentences contains outlines that are frequently transcribed incorrectly. Transcribe each shorthand outline in your notebook. Then compare your answers with the key located at the end of this chapter. Review any words you may have misspelled. Then write the outlines several times, until you can write them fluently.

1. May I  you to give  only when you are asked for it.
2. He found some weeds 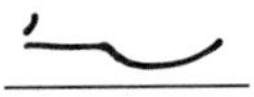 the flowers.
3. Open a  account at the bank.
4. The traps on the golf  were filled with  sand.
5. If Jean is  with you, tell her to bring her swim suit.
6. A  was set up to  the students.
7. The housing  was built within six months.

8. Ask your friends to _Nrl_ early for the cooking class.
9. When the _rgf_ rate went up, she was forced to sell her house.
10. _prcls_ your pitching arm in preparation for Tuesday's baseball _prcls_.
11. The letter was _rs_ three days after it was mailed.
12. You will, _trf_, take your lunch break early.
13. The _Npd_ bill carried a substantial interest rate.
14. We _ry_ you to pay your bills on time.

READING AND WRITING SHORTHAND

Assignments 4 and 5, except for those previewed, contain only words presented in Chapters and Units 1 through 12 of the text and *Study Guide*. Assignments 6 and 11 include vocabulary from Chapters and Units 1 through 32.

Assignment 4 — **Letter 1**. Read and write each preview word and phrase for Letter 1 until you can read and write each one rapidly and accurately. Then read and write the shorthand for Letter 1 to build your writing speed.

b,tn	fcer	ep	tbr,	vbn
Boatman	featuring	we hope	to borrow	have been
fsl	sec	tbjl	tNvil	tcsll
for so long	she can	to budget	to invite	to consult
trv				
to review				

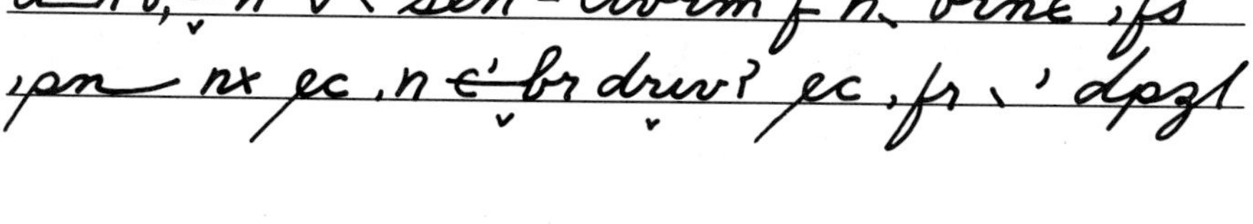

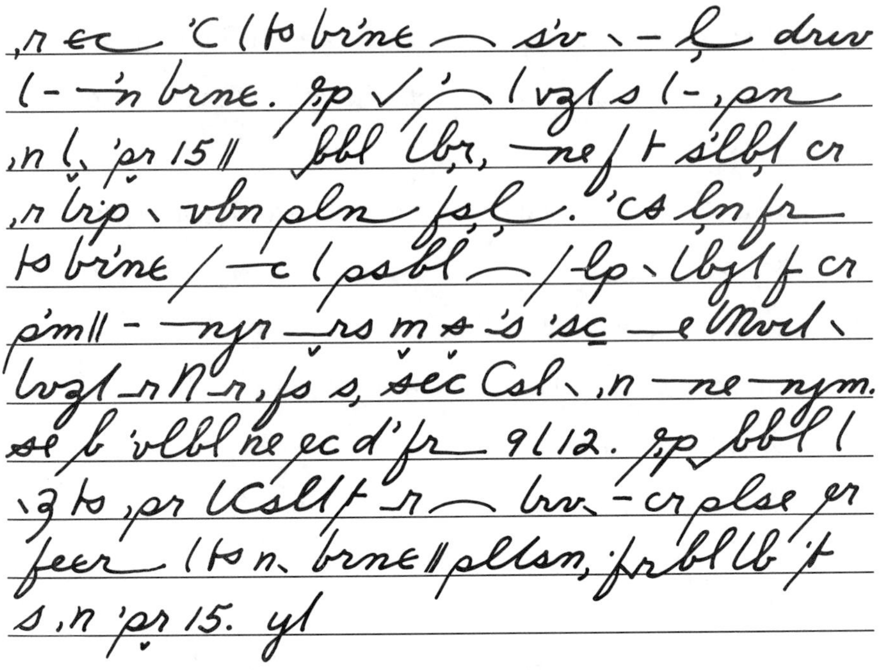

Assignment 5 — **Letter 2**. Read and write each of the preview words and phrases for Letter 2 until you can read and write each one rapidly and accurately. Then read and write the shorthand for Letter 2 to build your writing speed.

Cashwell Belwood to secure would be has not been

to cancel

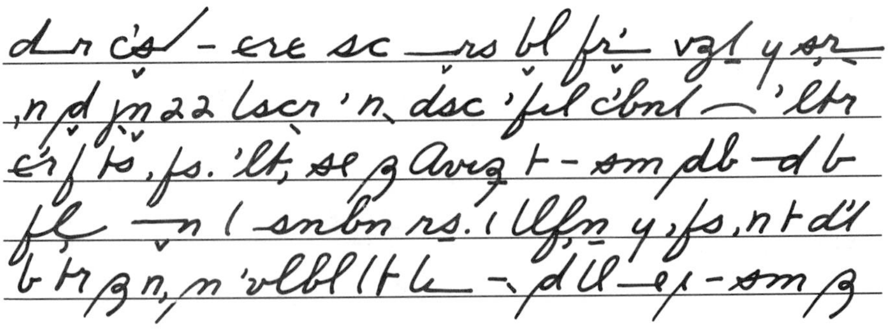

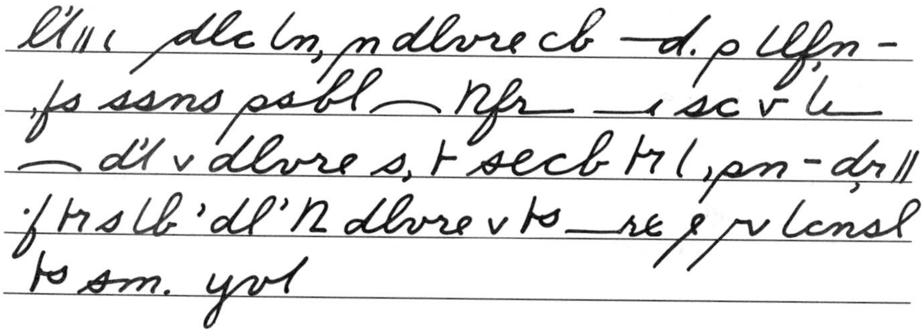

Assignment 6 — **Letter 3**. Read and write each of the preview words and phrases for Letter 3 until you can read and write each one rapidly and accurately. Then read and write the shorthand for Letter 3 to build your writing speed.

Waldonia Bristol blue crystal pre-sale post-sale

bargain We are now in a position to offer

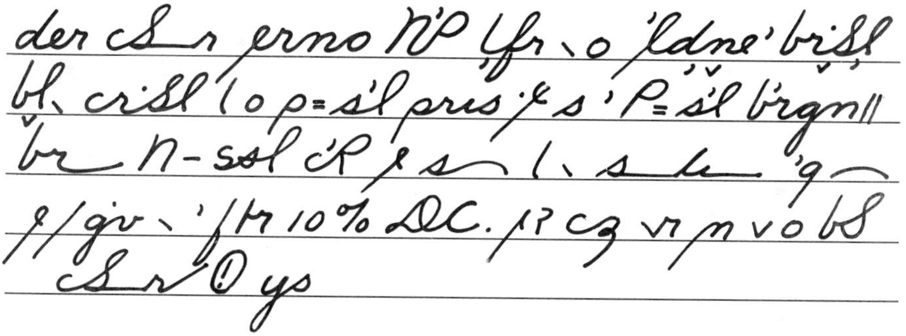

BUILDING SHORTHAND SPEED AND TRANSCRIPTION ACCURACY

Assignment 7 — **Self-testing**. Complete Unit 36 in your *Study Guide* before you proceed with the rest of this chapter.

Assignment 8 — **Taking tape dictation**. To write the letters in this chapter from dictation, use Cassette 20, Side A from *Theory and Speed Building Tapes*.

Assignment 9 — **Taking live dictation**. Write from dictation the material which is printed at the end of this chapter. Your instructor will dictate to you at various speeds.

Assignment 10 — **Own-note transcription**. Transcribe at your best typing rate an accurate copy of at least one of the pieces of correspondence you took in shorthand in Assignment 9. Type the assignment in the style requested by your instructor.

Assignment 11 — **Supplementary dictation**. If instructed to do so, read and write the additional material for this chapter found in Appendix B, "Supplementary Correspondence for Dictation."

Key to Assignment 1 — **Review Chart**

	A	B	C	D	E	F	G
1	ready	idle	earn	sign	lease	bread	eye/I
2	little	plan/ plain/ plane	rat/ rate	if	latter/ later	type	trip
3	back/ bake	locate	catalogue	copy	service	bought/ boat	on/own
4	buy	give	course/ coarse	very	factory	date	notice
5	number	soon	moment	member	committee	many/ money	settlement
6	informed	unable/ enable	damaged	energy	garage	until	invited
7	consider	would/ wood	council/ counsel	somewhere	twice	await	one/ won
8	tomorrow	judgment	unaware	mental	where/ were	enroll	consulted
9	delay	home	become	pleasure	hire/ higher	receipt	should/shed
10	which/ witch	their/ there	choose	reason	picture	these	weather/ whether
11	transmitting	adding	nothing	English	reviewing	bringing	something
12	cheque/ check	those	result	unusual	development	transferring	adopting

Key to Assignment 3 — **Spelling review**
1. advise/advice 2. among 3. chequing 4. course/coarse
5. coming 6. council/counsel 7. development 8. enrol
9. mortgage 10. Practise/practice 11. received 12. therefore
13. unpaid 14. urge

TRANSCRIPT OF SHORTHAND—ASSIGNMENT 4

Letter 1 Dear Mr. Boatman: Have you seen the advertisement for the new branch office opening next week on Chamber Drive? We can offer you (20) a deposit or chequing account at this branch and save you the long drive to the main branch. We hope you will want to (40) visit us at the opening on Tuesday, April 15.

You will be able to borrow money for that sailboat, (60) car, or trip you have been planning for so long. A cash loan from this branch will make it possible and will help you to (80) budget for the credit payment.

The manager, Mrs. M. Short, has asked me to invite you to visit her in (100) her office so she can counsel you on money management. She will be available any week day from (120) 9 to 12. We hope you will be able to use this opportunity to consult with her and to review the (140) credit policy we are featuring at this new branch.

Please let us know if you are able to (160) be with us on April 15. Yours truly, (*AW 176; SW 168; SI 1.32*)

TRANSCRIPT OF SHORTHAND—ASSIGNMENT 5

Letter 2 Dear Mr. Cashwell: The church secretary, Mrs. Belle Frame, visited your showroom on Wednesday, June 22, (20) to secure a new desk, a file cabinet, and a leather chair for this office. Although she was advised that the (40) shipment would be made by the following Monday, it has not been received. I telephoned your office on that date, (60) but there was no one available at that time who would tell me why the shipment was late.

I would like to know when (80) delivery can be made. Please telephone the office as soon as possible, and inform my secretary (100) of the time and date of delivery so that she can be there to open the door.

If there is to be a (120) delay in the delivery of this merchandise, we will have to cancel this shipment. Yours very truly, (Rushmore) (*AW 137; SW 139; SI 1.42*)

TRANSCRIPT OF SHORTHAND—ASSIGNMENT 6

Letter 3 Dear Customer: We are now in a position to offer you our Waldonia Bristol Blue crystal at our (20) pre-sale price, which is a post-sale bargain.

Bring in the special card we sent to you some time ago, and we will give you (40) a further 10 per cent discount. Why? Because you are one of our best customers! Yours sincerely, (*AW 59; SW 57; SI 1.35*)

TRANSCRIPTION TEST 1

- Your instructor will provide dictation material to be taken in shorthand.
- Transcribe each piece of dictation in an acceptable style as directed by your instructor.

CHAPTER 37

THEORY REVIEW OF CHAPTERS 13 THROUGH 16

Assignment 1 — **Theory Review.** The following sentence contains all the writing principles presented in Chapters 13 through 16. Study the writing principles and practise reading and writing this sentence until you can do so without hesitation and can quickly identify each writing principle.

Everybody left the annual school display quickly, including my friends.

SUMMARY OF WRITING PRINCIPLES

NT-ND	Write a curved stroke thus ⁀ to express the combinations *nt* or *nd*.
AN	Write a small longhand *a* to express the prefix *an*.
DIS-DES	Write a longhand capital *D* to express the prefixes *dis* and *des*.
QU	Write only *q* for the combination *qu*.
INCL ENCLOSE	Write a longhand capital *I* to express the combination *incl* and the following vowel and the word *enclose*.
LY	Write a short, disjoined dash close to the word to which it belongs to express the ending *ly*. Write words in full that end in *l* and then add the *ly* dash.
ADDING S	Write an upward, slanted, straight stroke joined to the last letter or symbol of a word to add *s* to a root word. This same stroke is used to add *s* to a word to form the possessive.
EVER-EVERY	Write a disjoined capital *V* for words *ever* and *every* and the prefixes and suffixes *ever-every*.

Assignment 2 — **Abbreviations and phrasing review.** Read and write the following sentences containing abbreviations and phrases until you can write them quickly and easily and without hesitation.

1. 

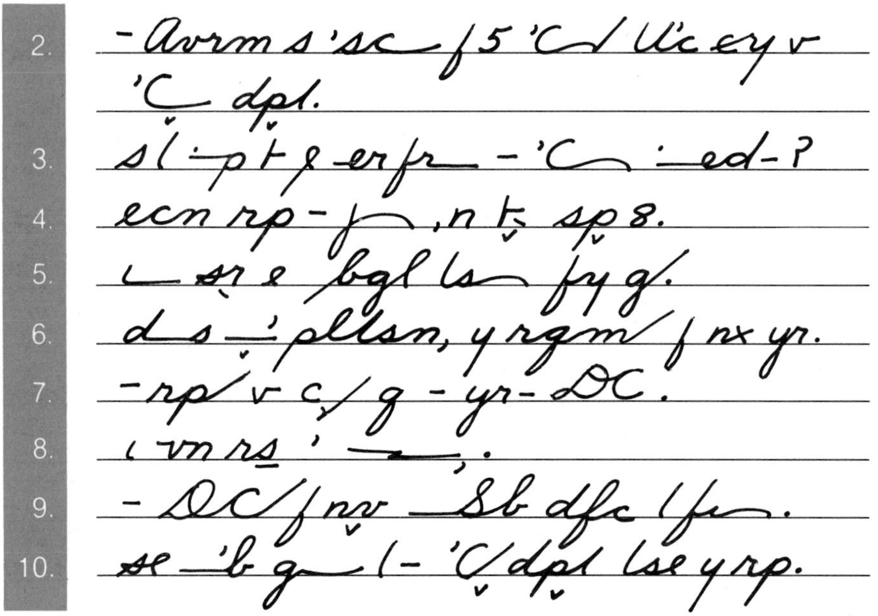

BUILDING TRANSCRIPTION SKILLS

Assignment 3 — **Transcription skills review — the semicolon.** Review the following rules governing the use of the semicolon in punctuating sentences joined by a transitional word. Then, transcribe the sentences, inserting the correct punctuation. The key to these sentences appears on page 228.

1. Place a semicolon before a transitional word or phrase that joins two sentences.

2. Place a comma after a transitional word or phrase that joins two sentences.

3. Common transitional words and phrases include: therefore, however, accordingly, consequently, in fact, as a result.

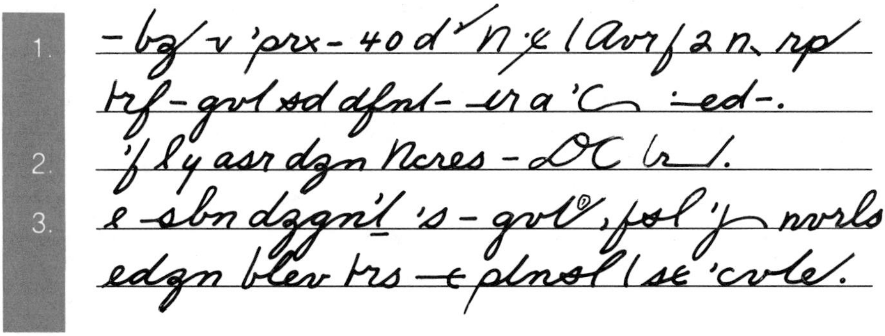

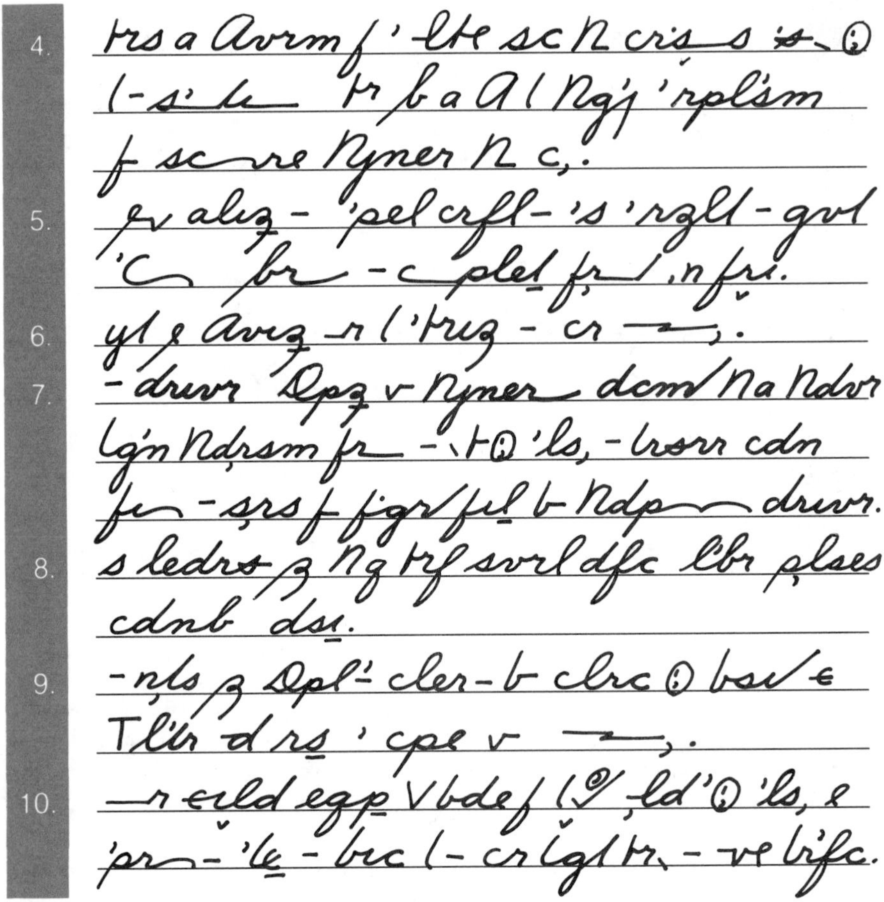

READING AND WRITING SHORTHAND

Assignments 4 and 5, except for those previewed, contain only words presented in Chapters and Units 1 through 16 of the text and *Study Guide*. Assignments 6 and 11 include vocabulary from Chapters and Units 1 through 32.

Assignment 4 — **Letter 1.** Read and write each preview word and phrase for Letter 1 until you can read and write each one rapidly and accurately. Then read and write the shorthand for Letter 1 to build your writing speed.

concerning | to submit | to begin | as well as | I am sure

would be glad

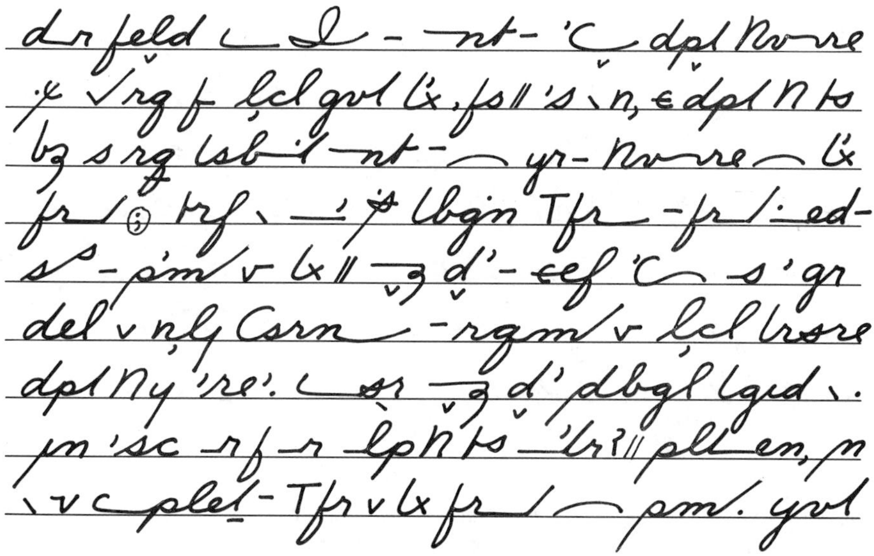

Assignment 5 — **Letter 2.** Read and write each of the preview words and phrases for Letter 2 until you can read and write each one rapidly and accurately. Then read and write the shorthand for Letter 2 to build your writing speed.

Lowe valued shoppers chains silver-framed

offering treasure you will be to encourage to shop

to choose

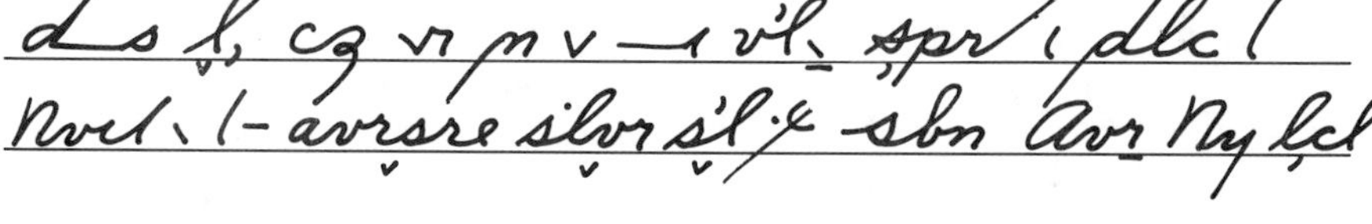

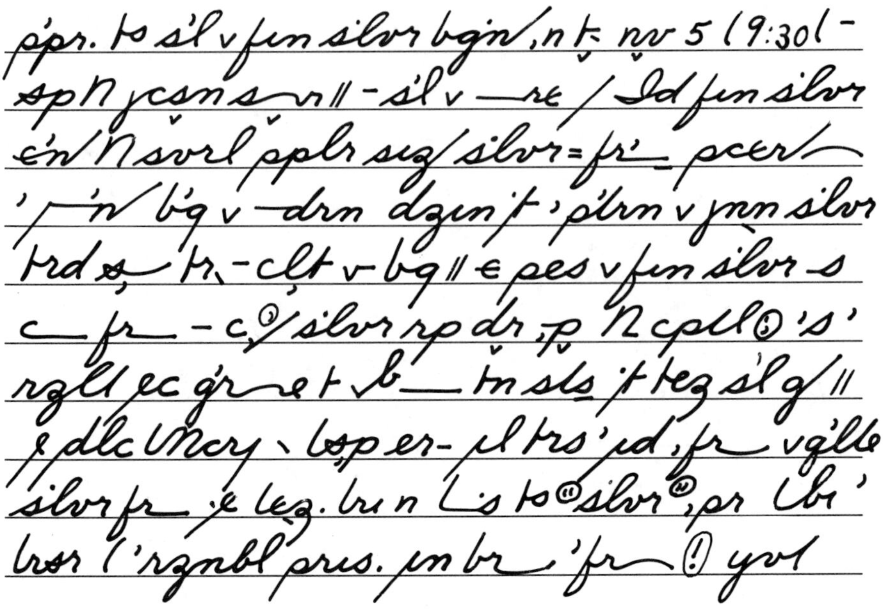

Assignment 6 — **Letter 3.** Read and write each preview word and phrase for Letter 3 until you can read and write each one rapidly and accurately. Then read and write the shorthand for Letter 3 to build your writing speed.

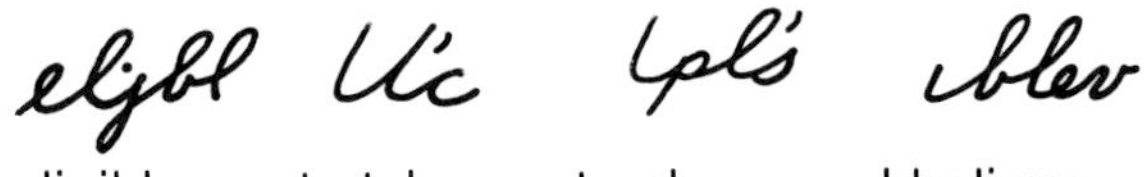

eligible to take to place I believe

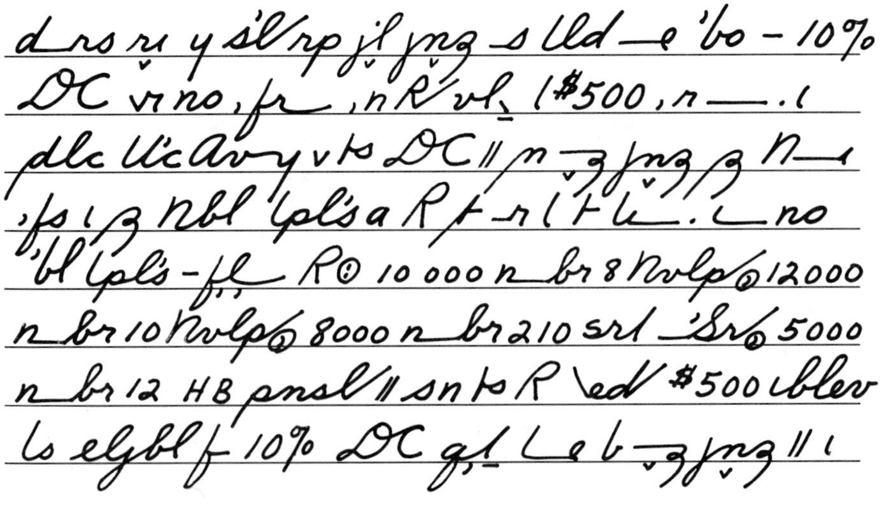

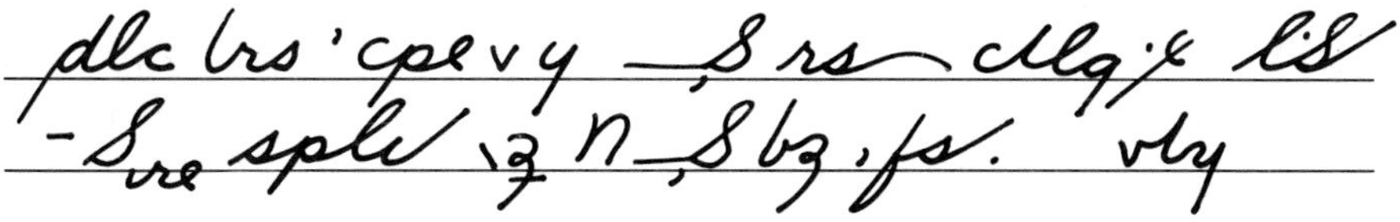

BUILDING SHORTHAND SPEED AND TRANSCRIPTION ACCURACY

Assignment 7 — **Self-testing.** Complete Unit 37 in your *Study Guide* before you proceed with the rest of this chapter.

Assignment 8 — **Taking tape dictation.** To write from dictation the sentences and letters in this chapter, use Cassette 21, Side A from *Theory and Speed-Building Tapes*.

Assignment 9 — **Taking live dictation.** Write from dictation the material which is printed at the end of this chapter. Your instructor will dictate to you at various speeds.

Assignment 10 — **Own-note transcription.** Transcribe at your best typing rate an accurate copy of at least one of the pieces of correspondence you took in shorthand in Assignment 9. Type the assignment in the style requested by your instructor.

Assignment 11 — **Supplementary dictation.** If instructed to do so, read and write the additional material for this chapter found in Appendix B, "Supplementary Correspondence for Dictation."

TRANSCRIPT OF SHORTHAND—ASSIGNMENT 2

1. I shall be glad to answer your questions.
2. The advertisement is asking for five accountants to take charge of the (20) Accounting Department.
3. Is it important that we hear from the accountant immediately?
4. He cannot represent (40) the gentlemen on Thursday, September 8.
5. I am sure he will be glad to send for your goods.
6. Dear Miss Maye: Please (60) let us know your requirements for next year.
7. The representatives of the companies question the yearly discount. (80)
8. I have not received a memorandum.

9. The discounts for November must be difficult to find.
10. She may be going (100) to the Accounts Department to see your representative. (111)

TRANSCRIPT OF SHORTHAND—ASSIGNMENT 3

1. The businesses have approximately forty days in which to advertise for two new representatives; (20) therefore, the government should definitely hire an accountant immediately.
2. After all, your answer does not (40) increase the discount terms.
3. He has been designated as the government's official agent; nevertheless, he does (60) not believe there is much potential to such activities.
4. There is an advertisement for a healthy (80) secretary in the Christmas issue; at the same time, there will be an ad to engage a replacement for the secondary (100) engineer in the company.
5. We have analysed the appeal carefully; as a result, the government (120) accountant will bring the completed forms on Friday.
6. Yet, we advised her to authorize the credit memo. (140)
7. The driver disposed of the engineering documents in an endeavor to gain endorsement from the youth; also, (160) the treasurer could not find the source for the figures filed by the independent driver.
8. His leadership was (180) in question; therefore, several difficult labor policies could not be decided.
9. The notice was displayed clearly (200) by the clerk; besides, each translator had received a copy of the memorandum.
10. Mr. Child equipped (220) everybody for Tuesday's holiday; also, he apparently attached the bike to the car to get through the heavy (240) traffic. (241)

TRANSCRIPT OF SHORTHAND—ASSIGNMENT 4

Letter 1 Dear Mr. Field: I am enclosing the monthly Accounting Department inventory which you will require for (20) the local government tax office.

As you know, each department in this business is required to submit monthly (40) and yearly inventory and tax forms; therefore, you may wish to begin transferring the forms immediately as (60) well as the payments of the tax.

Ms. Day, the chief accountant, has a great deal of knowledge concerning the requirements (80) of the local treasury department in your area. I am sure Ms. Day would be glad to guide you. Why (100) not ask her for her help in this matter?

Please let me know when you have completed the transfer of tax forms and payments. (120) Yours very truly, (*AW 120; SW 124; SI 1.45*)

TRANSCRIPT OF SHORTHAND—ASSIGNMENT 5

Letter 2 Dear Miss Lowe: Because you are one of my valued shoppers, I would like to invite you to the Anniversary (20) Silver Sale which has been advertised in your local paper. This sale of fine silver begins on Thursday, November (40) 5, at 09:30 at the shop in Jackson Centre.

The sale of merchandise will include fine silver chains in (60) several popular sizes, silver-framed pictures, and a woman's bag of modern design with a pattern of (80) genuine silver thread showing through the cloth of the bag.

Each piece of fine silver has come from the company's silver (100) representative, Dr. Hope, in the capital; as a result, we can guarantee that you will be more (120) than satisfied with these sale goods.

We would like to encourage you to shop early while there is a wide offering (140) of quality silver from which to choose. Try not to miss this "silver" opportunity to buy a treasure (160) at a reasonable price. Why not bring a friend! Yours very truly, (*AW 164; SW 171; SI 1.46*).

TRANSCRIPT OF SHORTHAND—ASSIGNMENT 6

Letter 3 Dear Mrs. Wright: Your sales representative, Jill Jones, has told me about the 10 per cent discount you are now (20) offering on orders valued at $500 or more. I would like to take advantage of this discount.

When (40) Ms. Jones was in my office, I was unable to place an order with her at that time. I am now able (60) to place the following order:

10 000 No. 8 envelopes
12 000 No. 10 envelopes
8 000 (80) No. 210 spirit masters
5 000 No. 12 HB pencils

Since this order exceeds $500, (100) I believe it is eligible for the 10 per cent discount quoted to me by Ms. Jones.

I would like to receive (120) a copy of your most recent catalogue which lists the stationery supplies used in most business offices. (140) Very truly yours, (*AW 137; SW 144; SI 1.47*)

CHAPTER 38

THEORY REVIEW OF CHAPTERS 17 THROUGH 20

Assignment 1 — **Theory Review.** The following sentence contains all the writing principles presented in Chapters 17 through 20. Study the writing principles and practise reading and writing this sentence until you can do so without hesitation and can quickly identify each writing principle.

The booklet outlines information and publicity on the self-service store

downtown.

SUMMARY OF WRITING PRINCIPLES

OUT	Write a small longhand *o* to express the prefix or suffix *out*.
SHUN	Write a short, vertical, downward stroke under the last letter or symbol of a word to express the *shun* sound and the preceding vowel.
SITY-CITY	Write a disjoined longhand capital *S* to express the combinations *sity-city* and the preceding vowel.
SELF	Write a small disjoined longhand *s* to express the prefix or suffix *self*.
ST	Write a longhand capital *S* to express the *st* combination.
OU-OW	Write a small longhand *o* to express *ou-ow*.

Assignment 2 — **Abbreviations and phrasing review.** Read and write the following sentences containing abbreviations and phrases until you can write them quickly and easily and without hesitation.

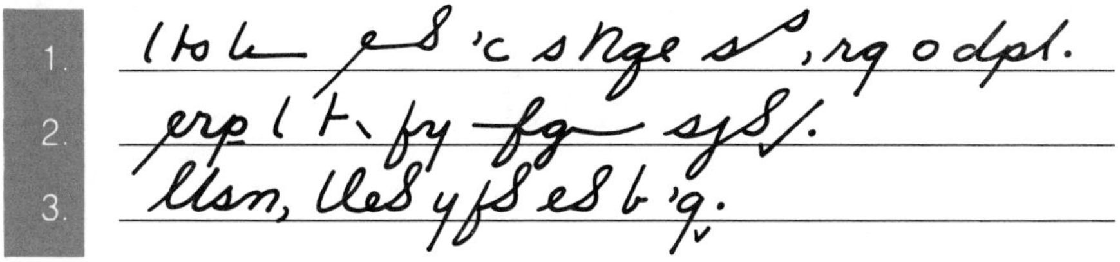

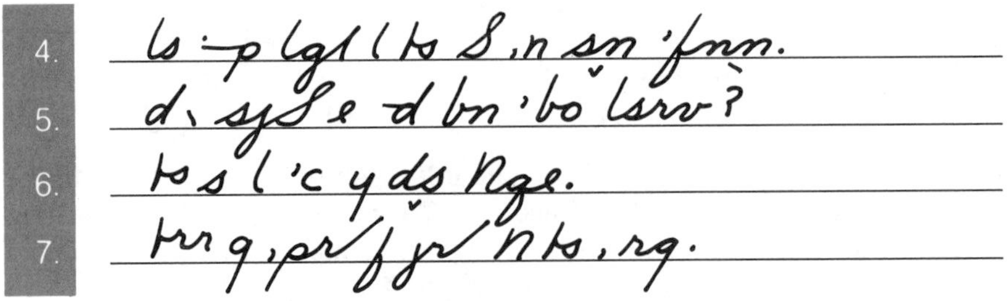

BUILDING TRANSCRIPTION SKILLS

Assignment 3 — **Transcription skills review—the apostrophe.** Review the following rules governing the use of the apostrophe, and then transcribe the sentences, inserting the correct punctuation. The key to these sentences appears on page 236.

1. **Forming the Singular Possessive.**
   To form the possessive of a singular word, add an apostrophe and an *s* to the word. Each possessive indicates "belonging to" or "of."

2. **Forming Contractions.**
   A contraction is a shortened form of the word or a group of words, for example: *can't* for *cannot*; *we've* for *we have*. Insert an apostrophe in a contraction to show that one or more letters have been omitted.

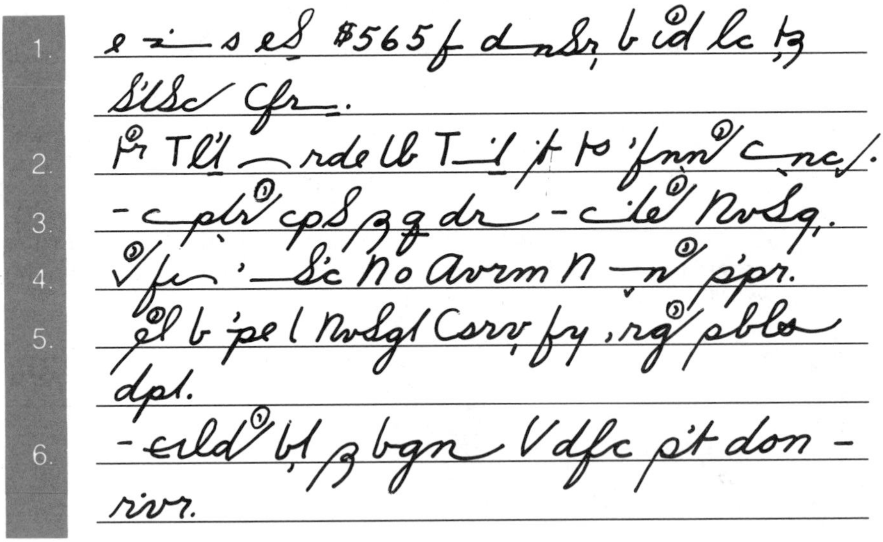

7. 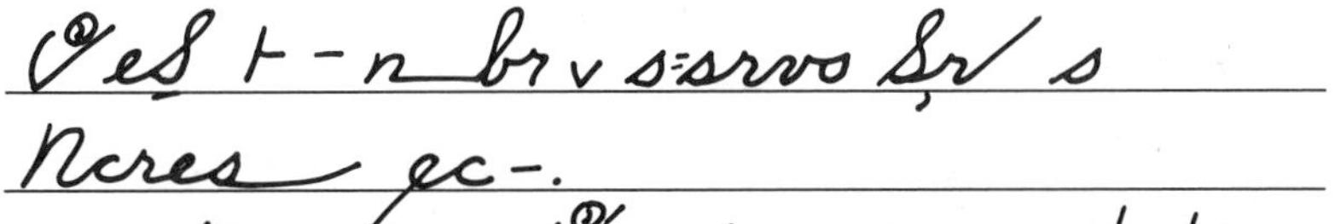

8. 

9. 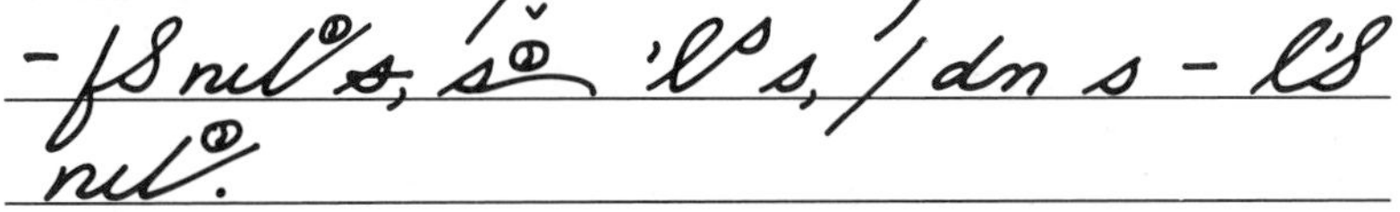

10. 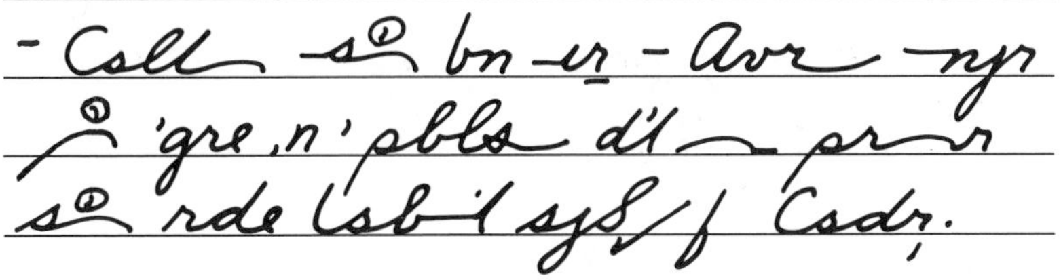

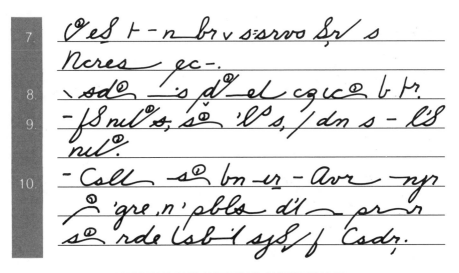

READING AND WRITING SHORTHAND

Assignments 4 and 5, except for those previewed, contain only words presented in Chapters and Units 1 through 20 of the text and study guide. Assignments 6 and 11 include vocabulary from Chapters and Units 1 through 32.

Assignment 4 — **Letter 1.** Read and write each of the preview words and phrases for Letter 1 until you can read and write each one rapidly and accurately. Then read and write the shorthand for Letter 1 to build your writing speed.

switching offset saved whatever considerations

values crew to satisfy please let us hear from

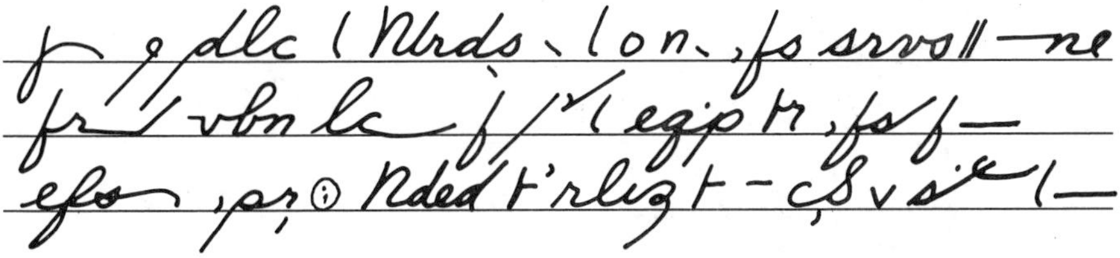

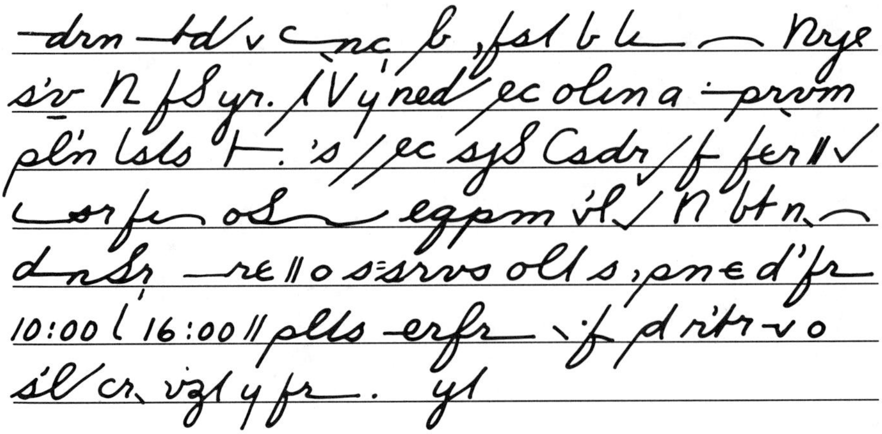

Assignment 5 — **Memorandum 1.** Read and write each of the preview words and phrases for Memorandum 1 until you can read and write each one rapidly and accurately. Then read and write the shorthand for Memorandum 1 to build your writing speed.

today's　making　established　I do not

as soon as possible　to determine　to do so

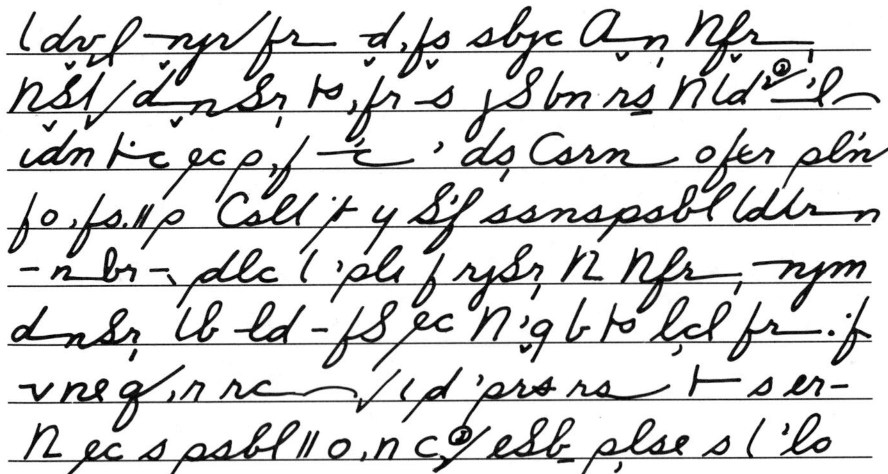

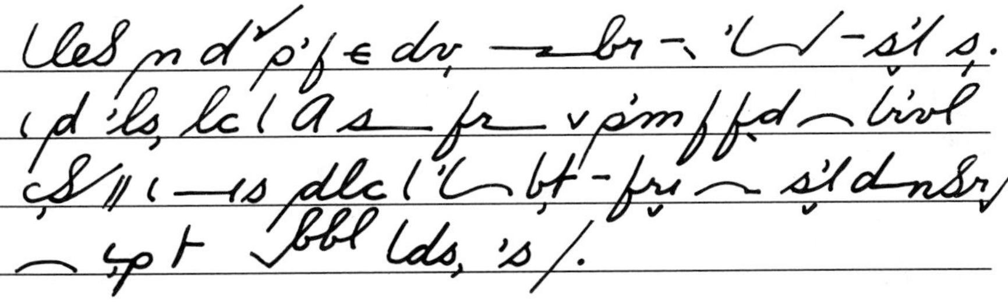

Assignment 6 — **Memorandum 2.** Read and write each of the preview words and phrases for Memorandum 2 until you can read and write each one rapidly and accurately. Then read and write the shorthand for Memorandum 2 to build your writing speed.

divisional wages keeping to have as many

please let me

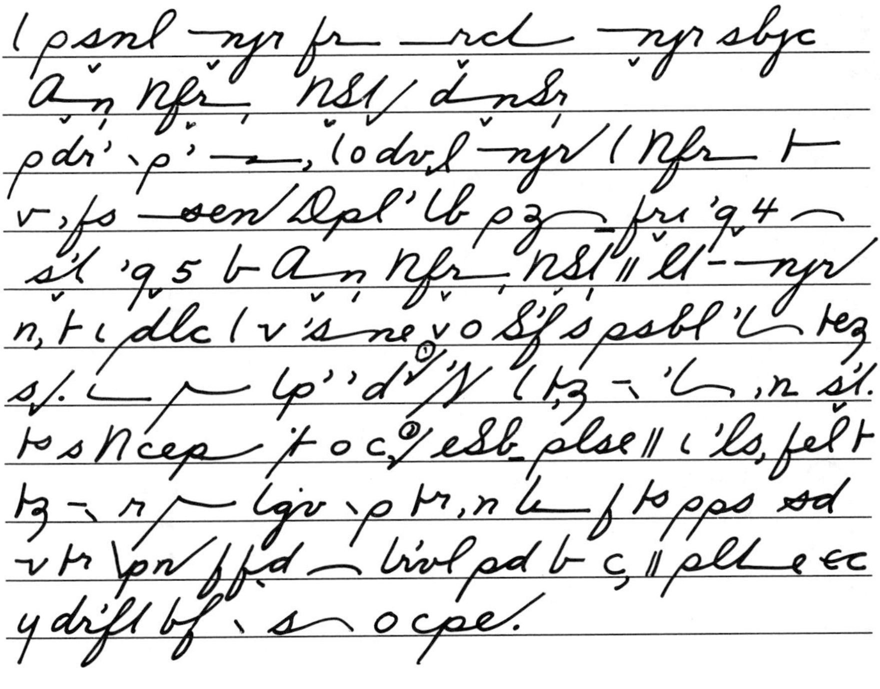

BUILDING SHORTHAND SPEED AND TRANSCRIPTION ACCURACY

Assignment 7 — **Self-testing.** Complete Unit 38 in your *Study Guide* before you proceed with the rest of this chapter.

Assignment 8 — **Taking tape dictation.** To write from dictation the sentences, letter, and memorandums in this chapter, use Cassette 21, Side A from *Theory and Speed-Building Tapes*.

Assignment 9 — **Taking live dictation.** Write from dictation the material which is printed at the end of this chapter. Your instructor will dictate to you at various speeds.

Assignment 10 — **Own-note transcription.** Transcribe at your best typing rate an accurate copy of at least one of the pieces of correspondence you took in shorthand in Assignment 9. Type the assignment in the style requested by your instructor.

Assignment 11 — **Supplementary dictation.** If instructed to do so, read and write the additional material for this chapter found in Appendix B, "Supplementary Correspondence for Dictation."

TRANSCRIPT OF SHORTHAND—ASSIGNMENT 2

1. At this time we must acknowledge his inquiry as well as organize our department.
2. We are pleased to thank you (20) for your manufacturing suggestions.
3. Let us know at least your first estimate by August.
4. It is important (40) to get to this street on Sunday afternoon.
5. Do you suggest he had been about to serve?
6. This is to acknowledge (60) your December inquiry.
7. There are good opportunities for juniors in this organization. (78)

TRANSCRIPT OF SHORTHAND—ASSIGNMENT 3

1. He, himself, estimated $565 for the demonstration, but I'd like those statistics (20) confirmed.
2. They're translated and ready to be transmitted with this afternoon's communications.
3. The computer's (40) capacity was questioned during the committee's investigation.

4. You'll find a mistake in our advertisement (60) in Monday's paper.
5. We'll be happy to investigate conservation for your organization's (80) publishing department.
6. The child's boat was beginning its difficult path down the river.
7. It's estimated that (100) the number of self-service stores is increasing weekly.
8. You shouldn't miss Wednesday's meeting because I can't be there. (120)
9. The first night's show isn't always so well done as the last night's.
10. The consultant hasn't been hired, the advertising (140) manager won't agree on a publishing date, and the printer isn't ready to submit suggestions for (160) consideration. (163)

TRANSCRIPT OF SHORTHAND—ASSIGNMENT 4

Letter 1 Gentlemen: We would like to introduce you to our new office service.

Many firms have been looking for ways to (20) equip their offices for more efficient operation; indeed, they realize that the cost of switching to (40) more modern methods of communication will be offset by the time and energy saved in the first year. (60) Whatever your needs, we can outline an improvement plan to satisfy them. As well, we can suggest considerations (80) for the future.

You will, I am sure, find outstanding equipment values in both new and demonstration merchandise. (100)

Our self-service outlet is open each day from 10:00 to 16:00.

Please let us hear from you if you would (120) rather have our sales crew visit your firm. Yours truly, (*AW 119; SW 125; SI 1.47*)

TRANSCRIPT OF SHORTHAND—ASSIGNMENT 5

Memorandum 1

TO: Divisional Managers
FROM: Head Office
SUBJECT: Administration Information Institutions Demonstration

This offer has just been received in today's mail, and I do not think we can put off making a decision concerning (20) our future plans for our office.

Please consult with your staff as soon as possible to determine the number (40) who would like to apply for registration in the information management demonstration to be held (60) the first week in August by this local firm. If you have any questions or recommendations, I would appreciate (80) receiving them as early in the week as possible.

Our own company's established policy is (100) to allow at least one day's pay for each division member who attends the Saturday session. I would also (120) like to add some form of payment for food and travel costs.

I, myself, would like to attend both the Friday and the (140) Saturday demonstrations, and I hope that you will be able to do so as well. (*AW 147; SW 155; SI 1.48*)

TRANSCRIPT OF SHORTHAND—ASSIGNMENT 6

Memorandum 2

TO: Personnel Manager
FROM: Marketing Manager
SUBJECT: Administration Information Institutions Demonstration

Please draw up a memo to our divisional managers to inform them of the office machines display to (20) be presented Friday, August 4, and Saturday, August 5, by the Administration Information Institution. (40)

Let the managers know that I would like to have as many of our staff as possible attend these sessions. (60) I am willing to pay a day's wages to those who attend on the Saturday. This is in keeping with our company's (80) established policy.

I also feel that those who are willing to give up their own time for this purpose (100) should have their expenses for food and travel paid by the company.

Please let me check your draft before you (120) send out copies. (*AW 113; SW 124; SI 1.53*)

CHAPTER 39

THEORY REVIEW OF CHAPTERS 21 THROUGH 24

Assignment 1 — **Theory Review.** The following sentence contains all the writing principles presented in Chapters 21 through 24. Study the writing principles and practise reading and writing this sentence until you can do so without hesitation and can quickly identify each writing principle.

The director instructed the employee to postpone the report at the special

conference on security.

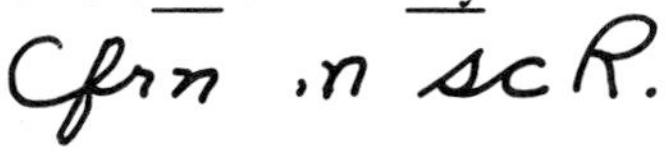

SUMMARY OF WRITING PRINCIPLES

SP	Write a small printed *s* to express the *sp* combination when no vowel occurs between the *s* and *p*.
CT	Omit *t* in the combination *ct* when *ct* ends a word because the *t* is lightly sounded. The *t* is also omitted when *ct* is followed by a common word ending such as *ed*, *ly*, *ing*, or *ive*.
INSTR	Write a disjoined longhand capital *N* to express the combination *instr* and the following vowel. Write the disjoined capital *N* close to the word to which it belongs.
RT-RD	Write a longhand capital *R* to express *rt-rd* when no vowel occurs between the two letters.
RITY	Write a disjoined capital *R* to express the combination *rity* and the preceding vowel.
OI-OY	Write a dotted *i* to express the sound of *oi-oy*.
NCE-NSE	Write a longhand small, disjoined *n* to express the combinations *nce-nse* and the preceding vowel.
POST-POSITION	Write a capital *P* thus  to express the prefix and suffix *post* and *position*.

Assignment 2 — **Abbreviations and phrasing review.** Read and write the following sentences containing abbreviations and phrases until you can write them quickly and easily and without hesitation.

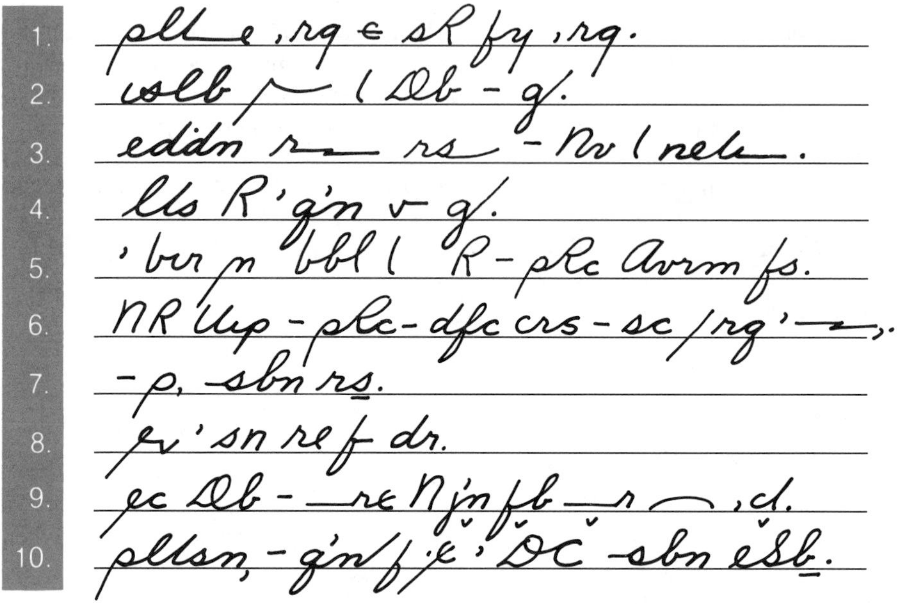

BUILDING TRANSCRIPTION SKILLS

Assignment 3 — **Transcription skills review — the dash and the hyphen.** Review the following rules governing the use of the dash and the hyphen, and then transcribe the sentences, inserting the correct punctuation. The key to these sentences appears on page 244.

1. Two or more words that are used as a single descriptive word should be hyphenated when they come before the word they describe.

2. The dash is used to set off parenthetical expressions and abrupt interruptions in thought.

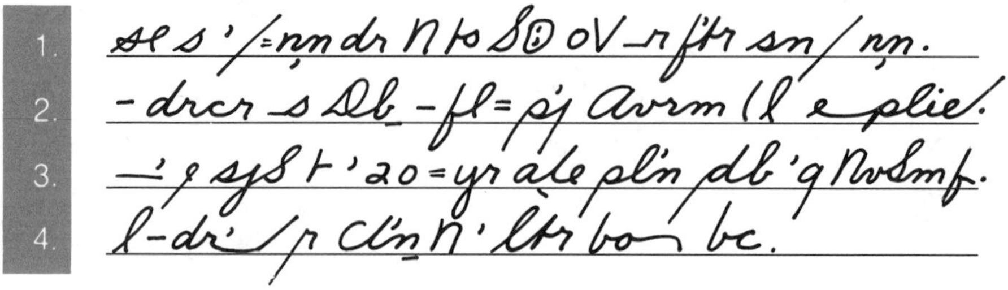

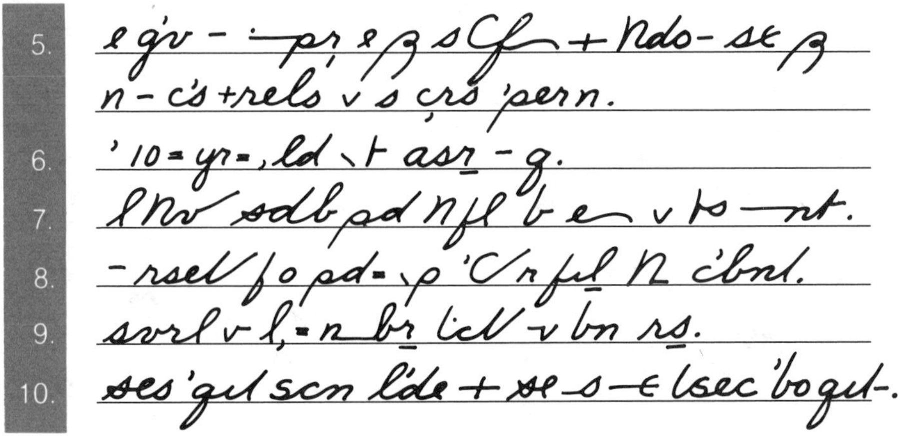

READING AND WRITING SHORTHAND

Assignments 4 and 5, except for those previewed, contain only words presented in Chapters and Units 1 through 24 of the text and *Study Guide*. Assignments 6 and 11 include vocabulary from Chapters and Units 1 through 32.

Assignment 4 — **Letter 1.** Read and write each of the preview words and phrases for Letter 1 until you can read and write each one rapidly and accurately. Then read and write the shorthand for Letter 1 to build your writing speed.

ready-to-wear specialty discriminate wholesale

low-priced dresses hand-blocked in your

have been able to apply to plan

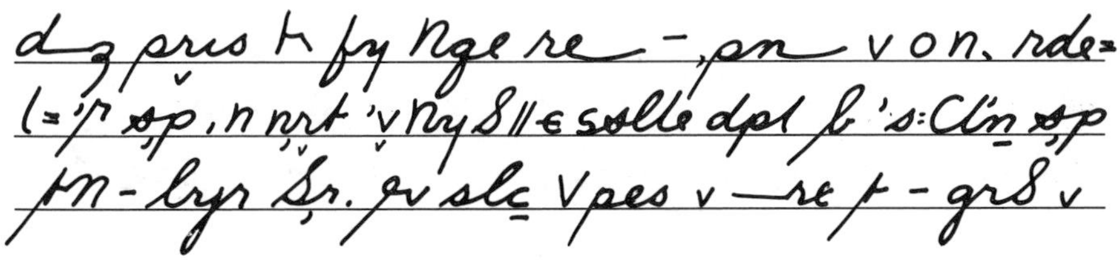

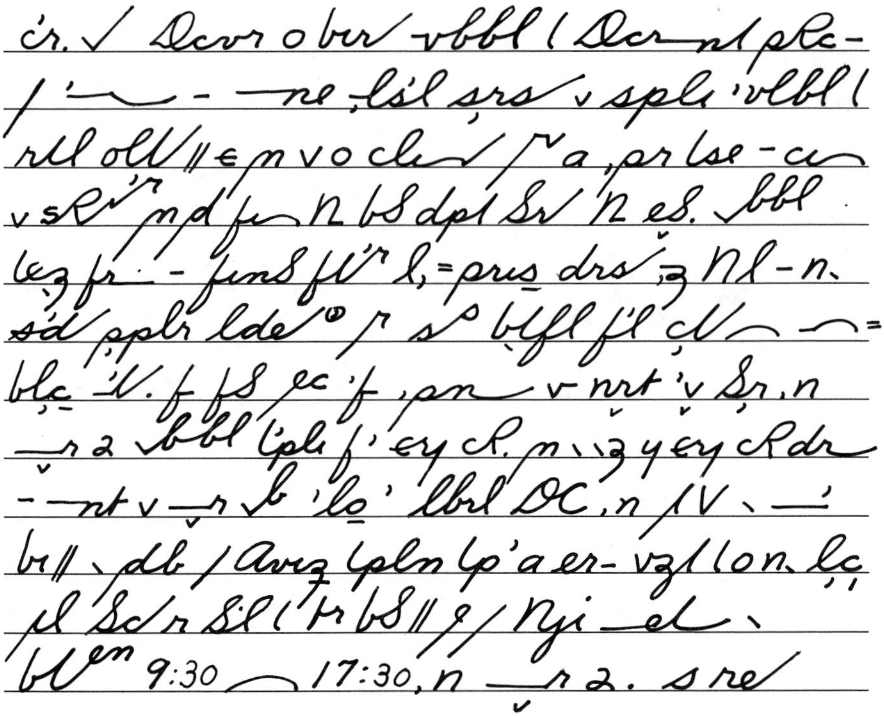

Assignment 5 — **Letter 2.** Read and write each of the preview words and phrases for Letter 2 until you can read and write each one rapidly and accurately. Then read and write the shorthand for Letter 2 to build your writing speed.

Toronto | obtained | degree | specialist | includes

jogging | we are pleased | to announce | she has been

will be held

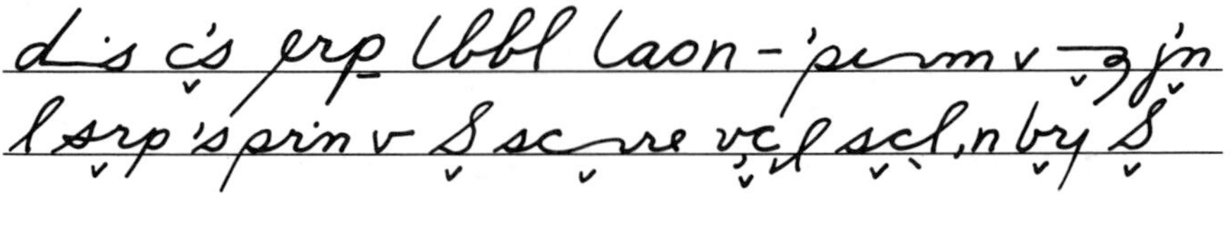

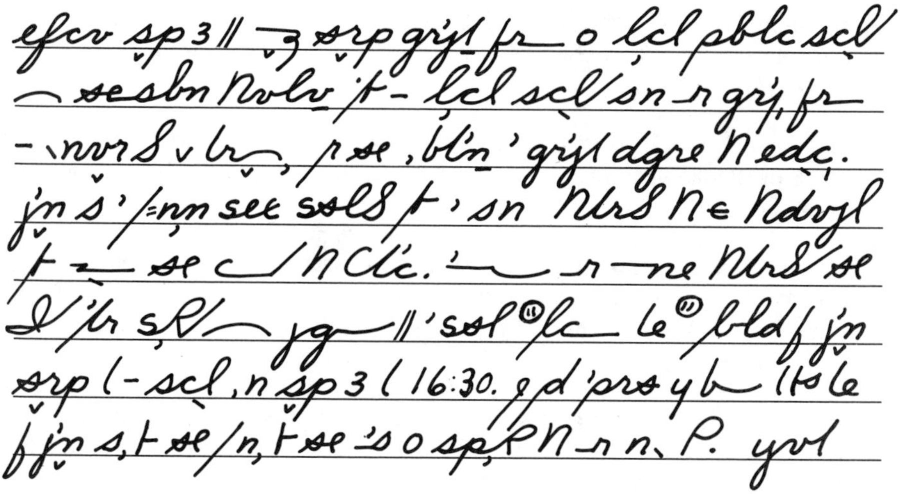

Assignment 6 — **Letter 3.** Read and write each of the preview phrases for Letter 3 until you can read and write each one rapidly and accurately. Then read and write the shorthand for Letter 3 to build your writing speed.

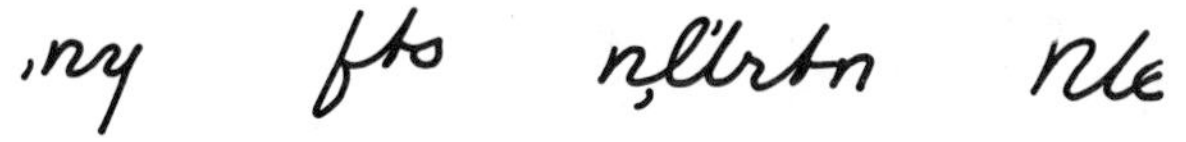

on your — for this — no later than — in touch

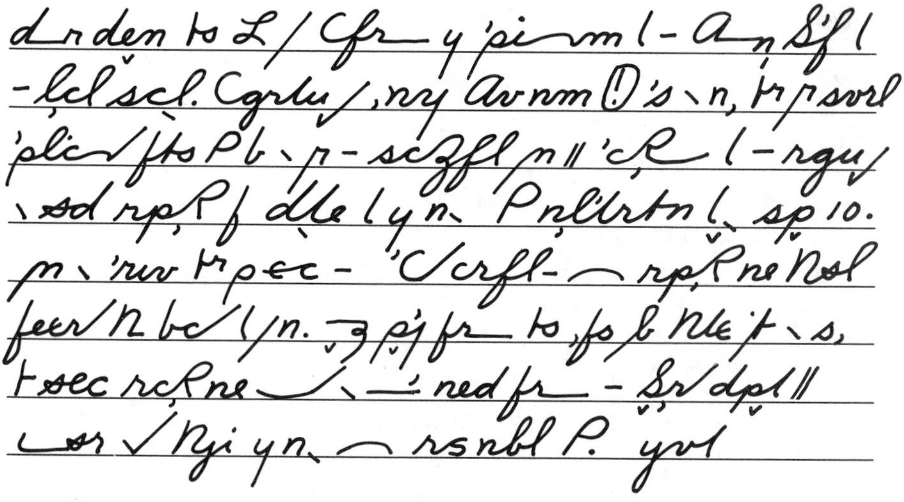

BUILDING SHORTHAND SPEED AND TRANSCRIPTION ACCURACY

Assignment 7 — **Self-testing.** Complete Unit 39 in your *Study Guide* before you proceed with the rest of this chapter.

Assignment 8 — **Taking tape dictation.** To write from dictation the sentences and letters in this chapter, use Cassette 22, Side A from *Theory and Speed-Building Tapes*.

Assignment 9 — **Taking live dictation.** Write from dictation the material which is printed at the end of this chapter. Your instructor will dictate to you at various speeds.

Assignment 10 — **Own-note transcription.** Transcribe at your best typing rate an accurate copy of at least one of the pieces of correspondence you took in shorthand in Assignment 9. Type the assignment in the style requested by your instructor.

Assignment 11 — **Supplementary dictation.** If instructed to do so, read and write the additional material for this chapter found in Appendix B, "Supplementary Correspondence for Dictation."

TRANSCRIPT OF SHORTHAND—ASSIGNMENT 2

1. Please let me organize each certificate for your organization.
2. I shall be willing to distribute the (20) goods.
3. He did not remember receiving the invoice at any time.
4. Let us order a quantity of the goods. (40)
5. A buyer will not be able to order the particular advertisement for us.
6. In order to type the (60) particularly difficult correspondence, the secretary will require a memo.
7. The purchase order (80) has been received.
8. We have a sincere regard for the doctor.
9. We can distribute the merchandise in January, (100) February, March, and October.
10. Please let us know the quantities for which a discount has been established. (120)

TRANSCRIPT OF SHORTHAND—ASSIGNMENT 3

1. She is a well-known doctor in this city; however, her father is not well known.
2. The director has distributed (20) the full-page advertisement to all employees.
3. May we suggest that a twenty-year annuity plan would (40) be a good investment for you.
4. All the drawings were contained in a leather-bound book.

5. He gave the impression (60) he was self-confident — undoubtedly, such was not the case — regardless of his coarse appearance.
6. A ten-year-old (80) youth answered the question.
7. All invoices should be paid in full by the end of this month.
8. The receipts for our paid-up (100) accounts are filed in the cabinet.
9. Several of the low-numbered tickets have been received.
10. She is a (120) quiet-spoken lady — she has much to speak about quietly. (129)

TRANSCRIPT OF SHORTHAND — ASSIGNMENT 4

Letter 1 Dear Ms. Price: Thank you for your inquiry regarding the opening of our new ready-to-wear shop on North Avenue (20) in your city.

Each specialty department will be a self-contained shop within the larger store. We have (40) selected every piece of merchandise with the greatest of care. You will discover our buyers have been able to (60) discriminate particularly well among the many wholesale sources of supply available to retail (80) outlets.

Each one of our clients will have an opportunity to see the kind of sportswear one would find in (100) the best department stores in the East. You will be able to choose from the finest footwear, low-priced dresses, hose in (120) all the new shades, popular ladies' wear, as well as beautiful fall coats and hand-blocked hats.

For the first week after (140) the opening of the North Avenue store on March 2, you will be able to apply for a charge card. When you (160) use your charge card during the month of March, you will be allowed a liberal discount on whatever you may buy. (180)

You would be well advised to plan to pay an early visit to our new location while stocks are still at their best. (200)

We will enjoy meeting you between 09:30 and 17:30 on March 2. Sincere regards, (*AW 217; SW 218; SI 1.40*)

TRANSCRIPT OF SHORTHAND — ASSIGNMENT 5

Letter 2 Dear Miss Case: We are pleased to be able to announce the appointment of Ms. Jane L. Sharpe as principal of the (20) City Secondary Vocational School on Bridge Street effective September 3.

Ms. Sharpe graduated from (40) our local public schools, and she has been involved with the local schools since her graduation from the University (60) of Toronto where she obtained a graduate degree in education. Jane is a well-known speech (80) specialist with a sincere interest in each individual with whom she comes in contact. Among her many (100) interests, she includes water sports and jogging.

A special "welcome tea" will be held for Jane Sharpe at the school on (120) September 3 at 16:30. We would appreciate your being at this tea for Jane so that she will know (140) that she has our support in her new post. Yours very truly, (*AW 141; SW 151; SI 1.49*)

TRANSCRIPT OF SHORTHAND—ASSIGNMENT 6

Letter 3 Dear Mr. Dean: This letter will confirm your appointment to the administration staff at the local school. (20) Congratulations on your advancement! As you know, there were several applicants for this post, but you were the successful (40) one.

According to the regulations, you should report for duty at your new post no later than Tuesday, (60) September 10. When you arrive there, please check the accounts carefully and report any unusual features in (80) the books at once. Ms. Page, from this office, will be in touch with you so that she can record any things you may need (100) from the Stores Department.

I am sure you will enjoy your new and responsible position. Yours very truly, (120) (*AW 114; SW 120; SI 1.47*)

CHAPTER 40

BUSINESS LETTER DICTATION AND TRANSCRIPTION

Assignment 1 — **Review Chart.** The chart below contains all the writing principles reviewed in chapters 37 through 39. Transcribe each word quickly and accurately. The numbers in the left column indicate the chapters in which each writing principle was first introduced. If you have difficulty reading and writing any outline, review the writing principle and practise reading and writing other words incorporating that principle. The key to this chart appears at the end of this chapter.

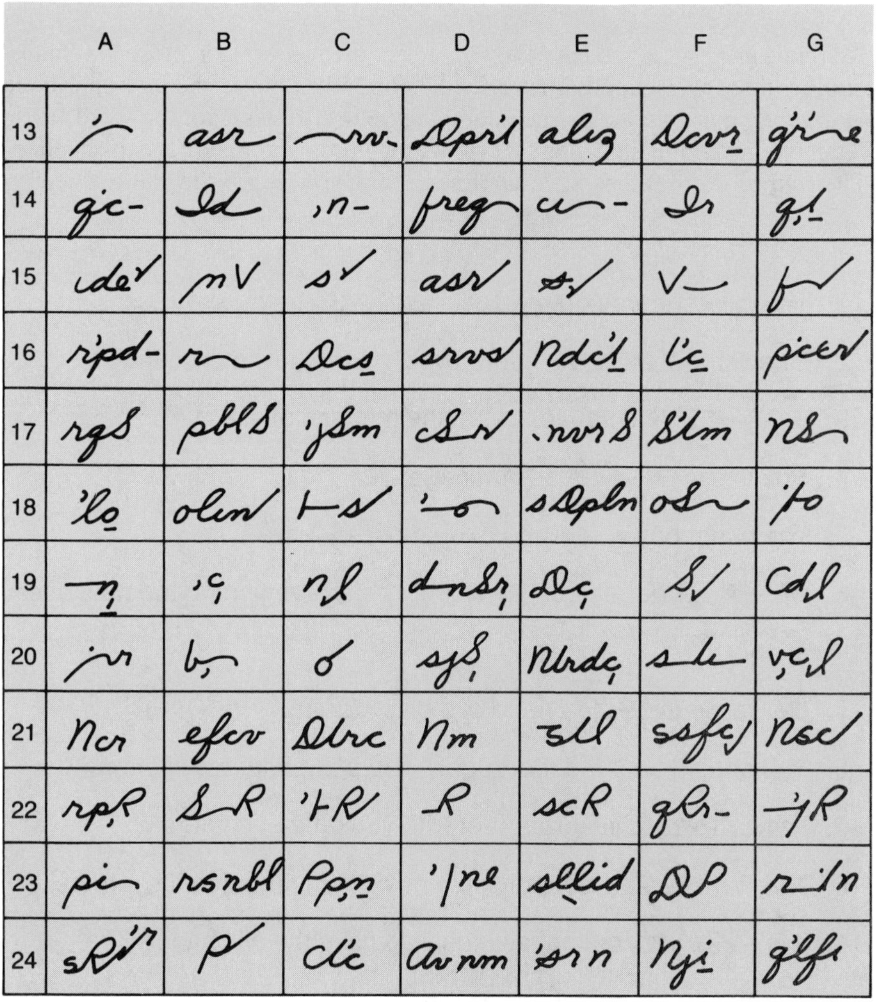
A B C D E F G
13
14
15
16
17
18
19
20
21
22
23
24

BUILDING TRANSCRIPTION SKILLS

Assignment 2 — **Spelling review.** Follow the steps outlined in Chapter 12 to check your ability to spell the following words correctly.

1. convenience
2. inventory
3. recommend
4. efficient
5. dependable
6. analyse
7. desperate
8. acquainted
9. entirely
10. adequate
11. desirable
12. combining
13. copying
14. considerable
15. guards
16. sincerely
17. library
18. annuity

Assignment 3 — **Spelling review.** Each of the following sentences contains outlines that are frequently transcribed incorrectly. Transcribe each shorthand outline in your notebook. Then compare your answers with the word list in Assignment 2 in this chapter. Review any words you may have misspelled. Then write the outlines several times, until you can write them fluently.

1. The cafeteria was opened as a  to the staff.
2. Check the  before ordering the new merchandise.
3. I  that you follow up the matter closely.
4. She is a most  manager.
5. The paper boy was found to be most .
6.  your objectives closely before beginning the new operation.
7. He was in  need of a place to live.
8. You should become thoroughly  with the system.
9. I am  in agreement with you on that point.
10. Take an 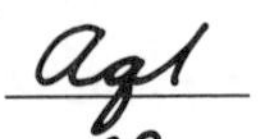 supply of First Aid equipment to the campsite.
11. It is , but not essential, to have the oil changed frequently.

12. You will have success with that recipe by Cbn certain ingredients properly.
13. She is now cpe the statement for the meeting.
14. There has been Csdrbl unnecessary waste of supplies.
15. The gR stood erect on Parliament Hill.
16. I sn hope you will visit us soon.
17. The lebrre will be open until 6 p.m.
18. The deferred ale comes due next year.

READING AND WRITING SHORTHAND

Assignments 4 and 5, except for those previewed, contain only words presented in Chapters and Units 1 through 24 of the text and *Study Guide*. Assignments 6 and 11 include vocabulary from Chapters and Units 1 through 32.

Assignment 4 — **Letter 1.** Read and write each of the preview words and phrases for Letter 1 until you can read and write each one rapidly and accurately. Then read and write the shorthand for Letter 1 to build your writing speed.

newest
Advertiser
city-wide
layout
turn-around
downtown
whomever
impress
Fast-print
to deliver
as soon as
to counsel
give us

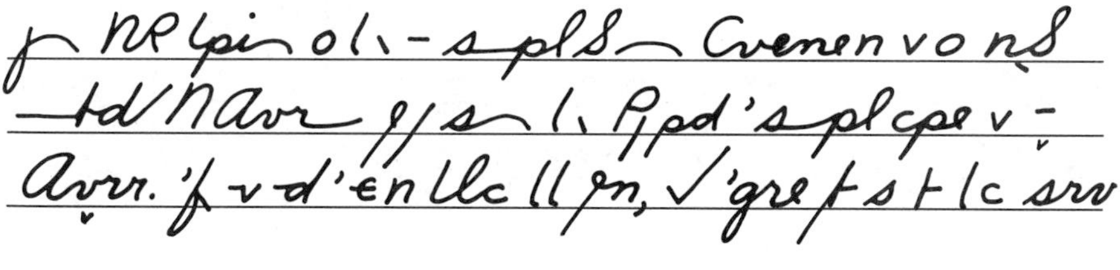

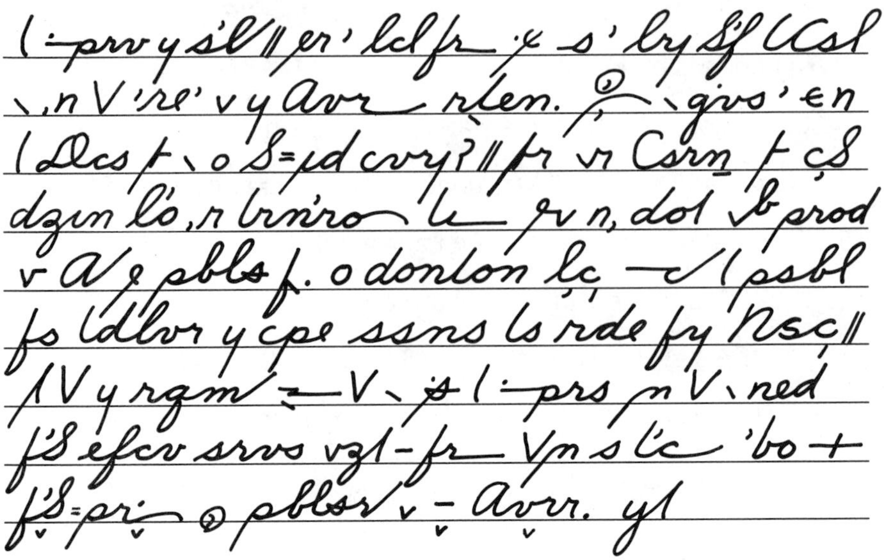

Assignment 5 — **Letter 2.** Read and write each of the preview words and phrases for Letter 2 until you can read and write each one rapidly and accurately. Then read and write the shorthand for Letter 2 to build you writing speed.

Townsend

exposure

considerably

to draw

I came

to thank you

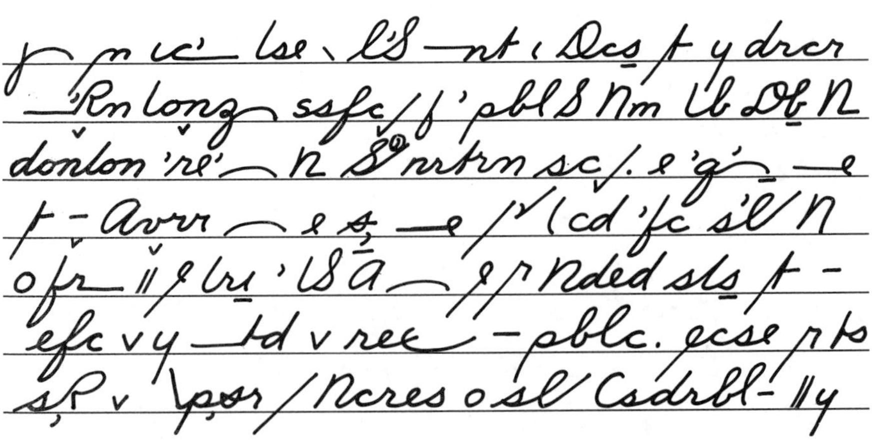

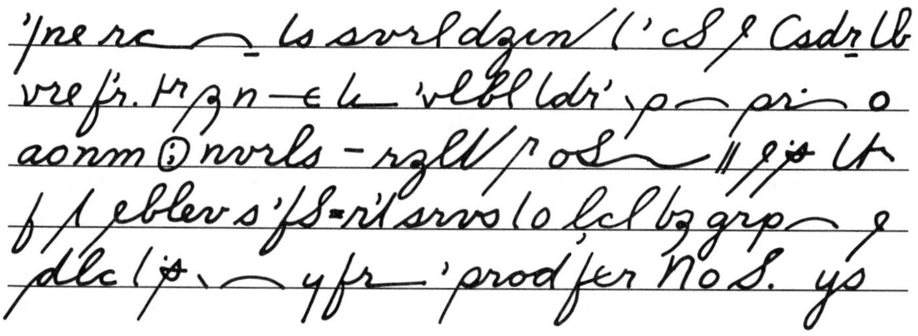

Assignment 6 — **Letter 3.** Read and write each of the preview words and phrases for Letter 3 until you can read and write each one rapidly and accurately. Then read and write the shorthand for Letter 3 to build your writing speed.

Hunter | created | RHOSP | holdings | existing | features

interim | declaration | to improve | to service | to determine

that these | in a few weeks | and are

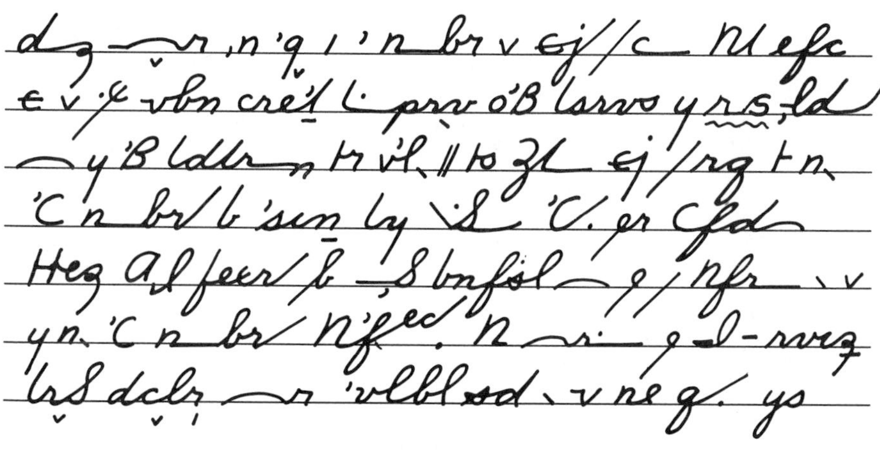

BUILDING SHORTHAND SPEED AND TRANSCRIPTION ACCURACY

Assignment 7 — **Self-testing.** Complete Unit 40 in your *Study Guide* before you proceed with the rest of this chapter.

Assignment 8 — **Taking tape dictation.** To write from dictation the letters in this chapter, use Cassette 22, Side A from *Theory and Speed-Building Tapes*.

Assignment 9 — **Taking live dictation.** Write from dictation the material which is printed at the end of this chapter. Your instructor will dictate to you at various speeds.

Assignment 10 — **Own-note transcription.** Transcribe at your best typing rate an accurate copy of at least one of the pieces of correspondence you took in shorthand in Assignment 9. Type the assignment in the style requested by your instructor.

Assignment 11 — **Supplementary dictation.** If instructed to do so, read and write the additional material for this chapter found in Appendix B, "Supplementary Correspondence for Dictation."

Key to Assignment 1 — **Review Chart.**

	A	B	C	D	E	F	G
13	want/ wand	answering	interview	desperate	analyse	discovered	guarantee
14	quickly	including	only	frequent	kindly	enclosure	quoted
15	ideas	whenever	says	answers	shows	everything	funds
16	rapidly	renting	discussed	services	indicated	talked	pictures
17	request	publicity	adjustment	customers	university	statement	instant
18	allowed	outlines	themselves	amount	self-discipline	outstanding	without
19	mentioned	occasion	national	demon- stration	discussion	stations	conditional
20	winter	bond	hours/ ours	suggestion	introduction	sometime	
21	instructor	effective	district	instrument	hospital	specifications	inspects
22	report	standard	authorities	heard/ herd	security	quarterly	majority
23	point	responsible	postponed	agency			remittance
24	sportswear	positions posts	contact	advancement		enjoyed	qualify

TRANSCRIPT OF SHORTHAND—ASSIGNMENT 4

Letter 1 Gentlemen: In order to point out to you the simplicity and convenience of our newest methods in (20) advertising, we will send to you, postage paid, a sample copy of The Advertiser. After you have had a (40) chance to look at it, we know you will agree with us that it can serve to improve your sales.

We are a local firm (60) which has a large staff to counsel you on every area of your advertising routine. Won't you give us a chance (80) to discuss with you our city-wide coverage?

Whether you are concerned with cost, design, layout, or turnaround (100) time, we have no doubt you will be proud of the ads we publish for you. Our downtown location makes it possible (120) for us to deliver your copy as soon as it is ready for your inspection.

Whatever your requirements, (140) whomever you wish to impress, whenever you need fast, effective service, visit the firm everyone is talking (160) about—Fast-print, publishers of The Advertiser. Yours truly, (*AW 167; SW 175; SI 1.46*)

TRANSCRIPT OF SHORTHAND—ASSIGNMENT 5

Letter 2 Gentlemen: When I came to see you last month, I discussed with your director, Martin Townsend, specifications (20) for a publicity instrument to be distributed in the downtown area and in the city's northern (40) sections. He acquainted me with The Advertiser, and he showed me ways it could affect sales in our firm.

We (60) tried a test ad, and we were indeed satisfied with the effect of your method of reaching the public. We can (80) see where this sort of exposure will increase our sales considerably.

Your agency recommended to us (100) several designs at a cost we considered to be very fair. There was not much time available to draw up and (120) print our announcement; nevertheless, the results were outstanding.

We wish to thank you for what we believe is a (140) first-rate service to our local business group, and we would like to wish you and your firm a proud future in our city. (160) Yours sincerely, (*AW 143; SW 164; SI 1.48*)

TRANSCRIPT OF SHORTHAND—ASSIGNMENT 6

Letter 3 Dear Ms. Hunter: On August 1 a number of changes will come into effect, each of which have been created (20) to improve our ability to service your RHOSP holdings and your ability to determine their value. (40)

This system change will require that new account numbers be assigned to your existing accounts. We are confident (60) that these additional features will be most beneficial and we will inform you of your new account numbers (80) in a few weeks. In the interim, we enclose the revised Trust Declaration and are available should you (100) have any questions. Yours sincerely, (*AW 95; SW 106; SI 1.54*)

TRANSCRIPTION TEST 2

- Your instructor will provide dictation material to be taken in shorthand.
- Transcribe each piece of dictation in an acceptable style as directed by your instructor.

CHAPTER 41

THEORY REVIEW OF CHAPTERS 25 THROUGH 28

Assignment 1 — **Theory Review.** The following sentence contains all the writing principles presented in Chapters and Units 25 through 28. Study the writing principles and practise reading and writing this sentence until you can do so without hesitation and can quickly identify each writing principle.

I forgot to explain that I prefer a change in letterhead design to give greater

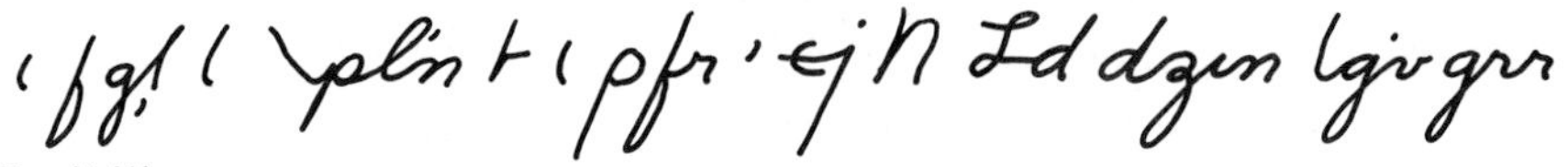

flexibility.

SUMMARY OF WRITING PRINCIPLES

FOR-FORE-FER-FUR	Write a disjoined longhand *f* for the prefixes *for-fore-fer-fur*. The disjoined *f* is used only when it represents a syllable.
BILITY	Write a longhand capital *B* to express the combination *bility* and the preceding vowel.
LETTER-LITER	Write a longhand capital *L* to express the combinations *letter-liter*.
PRE-PRI-PRO-PER-PUR	Write a small longhand disjoined *p* to express the combinations *pre-pri-pro-per-pur* when they begin a word containing more than one syllable. The disjoined *p* is used only when it represents a syllable. Write the disjoined *p* close to the remainder of the word.
AX-EX-OX	Write a long, straight, slanted, downward stroke thus \ to express the prefixes *ax*, *ex*, and *ox*. Be sure to slant the stroke so you will not confuse it with the letter *t*.
NGE	Write a dotted *j* to express the combination *nge*.

Assignment 2 — **Abbreviations and phrasing review**. Read and write the following sentences containing abbreviations and phrases until you can write them quickly and easily and without hesitation.

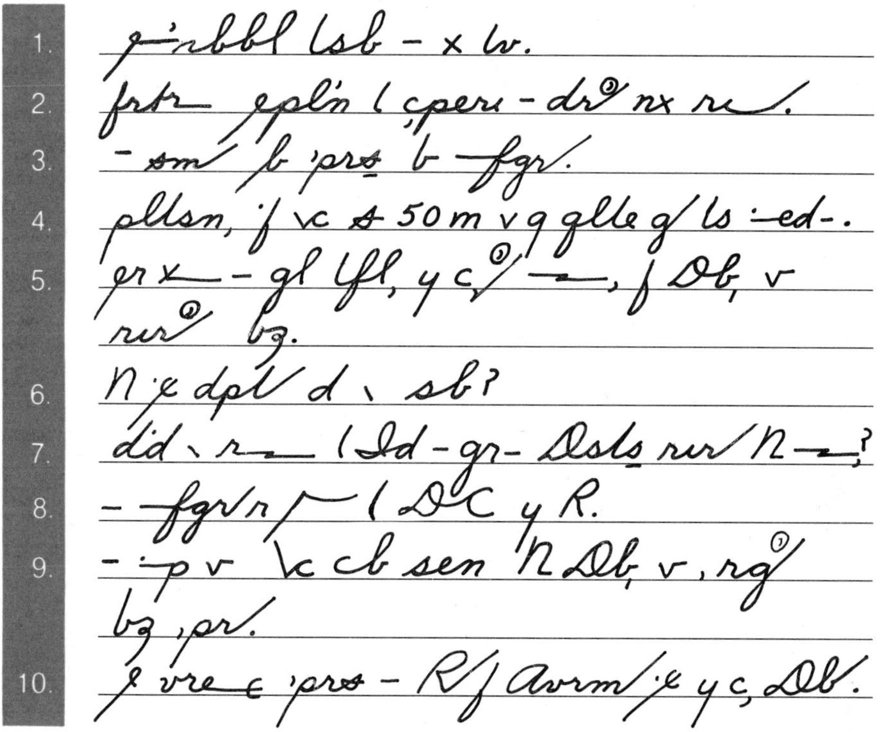

BUILDING TRANSCRIPTION SKILLS

Assignment 3 — **Transcription skills review** — **Transcribing numbers.** Review the following rules governing the writing of numbers, and then transcribe the sentences, inserting the correct form for each number. The key to these sentences appears on page 262.

1. Spell out numbers that begin a sentence.
2. Spell out isolated numbers from one to ten.
3. Use figures for other numbers (numbers of 11 and over, amounts of money, dates, percentages, and figures to denote time.)
4. In expressing metric quantities, the symbol is used with figures. (Example: 20 m; *but* twenty metres).

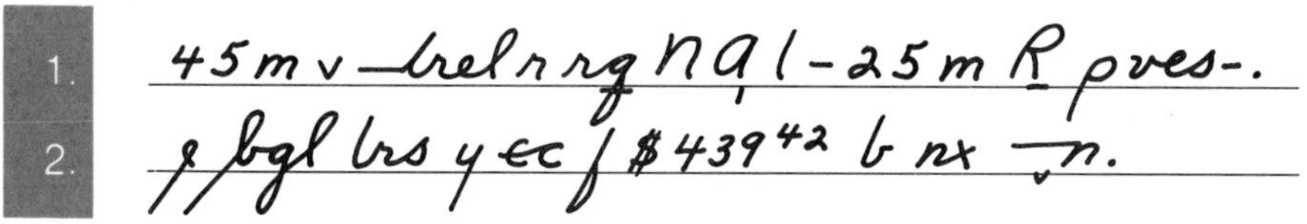

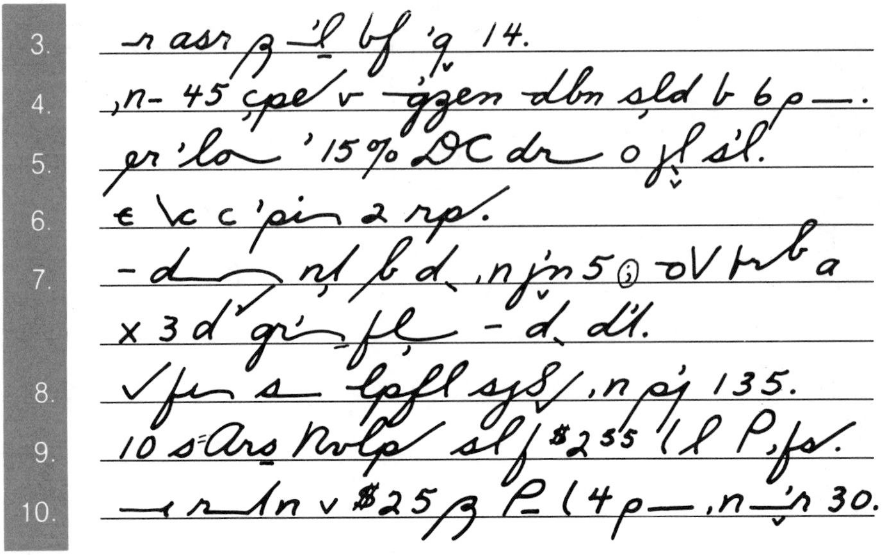

READING AND WRITING SHORTHAND

Assignments 4 and 5, except for those previewed, contain only words presented in Chapters and Units 1 through 28 of the text and *Study Guide*. Assignments 6 and 11 include vocabulary from Chapters and Units 1 through 32.

Assignment 4 — **Letter 1.** Read and write each of the preview words and phrases for Letter 1 until you can read and write each one rapidly and accurately. Then read and write the shorthand for Letter 1 to build your writing speed.

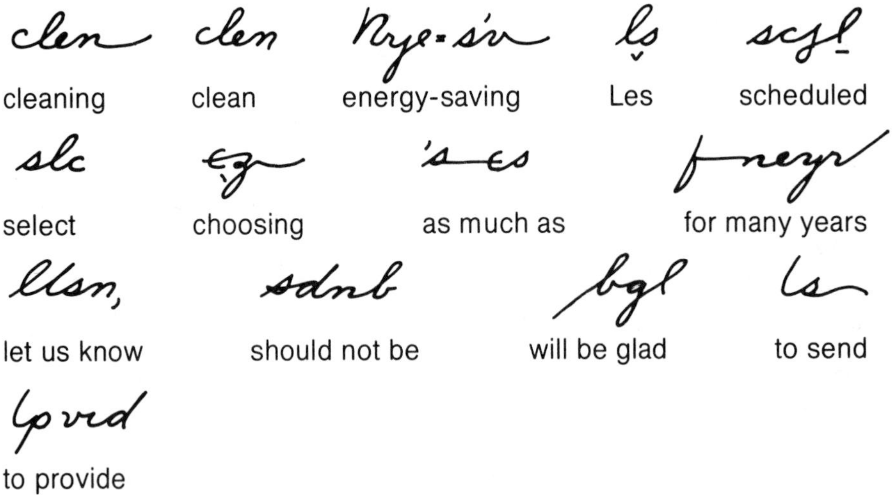

cleaning, clean, energy-saving, Les, scheduled

select, choosing, as much as, for many years

let us know, should not be, will be glad, to send

to provide

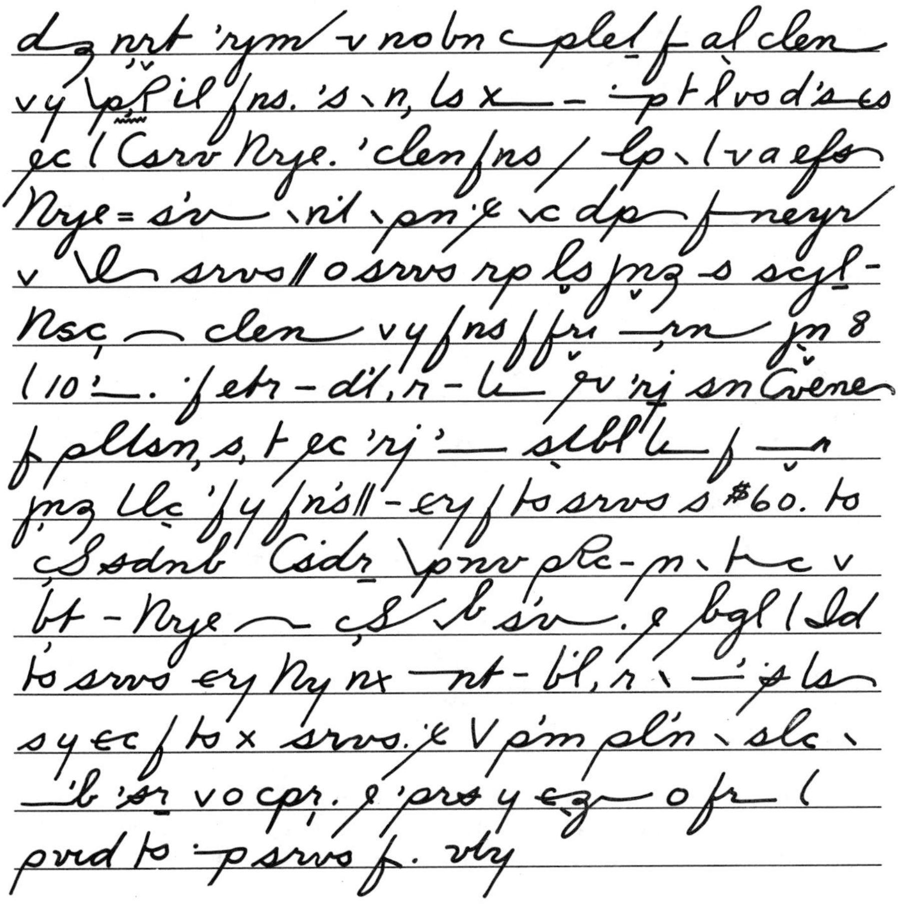

Assignment 5 — **Letter 2.** Read and write each of the preview words and phrases for Letter 2 until you can read and write each one rapidly and accurately. Then read and write the shorthand for Letter 2 to build your writing speed.

turning washing clothes electric typewriters

learning if you are to try to turn to conserve

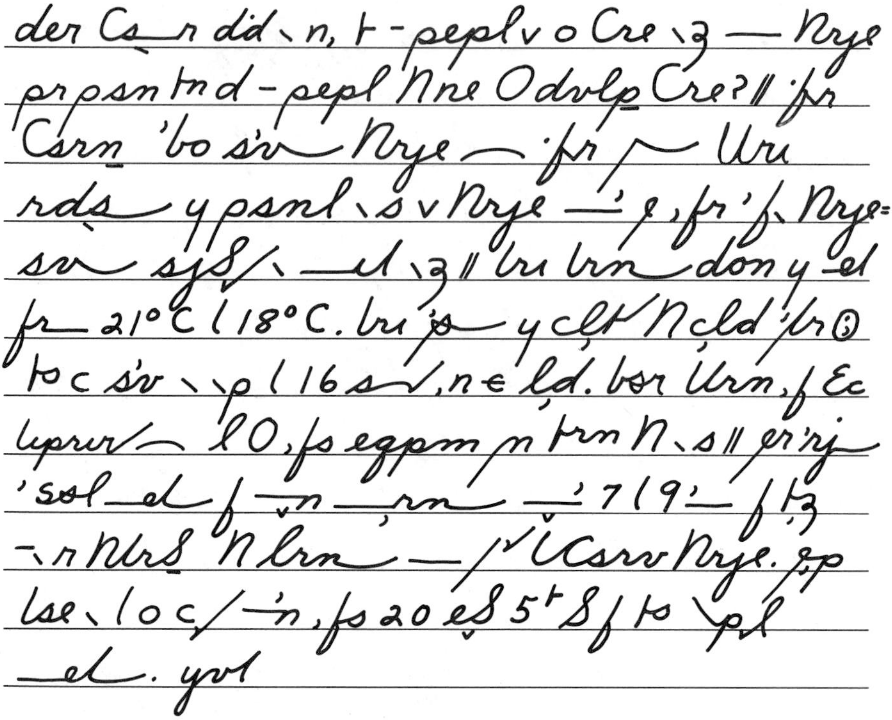

Assignment 6 – **Letter 3.** Read and write each of the preview words for Letter 3 until you can read and write each one rapidly and accurately. Then read and write the shorthand for Letter 3 to build your writing speed.

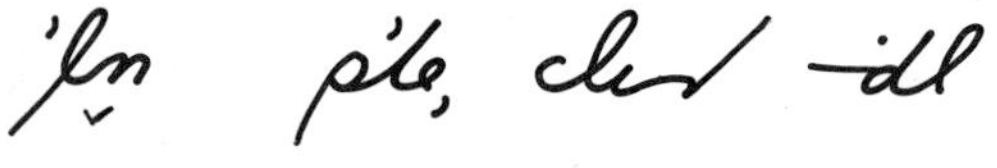

Whalen patio clients middle

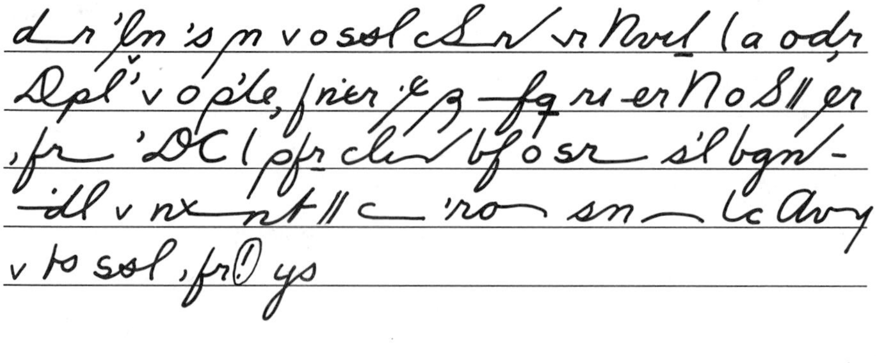

BUILDING SHORTHAND SPEED AND TRANSCRIPTION ACCURACY

Assignment 7 — **Self-testing.** Complete Unit 41 in your *Study Guide* before you proceed with the rest of this chapter.

Assignment 8 — **Taking tape dictation.** To write from dictation the sentences and letters in this chapter, use Cassette 19, Side B from *Theory and Speed-Building Tapes*.

Assignment 9 — **Taking live dictation.** Write from dictation the material which is printed at the end of this chapter. Your instructor will dictate to you at various speeds.

Assignment 10 — **Own-note transcription.** Transcribe at your best typing rate an accurate copy of at least one of the pieces of correspondence you took in shorthand in Assignment 9. Type the assignment in the style requested by your instructor.

Assignment 11 — **Supplementary dictation.** If instructed to do so, read and write the additional material for this chapter found in Appendix B, "Supplementary Correspondence for Dictation."

TRANSCRIPT OF SHORTHAND—ASSIGNMENT 2

1. We may not be able to substitute the extra television.
2. Furthermore, we plan to copyright the (20) doctor's next writings.
3. The shipments will be appreciated by the manufacturers.
4. Please let us know if you (40) can ship fifty metres of good quality goods to us immediately.
5. We are extremely glad to follow your (60) company's memorandum for distribution of the writer's business.
6. In which departments do you substitute? (80)
7. Did you remember to include the greatly dissatisfied writers in the memorandum?
8. The manufacturers (100) are willing to discount your order.
9. The importance of the executive can be seen in the distribution (120) of the organization's business opportunities.
10. We very much appreciate the orders for (140) advertisements which your company distributes. (148)

TRANSCRIPT OF SHORTHAND—ASSIGNMENT 3

1. Forty-five metres of material are required in addition to the twenty-five metres ordered previously. (20)
2. We will be glad to receive your cheque for $439.42 by next Monday. (40)
3. Her answer was mailed before August 14.
4. Only 45 copies of the magazine had been sold by 6 p.m. (60)
5. We are allowing a 15 per cent discount during our July sale.
6. Each executive can appoint two (80) representatives.
7. The demand note will be due on January 5; however, there will be an extra three days (100) granted following the due date.
8. You will find some helpful suggestions on page 135.
9. Ten self-addressed (120) envelopes sell for $2.55 at all post offices.
10. My remittance of $25 was (140) posted at 4 p.m. on March 30. (146)

TRANSCRIPT OF SHORTHAND—ASSIGNMENT 4

Letter 1 Dear Ms. North: Arrangements have now been completed for the annual cleaning of your EXPORT oil furnace. As you (20) know, it is extremely important that all of us do as much as we can to conserve energy. A clean furnace (40) will help you to have an efficient, energy-saving unit upon which you can depend for many years (60) of excellent service.

Our service representative, Les Jones, has scheduled the inspection and cleaning of your (80) furnace for Friday morning, June 8 at 10 a.m. If either the date or the time we have arranged is not (100) convenient for you, please let us know so that we can arrange a more suitable time for Mr. Jones to look after (120) your furnace.

The charge for this service is $60. This cost should not be considered expensive, particularly (140) when you think of both the energy and the costs you will be saving. We will be glad to include this service (160) charge in your next monthly bill, or you may wish to send us your cheque for this extra service. Whichever payment (180) plan you select, you may be assured of our co-operation. We appreciate your choosing our firm to provide (200) this important service for you. Very truly yours, *(AW 204; SW 209; SI 1.43)*

TRANSCRIPT OF SHORTHAND—ASSIGNMENT 5

Letter 2 Dear Consumer: Did you know that the people of our country use more energy per person than do the people (20) in any other developed country?

If you are concerned about saving energy and if you are willing (40) to try reducing your personal use of energy, may we offer a few energy-saving suggestions (60) you might use.

Try turning down your heat from 21°C to 18°C. Try washing (80) your clothes in cold water; this can save you up to 16 cents on each load. Be sure to turn off electric (100) typewriters and all other office equipment when they are not in use.

We are arranging a special meeting for (120) Monday morning, May 7, at 9 a.m., for those who are interested in learning more ways to conserve (140) energy. We hope to see you at our company's main office, 20 East Fifth Street, for this exceptional meeting. (160) Yours very truly, *(AW 152; SW 164; SI 1.5)*

TRANSCRIPT OF SHORTHAND—ASSIGNMENT 6

Letter 3 Dear Mr. Whalen: As one of our special customers, you are invited to an outdoor display of our (20) patio furniture which was manufactured right here in our city.

We are offering a discount to preferred (40) clients before our spring sale begins the middle of next month.

Come around soon, and take advantage of this special (60) offer! Yours sincerely, *(AW 58; SW 64; SI 1.55)*.

CHAPTER 42

THEORY REVIEW OF CHAPTERS 29 THROUGH 32

Assignment 1 — **Theory Review.** The following sentence contains all the writing principles presented in Chapters 29 through 32. Study the writing principles and practise reading and writing this sentence until you can do so without hesitation and can quickly identify each writing principle.

They undertake, with some success, to regulate, overcome, or control the

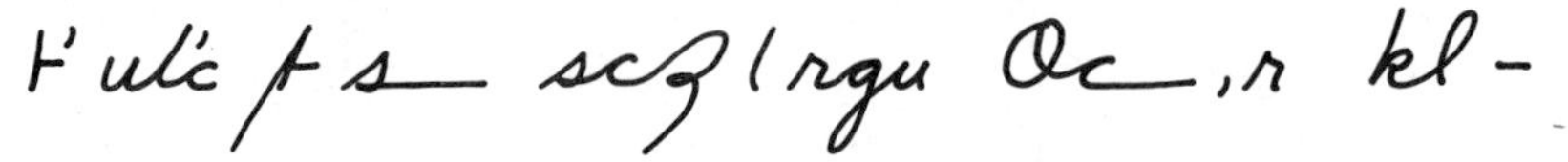

pain of bursitis with a prescription of modern electronic technology.

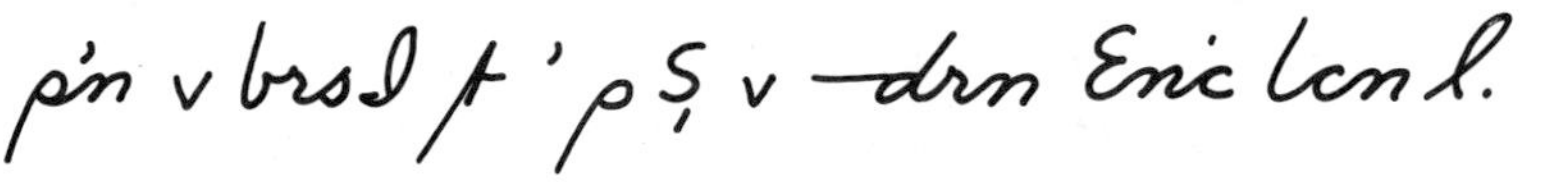

SUMMARY OF WRITING PRINCIPLES

UNDER	Write a small longhand *u* to express the combination *under*.
SYS-SESS-SUS-SIS-CESS-CIS	Write a longhand capital *Z* for the combinations *sys-sess-sus-sis-cess-cis*.
ULATE	Write a small longhand *u* to express the combination *ulate*.
OVER-OTHER	Write a joined or disjoined capital *O* to express *over* and *other*.
CONTR	Write a small longhand *k* to express the combination *contr* and the following vowel. Avoid writing extra strokes when writing the longhand *k*.
ITIS-ICITIS	Write a disjoined longhand capital *I* to express the combinations *itis-icitis*. Write it close to the word to which it belongs.
SCRIBE-SCRIPT	Write a printed capital *S* to express the combinations *scribe-script*. The *S* may be joined or disjoined.
ELECTR	Write a longhand capital *E* to express the combination *electr* and the following vowel.
OLOGY	Write a small longhand disjoined *l* to express the combination *ology*.

Assignment 2 — **Abbreviations and phrasing review.** Read and write the following sentences containing abbreviations and phrases until you can write them quickly and easily and without hesitation.

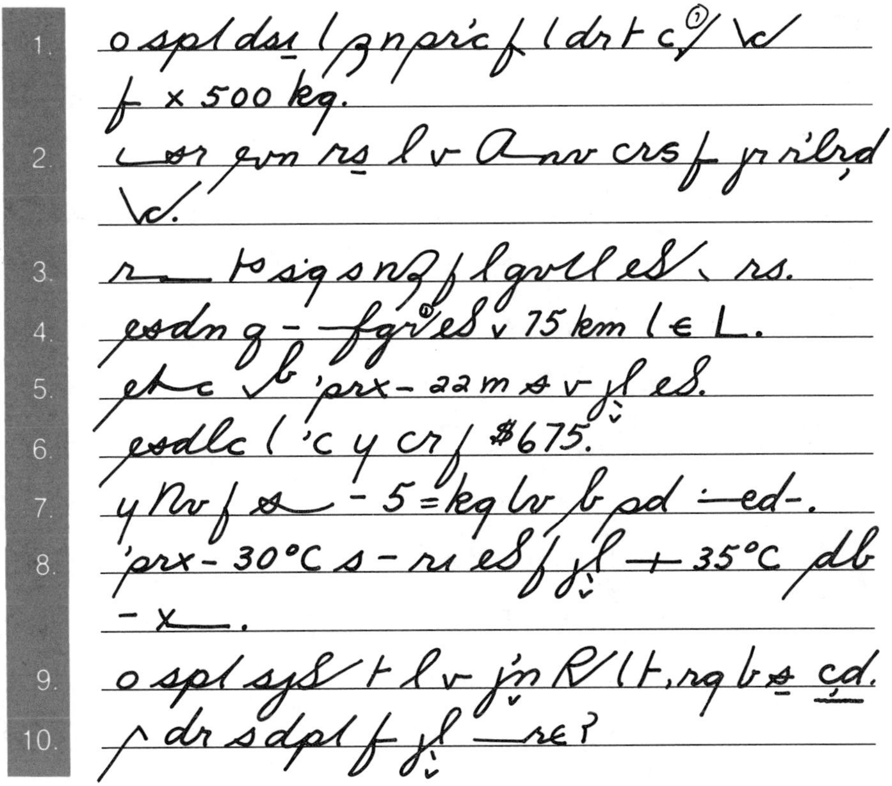

BUILDING TRANSCRIPTION SKILLS

Assignment 3 — **Transcription skills review—Capitalization.** Review the following rules governing the use of capitalization, and then transcribe the sentences, inserting the correct punctuation and capitalization. The key to these sentences appears on page 270.

1. Capitalize days of the week, months, and names of holidays. Do not abbreviate days of the week, or months, when transcribing.

2. Capitalize names of provinces, states, towns, streets, avenues, boulevards, and routes. These words are capitalized because they are proper nouns.

3. Capitalize geographical sections of a country. Capitalize compass points when they name specific geographical regions.

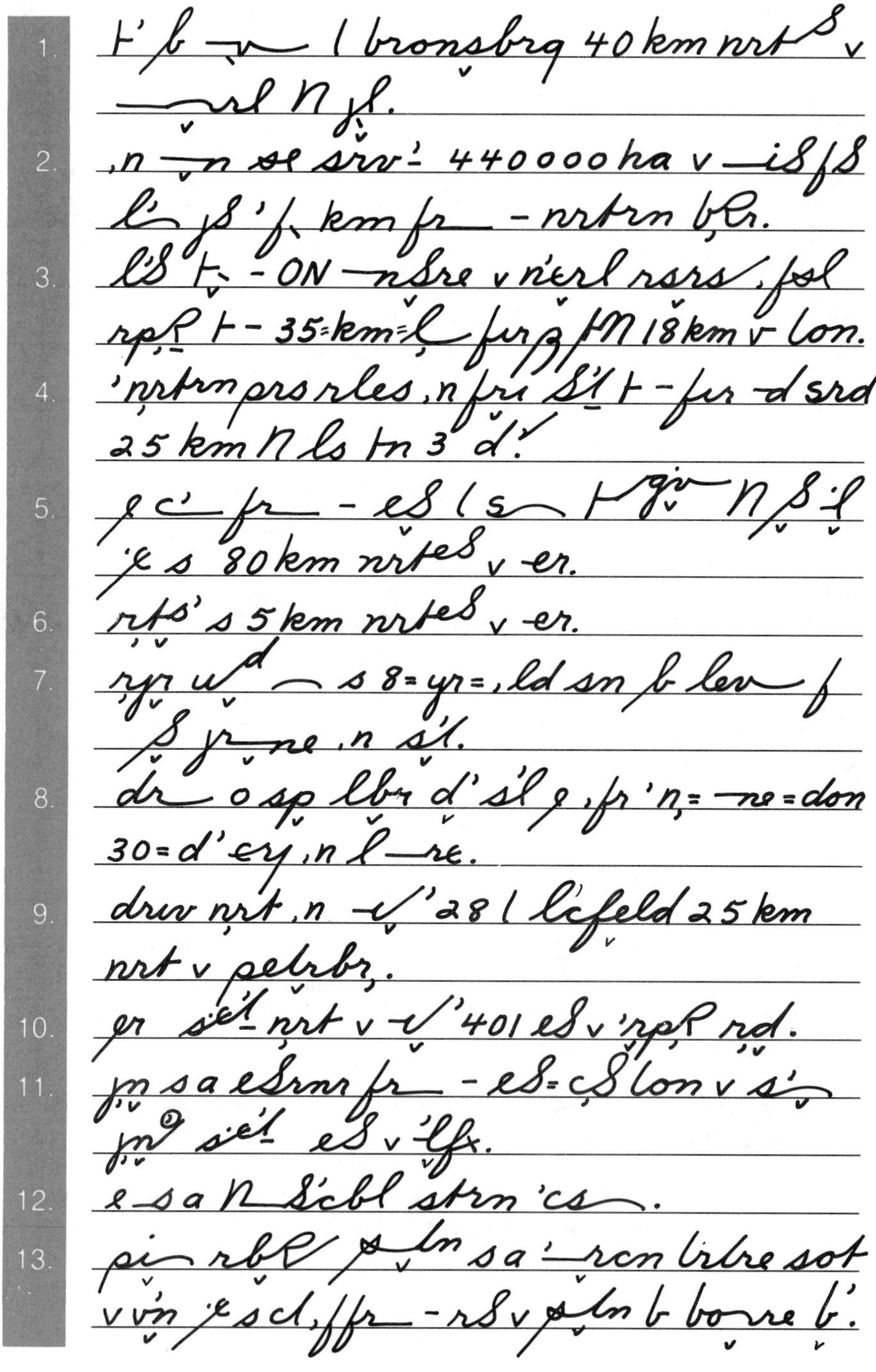

READING AND WRITING SHORTHAND

Assignments 4, 5, and 6, except for those previewed, contain only words presented in Chapters and Units 1 through 32.

Assignment 4 — **Letter 1.** Read and write each of the preview words and phrases for Letter 1 until you can read and write each one rapidly and accurately. Then read and write the shorthand for Letter 1 to build your writing speed.

Hatfield reserved parking Pat to settle

we shall be glad

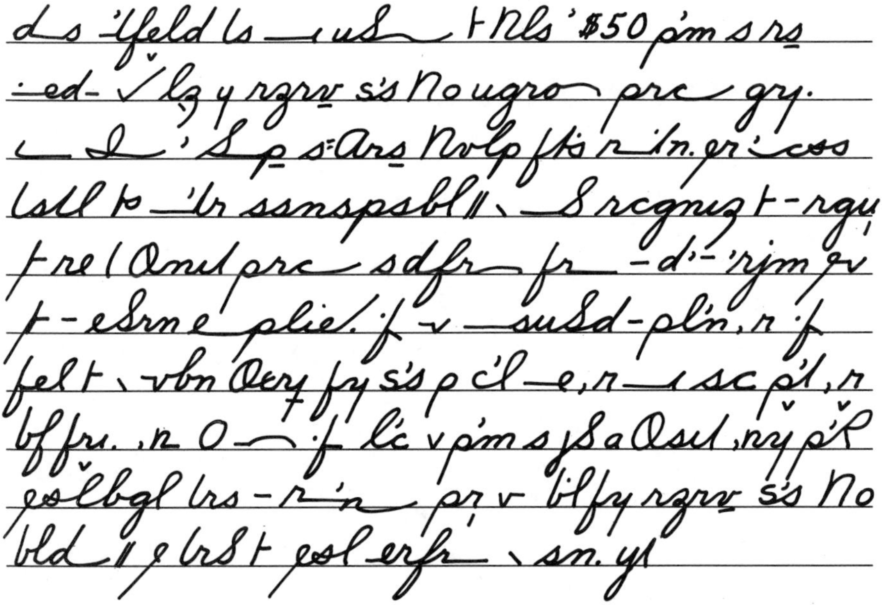

Assignment 5 — **Letter 2.** Read and write each preview word and phrase for Letter 2 until you can read and write each one rapidly and accurately. Then read and write the shorthand for Letter 2 to build your writing speed.

husband anticipated apologize debited Lance's

unintentional   to keep

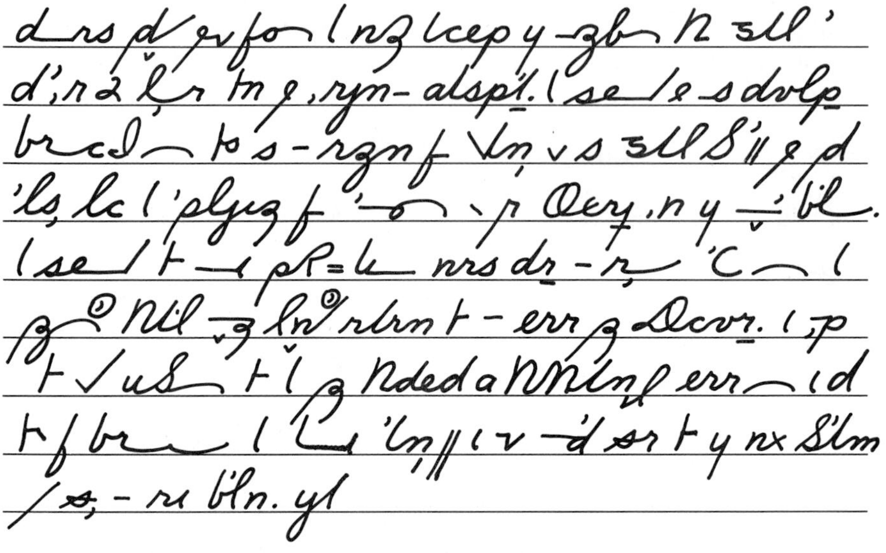

Assignment 6 — **Letter 3.** Read and write each of the preview words and phrases for Letter 3 until you can read and write each one rapidly and accurately. Then read and write the shorthand for Letter 3 to build your writing speed.

Weymark   minutes   Canada   United States   Great Britain

transmitters   time-saving   legal-size   to look   we shall be

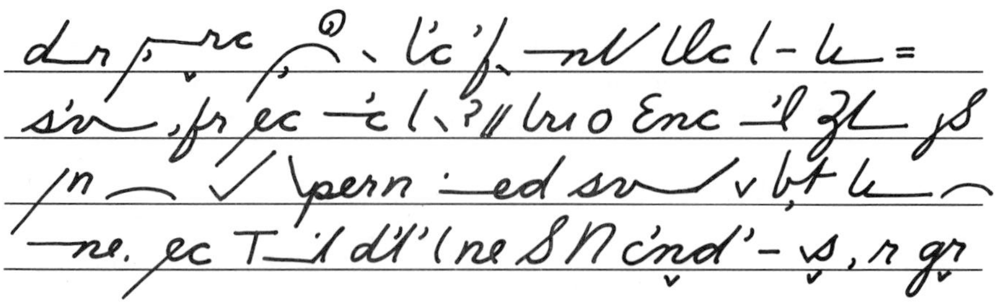

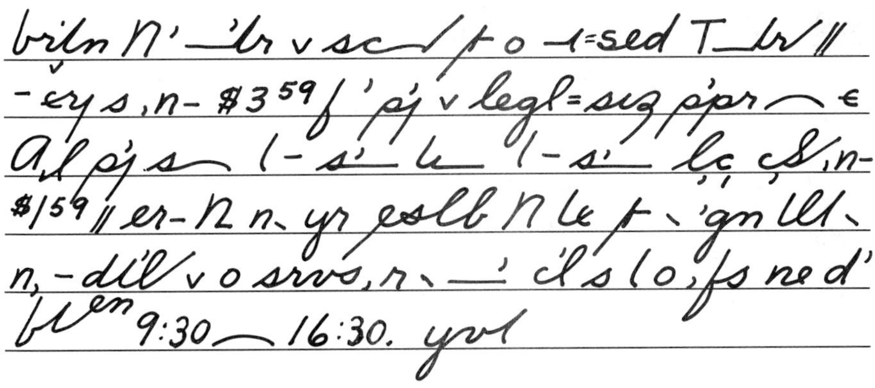

BUILDING SHORTHAND SPEED AND TRANSCRIPTION ACCURACY

Assignment 7 — **Self-testing.** Complete Unit 42 in your *Study Guide* before you proceed with the rest of this chapter.

Assignment 8 — **Taking tape dictation.** To write from dictation the sentences and letters in this chapter, use Cassette 19, Side B from *Theory and Speed-Building Tapes*.

Assignment 9 — **Taking live dictation.** Write from dictation the material which is printed at the end of this chapter. Your instructor will dictate to you at various speeds.

Assignment 10 — **Own-note transcription.** Transcribe at your best typing rate an accurate copy of at least one of the pieces of correspondence you took in shorthand in Assignment 9. Type the assignment in the style requested by your instructor.

Assignment 11 — **Supplementary dictation.** If instructed to do so, read and write the additional material for this chapter found in Appendix B, "Supplementary Correspondence for Dictation."

TRANSCRIPT OF SHORTHAND—ASSIGNMENT 2

1. Our superintendent decided it was not practical for you to debit that company's executives (20) for the extra 500 kg.
2. I am sure we have not received all of the administrative correspondence (40) for the junior railroad executives.
3. Remember, this signature is necessary for all governmental (60) estimates you receive.

4. We should not question the manufacturer's estimate of 75 km (80) to each litre.
5. We think you will be approximately 22 m short of the July estimate.
6. We should like (100) to acknowledge your credit for $675.
7. Your invoice for shipping the 5-kg (120) television will be paid immediately.
8. Approximately 30°C is the right estimate (140) for July—35°C would be the extreme.
9. Our superintendent suggests that all of the (160) January orders to that organization be shipped COD.
10. Will you debit his department for the July (180) merchandise? (182)

TRANSCRIPT OF SHORTHAND—ASSIGNMENT 3

1. They will be moving to Brownsburg, 40 km northwest of Montreal, in July.
2. On Monday, she (20) surveyed 440 000 ha of moist forest land just a few kilometres from the northern (40) border.
3. Last Thursday the Ontario Ministry of Natural Resources official reported that the (60) 35-km-long fire was within 18 km of the town.
4. A northern press release on Friday (80) stated that the fire had spread 25 km in less than three days.
5. We came from the East to spend Thanksgiving (100) in West Hill which is 80 km northeast of here.
6. Rothsay is 5 km northeast of here.
7. Roger (120) Underwood and his eight-year-old son will be leaving for West Germany on Saturday.
8. During our September (140) Labour Day sale, we offer a no-money-down 30-day charge on all merchandise.
9. Drive north on Highway 28 (160) to Lakefield, 25 km north of Peterborough.
10. We are situated north of Highway 401, (180) east of Airport Road.
11. Joan is an easterner from the east-coast town of St. John's, situated east of Halifax.

12. He (200) has an unmistakable southern accent.
13. Point Roberts, Washington, is an American territory south of Vancouver (220) which is cut off from the rest of Washington by Boundary Bay. (231)

TRANSCRIPT OF SHORTHAND—ASSIGNMENT 4

Letter 1 Dear Miss Hatfield: It is my understanding that unless a $50 payment is received immediately (20) you will lose your reserved space in our underground parking garage. I am enclosing a stamped, self-addressed (40) envelope for this remittance. We are anxious to settle this matter as soon as possible.

You must recognize (60) that the regulation with regard to overnight parking is different from the daily arrangement we have (80) with the Eastern employees. If you have misunderstood the plan or if you feel that you have been overcharged for (100) your space, please call me or my secretary, Pat Ore, before Friday. On the other hand, if the lack of payment (120) is just an oversight on your part, we shall be glad to receive the remaining portion of the bill for your (140) reserved space in our building.

We trust that we shall hear from you soon. Yours truly, *(AW 146; SW 153; SI 1.47)*

TRANSCRIPT OF SHORTHAND—ASSIGNMENT 5

Letter 2 Dear Mrs. Woods: We have found it necessary to keep your husband, Roger, in the hospital a day or two (20) longer than we originally anticipated. It seems he has developed bronchitis, and this is the (40) reason for the extension of his hospital stay.

We would also like to apologize for the amount you (60) were overcharged on your May billing. It seems that my part-time nurse debited the wrong account, and it wasn't (80) until Ms. Lance's return that the error was discovered. I hope that you will understand that it was indeed an (100) unintentional error, and I do thank you for bringing it to my attention.

I have made sure that your next (120) statement will show the right balance. Yours truly, *(AW 121; SW 128; SI 1.48)*

TRANSCRIPT OF SHORTHAND—ASSIGNMENT 6

Letter 3 Dear Mr. Weymark: Won't you take a few minutes to look at the time-saving offer we can make to you?

Try our (20) electronic mail system just once, and you will experience immediate savings of both time and money. (40) We can transmit data to any city in Canada, the United States, or Great Britain in a matter (60) of seconds with our high-speed transmitters.

The charge is only $3.59 for a page of (80) legal-size paper and each additional page sent at the same time to the same location costs only $1.59. (100)

Early in the new year we shall be in touch with you again to let you know the details of (120) our service, or you may call us at our office any day between 09:30 and 16:30. Yours (140) very truly, *(AW 128; SW 142; SI 1.40)*

CHAPTER 43

ABBREVIATIONS REVIEW

Assignment 1 — **Abbreviations Review Chart.** The chart below contains all the abbreviated words and some of the standard abbreviations in Forkner Shorthand. Transcribe each word quickly and accurately. The numbers in the left column identify the chapters in which each abbreviated word was first introduced. If you have difficulty reading and writing any outline, review, memorize, and practise writing each of these words. The key to this chart appears at the end of this chapter.

A
B
C
D
E
F
G
1/2
2/3
3/5
6/7
7/9
9/10
11/13
13/14/15
15/17/18
18/19
19/20/22
23
27/29/30

Assignment 2 — **Abbreviations and phrasing review.** Read and write the following sentences containing abbreviations and phrases until you can write them quickly and easily and without hesitation.

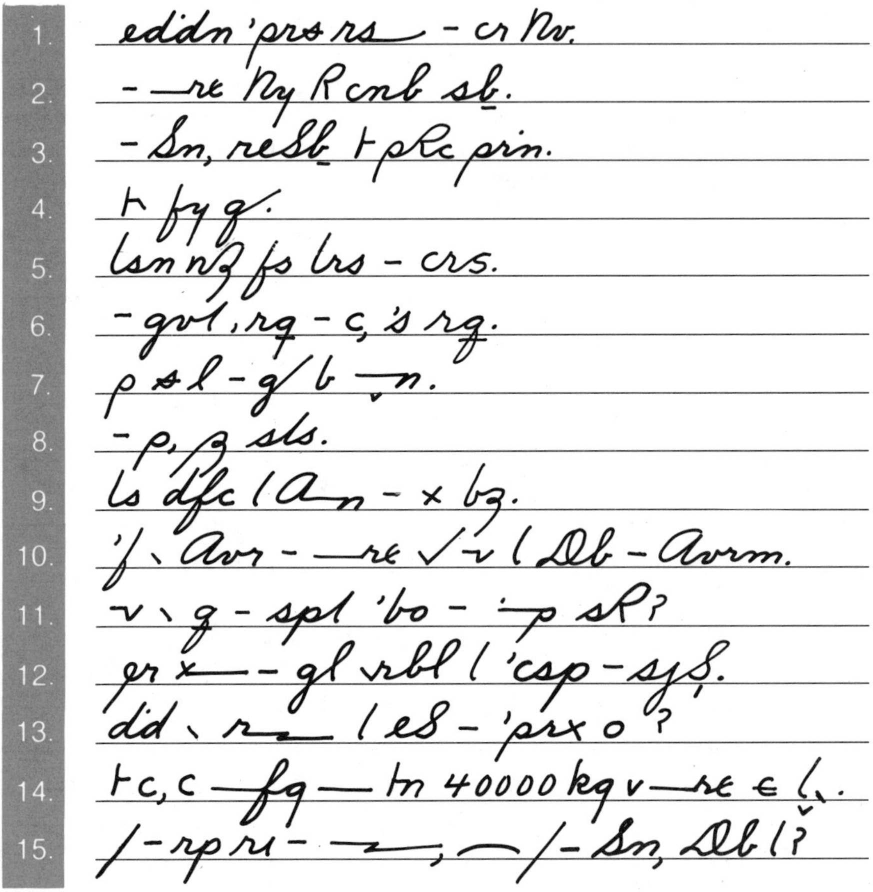

BUILDING TRANSCRIPTION SKILLS

Assignment 3 — **Transcription skills review — capitalization.** Review the following rule governing the use of capitalization, and then transcribe the sentences, inserting the correct punctuation and capitalization. The key to these sentences appears on page 280.

- Capitalize the names of businesses, organizations, associations, governmental agencies, schools, and colleges because they are proper nouns.

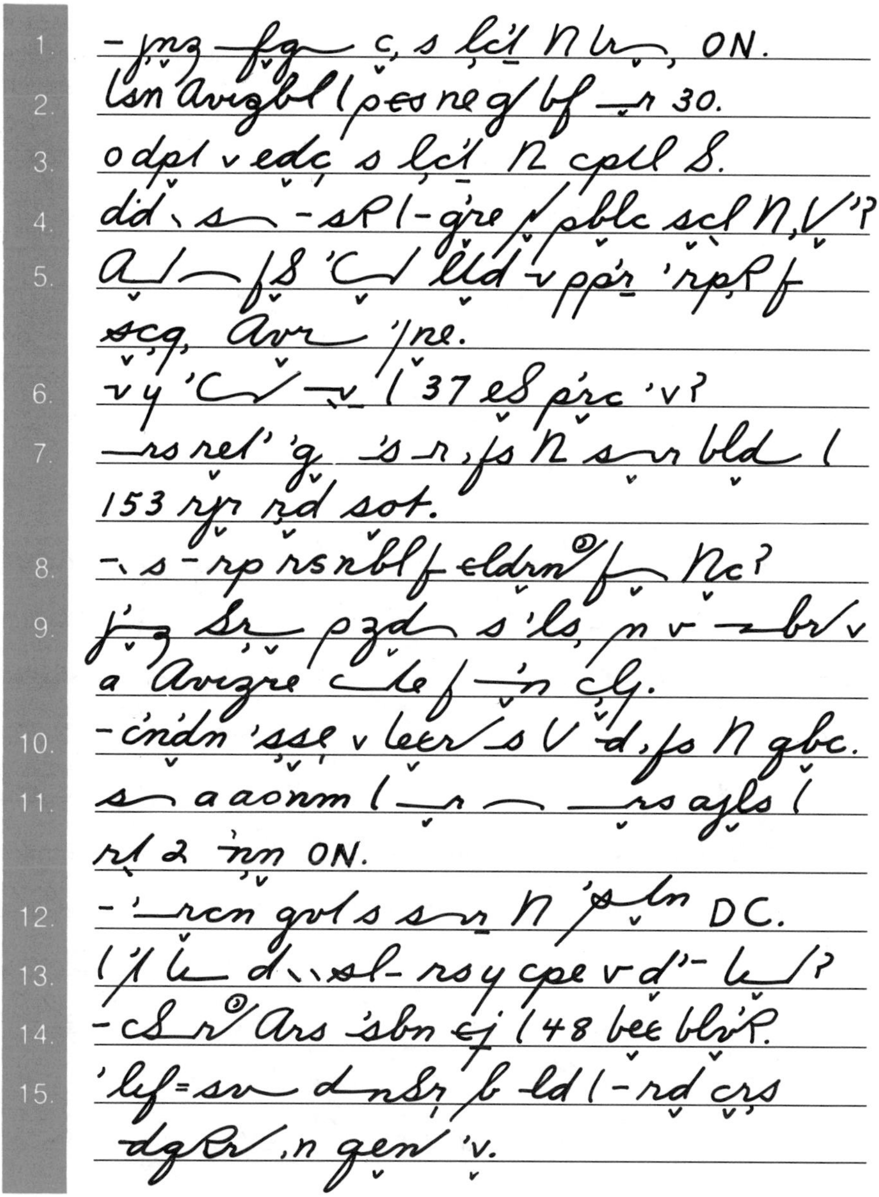

READING AND WRITING SHORTHAND

Assignments 4, 5, and 6, except for those previewed, contain only words presented in Chapters and Units 1 through 32.

Assignment 4 — **Letter 1.** Read and write each preview word and phrase for Letter 1 until you can read and write each one rapidly and accurately. Then read and write the shorthand for Letter 1 to build your writing speed.

Grant Temple guides capitalization Storey usage

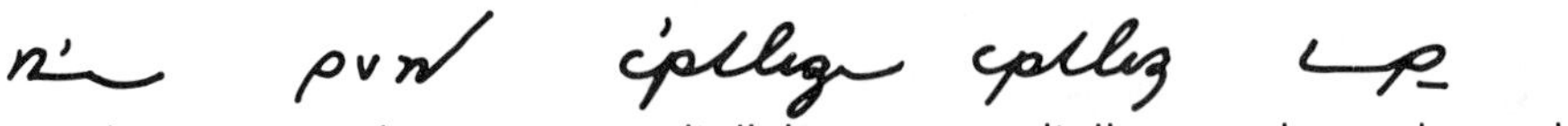

naming provinces capitalizing capitalize I am pleased

to learn there are I shall be able

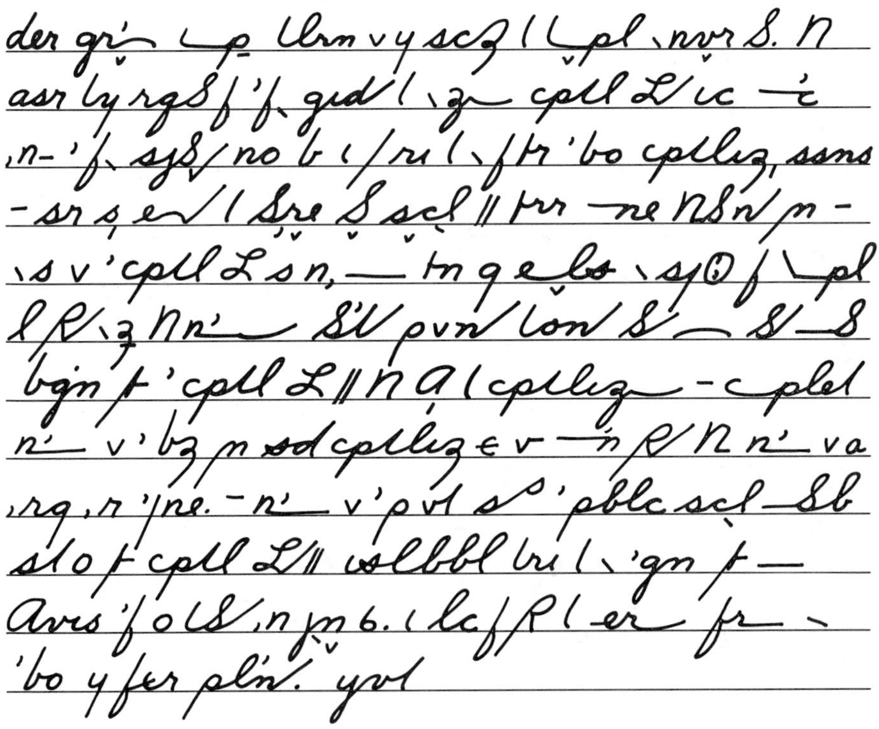

Assignment 5 — **Letter 2.** Read and write each preview word and phrase for Letter 2 until you can read and write each one rapidly and accurately. Then read and write the shorthand for Letter 2 to build your writing speed.

prompt community assets protect business-like

no doubt

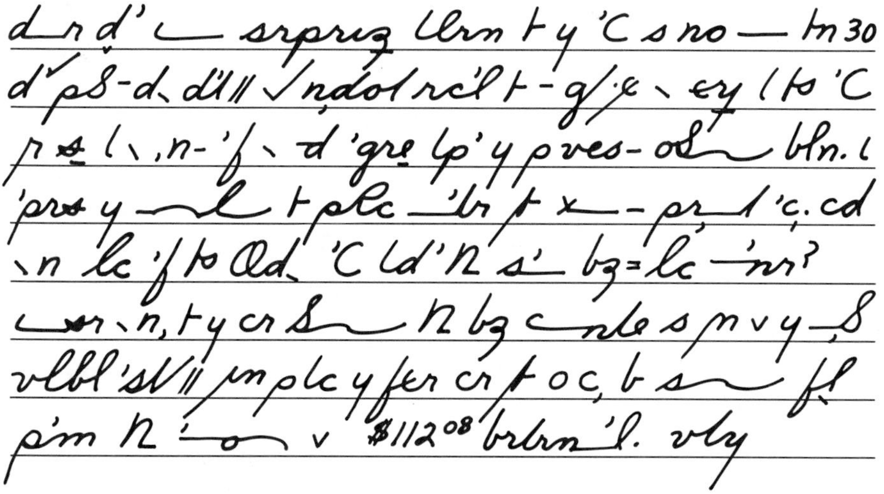

Assignment 6 — **Letter 3.** Read and write each of the preview words for Letter 3 until you can read and write each one rapidly and accurately. Then read and write the shorthand for Letter 3 to build your writing speed.

Chester Canadian colleague Shaw Communications

ON

Colleges Ontario achievers challenged intense

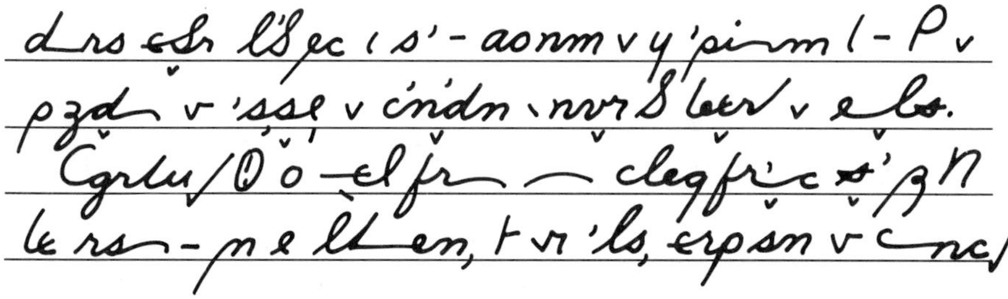

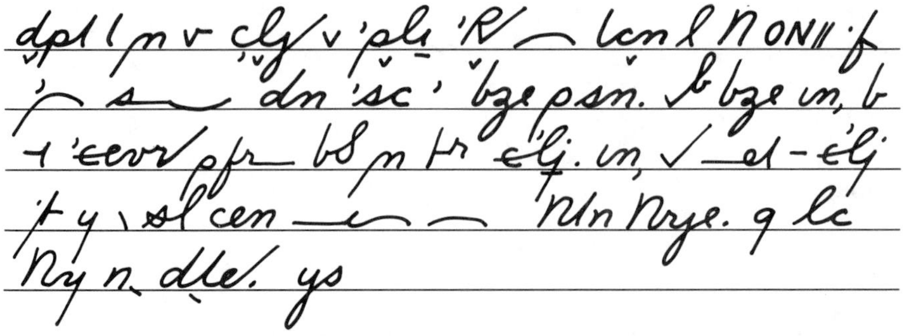

BUILDING SHORTHAND SPEED AND TRANSCRIPTION ACCURACY

Assignment 7 — **Self-testing.** Complete Unit 43 in your *Study Guide* before you proceed with the rest of this chapter.

Assignment 8 — **Taking tape dictation.** To write from dictation the sentences and letters in this chapter, use Cassette 20, Side B from *Theory and Speed-Building Tapes*.

Assignment 9 — **Taking live dictation.** Write from dictation the material which is printed at the end of this chapter. Your instructor will dictate to you at various speeds.

Assignment 10 — **Own-note transcription.** Transcribe at your best typing rate an accurate copy of at least one of the pieces of correspondence you took in shorthand in Assignment 9. Type the assignment in the style requested by your instructor.

Assignment 11 — **Supplementary dictation.** If instructed to do so, read and write the additional material for this chapter found in Appendix B, "Supplementary Correspondence for Dictation."

Key to Assignment 1 — **Abbreviations Review Chart.**

	A	B	C	D	E	F	G
1/2	can	for	go/good	he	is/his/us	the	all
2/3	be/by/bye/ but	it/at/to	of	your	not	next	and
3/5	do	as	right/ write	you	like	company/Co.	govern- ment
6/7	accept	am/more	great	opportunity	satisfy/ satis- factory	glad	after
7/9	any	are	will/well	appreciate	side	have	put/ please
9/10	receive	ship/ short	decide	each	merchandise	that/ thank	manufacture
11/13	advertise	has	business	memo/ memorandum	ask	difficult/ difficulty	year
13/14/15	represent/ representative	gentlemen	quantity	question	require	department	important/ importance
15/17/18	immediate	principle/ principal	administer	because	suggest	acknowledge	estimate
18/19	about	first	our/hour/ out	street	August	enquire	establish
19/20/22	organize/ organiza- tion	corre- spond/ corre- spondence	Mr.	certifi- cate	order	particular	distribute
23	sincere/ sincerely	remember	purchase order	invoice	October	regard	February
27/29/30	extra	extreme	executive	substitute	necessary	debit/ doctor	practical

TRANSCRIPT OF SHORTHAND—ASSIGNMENT 2

1. He did not appreciate receiving the credit invoice.
2. The merchandise in your order cannot be substituted. (20)
3. The stenographer re-established that particular principle.
4. Thank you for your questions.
5. It is not (40) necessary for us to receive the correspondence.
6. The government organized the company as required.
7. Please ship (60) all the goods by Monday.
8. The purchase order was satisfactory.
9. It is difficult to administer the (80) extra business.
10. After you advertise the merchandise, you will have to distribute the advertisement.
11. Have you (100) questioned the superintendent about the important certificate?
12. We are extremely glad you are able to (120) accept the suggestion.
13. Did you remember to estimate the approximate hour?
14. That company can (140) manufacture more than 40 000 kg of merchandise each Tuesday.
15. Will the representative write the (160) memorandum and will the stenographer distribute it? (170)

TRANSCRIPT OF SHORTHAND—ASSIGNMENT 3

1. The Jones Manufacturing Company is located in Toronto, Ontario.
2. It is not advisable (20) to purchase any goods before March 30.
3. Our Department of Education is located in the capital (40) city.
4. Did you send the certificate to the Gary Wills Public School in Ottawa?
5. Adams and Forest (60) Accountants Ltd. have prepared a report for the Chicago Advertising Agency.
6. Have your accountants (80) moved to 37 East Park Avenue?
7. Mrs. Rita August has her office in the Centre Building (100) at 153 Roger Road South.
8. Who is the representative responsible for the Children's Fund Incorporated? (120)
9. James Strong, President, is also one of the members of an advisory committee for Main College. (140)

10. The Canadian Association of Teachers has its head office in Quebec.
11. Send an announcement to Mr. and (160) Mrs. Angeles at Route 2, Hannon, Ontario.
12. The American government is centred in Washington, DC. (180)
13. At what time do you usually receive your copy of The Daily Times?
14. The customer's address has been changed (200) to 48 Beach Boulevard.
15. A life-saving demonstration will be held at the Red Cross headquarters on Queens (220) Avenue. (222)

TRANSCRIPT OF SHORTHAND—ASSIGNMENT 4

Letter 1 Dear Grant: I am pleased to learn of your success at Temple University. In answer to your request for a (20) few guides to using capital letters, I can make only a few suggestions now, but I will write to you (40) further about capitalization as soon as the senior session ends at Storey Street School.

There are many (60) instances when the use of a capital letter is no more than good English usage; for example, all words (80) used in naming states, provinces, towns, cities, and streets, must begin with a capital letter.

In (100) addition to capitalizing the complete name of a business, one should capitalize each of the main words (120) in the name of an organization or agency. The name of a private, as well as a public, school (140) must be set out with capital letters.

I shall be able to write to you again with more advice (160) after our tests on June 6. I look forward to hearing from you about your future plans. Yours very truly, *(AW 170; SW 179; SI 1.47)*

TRANSCRIPT OF SHORTHAND—ASSIGNMENT 5

Letter 2 Dear Mr. Day: I am surprised to learn that your account is now more than thirty days past the due date.

You will no doubt (20) recall that the goods which you charged to this account were shipped to you only after you had agreed to pay your (40) previously outstanding balance. I appreciate your handling that particular matter with extremely prompt (60) action. Could you not look after this overdue account today in the same business-like manner? I am sure you (80) know that your credit standing in the business community is one of your most valuable assets.

Why not (100) protect your future credit with our company by sending full payment in the amount of $112.08 (120) by return mail. Very truly yours, *(AW 127; SW 129; SI 1.42)*

TRANSCRIPT OF SHORTHAND—ASSIGNMENT 6

Letter 3 Dear Mrs. Chester: Last week I saw the announcement of your appointment to the position of President of (20) the Association of Canadian University Teachers of English. Congratulations! Our mutual (40) friend and colleague, Frank Shaw, was in touch recently, when he let me know that you are also chairperson of the (60) Communications Department at one of the Colleges of Applied Arts and Technology in Ontario. (80)

If you want something done, ask a busy person. You will be busy, I know, but high achievers perform best when they (100) are challenged. I know you will meet the challenge with your usual keen mind and intense energy. Good luck in your new (120) duties. Yours sincerely, *(AW 111; SW 124; SI 1.51)*

CHAPTER 44

BUSINESS LETTER DICTATION AND TRANSCRIPTION

Assignment 1 — **Review chart.** The chart below contains all the writing principles reviewed in chapters 41 and 42. Transcribe each word quickly and accurately. The numbers in the left column indicate the chapter in which the writing principle was first introduced. If you have difficulty reading or writing any word, review the writing principle and practise reading and writing other words incorporating that principle. The key to these words is at the end of this chapter.

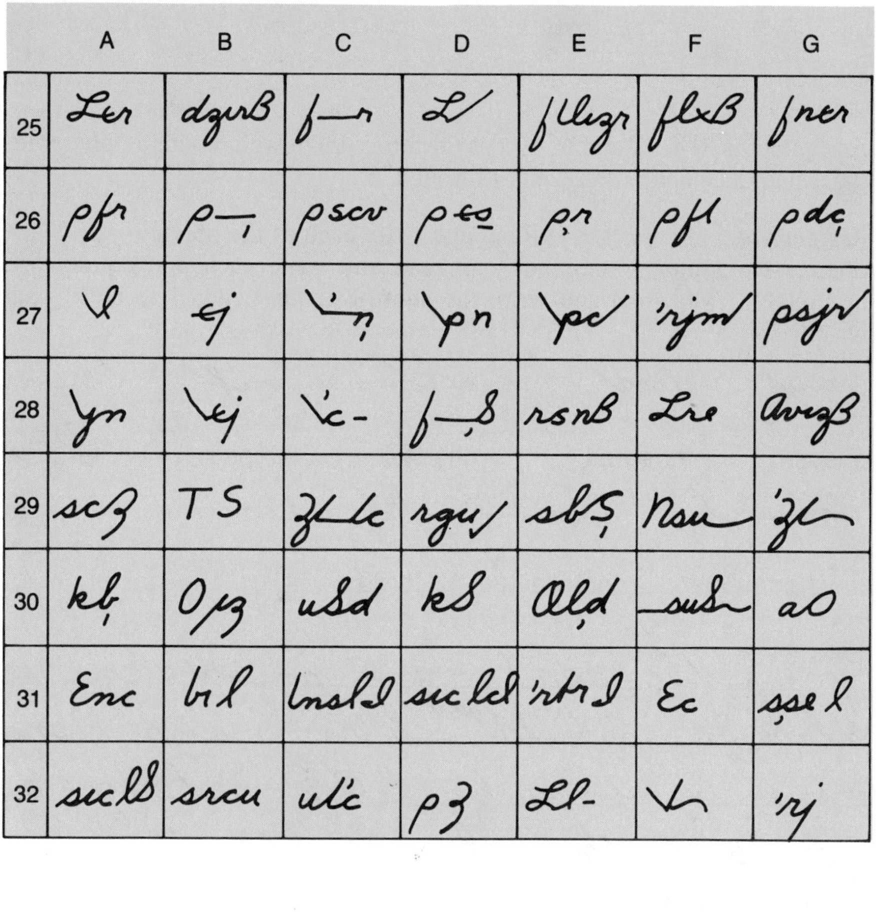
A
B
C
D
E
F
G
25
26
27
28
29
30
31
32

BUILDING TRANSCRIPTION SKILLS

Assignment 2 — **Spelling review.** Follow the steps outlined in Chapter 12 to check your ability to spell the following words correctly.

1. eligibility
2. advisability
3. furthermore
4. procedures
5. prospective
6. performed
7. pursue
8. oxygen
9. arrangements
10. achieve
11. mimeograph
12. superintendent
13. psychology
14. appendicitis
15. bursitis
16. tonsillitis
17. bronchitis
18. geologist
19. congratulations
20. governmental

READING AND WRITING SHORTHAND

Assignments 3, 4, 5, and 6, except for those previewed, contain only words presented in Chapters and Units 1 through 32.

Assignment 3 — **Letter 1.** Read and write each of the preview words and phrases for Letter 1 until you can read and write each one rapidly and accurately. Then read and write the shorthand for Letter 1 to build your writing speed.

arises ensures charts graphs terminal

developmental complicated to do to us

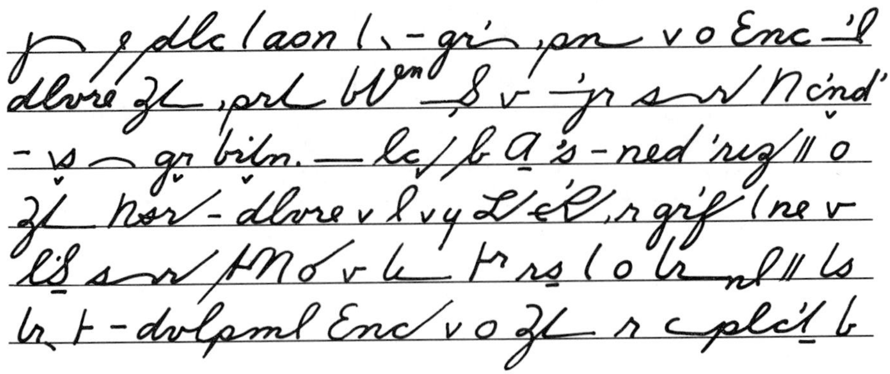

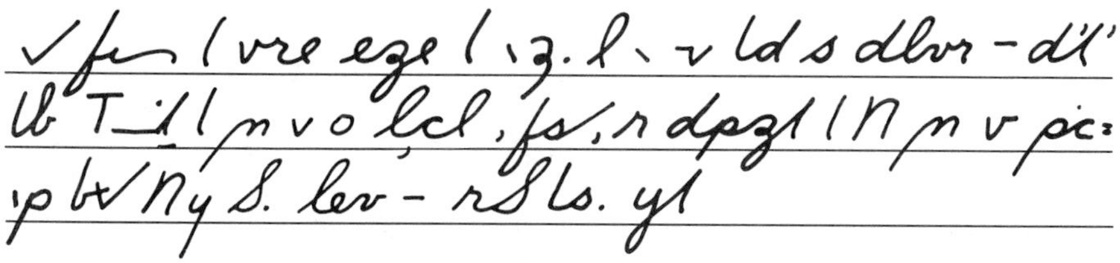

Assignment 4 — **Memorandum 1.** Read and write each of the preview words and phrases for Memorandum 1 until you can read and write each one rapidly and accurately. Then read and write the shorthand for Memorandum 1 to build your writing speed.

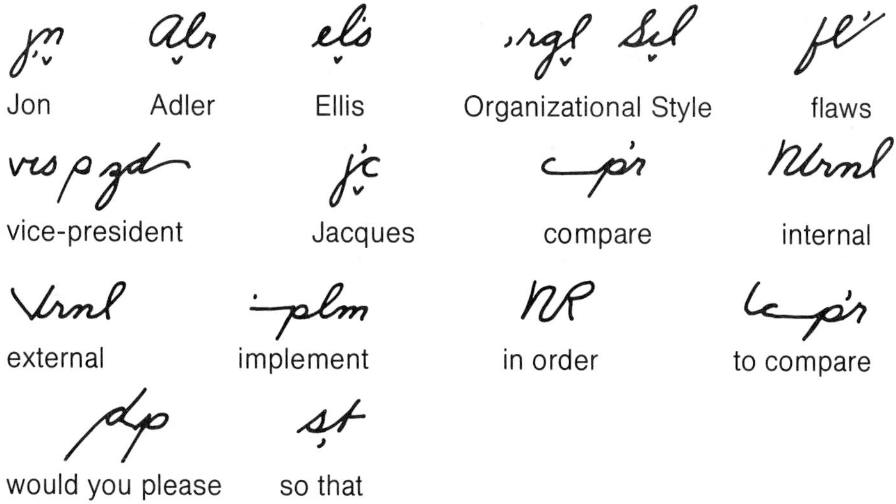
Jon
Adler
Ellis
Organizational Style
flaws
vice-president
Jacques
compare
internal
external
implement
in order
to compare
would you please
so that

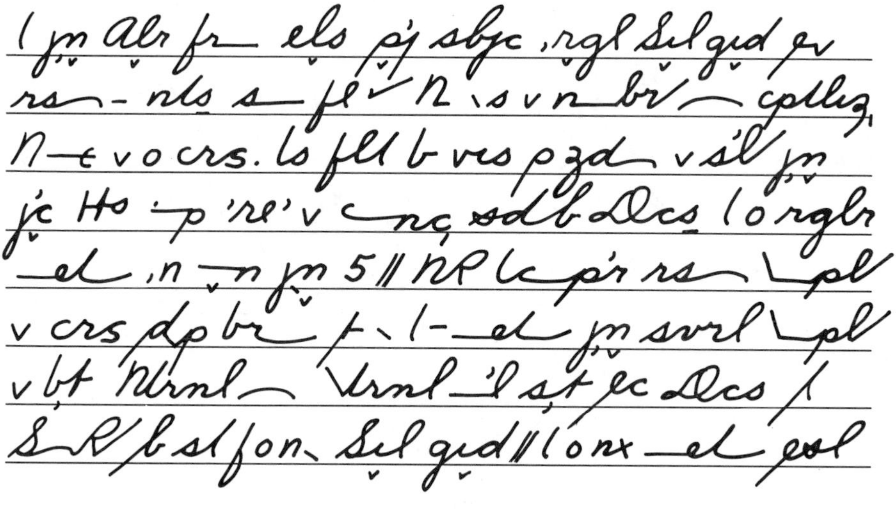

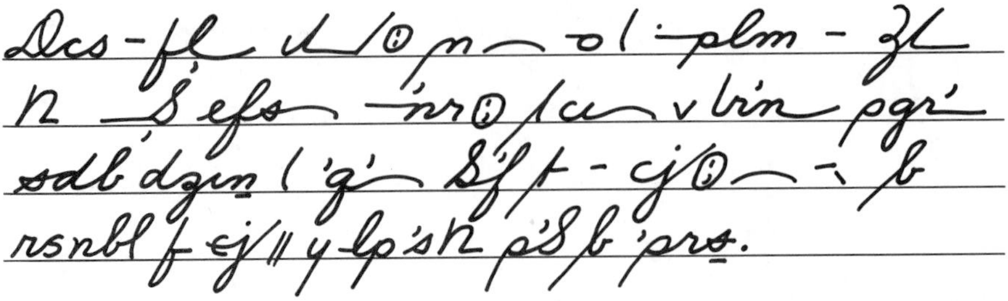

Assignment 5 — **Postcard 1.** Read and write the shorthand for Postcard 1 to build your writing speed.

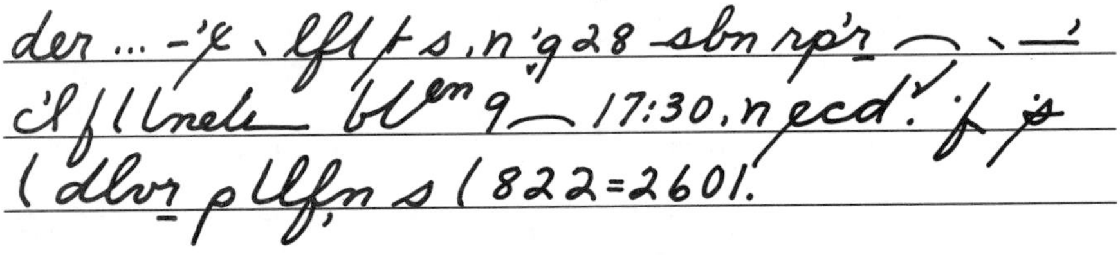

Assignment 6 — **Postcard 2.** Read and write each preview word and phrase for Postcard 2 until you can read and write each one rapidly and accurately. Then read and write the shorthand for Postcard 2 to build your writing speed.

Petcetera grooming boarding pet Guelph breeds

specialize cats we look

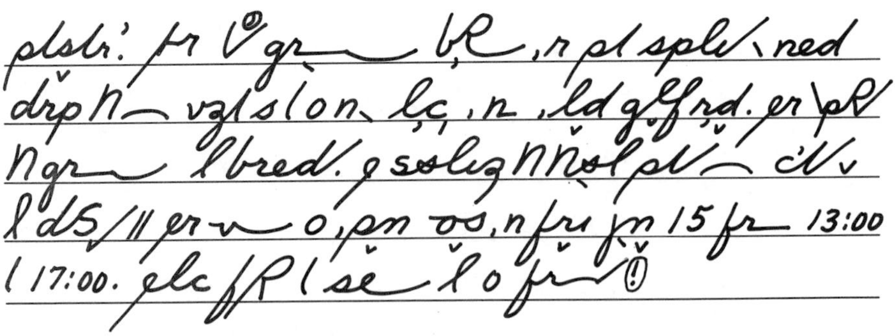

BUILDING SHORTHAND SPEED AND TRANSCRIPTION ACCURACY

Assignment 7 — **Self-testing.** Complete Unit 44 in your *Study Guide* before you proceed with the rest of this chapter.

Assignment 8 — **Taking tape dictation.** To write from dictation the letter, memorandum, and postcards in this chapter, use Cassette 20, Side B from *Theory and Speed-Building Tapes*.

Assignment 9 — **Taking live dictation.** Write from dictation the material which is printed at the end of this chapter. Your instructor will dictate to you at various speeds.

Assignment 10 — **Own-note transcription.** Transcribe at your best typing rate an accurate copy of at least one of the pieces of correspondence you took in shorthand in Assignment 9. Type the assignment in the style requested by your instructor.

Assignment 11 — **Supplementary dictation.** If instructed to do so, read and write the additional material for this chapter found in Appendix B, "Supplementary Correspondence for Dictation."

Key to Assignment 1 — **Review Chart**

	A	B	C	D	E	F	G
25	litera- ture	desira- bility	former	letters	fertili- zer	flexi- bility	furni- ture
26	prefer	permis- sion	prospec- tive	purchased	prior	profit	produc- tion
27	axle/ excel	change	exami- nation	expense	expects	arrange- ments	pas- sengers
28	oxygen	exchange	exactly	foremost	respon- sibility	liter- ary	advisa- bility
29	success	transcribe/ transcript	system- atic	regula- tions	subscrip- tion	insu- lating	assist- ant
30	contri- bution	other- wise	under- stood	contrast	over- load	misunder- standing	another
31	elec- tronic	biology	tonsil- litis	psycho- logical	arthritis	electric	sociol- ogy
32	psycho- logist	circulate	undertake	process	liter- ally	extend/ extent	arrange

TRANSCRIPT OF SHORTHAND—ASSIGNMENT 3

Letter 1 Gentlemen: We would like to announce to you the grand opening of our electronic mail delivery system (20) operating between most of the major centres in Canada, the United States, and Great Britain. More locations (40) will be added as the need arises.

Our system ensures the delivery of all of your letters, charts, (60) or graphs to any of the listed centres within hours of the time they are received at our terminal.

It is (80) true that the developmental electronics of our system are complicated, but you will find it very (100) easy to use. All you have to do is deliver the data to be transmitted to one of our local offices (120) or deposit it in one of the pick-up boxes in your city. Leave the rest to us. Yours truly, *(AW 130; SW 138; SI 1.48)*

TRANSCRIPT OF SHORTHAND—ASSIGNMENT 4

Memorandum 1

TO: Jon Adler
FROM: Ellis Page
SUBJECT: Organizational Style Guide

We have recently noticed some flaws in the use of numbers and capitalization in much of our correspondence. (20) It is felt by the vice-president of sales, Joan Jacques, that this important area of communication (40) should be discussed at our regular meeting on Monday, June 5.

In order to compare recent examples (60) of correspondence, would you please bring with you to the meeting, Jon, several examples of both internal and external (80) mail so that we can discuss what standards will be set for our new Style Guide.

At our next meeting, we shall (100) discuss the following items: when and how to implement the system in the most efficient manner; what kind (120) of training program should be designed to acquaint staff with the changes; and who will be responsible for the changes.

Your help, (140) as in the past, will be appreciated. *(AW 141; SW 146; SI 1.45)*

TRANSCRIPT OF SHORTHAND—ASSIGNMENT 5

Postcard 1 Dear ___________ The watch you left with us on August 28 has been repaired, and you may call for it at any time (20) between 09:00 and 17:30 on weekdays. If you wish it delivered, please telephone us (40) at 822-2601. *(AW 47; SW 44; SI 1.36)*

TRANSCRIPT OF SHORTHAND—ASSIGNMENT 6

PETCETERA

Postcard 2 Whether it's grooming, boarding, or pet supplies you need, drop in and visit us at our new location (20) on the Old Guelph Road. We are experts in grooming all breeds. We specialize in unusual pets and cats of (40) all descriptions.

We are having our Open House on Friday, June 15, from 13:00 to 17:00 (60). We look forward to seeing all our friends! *(AW 64; SW 67; SI 1.49)*

TRANSCRIPTION TEST 3

- Your instructor will provide dictation material to be taken in shorthand.
- Transcribe each piece of dictation in an acceptable style as directed by your instructor.

CHAPTER 45

BUSINESS LETTER DICTATION AND TRANSCRIPTION

Assignment 1 — **Spelling review.** Each of the following sentences contain outlines that are frequently transcribed incorrectly. Transcribe each shorthand outline in your notebook. Then compare your answers with the key located at the end of this chapter. Review any words you may have misspelled. Then write the outlines several times, until you can write them fluently.

1. Each piece of art has ______ own theme.
2. If the goods are misplaced, the fault is ______.
3. ______ not the intention of the exercise to make you feel inadequate.
4. I am ______ for the game.
5. We are ______ a half hour late for the game.
6. Give the incoming mail to the ______ office.
7. If you ______ the right attitude, you can adapt to the changes.
8. Have you ______ your students to speak ______ in class?
9. ______ who wishes may take ______ of the samples.
10. She left for school ______ ago.
11. Why not come over ______ and check the details for yourself.
12. She is ______ ready to cooperate in ______.

Assignment 2 — **Abbreviations and phrasing review.** Read and write the following sentences containing abbreviations and phrases until you can write them quickly and easily and without hesitation.

1.
2.

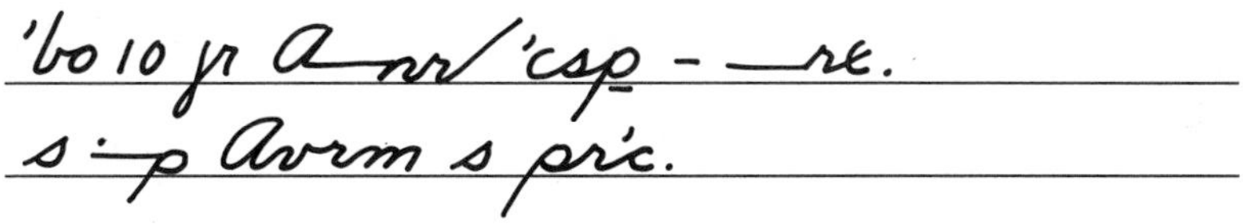

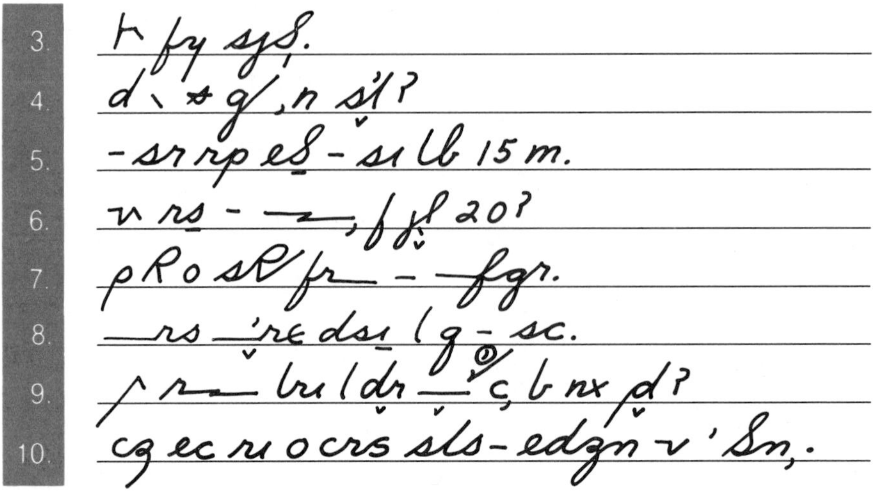

BUILDING TRANSCRIPTION SKILLS

Assignment 3 — **Transcription skills review—Quotation marks and the colon.** Quotation marks set out direct speech and material quoted from other sources. They are also used around some titles and around words used in special ways. A colon introduces what is to follow and is a mark of anticipation. Transcribe these sentences, inserting the correct punctuation. Compare your work with the key which appears on page 296.

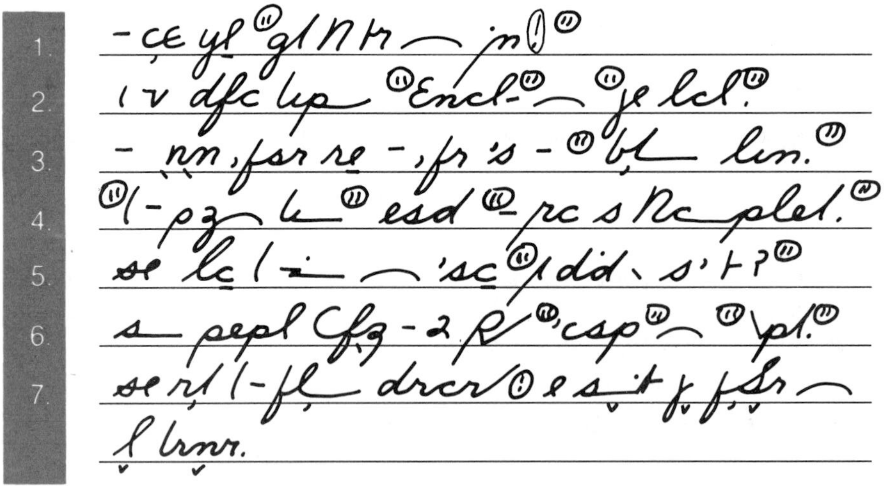

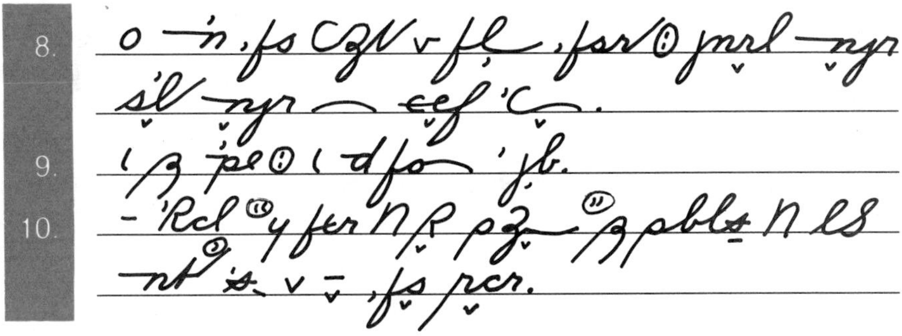
8.
9.
10.

READING AND WRITING SHORTHAND

Assignments 4, 5, and 6, except for those previewed, contain only words presented in Chapters and Units 1 through 32.

Assignment 4 — **Letter 1**. Read and write each preview word and phrase for Letter 1 until you can read and write each one rapidly and accurately. Then read and write the shorthand for Letter 1 to build your writing speed.

handbook before the we should if you can I shall be

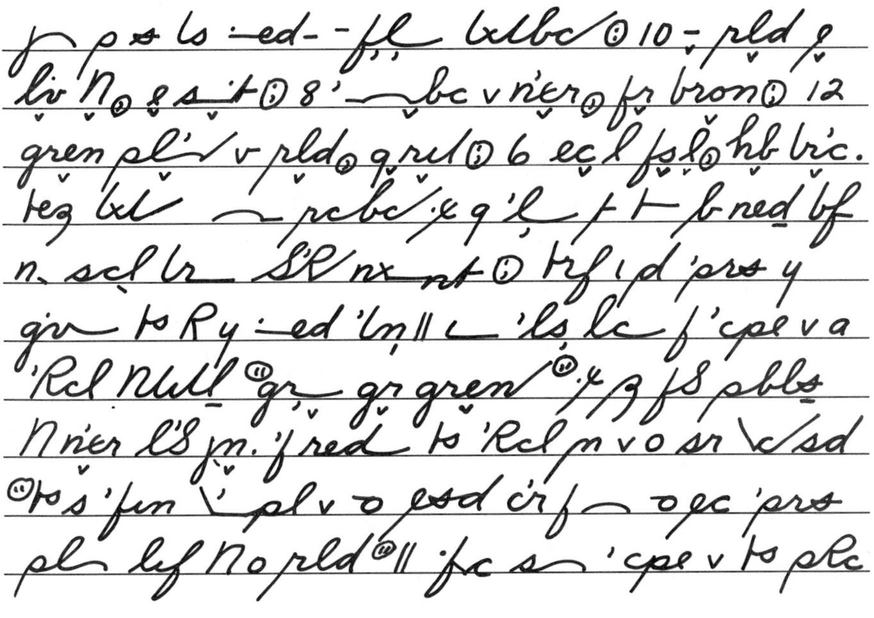

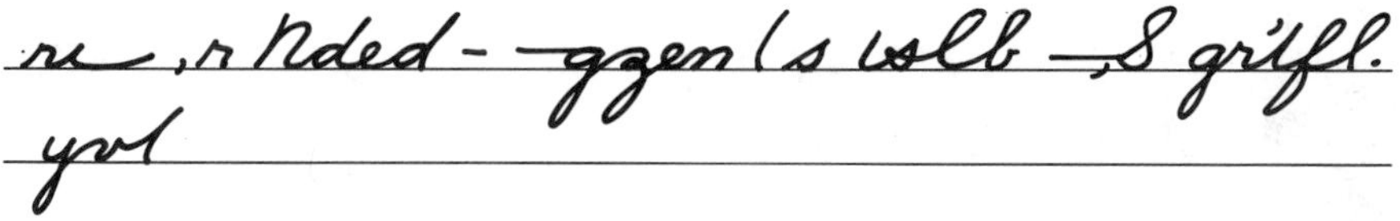

Assignment 5 — Letter 2. Read and write each of the preview words and phrases for Letter 2 until you can read and write each one rapidly and accurately. Then read and write the shorthand for Letter 2 to build your writing speed.

reorder supplier subsequently photocopy apologies

I am sorry we do not have we have had

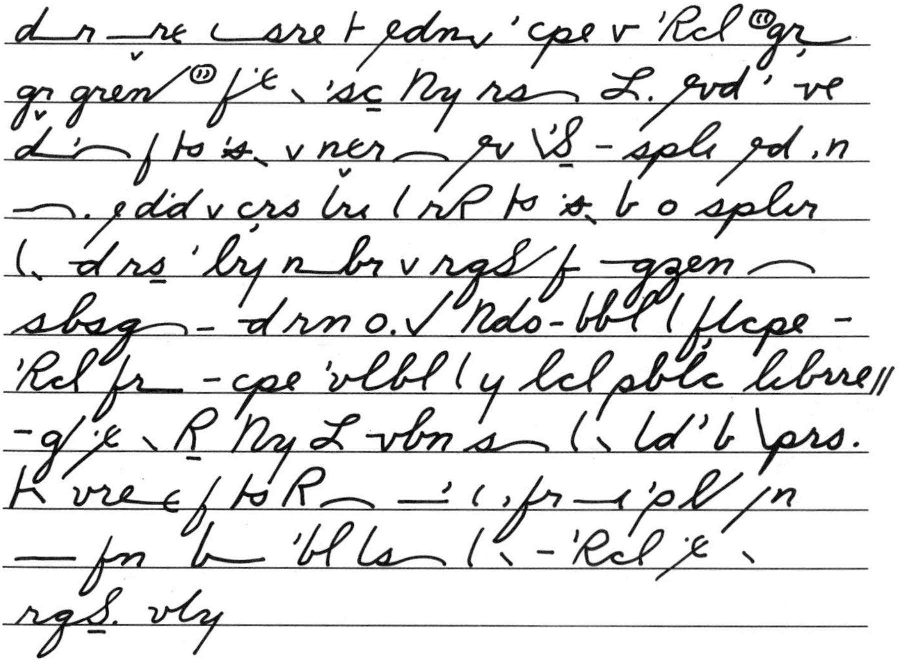

Assignment 6 — Letter 3. Read and write each of the preview words for Letter 3 until you can read and write each one rapidly and accurately. Then read and write the shorthand for Letter 3 to build your writing speed.

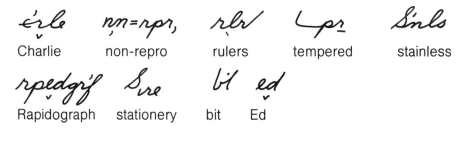

Charlie non-repro rulers tempered stainless

Rapidograph stationery bit Ed

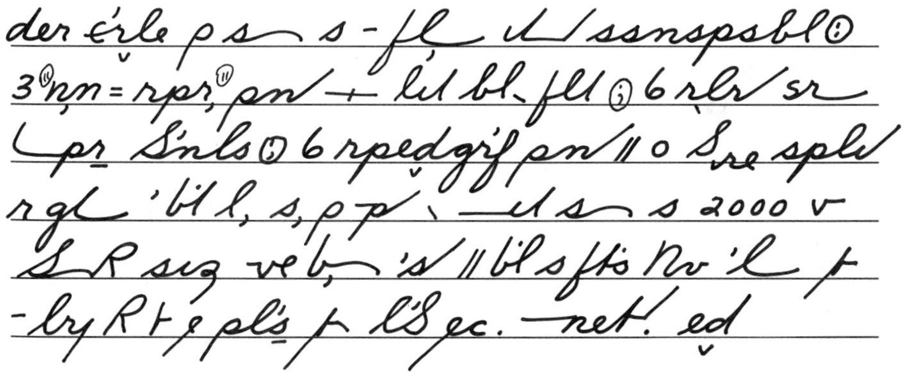

BUILDING SHORTHAND SPEED AND TRANSCRIPTION ACCURACY

Assignment 7 — **Self-testing**. Complete Unit 45 in your *Study Guide* before you proceed with the rest of this chapter.

Assignment 8 — **Taking tape dictation**. To write from dictation the sentences and letters in this chapter, use Cassette 21, Side B from *Theory and Speed-building Tapes*.

Assignment 9 — **Taking live dictation**. Write from dictation the material which is printed at the end of this chapter. Your instructor will dictate to you at various speeds.

Assignment 10 — **Own-note transcription**. Transcribe at your best typing rate an accurate copy of at least one of the pieces of correspondence you took in shorthand in Assignment 9. Type the assignment in the style requested by your instructor.

Assignment 11 — **Supplementary dictation**. If instructed to do so, read and write the additional material for this chapter found in Appendix B, "Supplementary Correspondence for Dictation."

Key to Assignment 1 — **Spelling review**
1. its 2. yours 3. It's 4. all ready 5. already 6. personnel 7. adopt 8. allowed/aloud 9. Anyone/any one 10. some time 11. sometime 12. always/all ways

TRANSCRIPT OF SHORTHAND—ASSIGNMENT 2

1. About ten junior administrators accepted the merchandise.
2. His important advertisement is practical. (20)
3. Thank you for your suggestion.
4. Do you ship goods on Saturday?
5. The senior representative estimated (40) the side to be 15 m.
6. Have you received the memorandum for July 20?
7. Please order our (60) certificates from the manufacturer.
8. Mrs. March decided to question the secretary.
9. Will you remember (80) to write to Dr. May's company by next Wednesday?
10. Because he can write our correspondence satisfactorily, he (100) does not have a stenographer. (106)

TRANSCRIPT OF SHORTHAND—ASSIGNMENT 3

1. The coach yelled, "Get in there and win!"
2. I have difficulty typing "electronically" and "geological." (20)
3. The union officer regarded the offer as the "bottom line."
4. "At the present time," he said, "the work is (40) incomplete."
5. She looked at him and asked, "Why did you say that?"
6. Some people confuse the two words "accept" and "except."
7. She (60) wrote to the following directors: E. Smith, J. Foster, and L. Turner.
8. Our main office consists of the following (80) officers: General Manager, Sales Manager, and Chief Accountant.
9. I was happy: I had found a job.
10. The (100) article "Your Future in Word Processing" was published in last month's issue of <u>The Office Worker</u>. (118)

TRANSCRIPT OF SHORTHAND—ASSIGNMENT 4

Letter 1 Gentlemen: Please ship to us immediately the following textbooks:

10 <u>The World We Live In</u>, E. Smith
8 <u>A</u> (20) <u>Handbook of Nature</u>, F. R. Brown

12 Green Plants Of The World, G. Wright
6 Ecology For Us All, H. B. Track

These (40) texts and the workbooks which go along with them will be needed before the new school term starts next month; therefore, I would (60) appreciate your giving this order your immediate attention.

I am also looking for a copy (80) of an article entitled "Growing Great Greens" which was first published in Nature last June. After reading this (100) article, one of our senior executives said, "This is a fine example of how we should care for and how (120) we can appreciate plant life in our world."

If you can send a copy of this particular writing, or, (140) indeed, the magazine itself, I shall be most grateful. Yours very truly, (*AW 149; SW 153: SI 1.43*)

TRANSCRIPT OF SHORTHAND—ASSIGNMENT 5

Letter 2 Dear Mr. March: I am sorry that we do not have a copy of the article "Growing Great Greens" for which you asked (20) in your recent letter. We have had a heavy demand for this issue of Nature, and we have exhausted (40) the supply we had on hand. We did, of course, try to reorder this issue, but our supplier, too, had received (60) a large number of requests for the magazine and subsequently had run out. You will undoubtedly be (80) able to photocopy the article from the copy available at your local public library.

The (100) goods which you ordered in your letter have been sent to you today by express. Thank you very much for this order, (120) and may I offer my apologies once more for not being able to send to you the article which you (140) requested. Very truly yours. (*AW 141; SW 146; SI 1.44*)

TRANSCRIPT OF SHORTHAND—ASSIGNMENT 6

Letter 3 Dear Charlie: Please send us the following items as soon as possible:

3 "non-repro" pens—light blue felt
6 (20) rulers, "spring tempered stainless"
6 "Rapidograph" pens

Our stationery supplies are getting a bit low, so perhaps (40) you might send us 2 000 of the standard size heavy bond as well.

Bill us for this invoice along with the large (60) order that we placed with you last week.

Many thanks. Ed (69) (*AW 69; SW 69; SI 1.39*)

CHAPTER 46

BUSINESS LETTER DICTATION AND TRANSCRIPTION

Assignment 1 — **Abbreviations and phrasing review**. Read and write the following sentences containing abbreviations and phrases until you can write them quickly and easily and without hesitation.

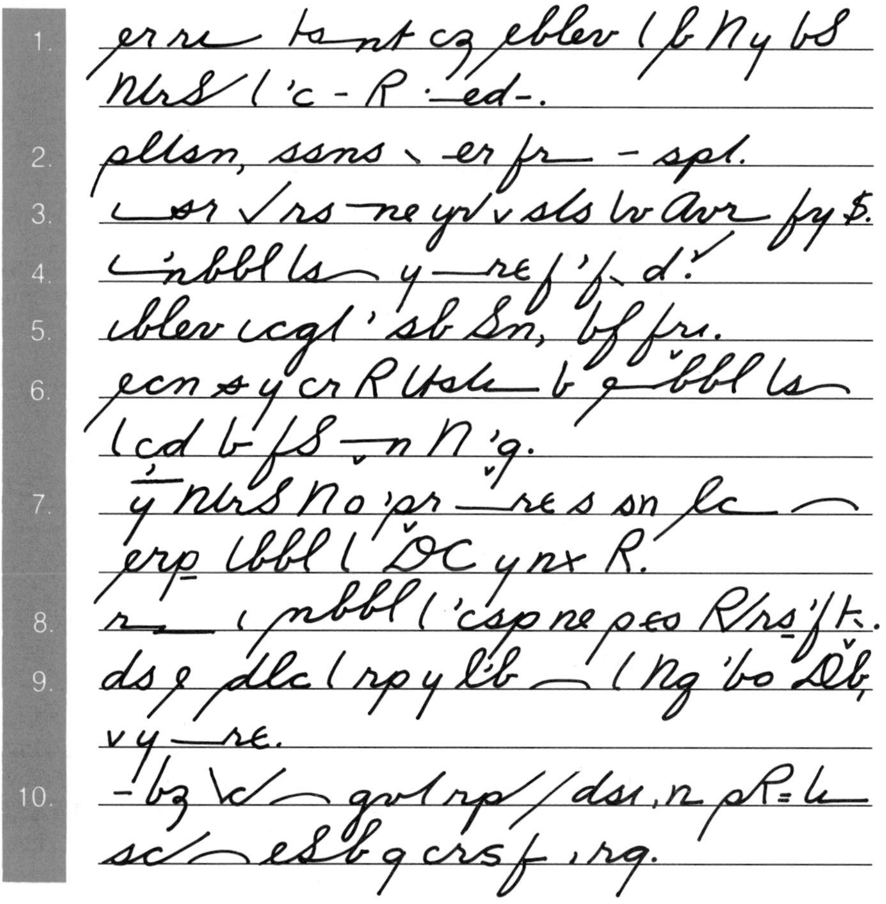
1.
2.
3.
4.
5.
6.
7.
8.
9.
10.

BUILDING TRANSCRIPTION SKILLS

Assignment 2 — **Transcription skills review** — Word division and paragraphs. Review and study the following rules governing paragraphs and word division. Then be sure to use these guidelines when you transcribe.

Paragraphs. A paragraph develops one main idea, and each sentence in that paragraph is used to develop the core theme.

Word Division. You may sometimes find it necessary to break a word at the end of a line of typing in order to keep an even right margin. Follow the rules below to guide you in dividing words.

- Divide words only when absolutely necessary.
- Divide only between syllables. Be guided by your dictionary.
- Words of one syllable are never divided.
- Do not set off a one-letter syllable at the beginning or at the end of a word.
- Divide unbroken compound words between the elements in the compound.
  Example: never- theless or neverthe- less.
- Divide hyphenated compound words at the hyphen in the compound.
  Example: Brother- in-law or brother-in- law.
- When two vowels that come together have separate sounds, divide between the vowels.
  Example: cre- ative.
- Whenever possible, try to divide a word close to the middle.
  Example: propri- etary.
- Always show the street number on the same line with at least the first element of the street name.

  Example: 288 Mountain
  Heights
  (*not* 288
  Mountain Heights)

Assignment 3 — **Word division**. In transcribing, we are often required to divide words at the end of a line. In your notebook, write each of the following words, using the hyphen to indicate the preferred position at which you may divide the word. Then compare your answers with the key located at the end of this chapter. Review any words you may have improperly divided. Then write the shorthand outlines for the words several times, until you can write them fluently.

1. activity	5. accommodate	9. graduation
2. introduce	6. supervise	10. valuable
3. investment	7. international	11. fluorescent
4. appreciation	8. circumstances	12. retroactive

READING AND WRITING SHORTHAND

Assignments 4, 5, and 6, except for those previewed, contain only words presented n Chapters and Units 1 through 32.

Assignment 4 — **Letter 1**. Read and write each of the preview words and phrases for Letter 1 until you can read and write each one rapidly and accurately. Then read and write the shorthand for Letter 1 to build your writing speed.

Rose recipe wheat flour millilitres roll

had been to buy

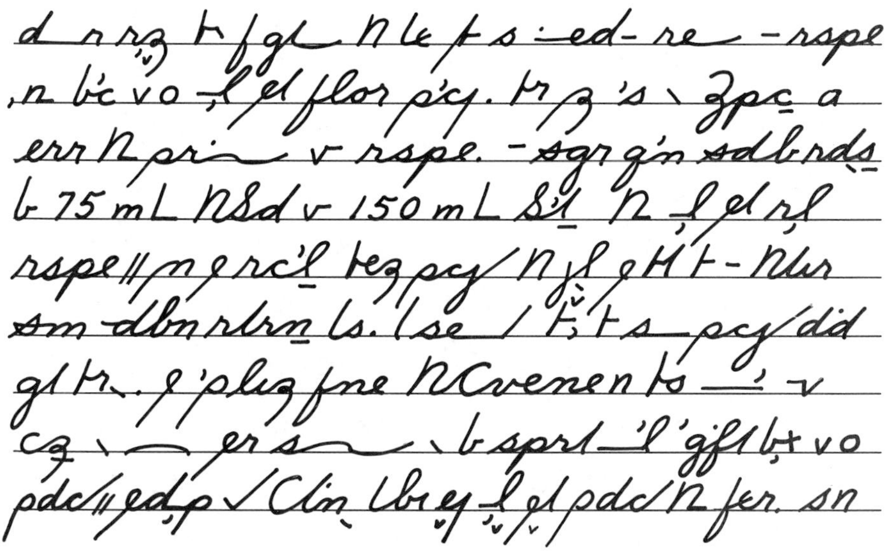

Assignment 5 — **Article 1**. Read and write each preview word and phrase for Article 1 until you can read and write each one rapidly and accurately. Then read and write the shorthand for Article 1 to build your writing speed.

communities	experiencing	proving	aquifer	sulphur
content	resulting	rotten	drinking	troubled
numerous	residents	emergencies	townspeople	taps
mineral	In order to make			

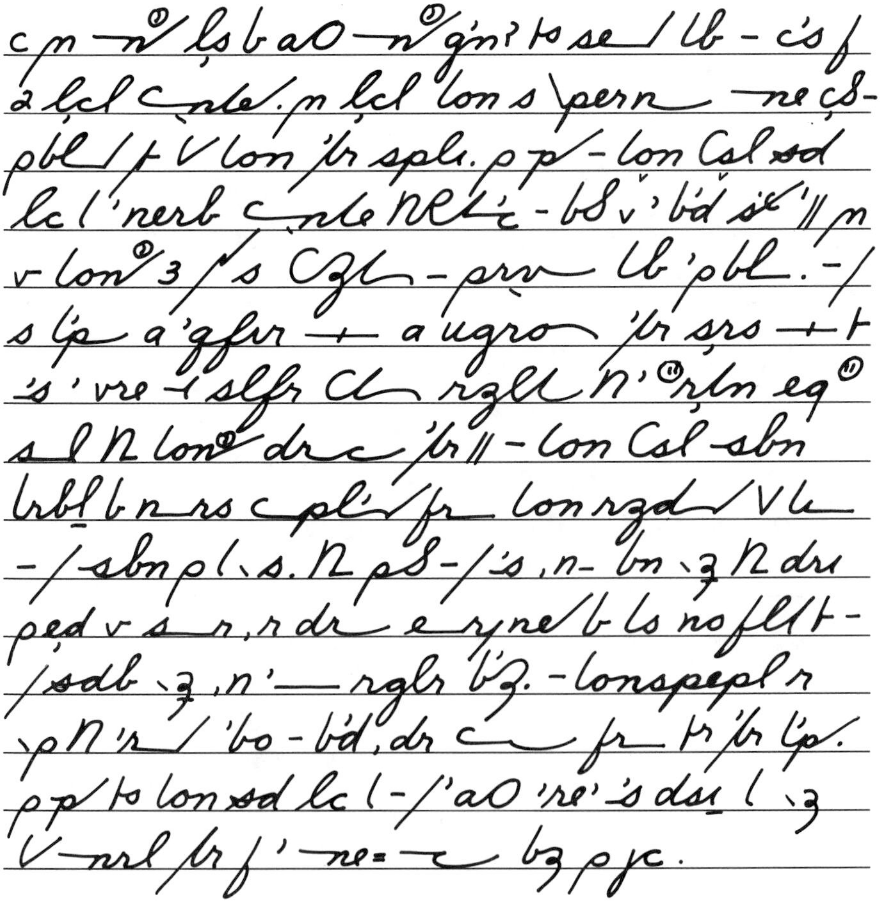

Assignment 6 — **Letter 2**. Read and write each preview word and phrase for Letter 2 until you can read and write each one rapidly and accurately. Then read and write the shorthand for Letter 2 to build your writing speed.

replacing Video Diskette command fashion styles

assembling bicycle for you

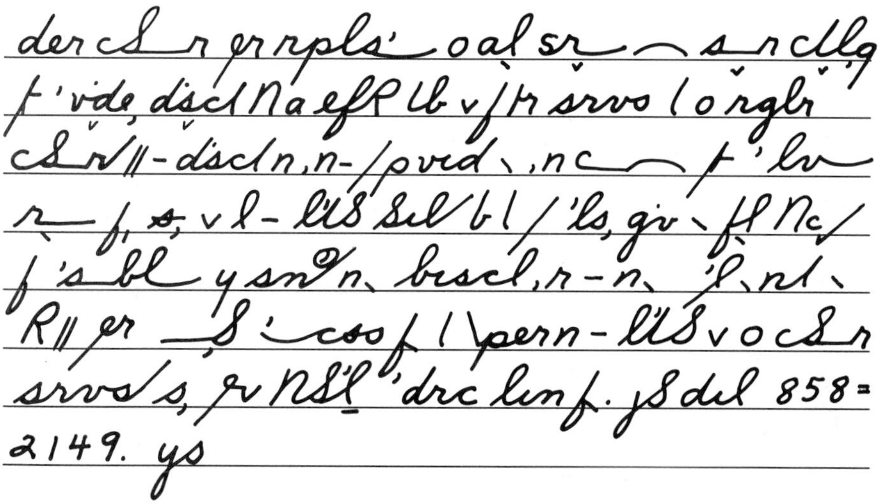

BUILDING SHORTHAND SPEED AND TRANSCRIPTION ACCURACY

Assignment 7 — **Self-testing**. Complete Unit 46 in your *Study Guide* before you proceed with the rest of this chapter.

Assignment 8 — **Taking tape dictation**. To write from dictation the sentences, the letters, and the article in this chapter, use Cassette 21, Side B from *Theory and Speed-Building Tapes*.

Assignment 9 — **Taking live dictation**. Write from dictation the material which is printed at the end of this chapter. Your instructor will dictate to you at various speeds.

Assignment 10 — **Own-note transcription**. Transcribe at your best typing rate an accurate copy of at least one of the pieces of correspondence you took in shorthand in Assignment 9. Type the assignment in the style requested by your instructor.

Assignment 11 — **Supplementary dictation.** If instructed to do so, read and write the additional material for this chapter found in Appendix B, "Supplementary Correspondence for Dictation."

TRANSCRIPT OF SHORTHAND—ASSIGNMENT 1

1. We are writing this month because we believe it will be in your best interests to acknowledge the order (20) immediately.
2. Please let us know as soon as you hear from the superintendent.
3. I am sure you will receive many years (40) of satisfactory television advertising for your dollar.
4. I may not be able to send your (60) merchandise for a few days.
5. I believe I can get a substitute stenographer before Friday.
6. We cannot ship your (80) credit order at this time, but we may be able to send it C.O.D. by the first Monday in August.
7. Your (100) interest in our April merchandise is sincerely welcome and we are pleased to be able to discount your next (120) order.
8. Remember, I will not be able to accept any purchase orders received after Thursday.
9. Dear Sir: (140) We would like to represent your laboratory and to inquire about distribution of your merchandise.
10. The (160) business executives and government representatives will decide on the part-time secretaries and (180) establish good correspondence for the organization. (190)

Key to Assignment 3 — **Word Division.**

1. activ- ity 2. intro- duce 3. invest- ment 4. appre- ciation or appreci- ation 5. accom- modate 6. super- vise 7. inter- national 8. circum- stances 9. gradu- ation 10. valu- able 11. flu-orescent 12. retro- active

TRANSCRIPT OF SHORTHAND—ASSIGNMENT 4

Letter 1 Dear Mr. Rose: Thank you for getting in touch with us immediately regarding the recipe on the back (20) of our whole wheat flour package. There was, as you suspected, an error in the printing of the recipe. The (40) sugar quantity should be reduced to 75 mL instead of the 150 (60) mL stated in the whole wheat roll recipe.

When we recalled these packages in July, we thought that (80) the entire shipment had been returned to us. It seems, though, that some packages did get through. We apologize (100) for any inconvenience this may have caused you, and we are sending you by separate mail a gift box of (120) our products.

We do hope you will continue to buy Edge Whole Wheat products in the future. Sincerely, (*AW 129; SW 138; SI 1.49*)

TRANSCRIPT OF SHORTHAND—ASSIGNMENT 5

Article 1 Can one man's loss be another man's gain? This seems to be the case for two local communities. One local (20) town is experiencing many costly problems with its town water supply. Perhaps the Town Council should look to (40) a nearby community in order to make the best of a bad situation.

One of the town's three wells is (60) consistently proving to be a problem. The well is tapping an aquifer—an underground water source—that (80) has a very high sulphur content, resulting in a "rotten egg smell" in the town's drinking water.

The Town (100) Council has been troubled by numerous complaints from town residents every time the well has been put to use. In the (120) past, the well has only been used in the dry period of the summer or during emergencies, but it is (40) now felt that the well should be used on a more regular basis. The townspeople are up in arms about the bad odor coming from their water taps. Perhaps this town should look at the way another area has decided (180) to use its mineral water for a money-making business project. (*AW 186; SW 193; SI 1.45*)

TRANSCRIPT OF SHORTHAND—ASSIGNMENT 6

Letter 2 Dear Customer: We are replacing our annual Spring and Summer Catalogue with a Video Diskette in (20) an effort to be of further service to our regular customers.

The diskette not only will provide you, (40) on command, with a living room fashion show of all the latest styles, but it will also give you full instructions (60) for assembling your son's new bicycle or the new wall unit you order.

We are most anxious for you to (80) experience the latest of our customer services, so we have installed a direct line for you. Just dial (100) 858-2149. Yours sincerely, (*AW 102; SW 107; SI 1.47*).

CHAPTER 47

BUSINESS LETTER DICTATION AND TRANSCRIPTION

Assignment 1 — **Abbreviations and phrasing review.** Read and write the following sentences containing abbreviations and phrases until you can write them quickly and easily and without hesitation.

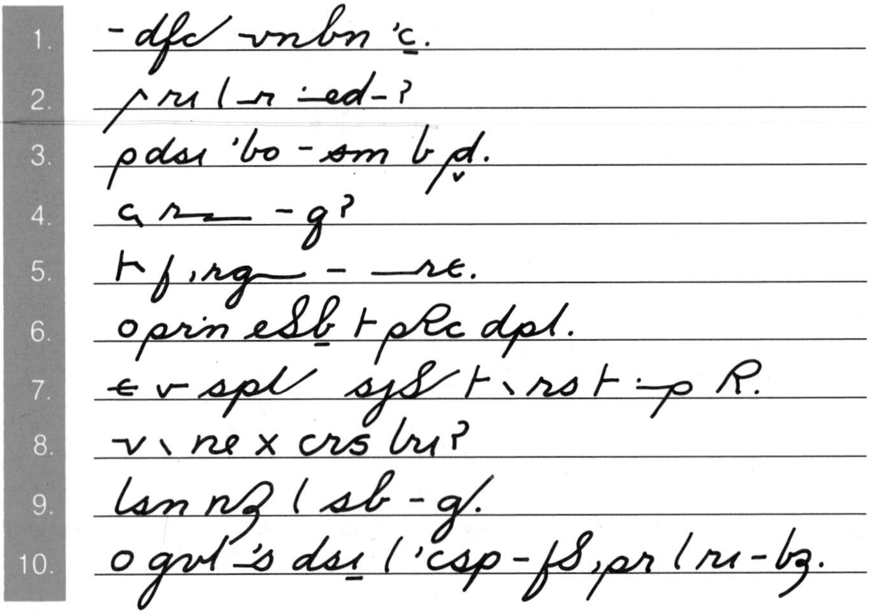

BUILDING TRANSCRIPTION SKILLS

Assignment 2 — **Transcription skills review—Paragraphs and subject-verb agreement.** A paragraph should be a progressive development of the subject, and it should flow logically from the previous paragraph. The verb must always agree with the subject of a sentence. A singular subject requires a singular verb; a plural subject requires a plural verb. Transcribe the following sentences; then take special note of the subject-verb agreement in number. Compare your work with the transcript which appears on page 311.

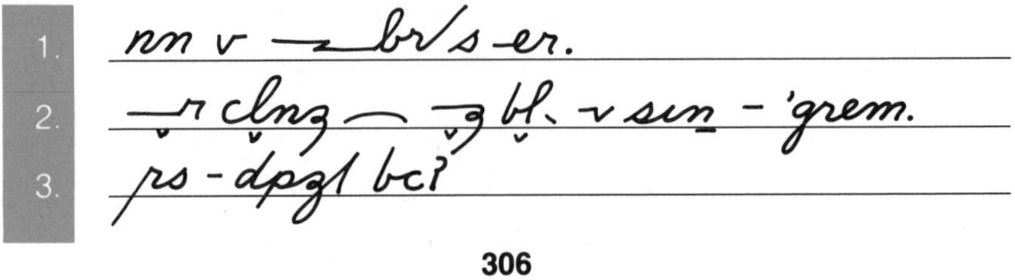

4.
5.
6.
7.
8.
9.
10.

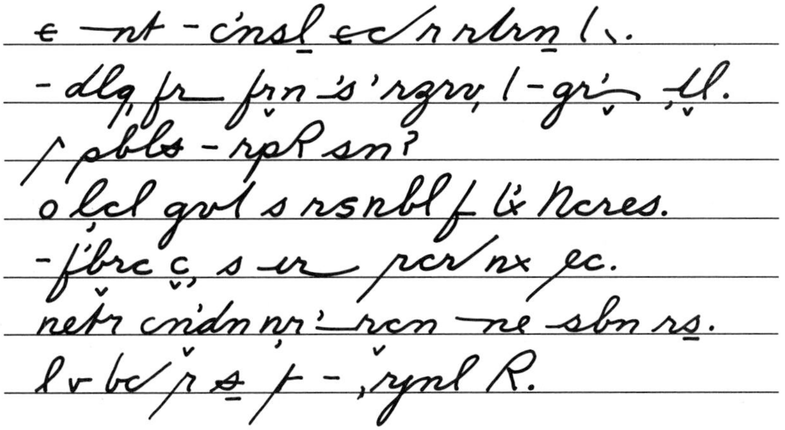

READING AND WRITING SHORTHAND

Assignments 3, 4, 5, and 6, except for those previewed, contain only words presented in Chapters and Units 1 through 32.

Assignments 3 — **Letter 1**. Read and write each preview word and phrase for Letter 1 until you can read and write each one rapidly and accurately. Then read and write the shorthand for Letter 1 to build your writing speed.

remarks   to give

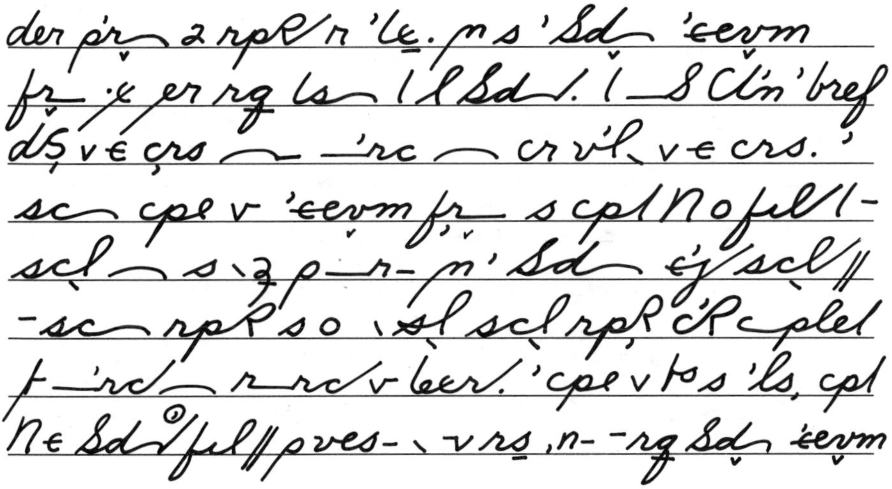

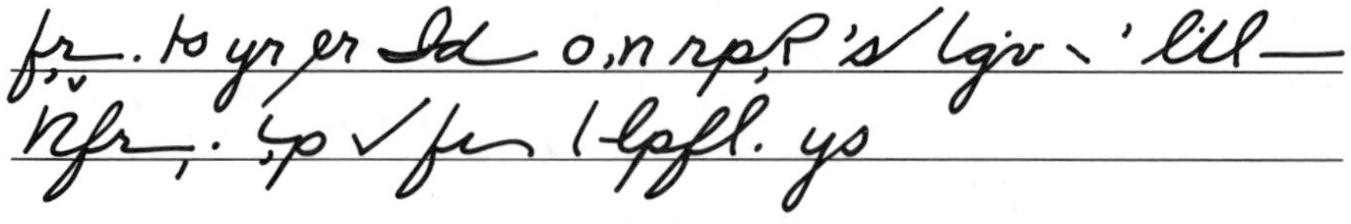

Assignment 4 — **Letter 2**. Read and write each preview word and phrase for Letter 1 until you can read and write each one rapidly and accurately. Then read and write the shorthand for Letter 1 to build your writing speed.

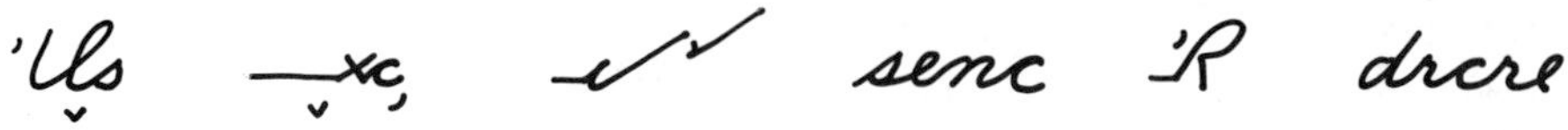

Atlas Mexico highways scenic heart directory

campgrounds explore discovery travelling to visit

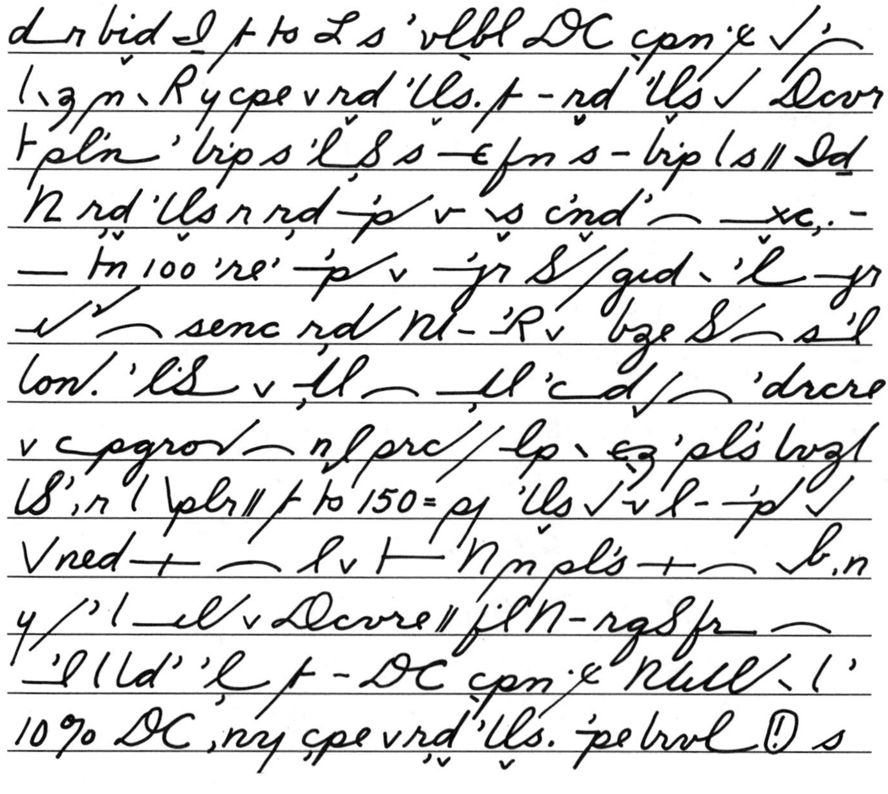

Assignment 5 — **Letter 3**. Read and write each of the preview words and phrases for Letter 3 until you can read and write each one rapidly and accurately. Then read and write the shorthand for Letter 3 to build your writing speed.

recession resounding sidelines wringing hands

worrying unprecedented economic shame periods

ignored sentiment recognized equities crisis

bargains portfolio boom era as bad as many times

great deal to sweeten

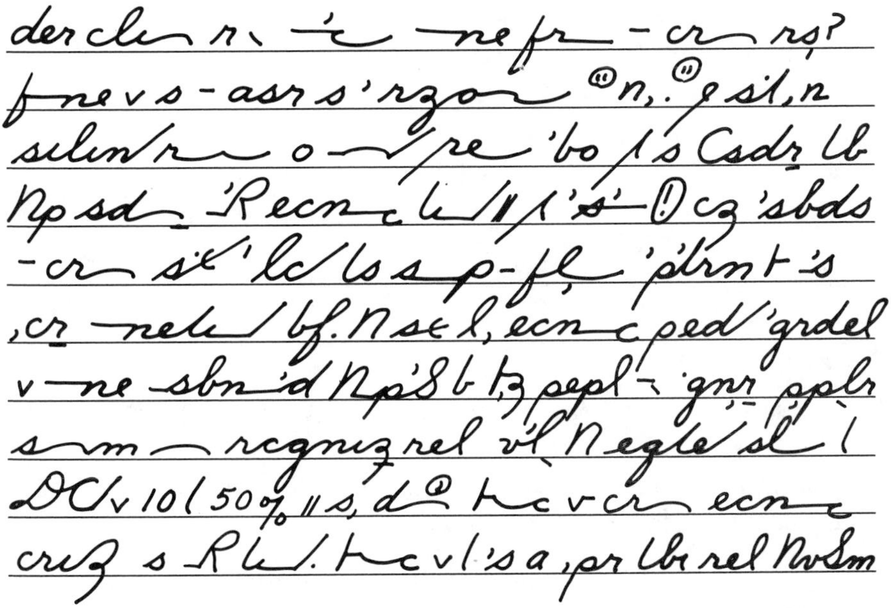

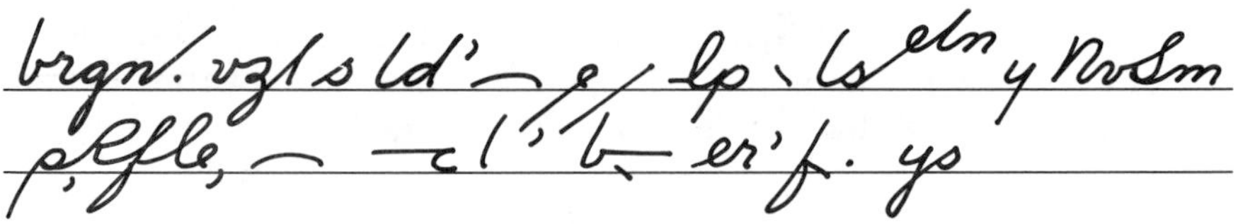

Assignment 6 — **Letter 4**. Read and write each preview word and phrase for Letter 4 until you can read and write each one rapidly and accurately. Then read and write the shorthand for Letter 4 to build your writing speed.

subsequently steward branches elections you're

useful to write

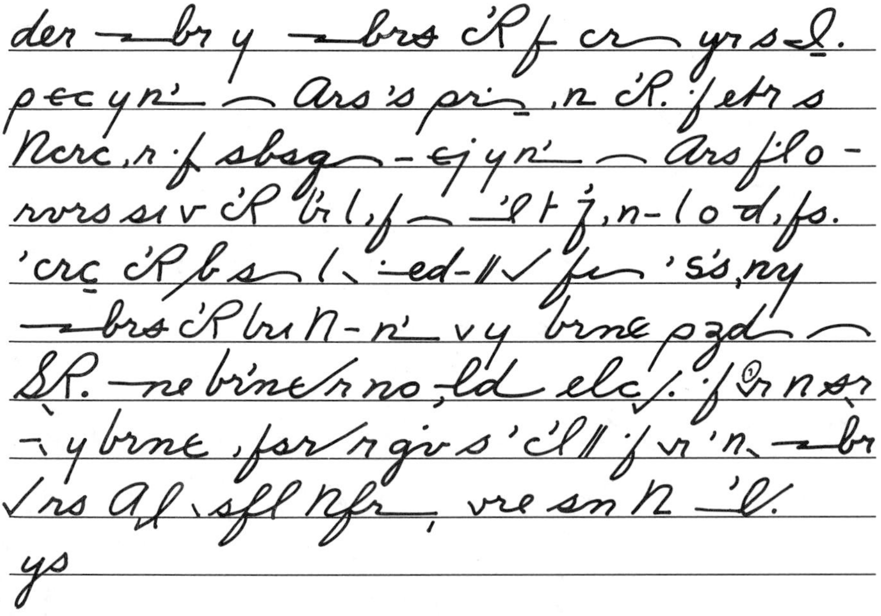

BUILDING SHORTHAND SPEED AND TRANSCRIPTION ACCURACY

Assignment 7 — **Self-testing**. Complete Unit 47 in your *Study Guide* before you proceed with the rest of this chapter.

Assignment 8 — **Taking tape dictation**. To write from dictation the sentences and letters in this chapter, use Cassette 22, Side B from *Theory and Speed-Building Tapes*.

Assignment 9 — **Taking live dictation**. Write from dictation the material which is printed at the end of this chapter. Your instructor will dictate to you at various speeds.

Assignment 10 — **Own-note transcription**. Transcribe at your best typing rate an accurate copy of at least one of the pieces of correspondence you took in shorthand in Assignment 9. Type the assignment in the style requested by your instructor.

Assignment 11 — **Supplementary dictation**. If instructed to do so, read and write the additional material for this chapter found in Appendix B, "Supplementary Correspondence for Dictation."

TRANSCRIPT OF SHORTHAND—ASSIGNMENT 1

1. The difficulties have not been acknowledged.
2. Will you write to her immediately?
3. Please decide about the shipment (20) by Wednesday.
4. Can you remember the question?
5. Thank you for organizing the merchandise.
6. Our principal established (40) that particular department.
7. Each of the superintendents suggests that you receive that important order. (60)
8. Have you any extra correspondence to write?
9. It is not necessary to substitute the goods.
10. Our government (80) has decided to accept the first opportunity to right the business. (94)

TRANSCRIPT OF SHORTHAND—ASSIGNMENT 2

1. None of the members is here.
2. Mr. Collins and Ms. Blue have signed the agreement.
3. Where is (20) the deposit book?
4. Each month the cancelled cheques are returned to you.
5. The delegation from France has a reservation at the Grand Hotel. (40)
6. Will you publish the report soon?
7. Our local government is responsible for the tax increase.
8. The Fabric (60) Company is hiring workers next week.
9. Neither Canadian nor American money has been received.
10. All of the (80) books were shipped with the original order. (87)

TRANSCRIPT OF SHORTHAND—ASSIGNMENT 3

Letter 1 Dear Parent: Two reports are attached. One is a Student Achievement Form which we are required to send to (20) all students. It must contain a brief description of each course and the mark and credit value of each course. A (40) second copy of the Achievement Form is kept in our files at the school and is used primarily when a student (60) changes schools.

The second report is our usual school report card complete with marks and remarks of the teachers. (80) A copy of this is also kept in each student's file.

Previously you have received only the required Student (100) Achievement Form. This year we are including our own report as well to give you a little more information. (120) I hope you will find it helpful. Yours sincerely, (*AW 129; SW 129;SI 1.39*)

TRANSCRIPT OF SHORTHAND—ASSIGNMENT 4

Letter 2 Dear Mr. Boyd: Enclosed with this letter is a valuable discount coupon which you will want to use when you (20) order your copy of Road Atlas. With the Road Atlas you will discover that planning a trip is almost as (40) much fun as the trip itself.

Included in the Road Atlas are road maps of the United States, Canada, and (60) Mexico. The more than one hundred area maps of major cities will guide you along major highways and (80) scenic roads into the heart of busy cities and small towns. A listing of hotel and motel accommodations, and (100) a directory of campgrounds and national parks will help you choose a place to visit, to stay, or to (120) explore.

With this 150-page Atlas you will have all the maps you will ever need—and all of them in one (140) place—and you will be on your way to miles of discovery.

Fill in the request form and mail it today along (160) with the discount coupon which entitles you to a 10 per cent discount on your copy of Road Atlas. Happy (180) travelling! Sincerely, (*AW 182; SW 184; SI 1.41*)

TRANSCRIPT OF SHORTHAND—ASSIGNMENT 5

Letter 3 Dear Client: Are you making money from the current recession? For many of us, the answer is a resounding (20) "no." We sit on the sidelines wringing our hands worrying about what is considered to be unprecedented (40) hard economic times.

What a shame! Because, as bad as the current situation looks, it is simply following (60) a pattern that has occurred many times before. In such low economic periods, a great deal of money (80) has been made in the past by those people who ignored popular sentiment and recognized real value in (100) equities selling at discounts of 10 to 50 per cent.

So, don't think of the current economic crisis as (120) hard times. Think of it as an opportunity to buy real investment bargains. Visit us today, and we will (140) help you to sweeten your investment portfolio and make it a boom era for you. Yours sincerely (*AW 145; SW 158; SI 1.52*)

TRANSCRIPT OF SHORTHAND—ASSIGNMENT 6

Letter 4 Dear Member: Your membership card for the current year is enclosed. Please check your name and address as printed on the (20) card. If either is incorrect, or if you subsequently change your name and address, fill out the reverse side of (40) the card, tear it off, and mail that half only to our head office. A corrected card will be sent to you immediately. (60)

You will find a space on your membership card to write in the name of your branch president and steward. Many (80) branches are now holding elections. If you're not sure who your branch officers are, give us a call.

If you are (100) a new member, you will receive additional useful information very soon in the mails. Yours sincerely, (*AW 122; SW 120; SI 1.40*)

CHAPTER 48

BUSINESS LETTER DICTATION AND TRANSCRIPTION

BUILDING TRANSCRIPTION SKILLS

Assignment 1 — **Spelling review**. Follow the steps outlined in Chapter 36 to check your ability to spell the following words correctly.

1. formerly	6. effectively	11. personal	16. nuclear
2. warranty	7. copyright	12. consequently	17. excess
3. preside	8. analysis	13. acceptable	18. access
4. appreciated	9. systematic	14. oversight	19. fertilizer
5. propose	10. possession	15. controller	20. forecast

Assignment 2 — **Spelling review**. The following sentences include the words in shorthand in the same order in which they appear in the list in Assignment 1 of this chapter. Transcribe each shorthand outline in your notebook. Compare your answers with the list in Assignment 1. Then write the outlines several times until you can write them fluently.

1. Carter was  president of the United States.
2. If the  on the car is still in effect, make a claim to the company.
3. Ask Julie to  over the meeting.
4. If you can deliver the order by next week, it will be very much .
5. Do you  sending the sales manager on that assignment?
6. If you write , your message will have impact.
7. It is a 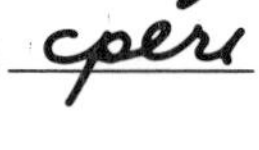 infringement to reproduce material from that book.
8. The  of the poem is brilliant.
9. Set up a  method for checking all documents.

10. He took ______ of his new house yesterday.
11. His new house is part of his ______ property.
12. The golfer practised her chip shots; ______, she lowered her handicap.
13. It is entirely ______ for you to attend the dinner.
14. It was an ______ on my part that you were not sent a copy of the letter.
15. The financial ______ prepared the income statement for the first quarter.
16. The ______ arms race is rather frightening.
17. Place all ______ baggage in compartment 2.
18. The economist has ______ to statistics to help him forecast accurately.
19. Add some ______ to the soil for a better yield next year.
20. The weather ______ predicts rain for tomorrow.

READING AND WRITING SHORTHAND

Assignments 3, 4, 5, and 6, except for those previewed, contain only words presented in Chapters and Units 1 through 32.

Assignment 3 — **Article 1**. Read and write each of the preview words and phrases for Article 1 until you can read and write each one rapidly and accurately. Then read and write the shorthand for Article 1 to build your writing speed.

beverage   movie   reservation   occurs   booking   to fly

you can make | will not be | has been received

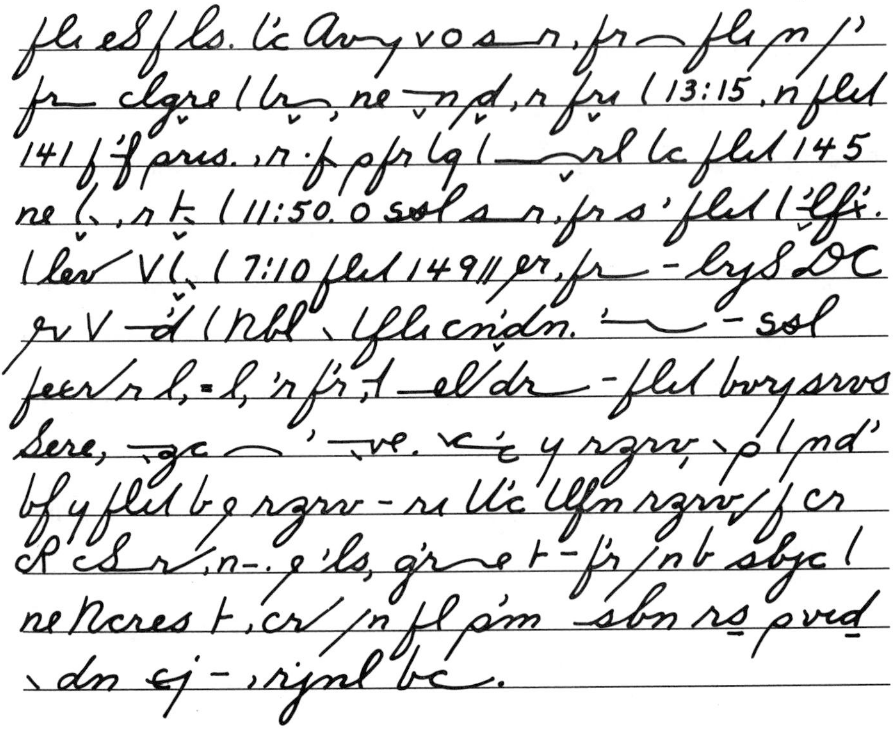

Assignment 4 — **Article 2.** Read and write each of the preview words and phrases for Article 2 until you can read and write each one rapidly and accurately. Then read and write the shorthand for Article 2 to build your writing speed.

lowest | midmorning | flights | refundable | repayment

midweek | weekend | destinations | if you will | at any time

you will not

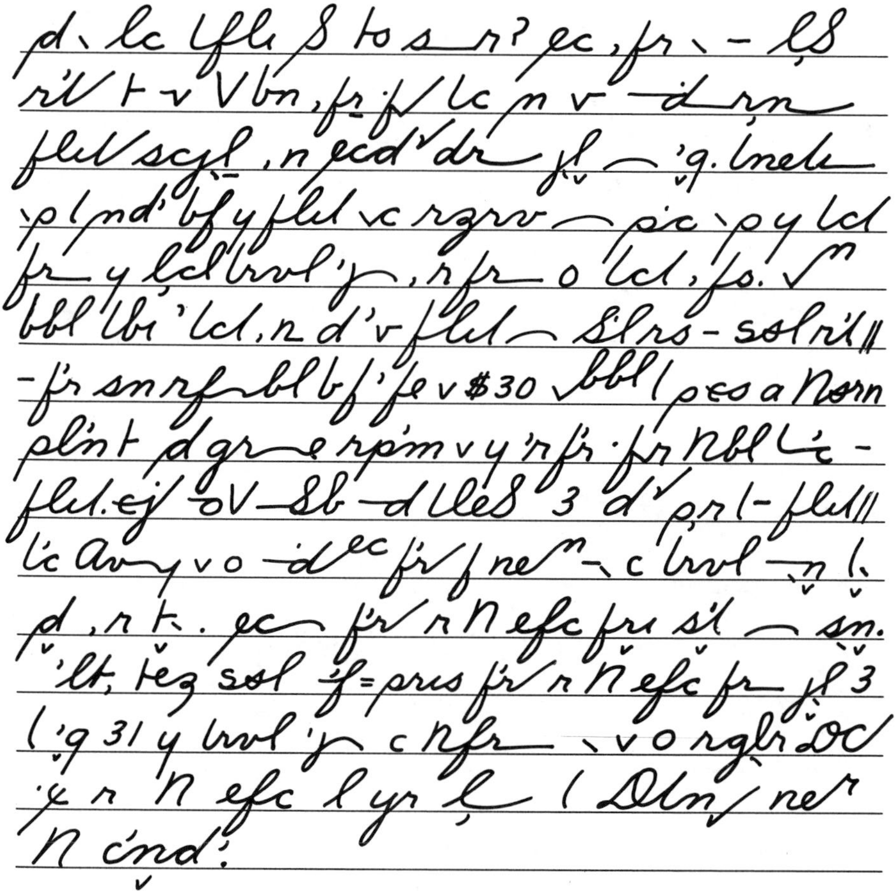

Assignment 5 — **Letter 1**. Read and write each of the preview words for Letter 1 until you can read and write each one rapidly and accurately. Then read and write the shorthand for Letter 1 to build your writing speed.

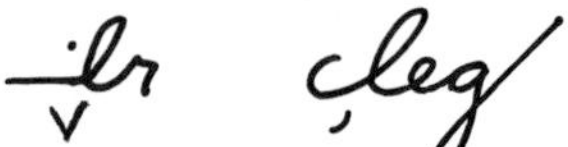

Miller colleagues

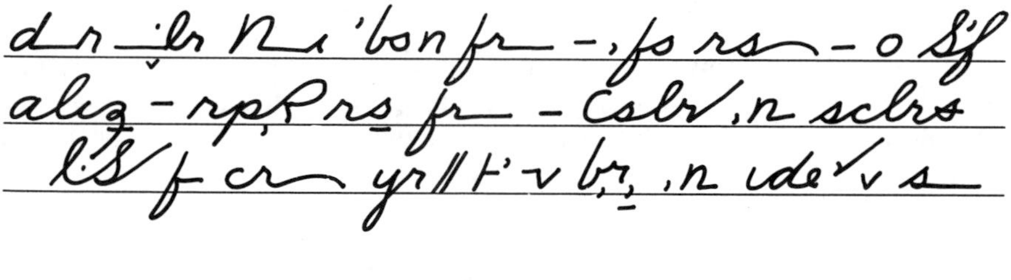

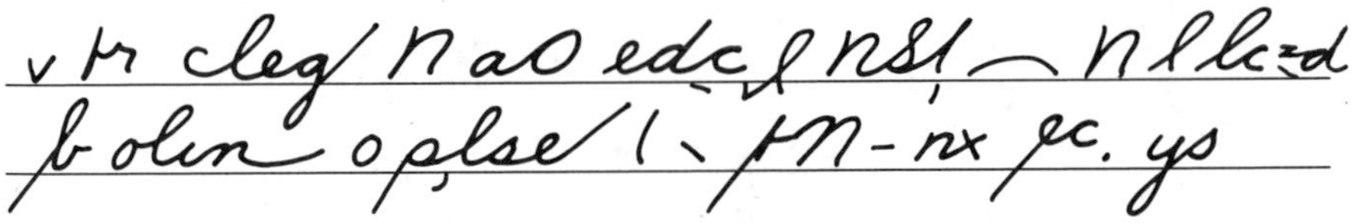

Assignment 6 — **Letter 2**. Read and write each preview word and phrase for Letter 2 until you can read and write each one rapidly and accurately. Then read and write the shorthand for Letter 2 to build your writing speed.

incentive within the

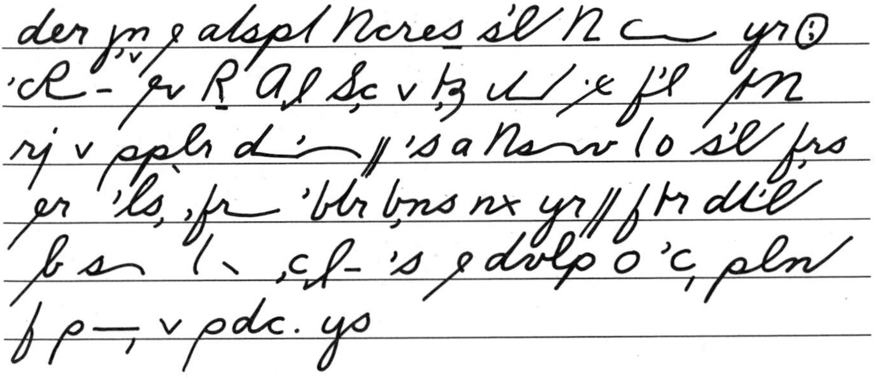

BUILDING SHORTHAND SPEED AND TRANSCRIPTION ACCURACY

Assignment 7 — **Self-testing**. Complete Unit 48 in your *Study Guide* before you proceed with the rest of this chapter.

Assignment 8 — **Taking tape dictation**. To write from dictation the articles and letters in this chapter, use Cassette 22, Side B from *Theory and Speed-Building Tapes*.

Assignment 9 — **Taking live dictation**. Write from dictation the material which is printed at the end of this chapter. Your instructor will dictate to you at various speeds.

Assignment 10 — **Own-note transcription**. Transcribe at your best typing rate an accurate copy of at least one of the pieces of correspondence you took in shorthand in Assignment 6. Type the assignment in the style requested by your instructor.

Assignment 11 — **Supplementary dictation**. If instructed to do so, read and write the additional material for this chapter found in Appendix B, "Supplementary Correspondence for Dictation."

TRANSCRIPT OF SHORTHAND—ASSIGNMENT 3

Article 1 Fly east for less. Take advantage of our summer offer and fly one way from Calgary to Toronto any (20) Monday, Wednesday, or Friday at 13:15 on Flight 141 for half price. Or, if you prefer to go to (40) Montreal, take Flight 145 any Tuesday or Thursday at 11:50. Our special summer offer (60) is a flight to Halifax. It leaves every Tuesday at 07:10, Flight 149.

We are offering the (80) largest discount we have ever made to enable you to fly Canadian. Among the special features are (100) low-low air fare, hot meals during the flight, beverage service, stereo music, and a movie. You can make your (120) reservation up to one day before your flight, but we reserve the right to take telephone reservations for (140) credit card customers only. We also guarantee that the fare will not be subject to any increase that (160) occurs once full payment has been received, provided you do not change the original booking. (*AW 166; SW 174; SI 1.49*)

TRANSCRIPT OF SHORTHAND—ASSIGNMENT 4

Article 2 Would you like to fly west this summer? We can offer you the lowest rates that have ever been offered if you will (20) take one of the midmorning flights scheduled on weekdays during July and August. At any time up to one day (40) before your flight, you can reserve and pick up your ticket from your local travel agent or from our ticket (60) office. You will not be able to buy a ticket on the day of the flight and still receive the special rate.

The fare (80) is not refundable, but for a fee of $30 you will be able to purchase an insurance plan (100) that would guarantee repayment of your air fare if you are unable to make the flight. Changes, however, must (120) be made at least three days prior to the flight.

Take advantage of our midweek fares for anyone who can travel (140) Monday, Tuesday, Wednesday, or Thursday. Weekend fares are in effect Friday, Saturday, and Sunday. Although these (160) special, half-price fares are in effect from July 3 to August 31, your travel agent can inform you of (180) our regular discounts, which are in effect all year long, to destinations anywhere in Canada. (*AW 198; SW 199; SI 1.40*)

TRANSCRIPT OF SHORTHAND—ASSIGNMENT 5

Letter 1 Dear Mr. Miller: In my absence from the office recently, our staff analysed the report received from the counsellors (20) on the scholarship lists for the current year.

They have borrowed on the ideas of some of their colleagues in (40) another educational institution and, in all likelihood, will be outlining our policies to you (60) within the next week. Yours sincerely, (*AW 59; SW 66; SI 1.52*)

TRANSCRIPT OF SHORTHAND—ASSIGNMENT 6

Letter 2 Dear John: We anticipate increased sales in the coming year; accordingly, we have ordered additional stock (20) of those items which fall within the range of popular demand.

As an incentive to our sales force, we are (40) also offering a better bonus next year.

Further details will be sent to you occasionally as we (60) develop our action plans for promotion of product. Yours sincerely, (*AW 63; SW 72; SI 1.52*)

TRANSCRIPTION TEST 4

- Your instructor will provide dictation material to be taken in shorthand.
- Transcribe each piece of dictation in an acceptable style as directed by your instructor.

*NOTE: Appendix A to Part A appears on page 155.

APPENDIX B

SUPPLEMENTARY CORRESPONDENCE FOR DICTATION

In this section there are 35 pieces of correspondence, sixty per cent of which are letters, thirty-one per cent of which are memorandums, and the other nine per cent of which are articles of interest. Providing a variety of new dictation matter, this Appendix gives an opportunity to apply the principles already learned through approximately ten per cent new vocabulary, all of which is previewed.

Phrases which have not already been reviewed in Chapters 33 through 48 are also previewed in this section. All dictation material is correlated chapter-by-chapter to PART B, each piece of correspondence carrying the corresponding chapter number to which it is appended.

Following each piece of dictation the actual words, the standard words, and the syllabic intensity are indicated in parentheses as *AW*, *SW*, and *SI*, respectively.

This material may be used as sight dictation and/or for transcription testing and is on Cassette 24 of *Theory and Speed-Building Tapes*.

Letter 33A

Preview. In your notebook, write each phrase several times.

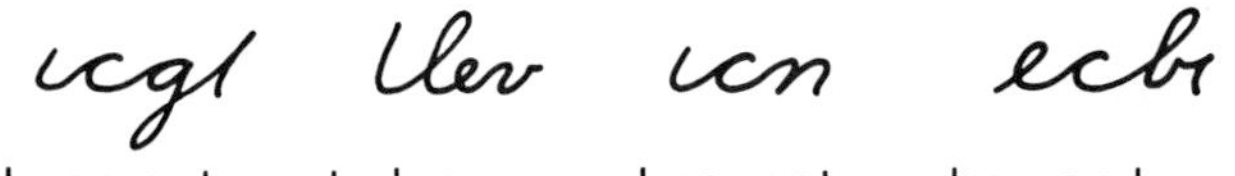

I can get — to leave — I cannot — he can buy

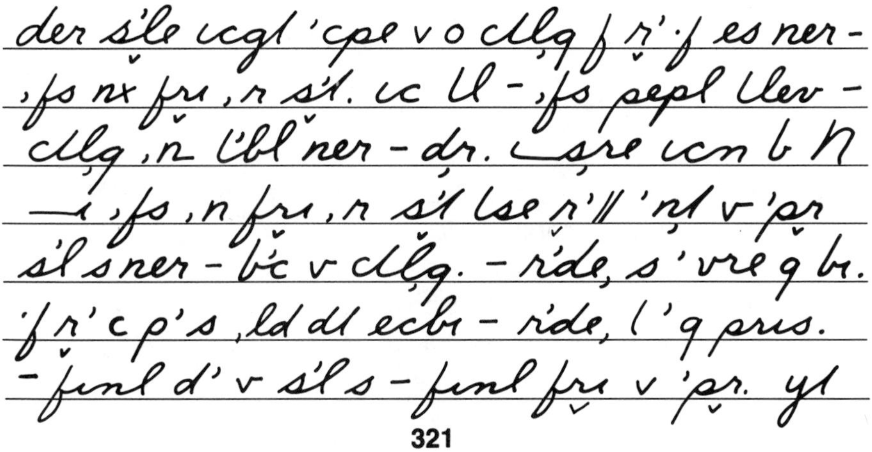

Dear Sally: I can get a copy of our catalogue for Ray if he is near the office next Friday or (20) Saturday. I can tell the office people to leave the catalogue on the table near the door. I am sorry I (40) cannot be in my office on Friday or Saturday to see Ray.

A note of the April sale is near the back (60) of the catalogue. The radio is a very good buy. If Ray can pay his old debt, he can buy the radio (80) at a good price. The final day of the sale is the final Friday of April. Yours truly, (*AW 104; SW 103; SI 1.31*)

Letter 33B

Preview. In your notebook, write each word and phrase several times.

nearby   I can offer   to know

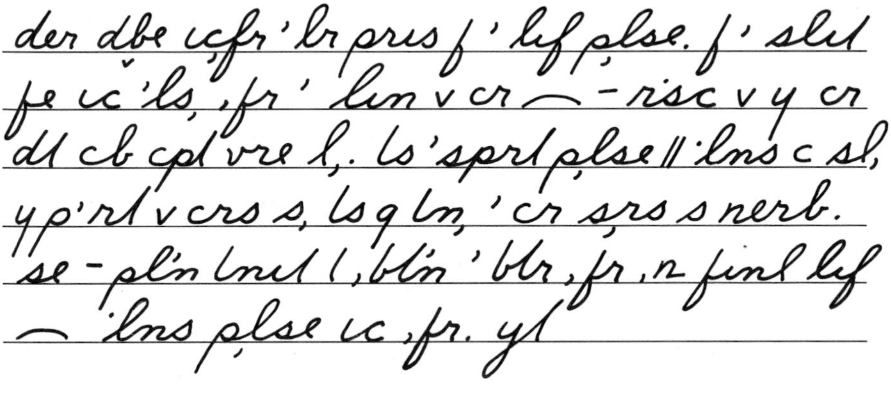

Dear Debby: I can offer a lower price for a life policy. For a slight fee, I can also offer a (20) line of credit, and the risk of your credit debt can be kept very low. It is a separate policy. (40)

Illness can slow your pay rate, of course, so it is good to know a credit source is nearby. See the plan tonight to (60) obtain a better offer on the final life and illness policy I can offer. Yours truly, (*AW 81; SW 77; SI 1.33*)

Letter 33C

Preview. In your notebook, write the phrases several times.

he sold he is able to sign

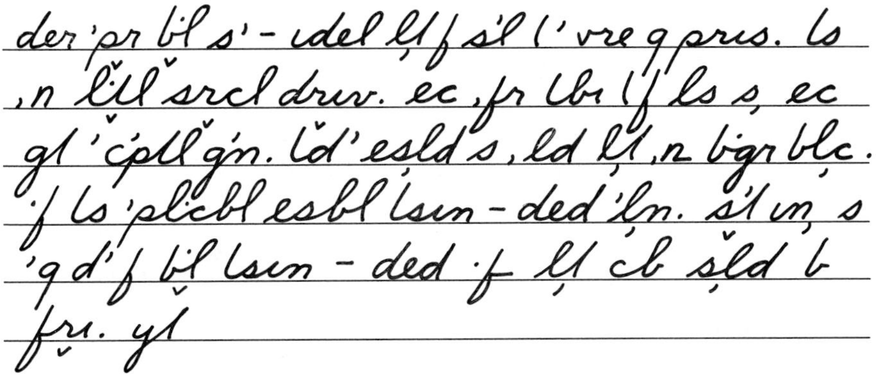

Dear April: Bill saw the ideal lot for sale at a very good price. It is on Little Circle Drive. He can (20) offer to buy it for less so he can get a capital gain. Today, he sold his old lot on the bigger block. If (40) it is applicable, he is able to sign the deed alone. Saturday, I know, is a good day for Bill to (60) sign the deed if the lot can be sold by Friday. Yours truly, (*AW 80; SW 91; SI 1.24*)

Memorandum 34A

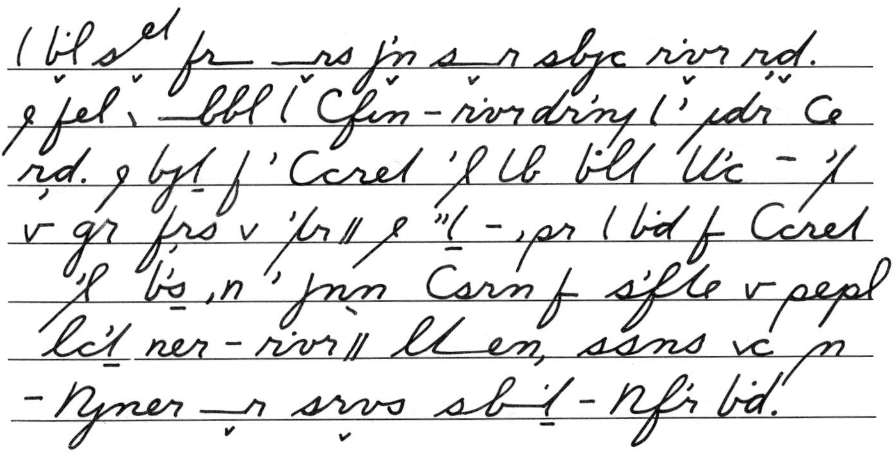

TO: Bill Sweet
FROM: Mrs. Jane Summer
SUBJECT: River Road

We feel you may be able to confine the river drainage to a wider county road. We budgeted for a (20) concrete wall to be built to take the weight of the great force of water.

We awaited the opportunity to (40) bid for the concrete wall based on a genuine concern for the safety of the people located near the river. (60)

Let me know as soon as you can when the engineer, Mr. Service, submitted the unfair bid. (*AW 77; SW 77; SI 1.40*)

Letter 34B

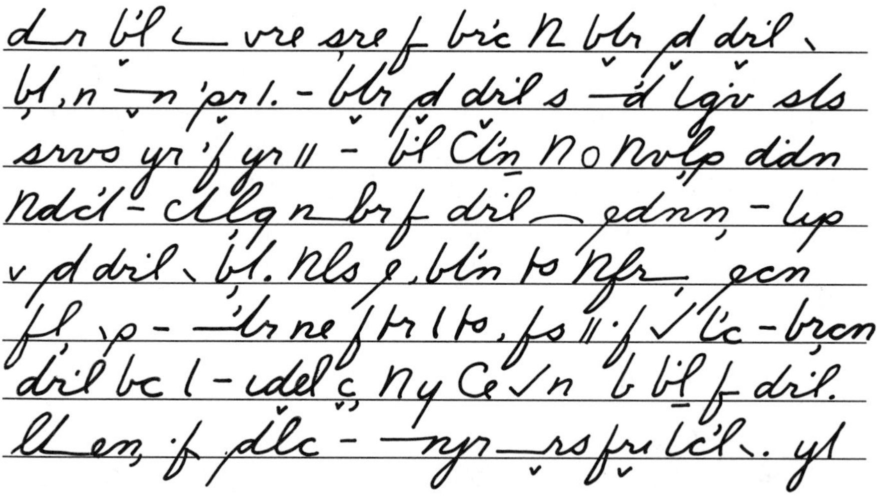

Dear Mr. Ball: I am very sorry for the break in the Better Wood Drill you bought on Monday, April 1. The (20) Better Wood Drill is made to give satisfactory service year after year.

The bill contained in our envelope did (40) not indicate the catalogue number for the drill, and we do not know the type of wood drill you bought. Unless we (60) obtain this information, we cannot follow up the matter any further at this office.

If you will take (80) the broken drill back to the Ideal Company in your county, you will not be billed for the drill. Let me know if (100) you would like the manager, Mrs. Friday, to call you. Yours truly, (*AW 116; SW 112; SI 1.40*)

Letter 34C

Preview. In your notebook, write the phrases several times.

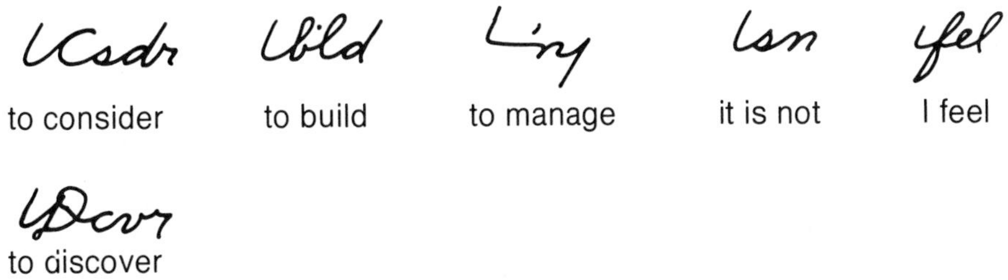
to consider
to build
to manage
it is not
I feel
to discover

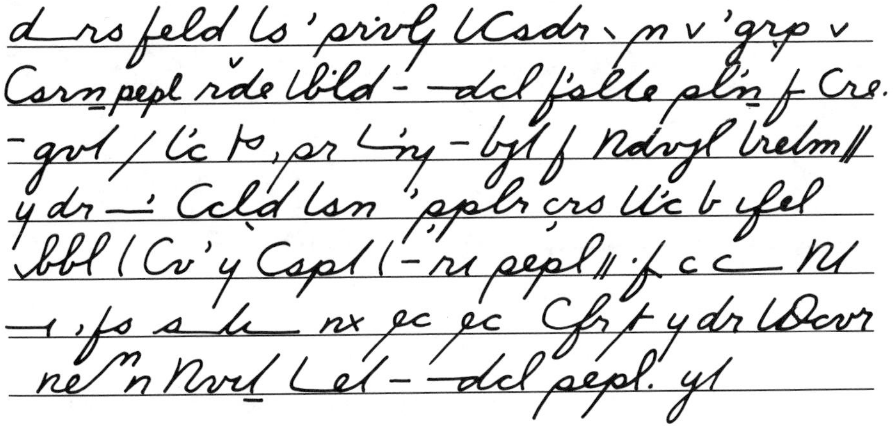

Dear Mrs. Field: It is a privilege to consider you one of a group of concerned people ready to build (20) the medical facility planned for the country. The government will take this opportunity to manage (40) the budget for individual treatment.

Your doctor may conclude it is not a popular course to take, but I (60) feel you will be able to convey your concept to the right people.

If you can come into my office sometime next week, (80) we can confer with your doctor to discover anyone not invited to meet the medical people. Yours (100) truly, (*AW 96; SW 101; SI 1.50*)

Letter 35A

Preview. In your notebook, write each word and phrase several times.

enlist interior decorating schemes lounge

cafeteria till to remodel

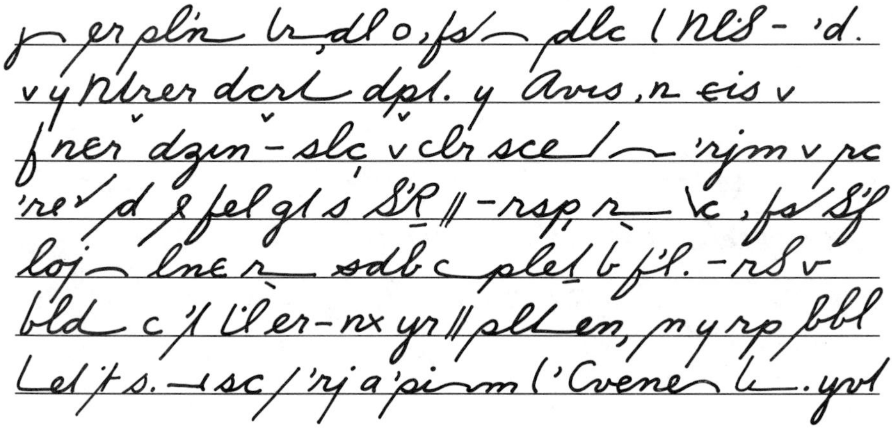

Gentlemen: We are planning to remodel our offices and would like to enlist the aid of your Interior (20) Decorating Department. Your advice on the choice of furniture design, the selection of color schemes, (40) and the arrangement of work areas would, we feel, get us started.

The reception room, executive offices, (60) staff lounge, and lunch room should be completed by fall. The rest of the building can wait till early next year.

Please let (80) me know when your representative will be able to meet with us. My secretary will arrange an appointment (100) at a convenient time. Yours very truly, (*AW 100; SW 105; SI 1.46*)

Letter 35B

Preview. In your notebook, write each of the words and phrases several times.

Walters plate window neighbor task unexpected

cannot be to respond we know you will be pleased

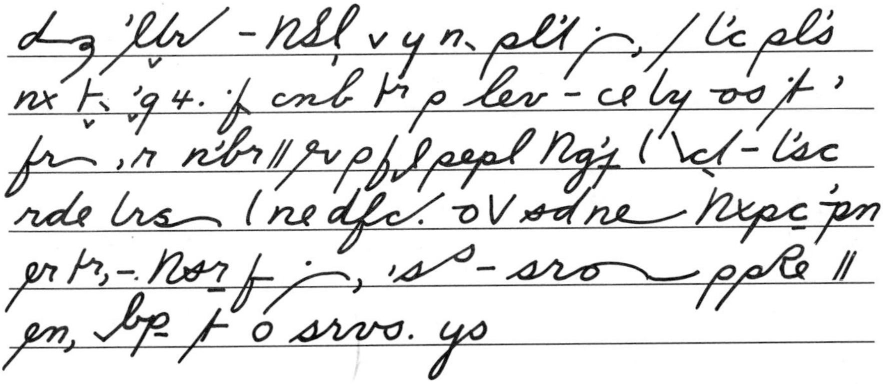

Dear Ms. Walters: The Installation of your new plate window will take place next Thursday, August 4. If you cannot (20) be there, please leave the key to your house with a friend or neighbor.

We have professional people (40) engaged to execute the task, ready to respond to any difficulties. However, should anything (60) unexpected happen, we are thoroughly insured for the window as well as the surrounding property.

We know you (80) will be pleased with our service. Yours sincerely, (*AW 79; SW 88; SI 1.52*)

Letter 35C

Preview. In your notebook, write each word several times.

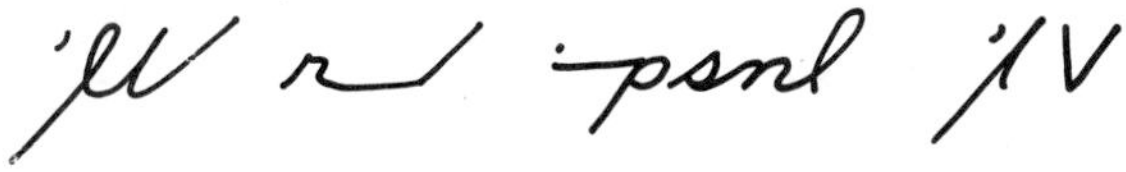

wallets rings impersonal whatever

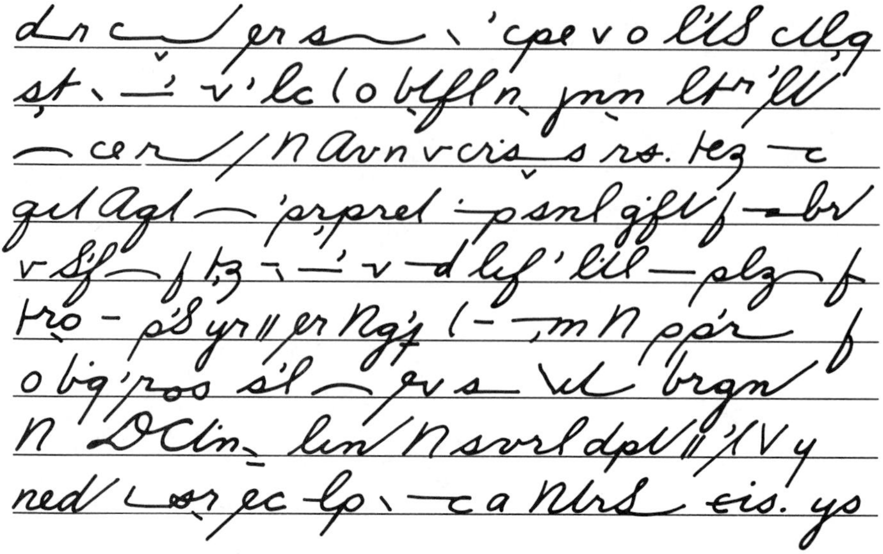

Dear Mr. Cummings: We are sending you a copy of our latest catalogue so that you may have a look at (20) our beautiful new genuine leather wallets and key rings well in advance of the Christmas rush. These make quite adequate (40) and appropriate impersonal gifts for members of the staff and for those who may have made life a little (60) more pleasant for you throughout the past year.

We are engaged at the moment in preparing for our big warehouse sale, (80) and we have some exciting bargains in discontinued lines in several departments.

Whatever your needs, I am (100) sure we can help you make an interesting choice. Yours sincerely, (*AW 109; SW 111; SI 1.40*)

Letter 36A

Preview. In your notebook, write each of the words and phrases several times.

Cashman

publisher

cookbook

that this

we feel

we are sure

your order

may be

is not

please let us know

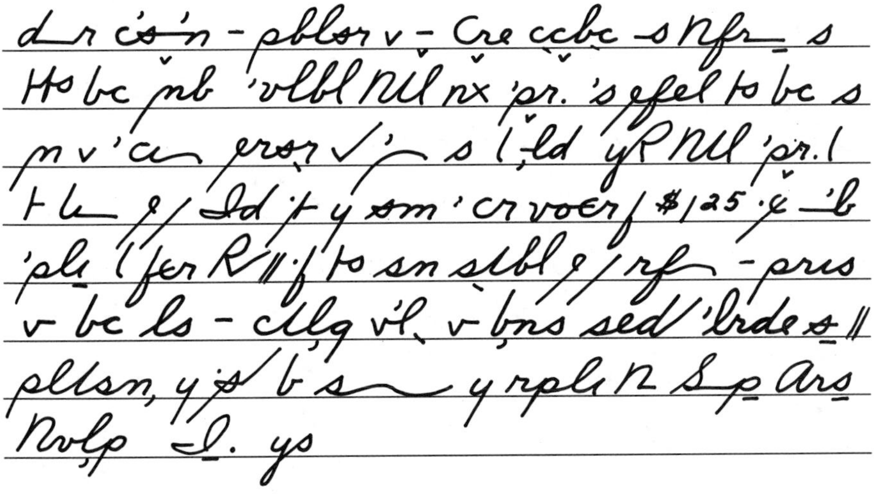

Dear Mr. Cashman: The publisher of <u>The Country Cookbook</u> has informed us that this book will not be available (20) until next April. As we feel this book is one of a kind, we are sure you will want us to hold your order (40) until April. At that time we will include with your shipment a credit voucher for $1.25 which may be (60) applied to future orders.

If this is not suitable, we will refund the price of the book less the catalogue (80) value of the bonus seeds already shipped.

Please let us know your wishes by sending your reply in the stamped, (100) addressed envelope enclosed. Yours sincerely, (*AW 110; SW 107; SI 1.36*)

Letter 36B

Preview. In your notebook, write each word and phrase several times.

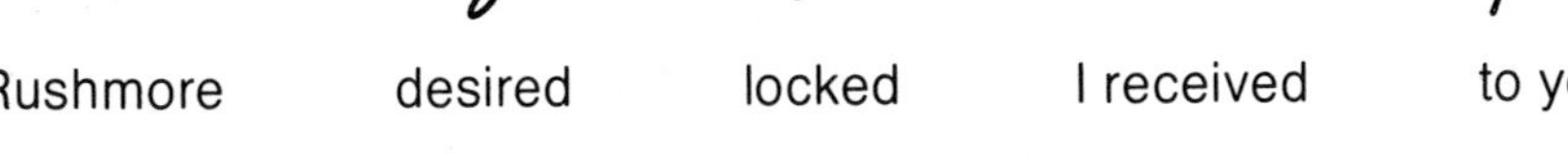

Rushmore desired locked I received to your

to telephone   your office   we regret   did not

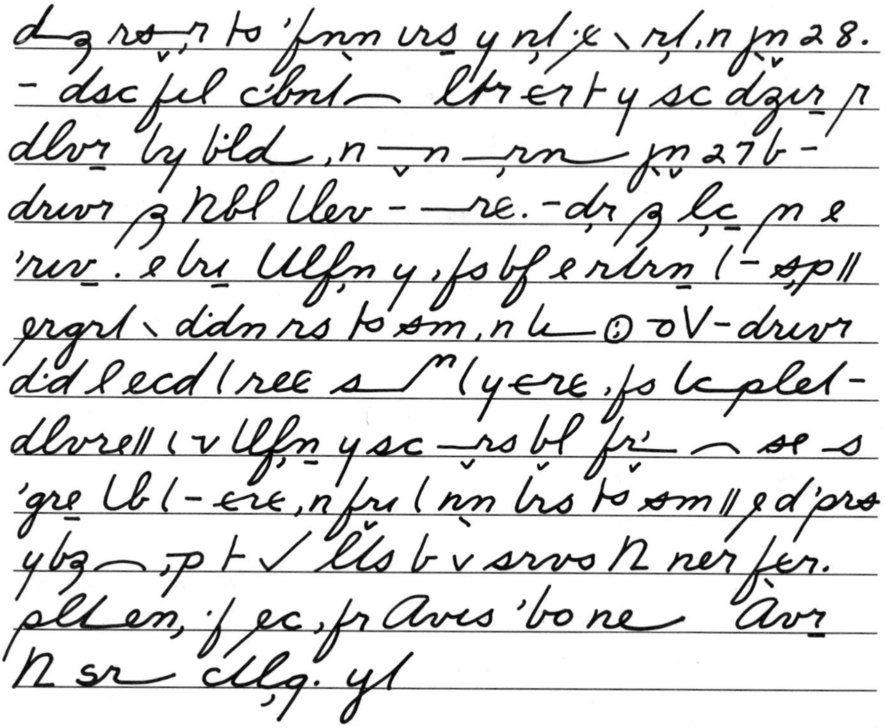

Dear Ms. Rushmore: This afternoon I received your note which you wrote on June 28. The desk, file cabinet, and (20) leather chair that your secretary desired were delivered to your building on Monday morning, June 27, (40) but the driver was unable to leave the merchandise. The door was locked when he arrived. He tried to (60) telephone your office before he returned to the shop.

We regret you did not receive this shipment on time; however, the driver (80) did all he could to reach someone at your church office to complete the delivery.

I have telephoned your secretary, (100) Mrs. Belle Frame, and she has agreed to be at the church on Friday at noon to receive this shipment.

We (120) do appreciate your business and hope that you will let us be of service in the near future. Please let me know (140) if we can offer advice about anything advertised in the spring catalogue. Yours truly, (*AW 154; SW 157; SI 1.43*)

Memorandum 37A

Preview. In your notebook, write each of the words and phrases several times.

erasers Myrtle newsprint ribbons substantially

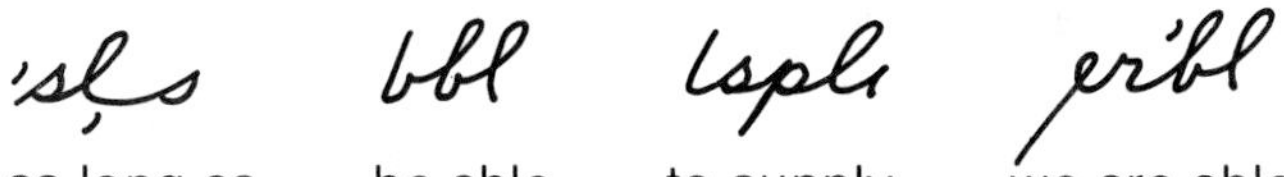

as long as be able to supply we are able

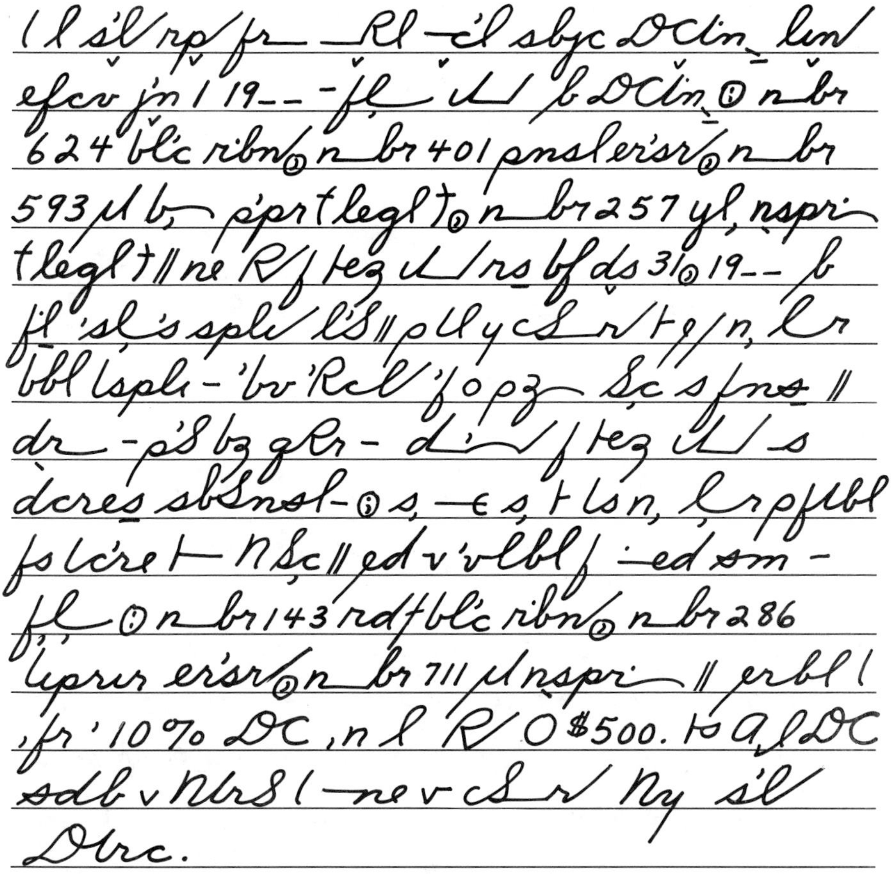

TO: All Sales Representatives
FROM: Myrtle McCall
SUBJECT: Discontinued Lines

Effective January 1, 19—, the following items will be discontinued:

No. 624 (20) black ribbons
No. 401 pencil erasers
No. 593 white bond (40) paper (legal)
No. 257 yellow newsprint (legal)

Any orders for these items received (60) before December 31, 19—, will be filled as long as supplies last.

Please tell your customers (80) that we will no longer be able to supply the above articles after our present stock is finished.

During (100) the past business quarter the demand for these items has decreased substantially; so much so, that it is no (120) longer profitable for us to carry them in stock.

We do have available for immediate shipment (140) the following:

No. 143 red/black ribbons
No. 286 typewriter erasers (160)
No. 711 white newsprint

We are able to offer a 10 per cent discount on (180) all orders over $500. This additional discount should be of interest to many of the (200) customers in your sales district. *(AW 174; SW 206; SI 1.49)*

Letter 37B

Preview. In your notebook, write each of the words several times.

dwelling contents inadequate replacement-cost

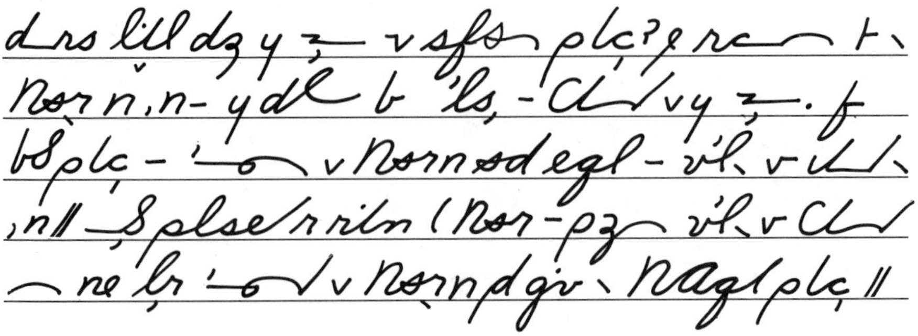

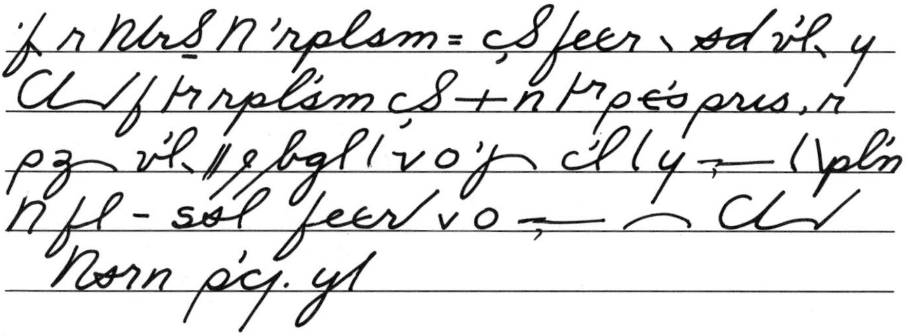

Dear Mrs. Little: Does your home have sufficient protection?

We recommend that you insure not only your dwelling (20) but also the contents of your home. For the best protection, the amount of insurance should equal the value (40) of the items you own.

Most policies are written to insure the present value of the contents, and any (60) lower amounts of insurance would give you inadequate protection.

If you are interested in a (80) replacement-cost feature, you should value your contents for their replacement cost—not their purchase price or present value. (100)

We will be glad to have our agent call at your home to explain in full the special features of our home and (120) contents insurance package. Yours truly, (*AW 116; SW 127; SI 1.54*)

Memorandum 38A

Preview. In your notebook, write each of the words and phrases several times.

morning's | Institutions | centralizing | preventing

duplication | trying | input | we received | we have been

we have not | we feel | we must | up to date

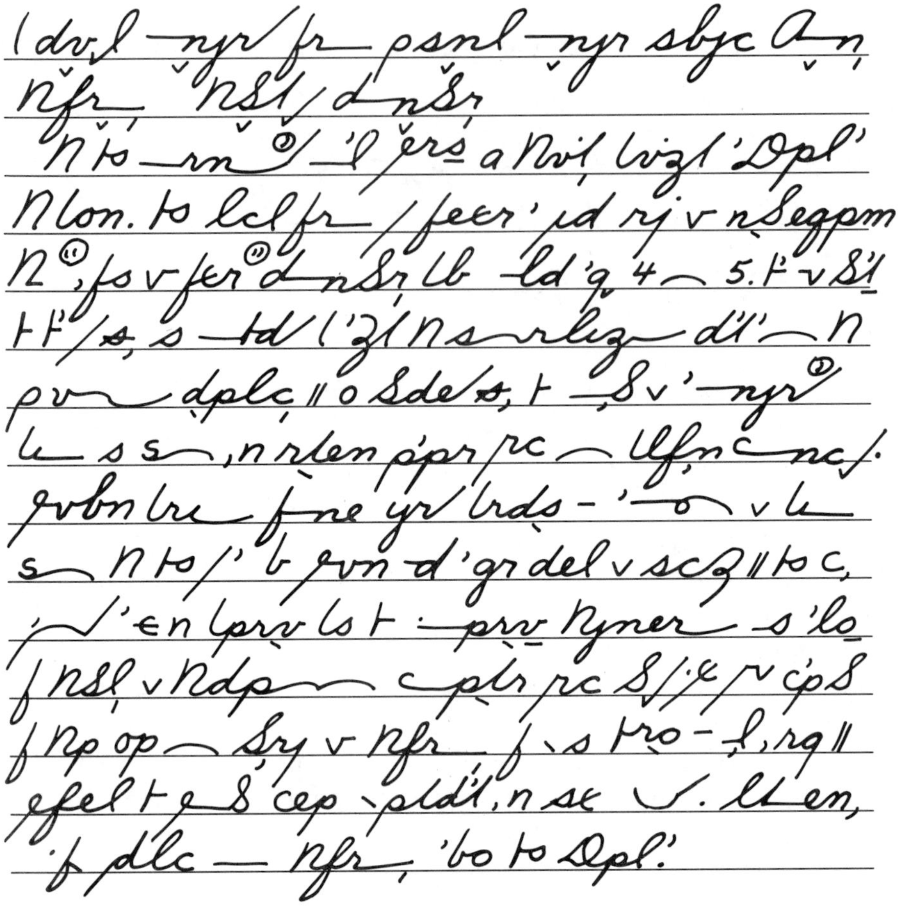

TO: Divisional Managers
FROM: Personnel Manager
SUBJECT: Administration Information Institutions Demonstration

In this morning's mail we received an invitation to visit a display in town. This local firm will feature (20) a wide range of the newest equipment in the "Office of the Future" demonstration to be held August 4 (40) and 5. They have stated that they will show us methods to assist in centralizing data and in preventing duplication. (60)

Our studies show that most of a manager's time is spent on routine paper work and telephone communications. (80) We have been trying for many years to reduce the amount of time spent in this way, but we have not (100) had a great deal of success.

This company wants a chance to prove to us that improved engineering has allowed (120) for installation of independent computer work stations which will have capacity for input, output, (140) and storage of the information for use throughout the whole organization.

We feel that we must keep up (160) to date on such things. Let me know if you would like more information about this display. (*AW 166; SW 196; SI 1.48*)

Memorandum 38B

Preview. In your notebook, write each of the words and phrases several times.

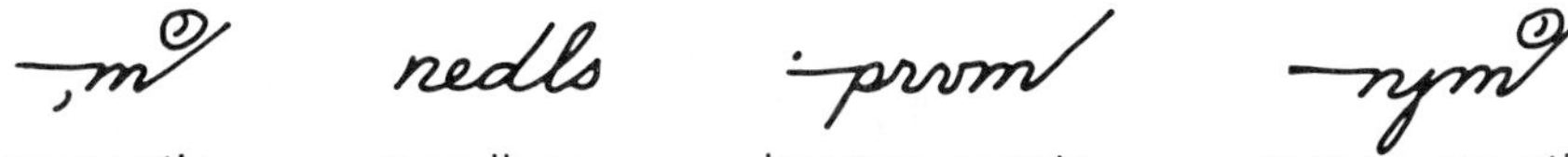

moment's needless improvements management's

very much this time do let me know

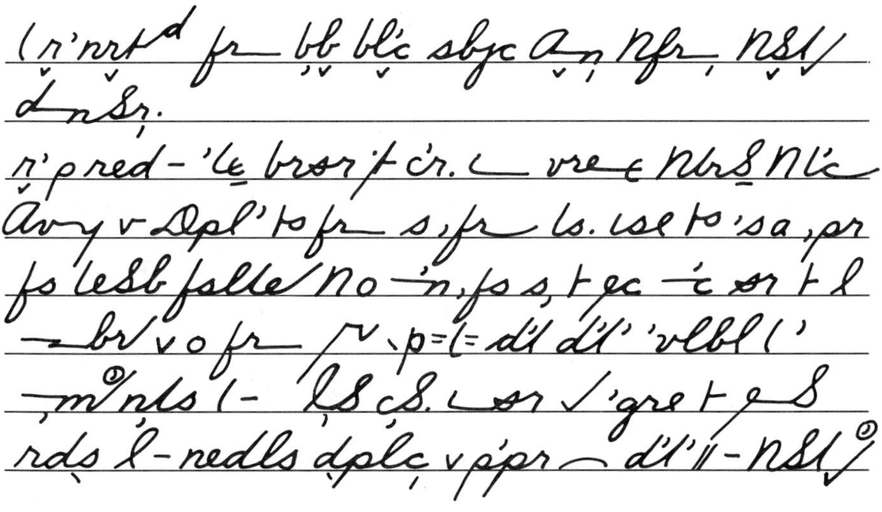

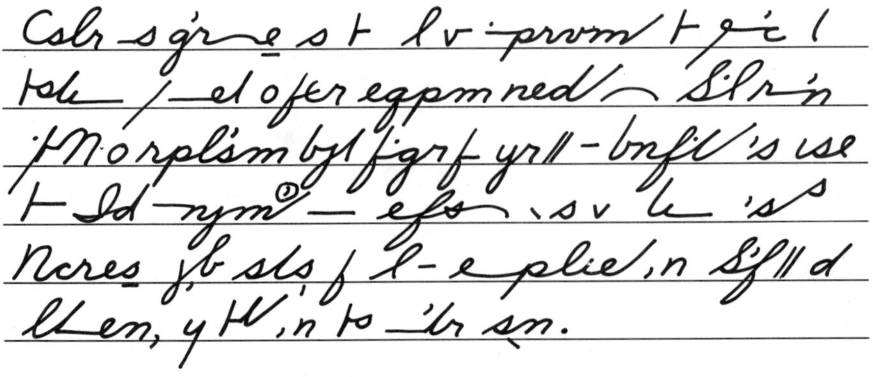

TO: Ray Norwood
FROM: Bob Black
SUBJECT: Administration Information Institutions Demonstration

Ray, please read the attached brochure with care. I am very much interested in taking advantage of the display (20) this firm is offering to us. I see this as an opportunity for us to establish facilities (40) in our main office so that we can make sure that all members of our firm will have up-to-date data available (60) at a moment's notice at the lowest cost. I am sure you will agree that we must reduce all the needless (80) duplication of paper and data.

The Institution's counsellor has guaranteed us that all of the (100) improvements that we make at this time will meet our future equipment needs and still remain within our replacement (120) budget figure for the year.

The benefits, as I see them, include management's more efficient use of time as (140) well as increased job satisfaction for all the employees on staff.

Do let me know your thoughts on this matter soon. (*AW 150; SW 161; SI 1.51*)

Memorandum 39A

Preview. In your notebook, write each word and phrase several times.

amendments agenda be sure

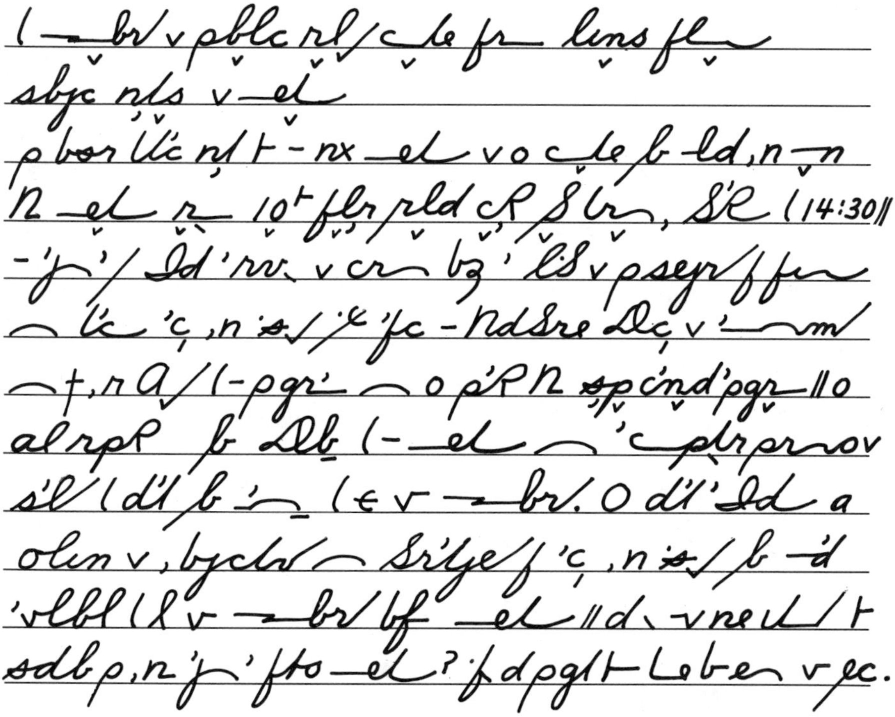

TO: Members of Public Relations Committee
FROM: Linus Fleming
SUBJECT: Notice of Meeting

Please be sure to take note that the next meeting of our Committee will be held on Monday in the Meeting Room, Tenth (20) Floor, World Court West, Toronto, starting at 14:30.

The agenda will include a review of current (40) business, a list of procedures for finding and taking action on issues which affect the industry, discussion (60) of amendments and/or additions to the program, and our part in the Shop Canada Program.

Our Annual Report (80) will be distributed at the meeting, and a computer printout of sales to date will be handed to each (100) of the members. Other data, including an outline of objectives and strategies for action on issues, (120) will be made available to all of the members before the meeting.

Do you have any items that should be put (140) on the agenda for this meeting? If you do, please get them to me by the end of the week. (*AW 151; SW 156; SI 1.45*)

Article 39B

Preview. In your notebook, write each of the words and phrases several times.

Glace Bay Nova Scotia miners' museum Centuries

mining cages canaries detect sewing bridles

pit ponies locomotives Amazon New York

highlight donning gear descent

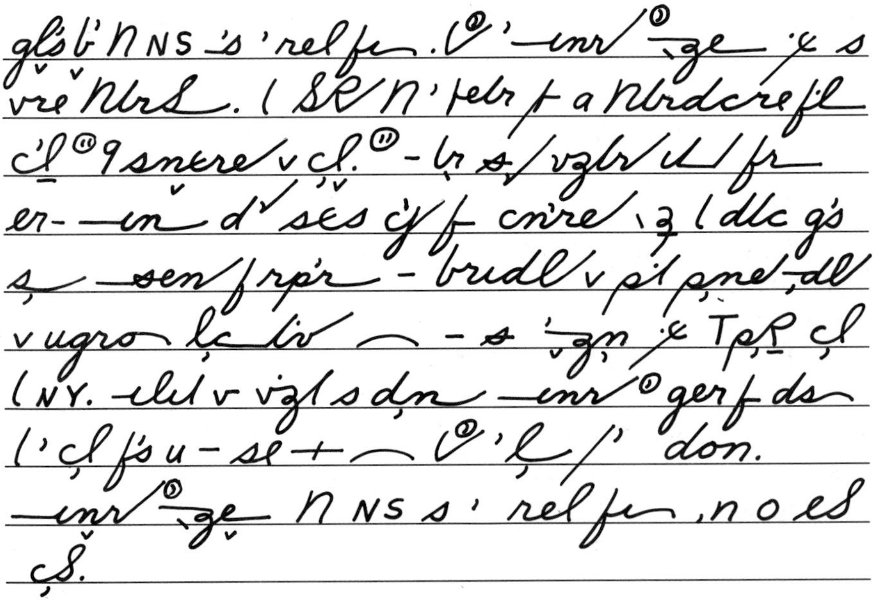

GLACE BAY, NOVA SCOTIA

Glace Bay in Nova Scotia has a real find. It's a miners' museum which is very interesting. It starts (20) in a theatre with an introductory film called "Nine Centuries of Coal." The tour shows visitors items from (40) early mining days, such as cages for the canaries used to detect gas, sewing machines for repairing the (60) bridles of pit ponies, models of underground locomotives, and the ship Amazon which transported coal to New (80) York. Highlight of the visit is donning miners' gear for the descent to a coal face under the sea—and it's a (100) long way down. Miners' Museum in Nova Scotia is a real find on our east coast. (*AW 110; SW 115; SI 1.46*)

Letter 40A

Preview. In your notebook, write each of the words several times.

Gardener owned operated designers illustrated

showings recognized selecting clothing interests

selection

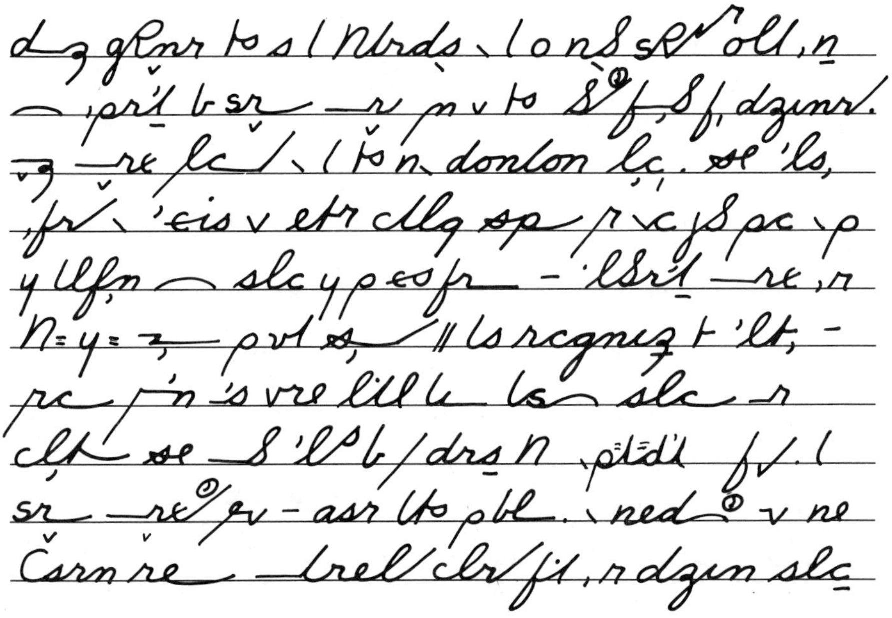

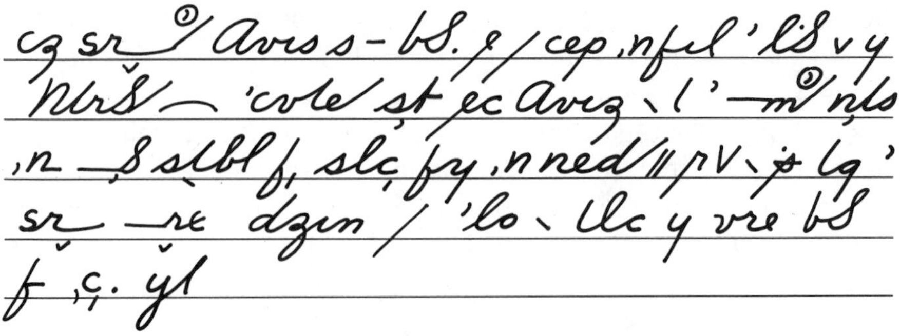

Dear Ms. Gardner: This is to introduce you to our newest sportswear outlet owned and operated by Spring (20) March, one of this city's foremost fashion designers. Ms. March welcomes you to this new downtown location. She (40) also offers you a choice of either catalogue shopping, where you can just pick up your telephone and select your (60) purchase from the illustrated merchandise or in-your-home private showings.

It is recognized that although the working (80) woman has very little time to spend selecting her clothing, she must always be well dressed in up-to-date (100) fashions. At Spring March's, we have the answer to this problem. You needn't have any concern regarding (120) materials, colors, fit, or design selected because Spring's advice is the best. We will keep on file a list of your (140) interests and activities so that we can advise you, at a moment's notice, on the most suitable fashion (160) selection for your own needs.

Wherever you wish to go, a Spring March design will allow you to look your very (180) best for the occasion. Yours truly, (*AW 177; SW 187; SI 1.48*)

Letter 40B

Preview. In your notebook, write each of the words several times.

householder unused Advertiser sporting

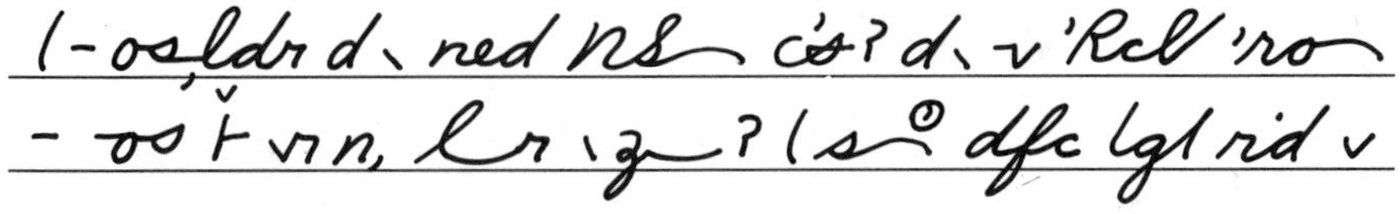

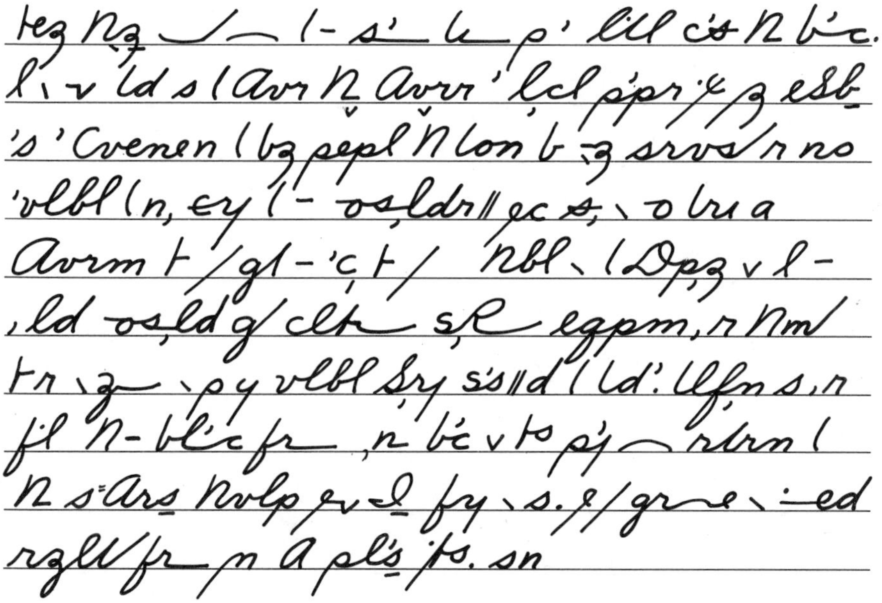

To the Householder: Do you need instant cash? Do you have articles around the house that you are no longer using? (20) It isn't difficult to get rid of these unused things and, at the same time, put a little cash in the (40) bank. All you have to do is to advertise in The Advertiser, a local paper which was established as (60) a convenience to business people in town but whose services are now available at no charge to the (80) householder.

We can show you how to write an advertisement that will get the action that will enable you to (100) dispose of all the old household goods, clothing, sporting equipment, or instruments that are using up your (120) valuable storage space.

Do it today. Telephone us, or fill in the blank form on the back of this page and return (140) it in the self-addressed envelope we have enclosed for your use. We will guarantee you immediate results (160) from one ad placed with us. Sincerely, (*AW 163; SW 167; SI 1.44*)

Memorandum 41A

Preview. In your notebook, write each of the words several times.

Match's evaluate attitude loyalty promotions

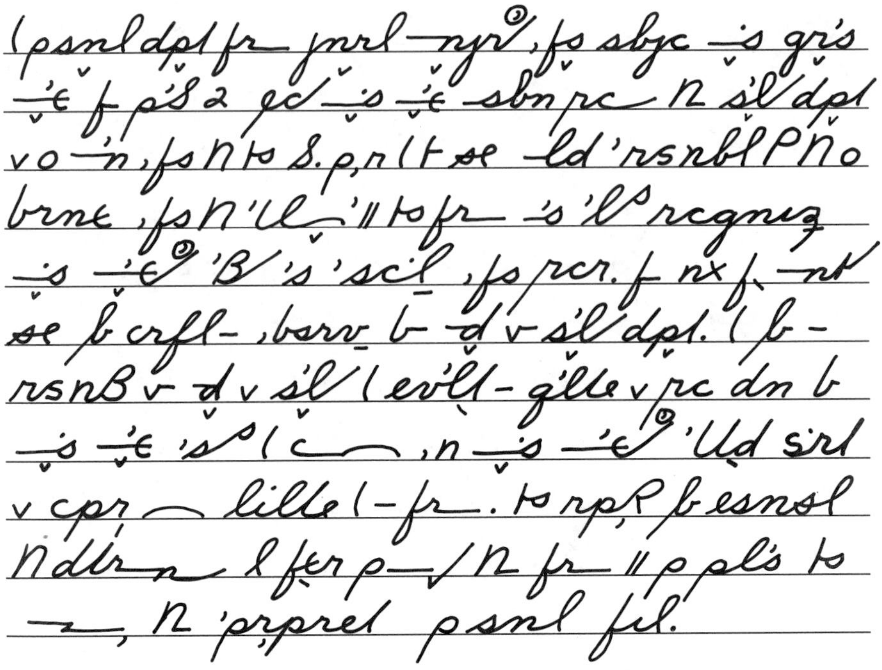

TO: Personnel Department
FROM: General Manager's Office
SUBJECT: Miss Grace Match

For the past two weeks Miss Match has been working in the Sales Department of our main office in this city. Prior (20) to that, she held a responsible position in our branch office in Atlanta.

This firm has always (40) recognized Miss Match's abilities as a skilled office worker. For the next few months she will be carefully observed by (60) the Head of the Sales Department. It will be the responsibility of the Head of Sales to evaluate (80) the quality of work done by Miss Match as well as to comment on Miss Match's attitude, spirit of (100) co-operation, and loyalty to the firm. This report will be essential in determining all future promotions (120) in the firm.

Please place this memo in the appropriate personnel file. (*AW 125; SW 132; SI 1.47*)

Memorandum 41B

Preview. In your notebook, write each of the words several times.

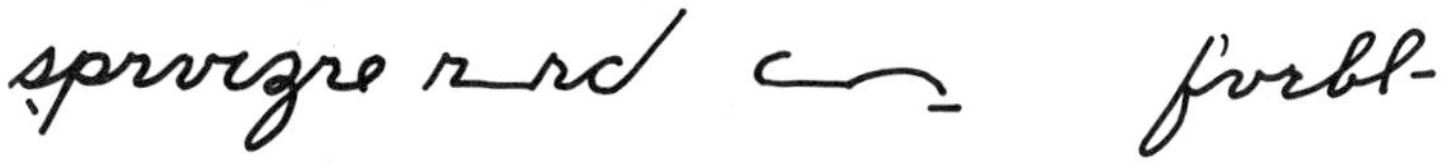

supervisory remarks commented favorably

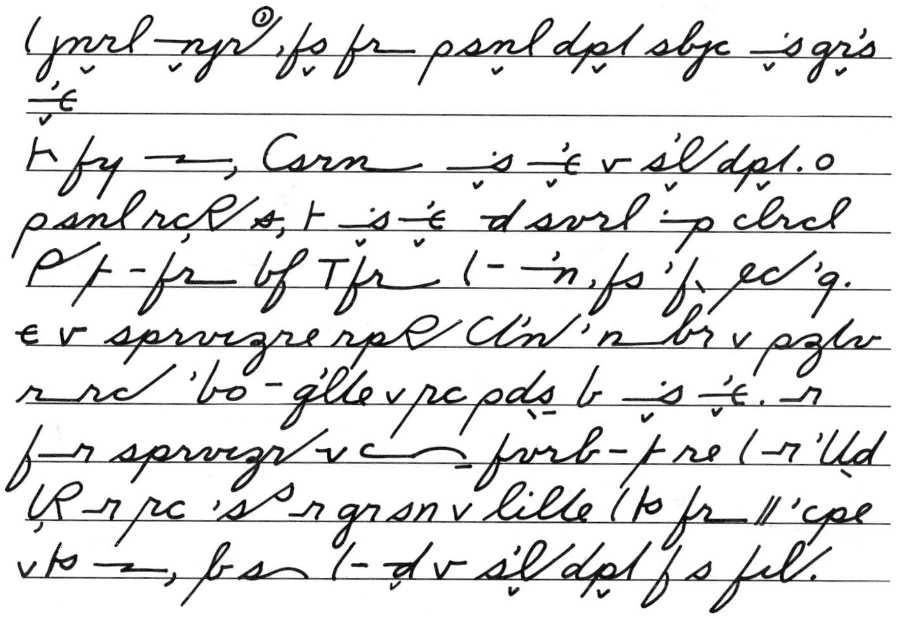

TO: General Manager's Office
FROM: Personnel Department
SUBJECT: Miss Grace Match

Thank you for your memo concerning Miss Match of the Sales Department. Our personnel records show that Miss Match (20) had several important clerical positions with the firm before transferring to the main office a few weeks (40) ago. Each of the supervisory reports contains a number of positive remarks about the quality (60) of work produced by Miss Match. Her former supervisors have commented favorably with regard to her (80) attitude toward her work as well as her great sense of loyalty to this firm.

A copy of this memo will (100) be sent to the Head of the Sales Department for his files. (*AW 101; SW 110; SI 1.53*)

Letter 41C

Preview. In your notebook, write each of the words several times.

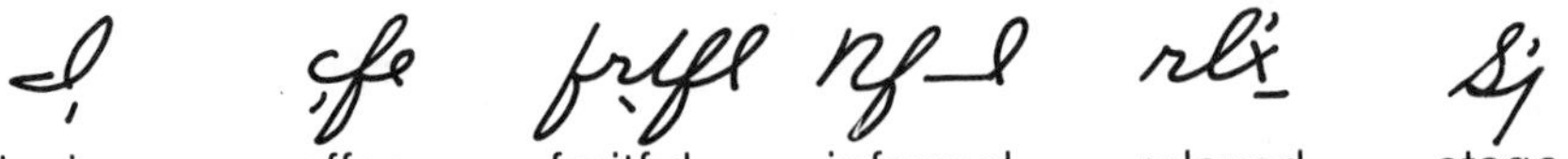

inclusion coffee fruitful informal relaxed stage

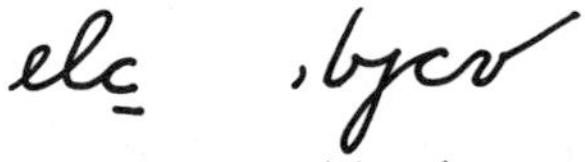

elected objectives

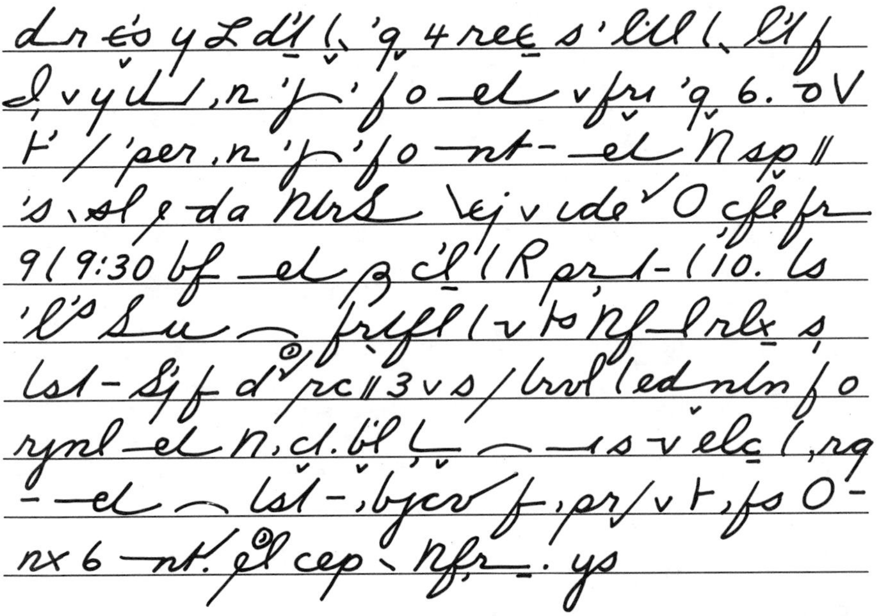

Dear Mr. Chase: Your letter dated Tuesday, August 4, reached us a little too late for inclusion of your (20) items on the agenda for our meeting of Friday, August 6. However, they will appear on the agenda (40) for our monthly meeting in September.

As usual, we had an interesting exchange of ideas over coffee (60) from 09:00 to 09:30 before the meeting was called to order promptly at 10:00. It is always stimulating (80) and fruitful to have this informal, relaxed session to set the stage for the day's work.

Three of us will travel to (100) Edmonton for our regional meeting in October. Bill, Tom, and myself have elected to organize the (120) meeting and to set the objectives for the operations of that office over the next six months. We'll keep you (140) informed. Yours sincerely, (*AW 130; SW 144; SI 1.55*)

Letter 42A

Preview. In your notebook, write each of the words several times.

transmissions solutions varied switching chart

graph specialized consultant technology

Kay Overstreet she will be glad

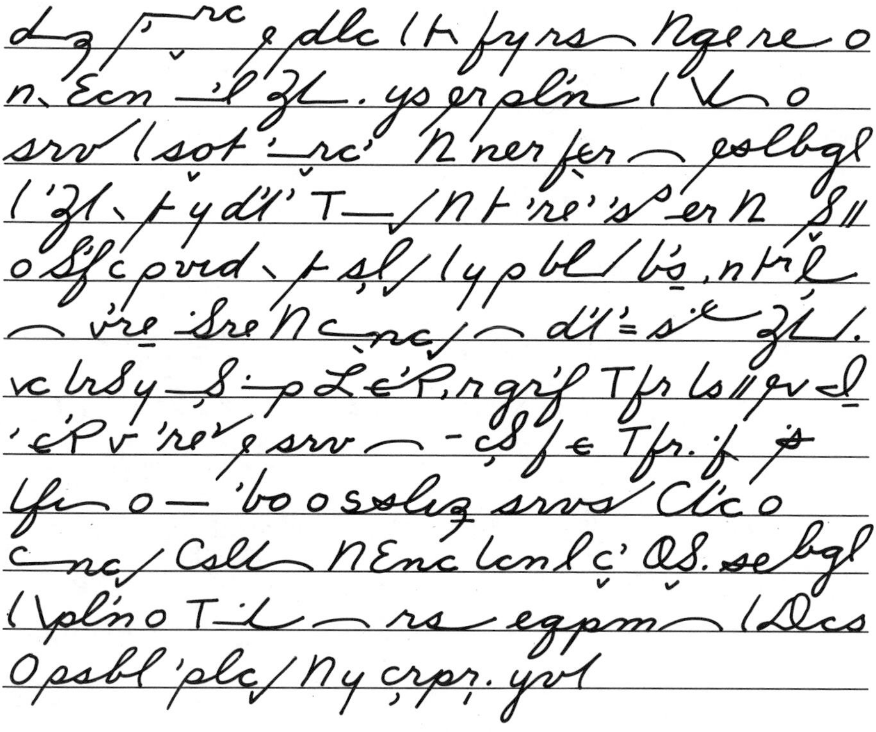

Dear Ms. Weymark: We would like to thank you for your recent inquiry regarding our new electronic mail (20) system. Yes, we are planning to extend our services to South America in the near future, and we shall be (40) glad to assist you with your data transmissions in that area as well as here in the West.

Our staff can provide (60) you with solutions to your problems based on their long and varied history in communications and data-switching (80) systems. You can trust your most important letter, chart, or graph transfer to us.

We have enclosed a chart of (100) the areas we serve and the cost for each transfer. If you wish to find out more about our specialized (120) services, contact our communications consultant in electronic technology, Kay Overstreet. She will be glad (140) to explain our transmitting and receiving equipment and to discuss other possible applications in (160) your corporation. Yours very truly, (*AW 151; SW 170; SI 1.48*)

Letter 42B

Preview. In your notebook, write each word and phrase several times.

response survey treated diagnosed marked

representing I can do if there is

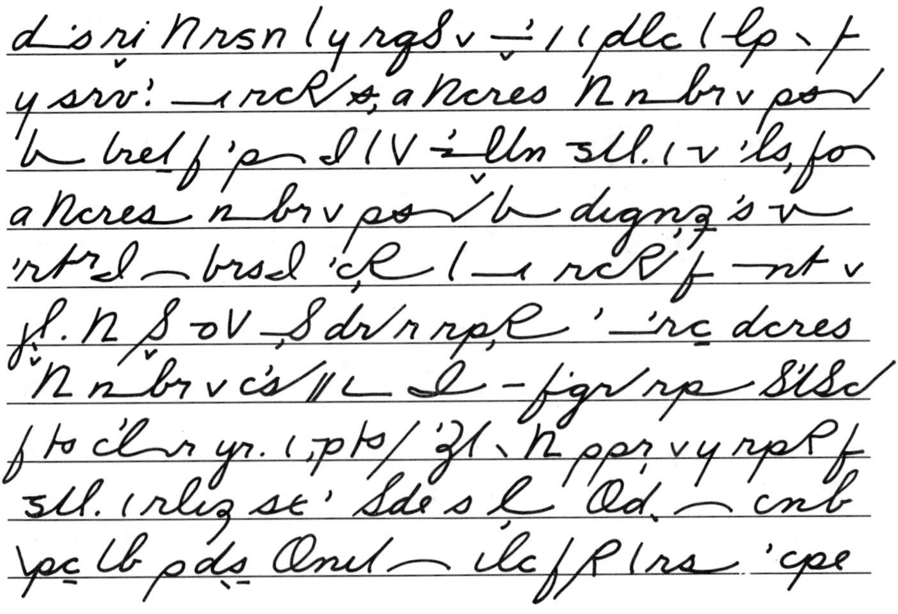

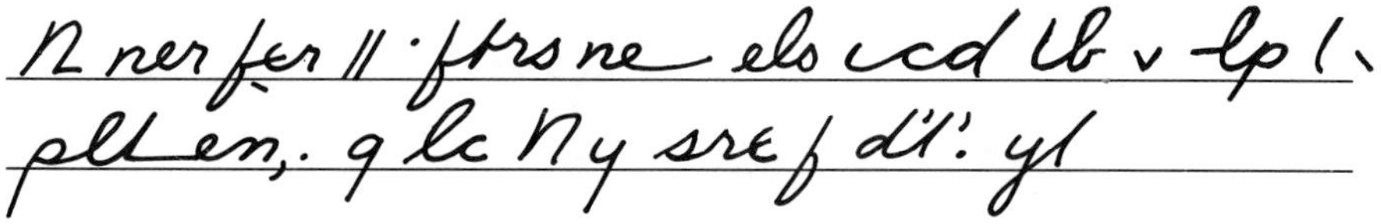

Dear Miss Roy: In response to your request of May 1, I would like to help you with your survey. My records show an (20) increase in the number of patients being treated for appendicitis at every Hamilton hospital. (40) I have also found an increasing number of patients being diagnosed as having arthritis and bursitis (60) according to my records for the month of July. In the West, however, most doctors are reporting a marked (80) decrease in the number of cases.

I am enclosing the figures representing statistics for this (100) calendar year. I hope this will assist you in the preparation of your report for the hospital. I (120) realize such a study is long overdue and cannot be expected to be produced overnight, and I look forward (140) to receiving a copy in the near future.

If there is anything else I can do to be of help to (160) you, please let me know. Good luck in your search for data. Yours truly, (*AW 160; SW 171; SI 1.50*)

Letter 43A

Preview. In your notebook, write each word and phrase several times.

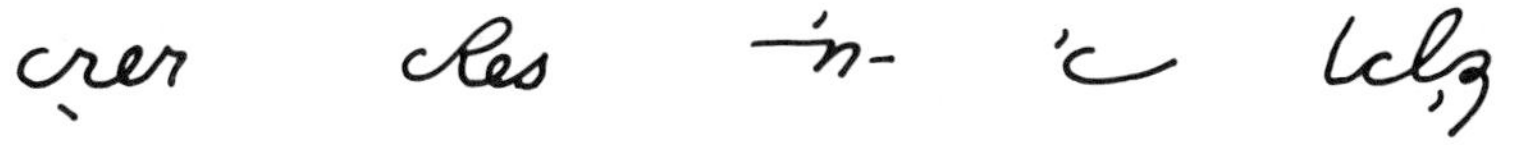

courier courteous mainly acting to close

from you we may you may be sure will be keeping

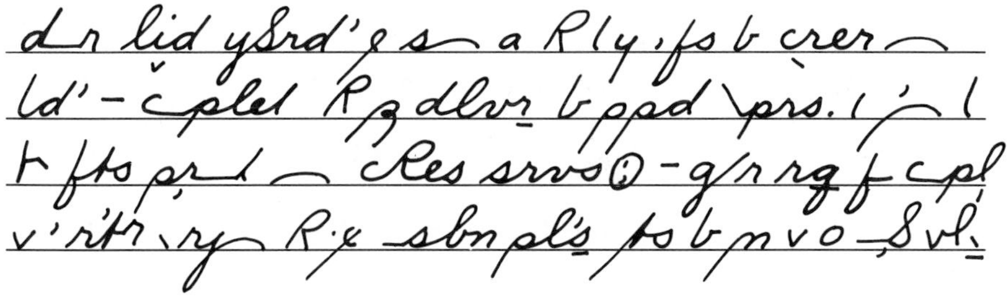

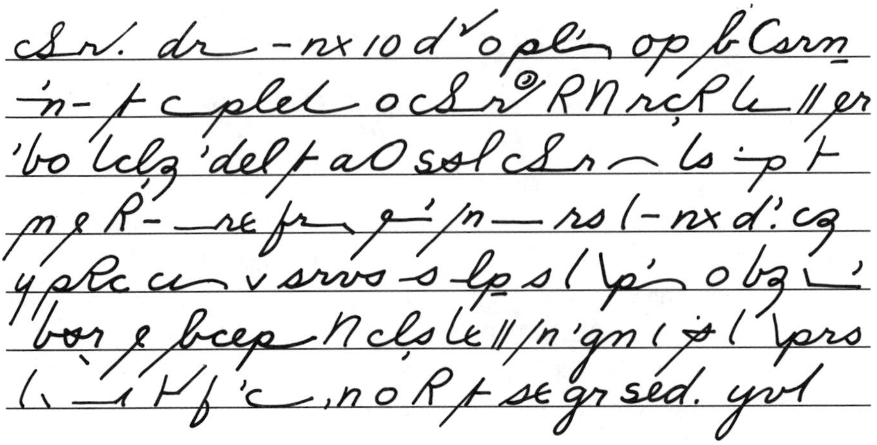

Dear Mr. Lloyd: Yesterday we sent an order to your office by courier, and today the complete order was (20) delivered by prepaid express. I want to thank you for this prompt and courteous service; the goods are required for the (40) completion of a rather urgent order which has been placed with us by one of our most valued customers. (60) During the next ten days our plant output will be concerned mainly with completing our customer's order in record (80) time.

We are about to close a deal with another special customer, and it is important that when we (100) order the merchandise from you, we may once more receive it the next day. Because your particular kind of (120) service has helped us to expand our business, you may be sure we will be keeping in close touch.

Once again, I wish to (140) express to you my thanks for acting on our order with such great speed. Yours very truly, (*AW 157; SW 156; SI 1.40*)

Letter 43B

Preview. In your notebook, write each word and phrase several times.

Carr casings confusion reconditioned to thank you

we regret   we can make

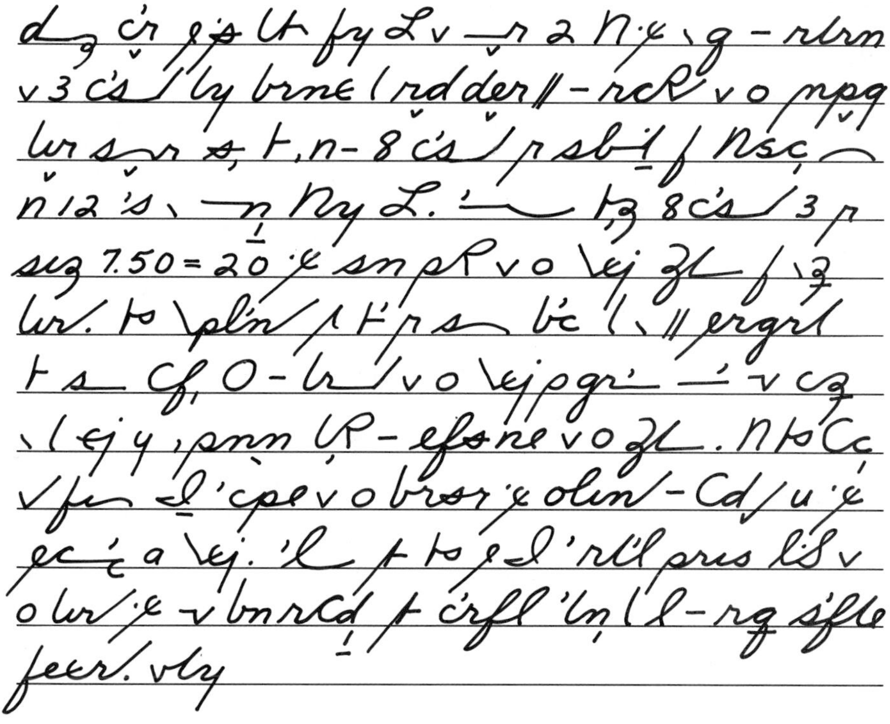

Dear Ms. Carr: We wish to thank you for your letter of March 2 in which you question the return of three casings to (20) your branch at Red Deer.

The records of our Winnipeg Tire Centre show that only eight casings were submitted for inspection (40) and not twelve as you mentioned in your letter. Among those eight casings, three were size 7.50-20 (60) which is not part of our exchange system for used tires. This explains why they were sent back to you.

We regret that some (80) confusion over the terms of our exchange program may have caused you to change your opinion toward the efficiency (100) of our system. In this connection, you will find enclosed a copy of our brochure which outlines the (120) conditions under which we can make an exchange. Along with this, we enclose a retail price list of our tires which have (140) been reconditioned with careful attention to all the required safety features. Very truly yours, (*AW 164; SW 158; SI 1.35*)

Memorandum 44A

Preview. In your notebook, write each of the words several times.

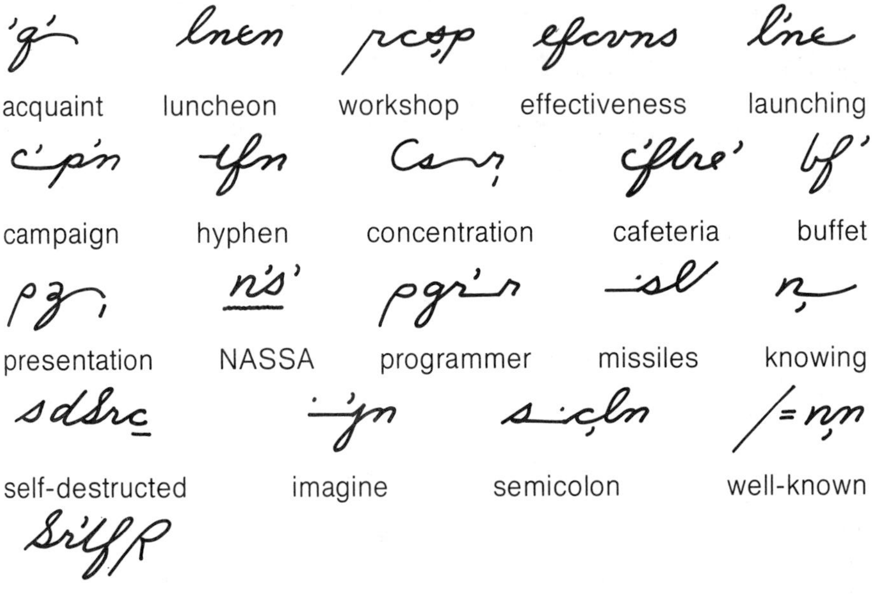

acquaint luncheon workshop effectiveness launching

campaign hyphen concentration cafeteria buffet

presentation NASSA programmer missiles knowing

self-destructed imagine semicolon well-known

straightforward

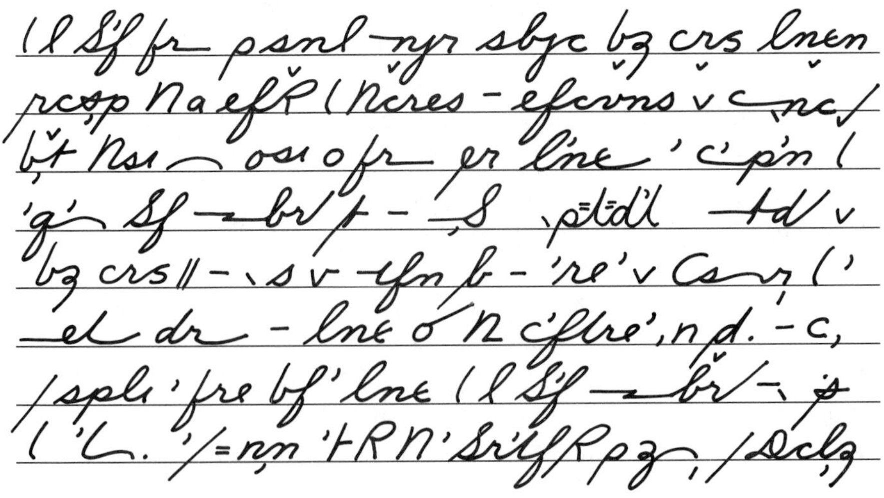

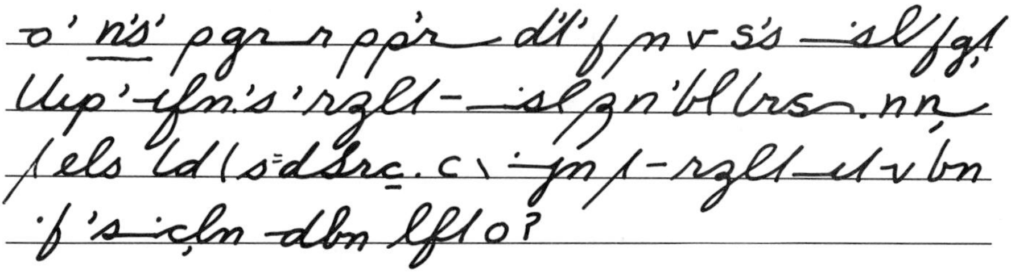

TO: All Staff
FROM: Personnel Manager
SUBJECT: Business Correspondence Luncheon Workshop

In an effort to increase the effectiveness of communications both inside and outside our firm, we are (20) launching a campaign to acquaint staff members with the most up-to-date methods of business correspondence.

The use (40) of the hyphen will be the area of concentration at a meeting during the lunch hours in the cafeteria (60) on Wednesday. The company will supply a free buffet lunch to all staff members who wish to attend. (80) A well-known authority in a straightforward presentation will disclose how a NASSA programmer preparing (100) data for one of the space missiles forgot to type a hyphen. As a result, the missile was not able to (120) respond. Not knowing what else to do, it self-destructed. Can you imagine what the result might have been if a (140) semicolon had been left out? (*AW 137; SW 146; SI 1.49*)

Letter 44B

Preview. In your notebook, write each word and phrase several times.

conversion refrigerator Beal freezer temperature

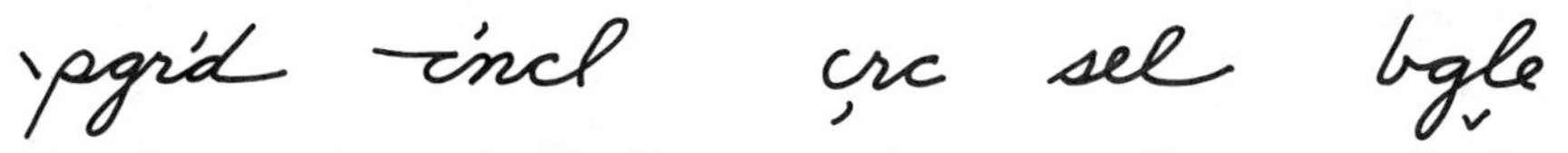

upgrading mechanical cork ceiling Begley

to cover we believe should not we do not have

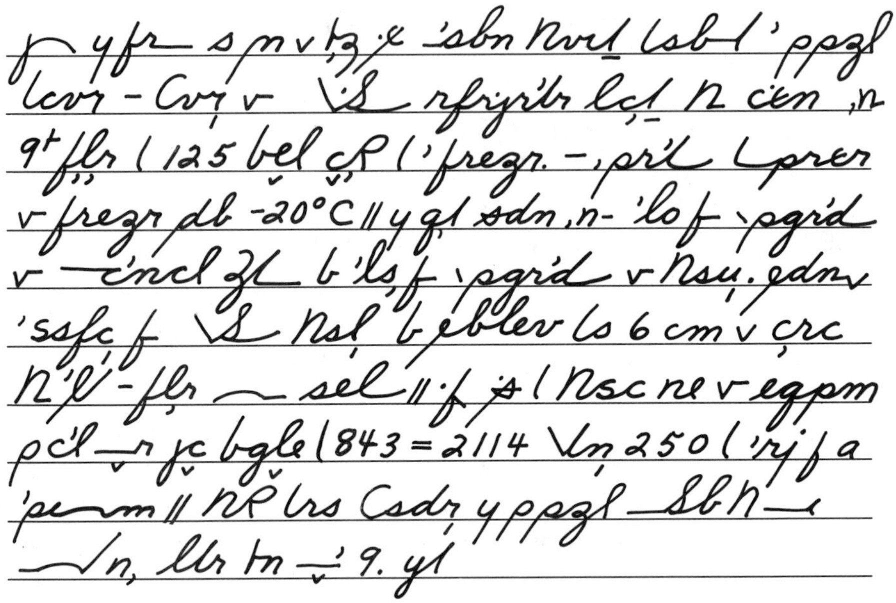

Gentlemen: Your firm is one of those which has been invited to submit a proposal to cover the conversion (20) of the existing refrigerator, located in the kitchen on the Ninth Floor at 125 Beal (40) Court, to a freezer. The operating temperature of the freezer would be −20°C. (60)

Your quote should not only allow for the upgrading of the mechanical system, but also for the upgrading (80) of the insulation. We do not have a specification for the existing insulation, but we (100) believe it is 6 cm of cork in the walls, the floor, and the ceiling.

If you wish to inspect any (120) of the equipment, please call Mr. J. C. Begley at 843-2114, Extension 250 (140) to arrange for an appointment.

In order to receive consideration, your proposal must be in (160) my hands no later than May 9. Yours truly, (*AW 156; SW 168; SI 1.5*)

Letter 45A

Preview. In your notebook, write each word and phrase several times.

flower | initial | Betty | Blake | Mechanics | introduced

texture | we are very happy | we look forward | to seeing

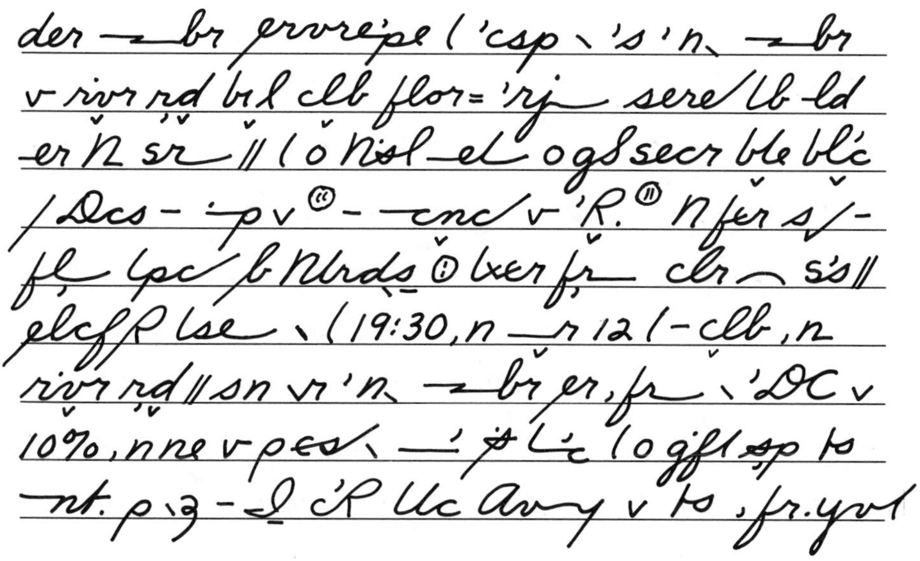

Dear Member: We are very happy to accept you as a new member of the River Road Biology Club (20) flower-arranging series to be held here in the spring.

At our initial meeting, our guest speaker, Betty Blake, (40) will discuss the importance of "The Mechanics of the Art." In future sessions, the following topics will be (60) introduced: texture, form, color, and space.

We look forward to seeing you at 19:30 on March 12 at the (80) Club on the River Road.

Since you are a new member, we are offering you a discount of 10 per cent on any (100) of the purchases you may wish to make at our gift shop this month. Please use the enclosed card to take advantage of (120) this offer. Yours very truly, (*AW 124; SW 126; SI 1.41*)

Letter 45B

Preview. In your notebook, write each of the words several times.

leisure policy's protected

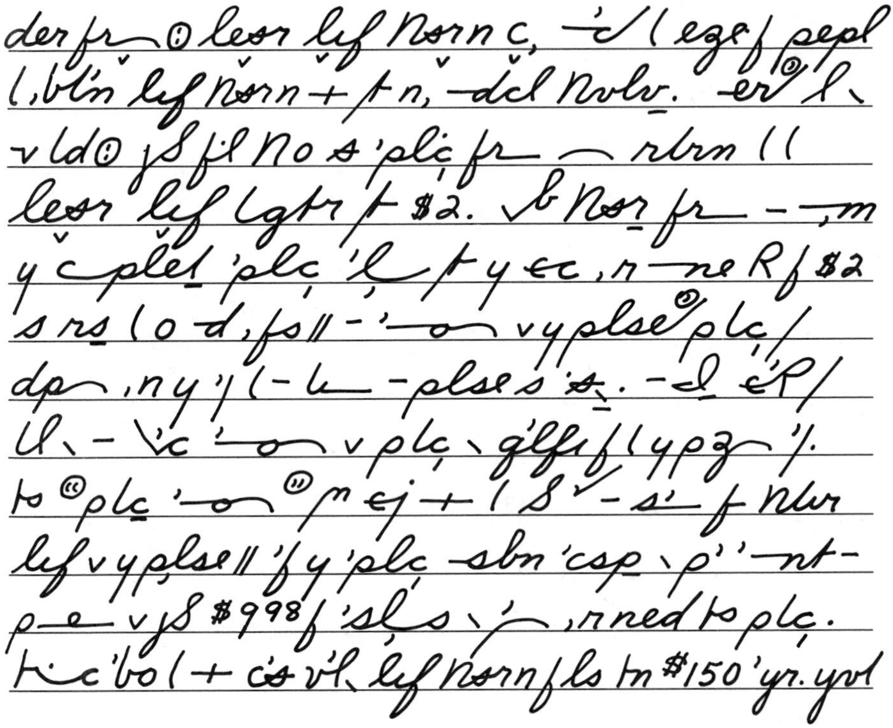

Dear Friend: Leisure Life Insurance Company makes it easy for people to obtain life insurance—with no (20) medical involved. Here's all you have to do: just fill in our short application form and return it to Leisure Life (40) together with $2.00. You will be insured from the moment your completed application, along with your cheque (60) or money order for $2.00, is received at our head office.

The amount of your policy's protection (80) will depend on your age at the time the policy is issued. The enclosed chart will tell you the exact amount (100) of protection you qualify for at your present age. This "protected amount" will not change—it stays the same for (120) the entire life of your policy.

After your application has been accepted, you pay a monthly premium (140) of just $9.98 for as long as you want or need this protection. Think about it — cash value life insurance (160) for less than $150 a year. Yours very truly, (*AW 169; SW 174; SI 1.43*)

Article 46A

Preview. In your notebook, write each of the words several times.

presence artesian flows re-establish spas

mineralized drink million convert layer depth

War flow disposing pumping basement

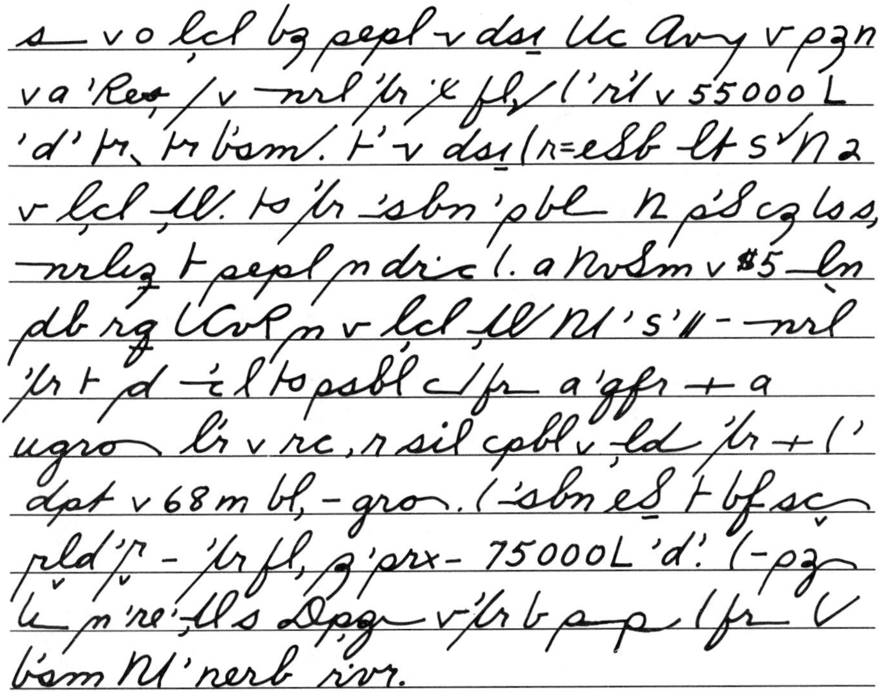

HEALTH SPAS

Some of our local business people have decided to take advantage of the presence of an artesian well (20) of mineral water which flows at a rate of 55 000 L a day through their basements. They have decided (40) to re-establish health spas in two of the local hotels. This water has been a problem in the past (60) because it is so mineralized that people will not drink it. An investment of $5 million would be (80) required to convert one of the local hotels into a spa.

The mineral water that would make all this (100) possible comes from an aquifer—an underground layer of rock or soil capable of holding water—at a (120) depth of sixty-eight metres below the ground. It has been estimated that before the Second World War the (140) water flow was approximately 75 000 L a day. At the present time, one area hotel (160) is disposing of the water by pumping it from its basement into a nearby river. (*AW 165; SW 177; SI 1.50*)

Letter 46B

Preview. In your notebook, write each of the words several times.

pool swimming solar kit community

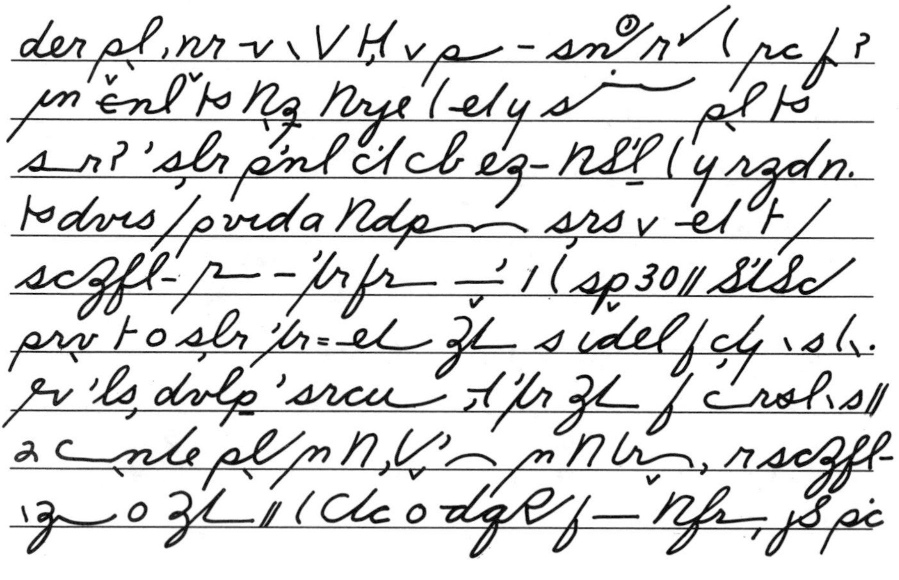

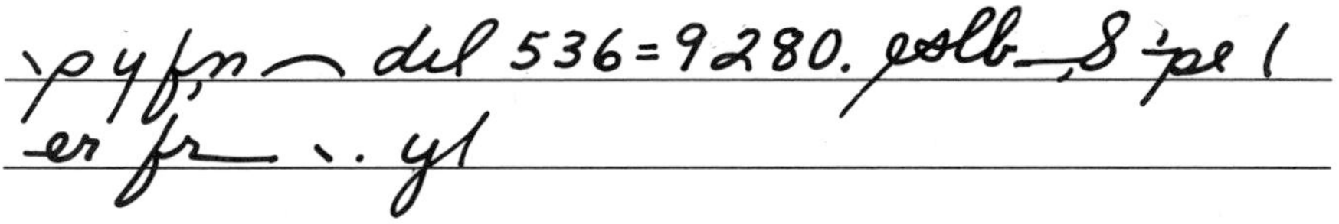

Dear Pool Owner: Have you ever thought of putting the sun's rays to work for you? Why not channel this unused energy (20) to heat your swimming pool this summer? A solar panel kit can be easily installed at your residence. (40) This device will provide an independent source of heat that will successfully warm the water from May 1 to (60) September 30.

Statistics prove that our solar water-heating system is ideal for cottage use too. We (80) have also developed a circulating hot water system for commercial use.

Two community pools, one (100) in Ottawa and one in Toronto, are successfully using our system.

To contact our headquarters (120) for more information, just pick up your phone and dial 536-9280. We shall be most happy to hear (140) from you. Yours truly, (*AW 134; SW 144; SI 1.50*)

Letter 47A

Preview. In your notebook, write each word and phrase several times.

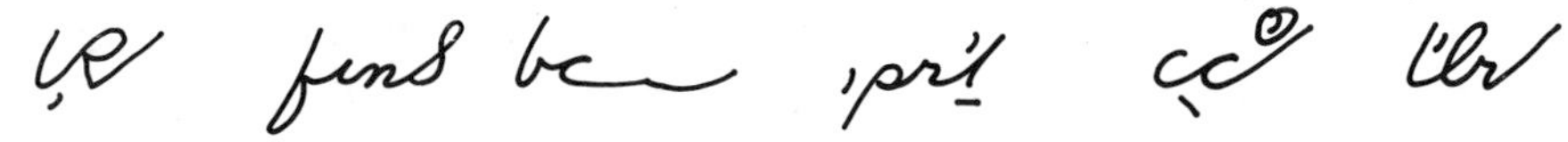

towards finest becoming operated Cooke's tailors

factor proportion gratifying I would like to make

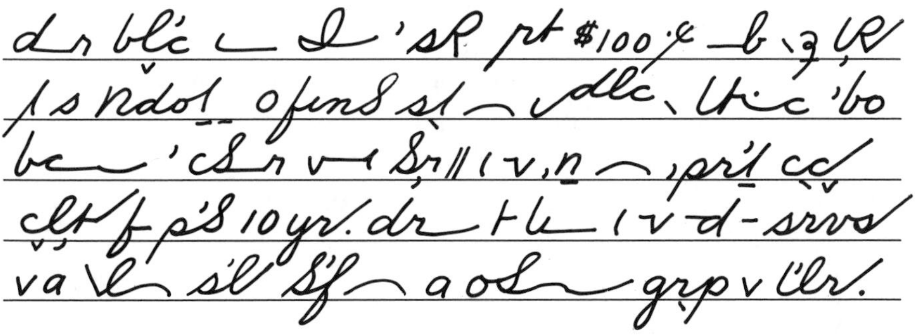

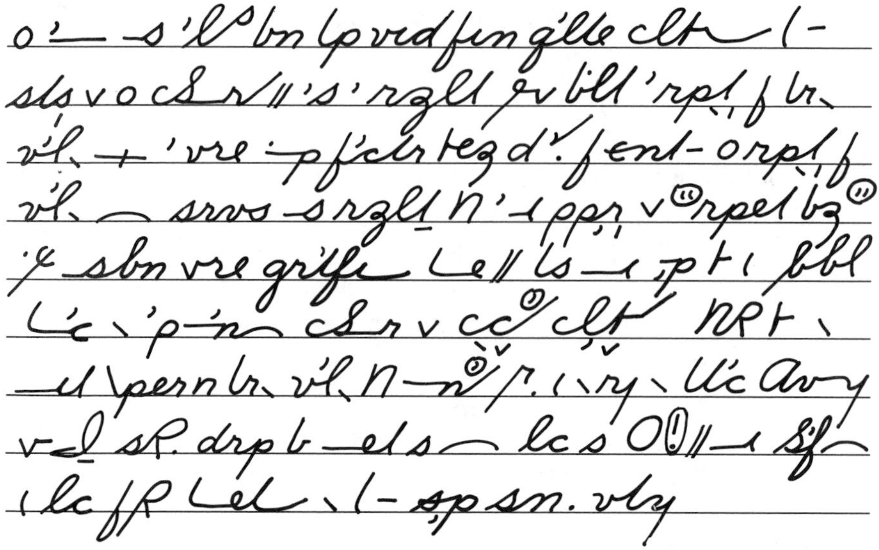

Dear Mr. Black: I am enclosing a certificate worth $100 which may be used towards what is (20) undoubtedly our finest suit, and I would like you to think about becoming a customer of my store.

I have (40) owned and operated Cooke's Clothes for the past ten years. During that time, I have had the services of an excellent (60) sales staff and an outstanding group of tailors. Our aim has always been to provide fine quality clothing to (80) the satisfaction of our customers.

As a result, we have built a reputation for true value—a very (100) important factor these days. Fortunately, our reputation for value and service has resulted in a (120) high proportion of "repeat business" which has been very gratifying to me.

It is my hope that I will be (140) able to make you a permanent customer of Cooke's Clothes in order that you might experience true value (160) in men's wear. I urge you to take advantage of the enclosed certificate. Drop by, meet us, and look us over! (180)

My staff and I look forward to meeting you at the shop soon. Very truly yours, (*AW 187; SW 194; SI 1.45*)

Memorandum 47B

Preview. In your notebook, write each word and phrase several times.

numeric separating hyphens imply at all times

each of the

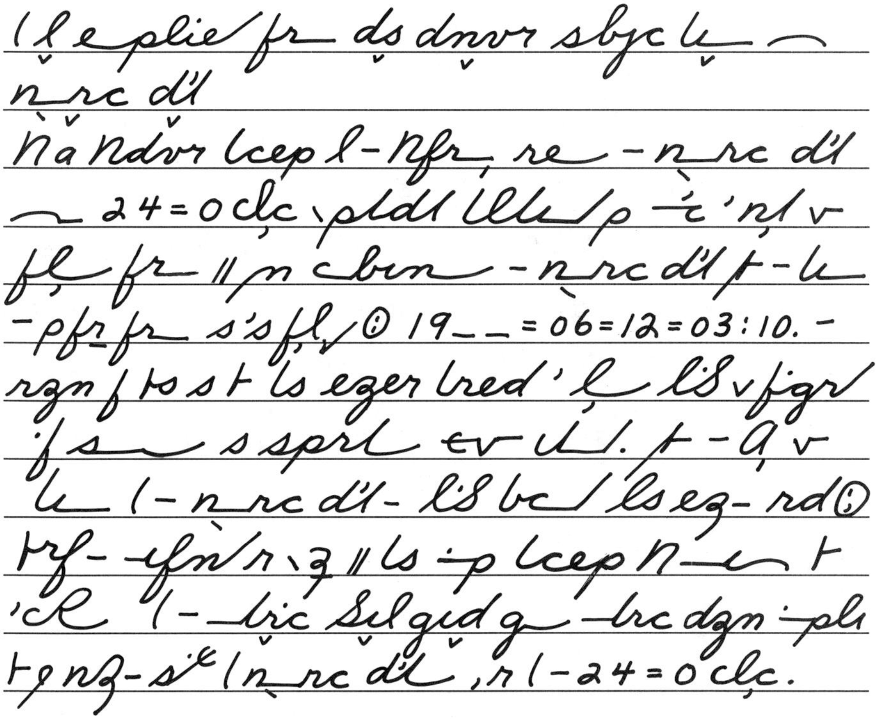

TO: All employees
FROM: D. S. Denver
SUBJECT: Time and Numeric Date

In an endeavor to keep all the information regarding the numeric date and the 24-hour clock (20) up to date at all times, please make a note of the following form.

When combining the numeric date with the time, (40) the preferred form is as follows: 19—06-12-03:10. The reason for this is that it is easier to (60) read a long list of figures if something is separating each of the items. With the addition of the time (80) to the numeric date, the list becomes less easily read; therefore, the hyphens are used.

It is important to (100) keep in mind that, according to the Metric Style Guide, going metric does not imply that we necessarily switch (120) to numeric dating or to the 24-hour clock. (*AW 121; SW 130; SI 1.47*)

Article 48A

Preview. In your notebook, write each word and phrase several times.

dressing preplanning dressed inflation fashionably

fashionable tips wardrobe mix-and-match

combinations assess poorly fitting altered

garment restyled mistake underestimate

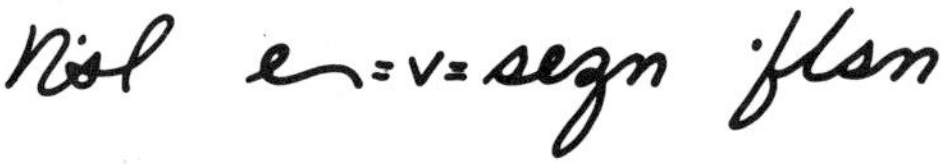

initial end-of-season if it is not

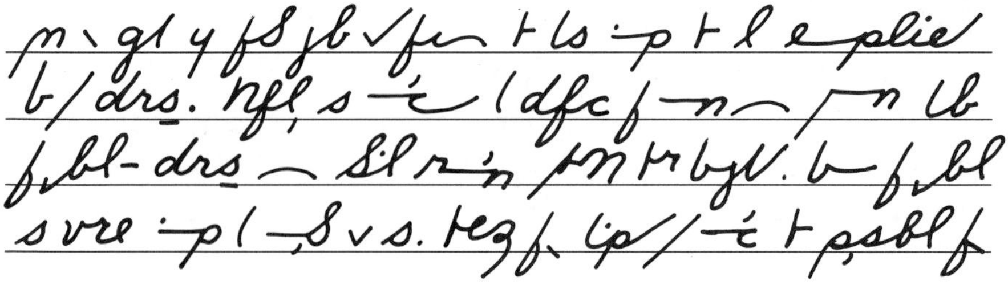

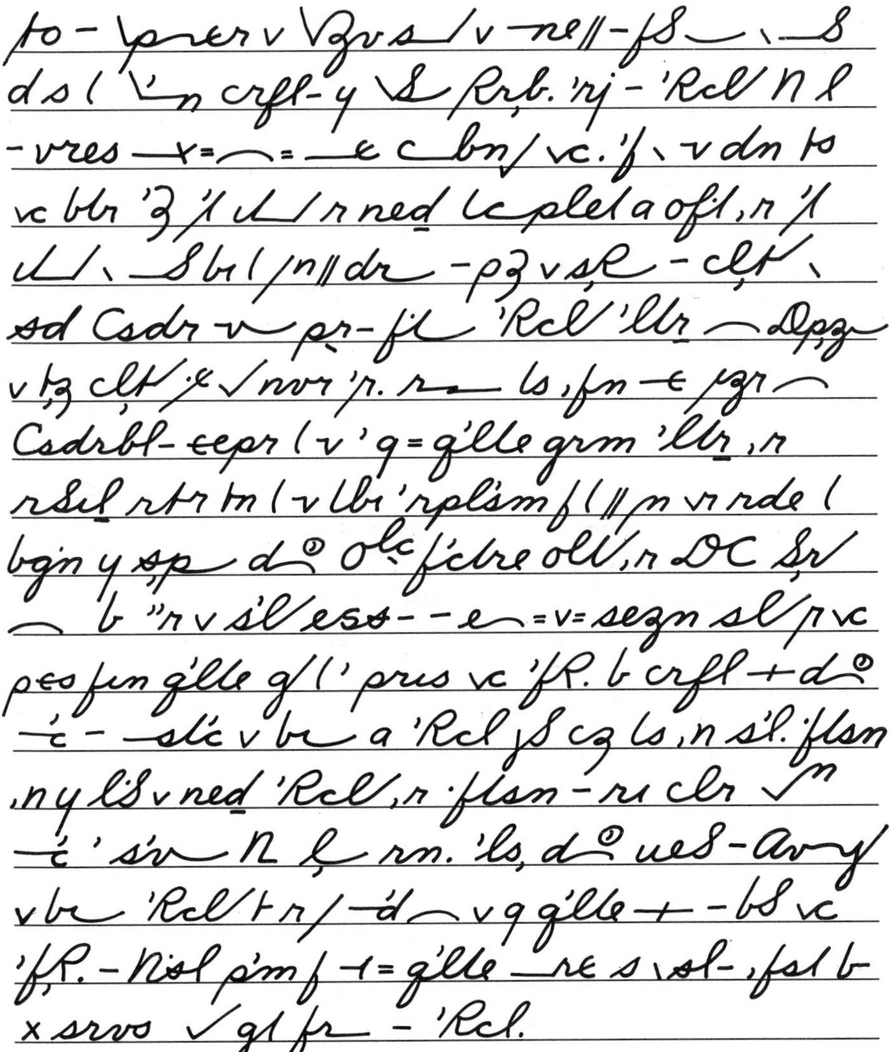

DRESSING WELL REQUIRES CONSIDERABLE PREPLANNING

When you get your first job, you will find that it is important that all employees be well dressed. Inflation is making (20) it difficult for men and women to be fashionably dressed and still remain within their budgets. Being (40) fashionable is very important to most of us. These few tips will make that possible for you without the (60) expenditure of excessive sums of money.

The first thing you must do is to examine carefully your existing wardrobe. Arrange the articles in all the various mix-and-match combinations you can. After you (100) have done this, you can better assess what items are needed to complete an outfit or what items you must buy (120) at once.

During the process of sorting the clothes, you should consider having poorly fitting articles (140) altered and disposing of those clothes which you will never wear. Remember, it is often much wiser and (160) considerably cheaper to have a good-quality garment altered or restyled rather than to have to buy a replacement (180) for it.

When you are ready to begin your shopping, don't overlook factory outlets or discount stores (200) and be aware of sales, especially the end-of-season sales, where you can purchase fine quality goods at a (220) price you can afford. Be careful—don't make the mistake of buying an article just because it is on sale. If (240) it is not on your list of needed articles or if it is not the right color, you will not make a saving (260) in the long run. Also, don't underestimate the advantages of buying articles that are well made and (280) of good quality—the best you can afford. The initial payment for high-quality merchandise is usually (300) offset by the extra service you will get from the article. (*AW 293; SW 313; SI 1.49*)

APPENDIX C

Abbreviations and Symbols

States, Districts, and Territories

Canadian Provinces and Territories

Summary of Writing Principles—Eight Sentences

ABBREVIATED WORDS

about	'bo	each	€	not	n
accept	'csp	establish	eSb	of	v
acknowledge	'c	extra	x	opportunity	,pr
administer	a‿n	extreme	x—	order	R
advertise	avr	first	fS	organization	,rg
after	'f	for	f	organize	,rg
all	l	glad	gl	our	o
am	—	go	g	out	o
and	⌐	good	g	particular	pRc
any	ne	great	gr	please	p
appreciate	'prs	has	-'s	practical	pric
are	r	have	⌐v	principal	prin
as	's	he	e	principle	prin
at	l	his	s	put	p
be	b	hour	o	quantity	q'n
because	cz	immediate	·ed	question	q
business	bz	importance	·p	receive	rs
but	b	important	·p	remember	r—
by/bye	b	inquire	nq	require	rq
can	c	is	s	right	ri
correspond	crs	it	l	satisfactory	sls
correspondence	crs	like	lc	satisfy	sls
difficult	dfc	merchandise	—rE	ship	s̶
difficulty	dfc	more	—	short	s̶
distribute	Db	necessary	nz	side	si
do	d	next	nx	sincere	sn

sincerely	sn	the	—	will	/
suggest	sjS	to	l	write	re
thank	T	us	s	you	\
that	T	well	/	your	y

STANDARD ABBREVIATIONS

approximate (approx.)	'prx	manufacture (mfg.)	—fg
avenue (ave.)	'v	memorandum (memo)	—,
certificate (cert.)	sR	Mr.	—r
Company (Co.)(company)	c,	Mrs.	—rs
credit (cr)	cr	Ms.	—z
debit (dr)	dr	purchase order (P.O.)	p,
department (dept.)	dpt	regard (re)	re
doctor (Dr.)	dr	represent (rep.)	rp
estimate (est.)	eS	representative (rep.)	rp
et cetera (etc.)	etc	secretary (sec.)	sc
executive (exec.)	\c	senior (Sr.)	sr
gentlemen (gent.)	jn	signature (sig.)	sg
government (govt.)	gvt	stenographer (steno)	Sn,
Incorporated (Inc.)	nc	street (St.)	S
invoice (inv.)	nv	substitute (sub.)	sb
junior (Jr.)	jr	superintendent (supt.)	spt
laboratory (lab.)	l'b	television (TV)	tv
Limited (Ltd.)	ltd	year (yr.)	yr

STANDARD SYMBOLS*

Celsius	C	dollar	$
centimeter/centimetre	cm	dollars	$
degree	°	gram	g
kilogram	kg	meter/metre	m
kilometer/kilometre	km	milligram	mg
liter/litre	L	millimeter/ millimetre	mm

*The metric symbols represent both singular and plural forms of the terms.

ABBREVIATIONS FOR DAYS AND MONTHS

Sunday (Sun.)	April (Apr.)
Monday (Mon.)	May
Tuesday (Tue.)	June
Wednesday (Wed.)	July (Jul.)
Thursday (Thu.)	August (Aug.)
Friday (Fri.)	September (Sep.)
Saturday (Sat.)	October (Oct.)
January (Jan.)	November (Nov.)
February (Feb.)	December (Dec.)
March (Mar.)	

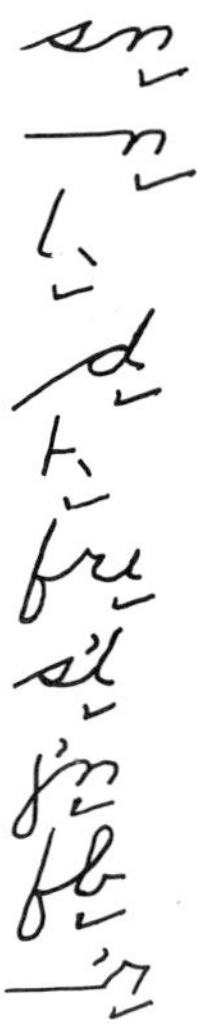

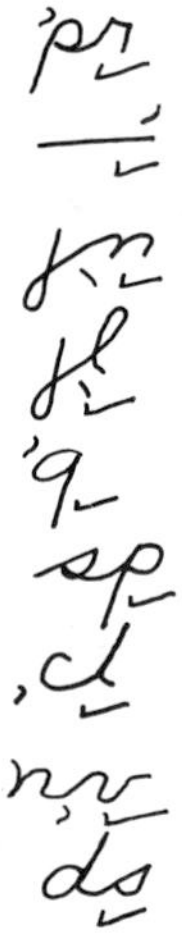

CANADIAN PROVINCES AND TERRITORIES

Alberta	AB	Nova Scotia	NS
British Columbia	BC	Ontario	ON
Labrador	LB	Prince Edward Island	PE
Manitoba	MB	Quebec	PQ
New Brunswick	NB	Saskatchewan	SK
Newfoundland	NF	Yukon Territory	YT
Northwest Territories	NT		

STATES, DISTRICTS, AND TERRITORIES

Alabama	AL	Montana	MT
Alaska	AK	Nebraska	NE
Arizona	AZ	Nevada	NV
Arkansas	AR	New Hampshire	NH
California	CA	New Jersey	NJ
Colorado	CO	New Mexico	NM
Connecticut	CT	New York	NY
Delaware	DE	North Carolina	NC
District of Columbia	DC	North Dakota	ND
Florida	FL	Ohio	OH
Georgia	GA	Oklahoma	OK
Guam	GU	Oregon	OR
Hawaii	HI	Pennsylvania	PA
Idaho	ID	Puerto Rico	PR
Illinois	IL	Rhode Island	RI
Indiana	IN	South Carolina	SC
Iowa	IA	South Dakota	SD
Kansas	KS	Tennessee	TN
Kentucky	KY	Texas	TX
Louisiana	LA	Utah	UT
Maine	ME	Vermont	VT
Maryland	MD	Virginia	VA
Massachusetts	MA	Virgin Islands	VI
Michigan	MI	Washington	WA
Minnesota	MN	West Virginia	WV
Mississippi	MS	Wisconsin	WI
Missouri	MO	Wyoming	WY

SUMMARY OF WRITING PRINCIPLES

The following eight sentences contain all of the writing principles in Forkner Shorthand.

Chapters 1—4

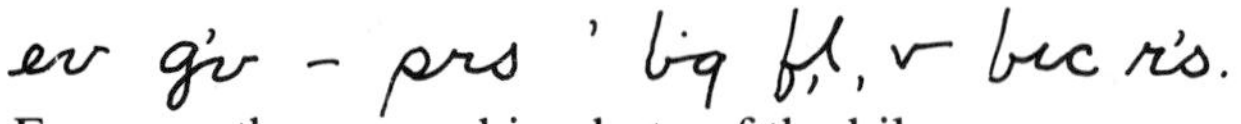

Eve gave the press a big photo of the bike race.

Sound of long *e*	Sound of short *i*	Sound of long *i*
Sound of short *e*	Sound of *t*	Sound of hard *c* and *k*
Sound of *a*	Sounds of *o*	Sound of soft *c*

Chapters 5—8

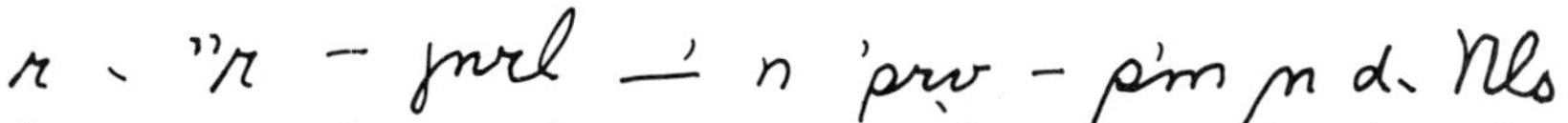

Are you aware the general may not approve the payment when due unless

he is consulted?

awa-away	Sound of *m*	Prefixes *in-en-un*
Sounds of *w-wh*	Sounds of *u-oo*	Prefixes *con-coun-count*
Sound of soft *g* and *j*	Syllable *ment*	*d* or *ed* added to a root word

Chapters 9—12

She advised her children to transfer the deposit this evening.

Sound of *sh*	Sound of *h*	Prefixes *be-de-re*
Prefix *ad-add*	Sound of *ch*	Sound of *th*
Sound of hard *s* and *z*	Prefix *trans*	Sounds of *ng-ing-thing*

SUMMARY OF WRITING PRINCIPLES

Chapters 13—16

Everybody left the annual school display quickly, including my friends.

Prefix or suffix *ever-every*	*qu*	*nt-nd*
Prefix *an*	*ly*	Adding *s* to root words
Prefixes *dis-des*	*incl-enclose*	

Chapters 17—20

The booklet outlines information and publicity on the self-service store

downtown.

Prefix or suffix *out*	*sity-city*	*st*
Sound of *shun*	Prefix or suffix *self*	Sound of *ou-ow*

Chapters 21—24

The director instructed the employee to postpone the report at the special

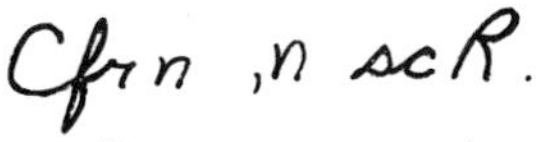

conference on security.

ct	*post-position*	nce-nse
instr	*rt-rd*	*rity*
Sound of *oi-oy*	*sp*	

SUMMARY OF WRITING PRINCIPLES

Chapters 25—28

I forgot to explain that I prefer a change in letterhead design to give greater

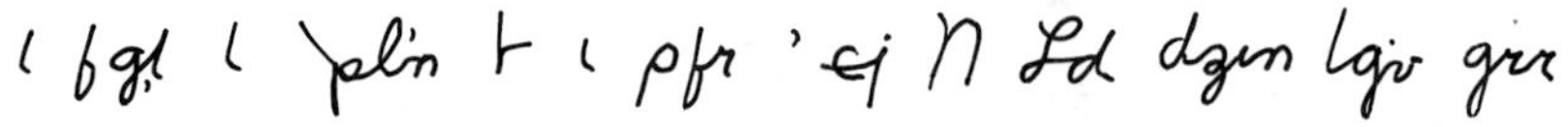

flexibility.

Prefixes *for-fore-fer-fur*
Prefixes *ax-ex-ox*

Prefixes *pre-pri-pro-per-pur*
nge

letter-liter
bility

Chapters 29—32

They undertake, with some success, to regulate, overcome, or control the

pain of bursitis with a prescription of modern electronic technology.

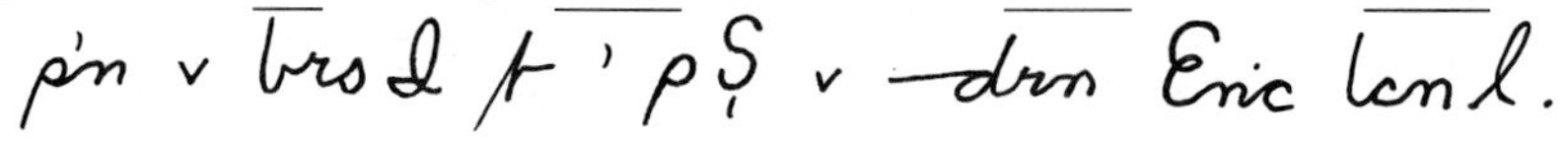

under
Syllables *sys-sess-sus-sis-cess-cis*
ulate

over-other
contr
itis-icitis

scribe-script
electr
ology